NORTHERN LANDSCAPES

The Struggle for Wilderness Alaska

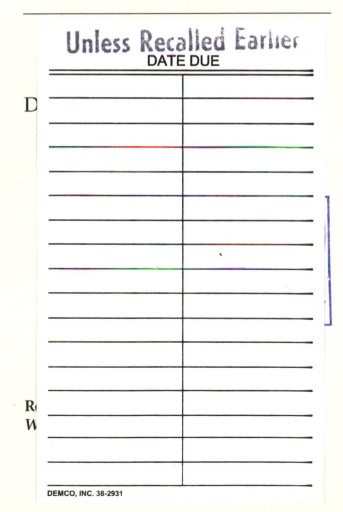

An RFF Press book
Published by Resources for the Future
1616 P Street NW
Washington, DC 20036–1400
USA
www.rffpress.org

Library of Congress Cataloging-in-Publication Data

Nelson, Daniel, 1941-
  Northern landscapes : the struggle for wilderness Alaska / Daniel Nelson.
    p. cm.
  Includes bibliographical references and index.
  ISBN 1-891853-84-8 (hardcover : alk. paper) -- ISBN 1-891853-85-6 (pbk. : alk. paper)
  1. Nature conservation--Alaska--History. I. Title.
  QH76.5.A4N46 2004
  333.72'09798--dc22

                          2004010084

f e d c b a

The paper in this book meets the guidelines for permanence and durability of the Committee on Production Guidelines for Book Longevity of the Council on Library Resources.

This book was designed and typeset in Giovanni Book and Myriad MM by Maggie Powell. It was copyedited by Sally Atwater. The cover was designed by Maggie Powell. Cover photo of Northern Lights, Girdwood, Alaska, by Eric Teela.

ISBN 1891853-84-8 (cloth)   ISBN 1891853-85-6 (paper)

About Resources for the Future and RFF Press

Resources for the Future (RFF) improves environmental and natural resource policymaking worldwide through independent social science research of the highest caliber. Founded in 1952, RFF pioneered the application of economics as a tool for developing more effective policy about the use and conservation of natural resources. Its scholars continue to employ social science methods to analyze critical issues concerning pollution control, energy policy, land and water use, hazardous waste, climate change, biodiversity, and the environmental challenges of developing countries.

RFF Press supports the mission of RFF by publishing book-length works that present a broad range of approaches to the study of natural resources and the environment. Its authors and editors include RFF staff, researchers from the larger academic and policy communities, and journalists. Audiences for publications by RFF Press include all of the participants in the policymaking process—scholars, the media, advocacy groups, NGOs, professionals in business and government, and the public.

ABOUT THE AUTHOR

Daniel Nelson is professor of history emeritus at the University of Akron, where his specialties included economic, labor, and environmental history. His publications include *Managers and Workers: Origins of the Twentieth Century Factory System; Frederick W. Taylor and the Rise of Scientific Management;* and *Shifting Fortunes: The Rise and Decline of American Labor from the 1820s to the Present,* as well as more than fifty articles.

CONTENTS

To Lorraine, with love

ACKNOWLEDGMENTS

I am grateful to the more than two dozen participants in this story who shared their recollections of the events of the 1960s and 1970s. I am particularly indebted to Peg Tileston, Mark Hickok, Richard Gordon, and Helen Nienhauser, who permitted me to use their personal papers or other fugitive materials, including several important newsletters, that were not available elsewhere.

The librarians and archivists of the following institutions were unfailingly helpful in locating documents and other materials: University of Akron, Alaska State Library, University of Alaska–Fairbanks, University of Alaska–Anchorage, University of Arizona, University of California–Berkeley, Carter Presidential Library, Denver Public Library, National Park Service, and University of Washington. The University of Akron Faculty Research Committee generously financed the early stages of my research.

Richard Gordon, Jack Hession, Theodore Catton, and Mark Harvey read the entire manuscript and offered valuable critiques. Jeffrey Stine and former Representative John Seiberling read the chapters on ANILCA and made similarly valuable comments. I am grateful to all of them for their time and assistance.

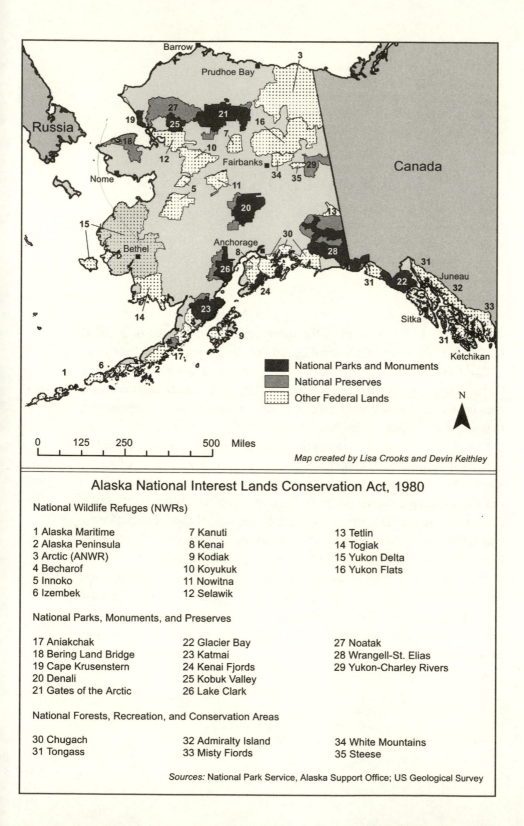

Map created by Lisa Crooks and Devin Keithley

Alaska National Interest Lands Conservation Act, 1980

National Wildlife Refuges (NWRs)

1 Alaska Maritime
2 Alaska Peninsula
3 Arctic (ANWR)
4 Becharof
5 Innoko
6 Izembek

7 Kanuti
8 Kenai
9 Kodiak
10 Koyukuk
11 Nowitna
12 Selawik

13 Tetlin
14 Togiak
15 Yukon Delta
16 Yukon Flats

National Parks, Monuments, and Preserves

17 Aniakchak
18 Bering Land Bridge
19 Cape Krusenstern
20 Denali
21 Gates of the Arctic

22 Glacier Bay
23 Katmai
24 Kenai Fjords
25 Kobuk Valley
26 Lake Clark

27 Noatak
28 Wrangell-St. Elias
29 Yukon-Charley Rivers

National Forests, Recreation, and Conservation Areas

30 Chugach
31 Tongass

32 Admiralty Island
33 Misty Fiords

34 White Mountains
35 Steese

Sources: National Park Service, Alaska Support Office; US Geological Survey

WASHINGTON, DECEMBER 1980

On the evening of December 1, 1980, more than 500 people crowded into the Palladian Room of Washington's Shoreham Hotel. They came to celebrate the passage of the Alaska National Interest Lands Conservation Act (ANILCA), "the greatest conservation bill in history," in the words of Interior Secretary Cecil Andrus. President Jimmy Carter would sign the act the following morning. Most of those who attended the Shoreham party were youthful activists associated with one of more than three dozen organizations, headed by the Sierra Club, the Wilderness Society, the Audubon Society, and the Friends of the Earth, which had formed a formidable partnership, the Alaska Coalition, and pushed the ANILCA legislation. A large number came from Alaska itself, where they had participated in one or more of the groups that had spearheaded the initial drive to preserve parts of the immense state and later played a central role in the national effort. "What a well-dressed army it was," noted a reporter for the *Washington Post*; "I've never seen the Alaska people so dressed up." Dee Frankfourth, an Alaskan who had risen from an intern's position with the Anchorage-based Alaska Center for the Environment to a major role in the Alaska Coalition, observed wistfully that "this is as close to a wedding as I'll ever get."[1]

Other partygoers emphasized the bittersweet character of the celebration. Edgar Wayburn, who had headed the Sierra Club's ambitious campaign to preserve Alaska's lands for more than a decade, explained that "on the third of November I was emphatic that we should get a better bill. On the fourth I said, 'Let's get this one through.'" The difference had been Carter's defeat at the hands of Republican Ronald Reagan, who had made no secret of his hostility to environmentalism. The Republicans had also taken control of the Senate in the 1980 election. With the Democrats in charge, it had taken nearly three years of concerted activity to pass the Alaska bill. The Republicans were certain to be less cooperative. The Sierra Club's Jack Hession, who had worked full time on Alaska issues for a decade, bravely promised a new effort to improve the act, but few colleagues shared his optimism.[2]

Some Alaska environmentalists were even less happy with the outcome of the Washington campaign. Ron Hawk and Kay Greenough, former co-executive directors of the Southeast Alaska Conservation Council, a coalition of environmental groups in the rugged, wet panhandle area of southeastern Alaska, had become so unhappy that they and some of their colleagues had broken with the Alaska Coalition and lobbied against the bill.[3] Their opposition called attention to the shortcomings of ANILCA and to the certainty that the new law would not be the final word in the struggle to control Alaska's land and resources.

At 9:30 on the morning of December 2, many of those who had attended the Shoreham party gathered in the East Room of the White House for the speeches and signing. Carter arrived, looking "tired and drawn."[4] In his remarks the president was gracious, praising congressional and Alaska Coalition leaders. Representatives John F. Seiberling (D-OH) and Morris Udall (D-AZ), who had orchestrated the legislation's overwhelming victories in the House of Representatives, compared Carter to Theodore Roosevelt. Senator Henry Jackson (D-WA), chairman of the Senate Energy Committee and principal author of the final bill that Carter signed, followed Udall. For years Jackson had been one of the environmentalists' congressional champions. In the Alaska battle, however, he had played a different and less supportive role, indicative of the conflicting political pressures that had delayed and at times threatened the legislation. Jackson described the bill as "a lasting monument in striking a balance between development on the one hand, and preservation and conservation on the other." He praised Carter, Andrus, and Udall but also Alaska's Republican Senator Ted Stevens, who, he insisted, "stuck his neck out over and over again, [and] kept us together on the Senate side."

Stevens then stepped to the podium. A staunch defender of Alaska business interests and an equally vigorous opponent of the Alaska Coalition, he agreed that there was "balance" in the bill "because it will fulfill the commitment of the Statehood Act." He recalled that his goal had been to "get a bill that would fulfill our hopes and aspirations. ... This bill did not do that for us, and I think for some of you, it didn't meet all of your goals, either. So, we're not finished, Mr. President. We've just really started."[5]

Secretary Andrus followed Stevens. He insisted that economic growth and environmental protection were compatible goals. "In these times of need for energy and minerals," people had shown that "they are also concerned about the environment in which they live." He described ANILCA, which had been the president's foremost environmental goal, as a "hallmark" of the Carter approach to resource issues.[6]

Andrus was understandably upbeat. ANILCA preserved more than 107 million acres, more than one-quarter of Alaska and one-half of the federal land in the huge state, including a large percentage of Alaska's most spectacular mountains, fiords, wetlands, and unusual geologic features. The 44 million acres set aside for national parks more than doubled the size of the national park system. The 57 million acres designated as wilderness more than tripled the acreage of the wilderness preservation system. The act's 59 million acres of wildlife refuges would provide sanctuaries for millions of birds, mammals, and other animals and more than doubled total refuge acreage; 26 new wild and scenic rivers and 1.3 million adjacent acres of land nearly doubled the number and tripled the acreage of wild and scenic rivers; and 3 million additional acres of national forests created opportunities for a variety of users.[7] At the time these designations had little significance outside the federal bureaucracy; the land was almost wholly undeveloped and the handful of people who happened to live there would hardly notice the change. Their real significance would not be apparent for 20, 50, or 100 years.

The events of December 1–2 directly or indirectly captured the essence of one of the defining political struggles of the 20th century. It had begun in the 1950s, as the social and environmental costs of the postwar economic boom became evident, even in faraway Alaska. The struggle intensified in the 1960s and 1970s, as the pace of Alaskan industrialization increased and the discovery of a vast new oil field on the Arctic coast forced elected officials to make decisions about the future of Alaska's public lands. Yet the decisive development of that period was not the changing economy but the emergence, in Alaska and elsewhere, of a politically assertive environmental movement, which had roots in the established conservation organizations but added new, broader perspectives on the challenges facing society. Underlying its activist agenda was a pervasive sense of the "environment as a living system—a web of life or ecosystem," in the words of political scientist Richard N. L. Andrews, that made it more than the sum of its parts.[8] The new perspectives, together with a commitment to immediate, decisive action, ensured that Alaska's chosen path to prosperity would not go unchallenged.

In practical terms environmentalists had two broad interests. First, they sought to extend traditional conservation goals, such as wildlife preservation, outdoor recreation, and public land management that emphasized noneconomic values and the preservation of unique areas and resources. By the 1960s this goal had led them to embrace related causes, including legal protections for endangered plants and animals and government support for a national system of long-distance hiking trails, but the demand for parks, wildlife refuges, and legally recognized natural areas and the reform of public agencies devoted to land and natural resource stewardship remained paramount. Empty, beautiful, and comparatively pristine Alaska was an obvious place to realize these ends, and ANILCA would be one of the environmentalists' most notable achievements.

The second major thrust of environmentalism was even more ambitious. The postwar economic boom had provided mounting evidence of the short- and especially the long-term costs of economic growth, and environmentalists grappled with ways to reduce or mitigate those effects. One obvious target was industrial pollution, especially pollution resulting from the reckless use of new technologies, such as chemical pesticides and nuclear energy. Alaska played a role in this effort, too. It first became familiar to many Americans as a proposed site for nuclear weapons tests. After the mid-1950s, and especially after 1967, it also emerged as the frontier of the North American oil industry. The contrast between Alaska's natural, unspoiled beauty and the predictable effects of nuclear explosions and wholesale oil exploration was stark and compelling. The effort to minimize the environmental impact of oil exploration and development was also closely related to the campaign to set aside public lands as parks and wilderness areas. Together they made the fate of Alaska a critical measure of the larger effort to address the costs of economic growth and technological innovation.

This role would have astounded Alaskans of earlier years. For most of its history Alaska had been, in the economic sense, a poor place, where profitable activity had been problematic. Yet the lush rain forest of the Southeast, the seemingly abundant fish and other marine life, the presence of gold and other valuable minerals, and the likelihood of petroleum, natural gas, and other resources suggested limitless opportunity. The contrast between the often unpleasant reality and the apparent potential was striking, superficially inexplicable, and a source of great frustration to many Alaskans. Out of that frustration emerged a consensus that became the foundation of Alaska political life: Alaskans were victims of distant forces that made it impossible for them to share the prosperity and comforts that other Americans enjoyed. These forces included outside corporate interests and the federal government, which was the formal owner of virtually all of Alaska until the 1960s. Though many Alaskans, including most of the large Native minority, cherished its relative emptiness, the politically active, largely urban population became committed to the idea that Alaska's natural resources could and should make them indistinguishable from affluent residents of Pennsylvania or California.

People in other areas of the American West had addressed similar concerns through self-government, and that became the panacea for white Alaskans in the years leading to the Statehood Act of 1958. After an extended campaign, they won a remarkably generous settlement that included a grant of 104 million acres (more than the total acreage of 45 other states), approximately 30 percent of Alaska. Moreover, Alaska's leaders could select the land piecemeal over the next quarter-century. Given the new state's political culture, this novel concession was an invitation to resource exploitation. The state would be the mechanism through which Alaska's entrepreneurial community achieved its long-awaited destiny. As Senator Stevens noted 20 years later, his and his supporters' aim was still to "fulfill the commitment of the Statehood Act."

Alaska's boosters (or boomers or Superboosters, depending on the source)[9] continued to dominate its economy and politics in the 1960s. Until the end of the decade they had little to show for their efforts. The state's traditional industries, fishing and mining, continued to languish and most of the boosters' grandiose plans had failed. As late as 1967 the state had patented only 5 million acres of land, individuals only half a million. A leading social scientist concluded that Alaska remained in a "precarious position."[10] At that point, however, the discovery of a genuine bonanza on the Arctic coast seemed at last to fulfill the boosters' predictions. A small number of Alaskans became wealthy through oil lease speculations. Others hoped to profit from business generated by the oil fields and the construction of an oil pipeline to the Pacific coast. Still others expected to benefit from a more secure and generous state government. But—and this was the irony of the Alaska story—the Prudhoe Bay discoveries occurred just as public opinion in the United States, and to a degree in Alaska, began to question the boosters' values and objectives and the desirability of resource exploitation as a formula for prosperity. The resulting conflict became one of the classic political confrontations of the "environmental decade" (proclaimed by President Richard M. Nixon in January 1970) and an example of how environmentalists, operating through a network of activist organizations in Alaska and across the country, changed a long-entrenched pattern of political behavior that had been reinforced by the Prudhoe Bay discoveries. The White House ceremony of December 2, 1980, was a measure of their success. The legacy of that event includes parks and wildlife refuges that preserve the most attractive and inspiring areas of Alaska, a compelling example of political activism and mobilization, and a continuing debate over the future of Alaska's land and other resources.

PART I

Seedtime:
Alaska to the 1960s

White men, uncontrolled and uncontrollable, already swarm over the Alaskan coast ...

—George Bird Grinnell, naturalist, 1899

We are ready to start pumping the wealth of our resources in an ever-increasing flow into the veins of the new state of Alaska, and into the commerce of the United States.

—Edward J. Rusing, Fairbanks banker, 1957

Many Alaskans, including political leaders, think of themselves as heroes in a TV western. In the northern version of the last frontier ... wilderness is to be despoiled and destroyed as valueless, a nuisance, or a threat.

—George W. Rogers, economist, 1971

CHAPTER 1

THE EMERGENCE OF ALASKA

In 1899 Edward H. Harriman, like a small but growing number of adventurous individuals, vacationed in Alaska. Harriman, however, was far from a typical tourist. A shrewd, aggressive financier who was putting together a railroad empire and making himself one of the richest men in the world, Harriman set out to hunt Alaska brown bear in a style befitting a man of his wealth and station. Having leased the *George H. Elder*, a luxurious steam yacht with room for more than 100 guests and crew, Harriman began to reconsider the purpose of his trip. By the time the *Elder* left Seattle on May 31, 1899, he had recruited 25 of the country's leading scientists, including naturalists John Muir, John Burroughs, and George Bird Grinnell, together with artists and photographers, a medical staff, a chaplain, laborers, and 11 family members. Though Harriman still hoped to shoot a bear, his hunting trip had evolved into an expensive, high-profile scientific expedition to the little-known northern wilderness that had been acquired from Russia only 30 years earlier and had become a U.S. territory in 1881. Historians have characterized the voyage as the "last grand expedition of the nineteenth century."[1]

For two months the *Elder* cruised the Alaska coast (at one point even crossing to Siberia) as the passengers and crew admired the majestic mountains and lush forests. The most illuminating moments, however, resulted from contacts with the new society that was emerging in the Far North. Three events in particular stood out. The first was a visit to the great Treadwell gold mine on Douglas Island, across the Gastineau Channel from Juneau, Alaska's largest town. The Treadwell operation dated from the early 1880s and was one of the territory's most successful industrial enterprises. By 1899 it had become a source of controversy. The Harriman party quickly grasped the downside of Treadwell's success. Several visitors complained about the noise of the mill, where gold was separated from rock. John Burroughs thought Niagara Falls was "a soft hum beside it." He and his colleagues were equally appalled at the devastated forests of Douglas Island, which the Treadwell managers had appropriated for the mine, and the seemingly degraded employees, who earned modest wages producing the Treadwell bonanza.[2]

The second incident occurred the following day during a visit to Skagway, the raucous boomtown that had emerged in the wake of the famous Klondike gold rush. Skagway had sprung up in 1897 with the influx of miners; five years after Harriman's visit it would be nearly a ghost town, as other Alaska gold rushes, disease, and financial failure winnowed the local population. In 1899 the visiting scientists were more appalled than impressed. Greed and irresponsibility were everywhere evident in the shabby buildings, lack of community institutions, and unruly behavior. Muir, who had visited Skagway at the start of the rush, viewed the changes of the intervening years as conclusive evidence of the corrosive effects of the strike-it-rich mentality. He wrote of the "poor, deluded, self-burdened" men he found there.[3]

The third was a visit to the settlement of Metlakatla, on Annette Island, near the southern border of Alaska, where a charismatic Scottish missionary, William Duncan, had created Alaska's first Native reservation and a model of how Alaska's Native population might be incorporated into American society. Duncan had brought a large group of Tsimshian followers from his former mission in British Columbia, won reservation status for Annette Island from Congress, and created a series of successful industries, including a salmon cannery. By the turn of the century Metlakatla had become a showcase of enlightened paternalism. Grinnell, a crusader for Native rights, wrote admiringly that Duncan had changed "these Indians from the wildmen that they were when he first met them, to the respectable and civilized people they are now." Harriman, ever alert to economic opportunity, had a more practical observation. Metlakatla had demonstrated that Natives "could be largely used in the development of the territory."[4]

During their brief visit, Harriman's scientists thus identified several enduring features of Alaska society. One was the difficulty of making a living in an environment where most agricultural and industrial activities were difficult, if not impossible. A second was the role of large corporations in Alaska's economic life. Closely related were the social and environmental costs of mining and other forms of natural resource exploitation. The visitors also indirectly noted the prevailing uncertainty about the role of the Native population, which was not only large (and a majority of the total population before 1898 and in the 1920s and 1930s) but also potentially more powerful legally and politically than any other Native American community. What they failed to note, because it was so obvious, was the role of government in the territory. The federal government owned Alaska and its resources, and federal agencies had responsibility for most governmental functions. Congress gradually provided for representative government (Alaska gained an appointed governor and a handful of officials with the creation of the territory in 1881, an elected nonvoting congressional representative in 1906, and a territorial legislature in 1912), but federal policy would be the critical dynamic in Alaska's economic and political life during the territorial period and a formidable influence afterward.

A "COLONIAL" ECONOMY

During the four decades that followed the Harriman visit, Alaska grew slowly and fitfully. After doubling in the 1890s to 64,000, its population briefly stabilized, then declined, and recovered only in the mid-1930s, when the Roosevelt administration's gold policies inspired a new mining boom. Even with this stimulus, Alaska badly trailed every western state during the first third of the century. In 1900 it had one and a half times the population of empty Nevada; on the eve of World War II, Nevada, still the least-populated state, had one and a half times the population of Alaska.[5] The memory of the turn-of-the-century boom continued to inspire hopes of new bonanzas, but most Alaskans eked out a living as fishermen or miners and wondered why, amid so much apparent wealth, they had so few opportunities.

The area that the Harriman party visited, the long southeastern panhandle from Juneau south to the Canadian border, remained a region of small, relatively stable communities based on fishing and salmon canning. Ketchikan, in the far south, grew from fewer than 500 residents in 1900 to 4,700 in 1940 and became Alaska's second-largest city. Wrangell and Petersburg had about 1,300 residents each in 1940, and Sitka, the picturesque former capital, had just over 1,000 inhabitants in 1930, when it, too, began to grow. Juneau, the one southeastern community with a diversified economy, had the most impressive record. It succeeded Treadwell as the gold mining center of the Southeast, became the territorial capital in 1912, and grew into Alaska's largest city. By 1940 it counted more than 5,700 residents. Yet towering mountains severely limited its physical expansion and led to congestion and overcrowding. On arriving in 1939, the new territorial governor, Ernest Gruening, described it as "slummy."[6] Facing outward to the sea, Juneau, like the other southeastern towns, had only a passing interest in the vast expanse of Alaska that lay to the north and west, or even in the densely forested islands and mountainsides that rose from the sea on every side.

Although life in Southeast Alaska was reasonably stable and prosperous—even idyllic for those who appreciated the area's majestic mountains, glaciers, and forests—it depended on simple extractive activities and powerful outsiders. Southeastern Alaska might have abundant fish, but it was far from international markets and operated in a competitive environment that kept prices low. San Francisco and Seattle merchants and bankers supplied much of the region's capital and soon dominated salmon canning and ocean transportation. Only slightly less threatening was the outsiders' control of the canneries. Salmon canning grew rapidly in the late nineteenth century and led to the formation of a business combination, the Alaska Packers Association (APA), in 1893. For several decades the association controlled the industry in Southeast Alaska. (As fishing developed in the even richer Bristol Bay region of southwestern Alaska, the APA share of the Alaska industry lessened, but other large operators exercised similar powers there.) APA canneries hired Natives or Asian immigrant workers, paid low wages, and kept them physically isolated, minimizing their economic impact. The canneries also promoted the use of fish traps, which blocked the mouths of streams and devastated the salmon population. In response to complaints, the canners lobbied successfully for federal regulation and then, through their Washington contacts, controlled the faraway and ineffectual federal regulators. (In the early twentieth century, the Fisheries Service, the regulatory agency, typically had only one or two employees in Southeast Alaska.)[7] The 1924 White Act provided for more aggressive regulation. Yet fish traps were still permitted, and Congress appropriated too little money to make the regulations meaningful. In this environment the industry expanded rapidly to the mid-1930s and then crashed. The total catch fell by nearly 50 percent between 1935 and 1940 and continued to fall in the 1940s, creating widespread hardship. Fishing remained a "sick" industry through the 1950s, spurring an increasingly desperate search for alternatives.[8]

The canners were no less active in Juneau. Through vigorous lobbying they dominated the territorial legislature and prevented tax increases on canned salmon. Since the salmon tax was the territory's principal revenue source, the canners' political muscle ensured that local government would remain small and ineffectual. Their activities were often cited as another example of Alaska's colonial status.

In the meantime, the Seattle Chamber of Commerce worked to control ocean shipping and other Alaska resources. Historian Jeanette Nichols spelled out an important corollary to this role:

> Quick upon the heels of the economic adoption of Alaska by Seattle business men came the political adoption of the territory by Washington politicians. ... Seattle business soon acquired a vested interest in Alaska which demanded the closest possible attention to the policy of Congress and the administration. ... Insignificant and few indeed would be the Alaskan issues which could be settled without consulting the wishes of these highly organized combinations.[9]

Seattle domination of the shipping industries would be the most persistent of Alaskans' grievances. The Jones Act of 1920 (named for Senator Wesley Jones, of Washington), which banned Canadian shipping companies from the Alaska trade and sealed the Seattle monopoly, was for decades the preeminent badge of Alaska's vassalage.

Interior Alaska, extending roughly from Juneau north nearly 700 miles to the Yukon River (but excluding the vast coastal area to the west), was no less troubled. The interior, together with coastal entry points like Skagway and Valdez, was tied to the highly speculative gold mining industry that dated from the 1860s, attracted worldwide attention in 1897–1898 with the great Klondike rush, and peaked in the following decade. Apart from the Klondike rush, the most important rushes were at Nome on the Seward Peninsula, in far northwestern Alaska, in 1898, and around the new town of Fairbanks, in the Tanana Valley, in 1902. Nome briefly succeeded Dawson City, Yukon, as the largest community in northwestern North America, but Fairbanks soon surpassed it and remained the largest interior town of the pre–World War II years.

Interior Alaska was even more dependent on large corporations and outside capital than the southeast. Relatively few prospectors struck it rich; in the Klondike, for example, only about one percent enjoyed any significant success.[10] Those who remained usually became employees of the large mining companies that followed in their wake and quickly dominated the industry and region. The most famous and notorious of these concerns was known as the Alaska Syndicate. The syndicate's leader, Stephen Birch, had bought claims to high-grade copper deposits in the Wrangell Mountains of south-central Alaska and enlisted the assistance of the Guggenheim family, the dominant influence in the hard-rock mining industry, and J.P. Morgan, the nation's leading investment banker. The syndicate soon overshadowed the Treadwell companies and the Seattle firms and seemingly threatened the thousands of prospectors and small capitalists, many of whom soon agreed with the *Nome Gold Digger* that the Alaska Syndicate was a "vampire which has already started its blood sucking operations, and is laying its plans for the complete subjugation of the country to its will."[11]

To advance his plans, Birch bought out Alaska promoter John Rosene, whose interests included a railroad right-of-way from the coast to the area near the syndicate's property, and a steamship line, which would transport the ore to a Guggenheim smelter in Tacoma. The projected railroad would also provide a convenient overland connection with the Yukon River. Apart from these assets, Rosene's holdings included steamship connections with the Seward Peninsula and the mouth of the Yukon River, lifelines for residents of Nome and the vast Yukon Valley; stores and other properties in the Nome area; and a large salmon canning operation in Southeast Alaska. For the Guggenheims, who had recently bought up the leading mining firms of the Klondike region, the syndicate's potential was intoxicating. Their biographer reports that their "ambition had become nothing less than to control all the natural resources of Alaska."[12]

Their inflated hopes soon gave way to a modest but profitable reality. Birch and his backers concluded that most of the Rosene holdings were worthless and by 1915 had eliminated everything except the mining and transportation properties. Government restrictions on the development of the Bering River coalfield also foiled the plan for a railroad empire. What remained was still formidable: North America's richest copper mine, a short but essential railroad to the mine site, and a steamship line. Meanwhile, the money poured in. Despite an expenditure of more than $23 million to complete the Copper River and Northwestern Railroad, the syndicate was immediately profitable. In the mid-1910s, it reorganized as a public corporation, the Kennecot Copper Company. Over its lifetime the Kennecot mine alone produced revenues of $300 million and profits of $100 million.[13]

As recent historians have noted, the Alaska Syndicate was exactly the kind of business that Alaska business and political leaders always insisted they needed. It had abundant capital, expert management, and advanced technology. During World War I, it made the Kennecot community a model town. An important factor in its success, notes historian Melody Webb Grauman, was "a definite shift in decision making from wealthy owners to efficient managers."[14]

Why, then, was the Alaska Syndicate controversial? One answer is that some of the criticism was self-serving: syndicate enemies were unhappy because they were excluded from sharing in its ventures. Syndicate managers were also imperious and ruthless in relations with their Alaska neighbors. A violent altercation in 1906 between syndicate workers and employees of a competing railroad became an ominous symbol of the organization's potential. And like the salmon canners, the syndicate employed Washington lobbyists to avoid local taxation.[15]

In view of contemporary anxiety over the power of "trusts," it is not surprising, then, that the syndicate became a catalytic presence in Alaska politics. The principal beneficiary was James Wickersham, a judge and attorney who became Alaska's most important and durable pre–World War II political figure. Running against the syndicate, Wickersham was elected Alaska's congressional delegate in 1908, won every subsequent election through 1918, and won again in 1930. He ran variously as a Republican, Progressive Republican, Independent, and quasi- Democrat.[16] Although he proved endlessly protean, there were two constants in his career: his opposition to the syndicate and the "Guggs," and his identification with the economic ambitions of Alaska speculators and promoters. Thanks to Wickersham, suspicion of big business became a prominent feature of Alaska political life. But as the syndicate became respectable, Wickersham and a growing number of imitators found a new bogeyman. By the mid-

1910s the federal government—remote, insensitive, enormously powerful, controlled by interests like the Guggs and the Seattle merchants—had become the preeminent enemy of Alaska enterprise. The fact that the government also provided services and subsidies, such as the government-owned railroad authorized in 1914, did little to mollify Wickersham and his allies.

Alaska's third and largest economic region consisted of the western coastal area (minus the Nome mining region), the Arctic, and most of the interior river valleys. Mostly flat, wet, inhospitable, and unappealing to outsiders, these lands were home to a vast array of wildlife and most of Alaska's Native peoples. Natives engaged in hunting, trapping, fishing, berry picking, and related activities. Geographically scattered and ethnically diverse, they included Inupiat and Yupik Eskimos, who occupied the northern and western Arctic coasts and the western and southwestern Pacific coasts, respectively; the Aleuts, who lived on the far-flung Aleutian Islands; and various tribes, notably the Athabascans of the interior Yukon Valley and the Tlingit and Haida of the southeast. In aggregate, the Native population may have peaked at 75,000 in the mid-eighteenth century.[17] The arrival of Russian fur traders and the introduction of European diseases, such as smallpox, influenza, and tuberculosis, cut it in half by the 1830s and contributed to a continuing decline in the following decades. In Southeast Alaska, for which the best data exist, the Native population had fallen to 5,800 by 1900 and to a low of 5,200 in 1920. The addition of William Duncan's nearly 1,000 Tsimshians in 1887 only partly offset the decline.

Most Natives continued to live off the land. In the southeast and southwest, where salmon were the principal foodstuff, semipermanent villages were the rule. Clans and family groups had "well-defined tracts of land and sea, and in certain cases, trade trails to the interior."[18] In other areas, scarce and migrating animal populations made mobility a necessity. The Athabascans of the upper Yukon, for example, developed villages only in the nineteenth century as trapping (in response to trading opportunities at Hudson's Bay Company outposts) succeeded hunting.[19] Most other groups moved frequently and ranged widely. In the words of anthropologist Ernest Burch, "there was no usable land that was never used."[20]

By the late nineteenth century the government's relationship with the aboriginal tribes in the American West had reached a turning point. In 1871 a disillusioned Congress banned additional treaties with Native tribes. Seventeen years later it passed the Dawes Act, which provided for phasing out the reservation system. (Metlakatla, dating from 1884, was thus an exception to the general policy.) These initiatives had a distinctive effect in Alaska: since there had been no treaties, Alaska Natives did not give up their claims to the land based on traditional uses. The potential scope of those claims attracted little notice at the time, or for many years afterward. The distinguished Alaskan economist George Rogers would write in the late 1950s that Alaska authorities "either blithely ignored the existence of prior claims ... or put off the final reckoning."[21]

The other critical factor in Alaska was the role of Christian missionaries. They came to Alaska to convert and to persuade Natives to embrace white culture, but they soon faced an obstacle that forced them to postpone, and partially abandon, their "civilizing" mission. That obstacle, in the words of Hudson Stuck, Episcopal archdeacon of Alaska from 1904 to 1920, was an abundance of "low-down white men," determined to cheat and corrupt the Natives.[22] Stuck's colleagues emphatically agreed. "Unprincipled," "degenerate," "dishonest" white men plied guileless Natives with liquor, took their property, corrupted Native women, and left chaos in their wake.

Given the size of Alaska and its dispersed population, there were two obvious ways to confront that menace. The first was most effectively represented by William Duncan's Metlakatla. By the time of the Harriman visit, it had become precisely what liberal advocates of reservations had envisioned. Yet neither Duncan nor his contemporaries grasped the irony of their approach—modernizing by scorning modern influences and contacts. Though his example helped keep the reservation idea alive for a half-century, Metlakatla did not strike most missionaries or government officials as a practical solution to Alaska's problem. Duncan's personality was too large an influence, and the migratory habits of most Alaska Natives made the enclave idea unrealistic. As a result, a second, somewhat different approach prevailed.

Its principal advocate was an energetic Presbyterian minister, Sheldon Jackson, who brokered an 1880 agreement among Protestant churches to divide Alaska into informal enclaves and persuaded Congress to authorize publicly financed schools, which would constitute a de facto Native school system.[23] Jackson was appointed general agent of the new board of education in 1884 and held that position for 23 years. In that role he was able to obtain public subsidies for many fledging mission schools and encourage the creation of others. Under his regime, Native youths received a basic education and vocational skills in a controlled environment, free from the corrupting influences of white society.

Like Duncan, Jackson sought to isolate Alaska Natives so that they would experience only the positive, uplifting features of the outside world. Over time, however, Jackson's approach became increasingly problematic. The missionaries hoped to equip Native children to enter white society at a higher, more refined level. But the Native education program proved a disappointment; the federal subsidy was too small to achieve its original goal, and private support declined. There were also cultural barriers that challenged the missionaries' premises. When Natives attempted to find jobs or housing in white communities, they faced intense hostility and prejudice. Though most Natives became at least nominal church members, their conversion was not accompanied by significant economic or political progress.

Native disillusionment was reflected in the creation of the Alaska Native Brotherhood (ANB) in 1912 and the Alaska Native Sisterhood in 1915. Founded by the southeastern Native elite, ANB was militantly assimilationist, admitting only Christians and English speakers. ANB members were acutely aware of the problems that even educated Natives faced. Though they endorsed a variety of self-help projects, their organization was best suited for political action. And there was much political work to do. Apart from the deficiencies of the education program, land had become a major issue. Between 1902 and 1907 President Roosevelt had set aside most of Southeast Alaska as the Tongass National Forest, effectively dismissing the Natives' claims. Congressional legislation authorizing payment or a lawsuit could correct the oversight, but most ANB leaders considered that an impossible hurdle. Only when Wickersham proposed legislation authorizing a lawsuit against the government (described in his diary as a "scheme" to obtain a large legal fee) did ANB embrace it. He introduced the bill in 1931, marking the formal beginning of the Native land claims movement.[24]

CONSERVATION IN ALASKA

One important challenge to the status quo—and in part to the local perception of the federal government as an ally of the corporations that exploited Alaska's natural resources—was the emergence of the conservation movement during the first decade of the twentieth century. Conservation reflected growing interest in preserving parts of the national domain and countering the irresponsible behavior of timber and mining companies. Pressured by a growing number of private scientific, educational, and recreational groups, Congress set aside areas of unusual beauty and aesthetic interest as parks, beginning with Yellowstone in 1872. Under an 1891 law, the president gained authority to create forest "reserves," or national forests. Congress later passed the Antiquities Act (1906), which enabled the president to create national monuments, and the Weeks Act (1910), which provided for the purchase of privately owned lands. Yet there was little effort to spell out the meaning of federal management until the Theodore Roosevelt administration. Long an avid hunter and naturalist, Roosevelt endorsed the ideas of Gifford Pinchot, the head of the Bureau of Forestry (after 1905, when Congress transferred the forest reserves to the Agriculture Department, the Forest Service), which managed the reserves. Pinchot advocated public ownership and commodity production under expert management—the so-called wise use of public resources. Forest Service professionals would reconcile the demands of competing users and ensure that logging and other extractive activities did not exceed the forest's natural growth or cause permanent harm. With Roosevelt's encouragement, these ideas became the basis of Forest Service policy and a major feature of American conservation.[25]

Roosevelt quickly turned his attention to Southeast Alaska's lush forests. In 1902, utilizing his authority under the 1891 act, he created the Alexander Archipelago Forest Reserve, covering the sparsely inhabited islands along the coast, and in 1907, on the recommendation of the Forest Service, extended the reserve to the mainland and renamed it the Tongass National Forest. A 1909 order enlarged the Tongass to 17 million acres, embracing most of Southeast Alaska. It became and remained the largest national forest.[26] Many local loggers applauded the president's action for introducing order and system to Alaska's forests. Others complained. The most vocal opponents were administrators of the General Land Office, which had had jurisdiction over the land. Commissioner Richard Ballinger, a former Seattle mayor and promoter of Puget Sound business interests, became the most outspoken opponent of the Tongass National Forest.

Roosevelt's other conservation initiatives in Alaska were equally controversial. In 1907, again acting on Forest Service recommendations, he created the 5-million-acre Chugach National Forest, which included most of the land bordering Prince William Sound just north of the Tongass. He explained his action—which Ballinger also strenuously opposed—as an effort to thwart the "land thieves." At the same time he withdrew Alaska coal lands from the public domain until a leasing system could be devised. Roosevelt left little doubt that he had the Alaska Syndicate in mind when he attacked outsiders who sought "to develop Alaska by exploiting the coal fields purely in their own interest."[27]

Roosevelt's actions also brought the conflict between Pinchot and Ballinger to a head. When President Taft appointed Ballinger as secretary of the Interior in 1909, Ballinger ordered his subordinates to honor a series of coal land claims filed by Clarence Cunningham on behalf of a group of Seattle-area speculators before Roosevelt's withdrawal order had gone into effect. Cunningham had agreed to sell his coal to the syndicate. Through a series of misunderstandings, Ballinger and Pinchot were drawn into open conflict, Pinchot was fired, and Roosevelt entered the dispute as Pinchot's ally. Ultimately, Roosevelt and Taft became enemies and the Republican Party split. Though other factors were involved, at heart the conflict was a dispute over conservation and the role of the federal government in managing natural resources.[28]

In the following years federal policy became less controversial. Though it did not address the stranglehold of the Seattle merchants or the Natives' grievances (as Wickersham and his imitators eagerly reminded voters), Washington was generally an accommodating landlord. In 1914 Congress passed a coal leasing law and authorized a government-owned railroad. Federal agencies promoted a variety of development plans. In a notable effort to create a more diversified economy, the Forest Service, for example, sought to create a wood products industry in Southeast Alaska. By the early 1920s Alaska mills provided nearly all the territory's lumber and had developed an export business. Government foresters were particularly optimistic about the prospects for pulp and paper production. By 1922 two mills were in operation and a third was on the drawing board. The two mills soon failed because of poor market conditions and high shipping costs, but the Forest Service was undeterred. In the late 1920s it offered a long-term contract to John Bellaine, a Seattle promoter who had been active in Alaska for many years. Bellaine agreed to invest more than $2 million. The collapse of the economy in the early 1930s killed this plan, as well as other timber projects. Nevertheless, Forest Service Chief William Greeley retained "a deep personal interest in the development of a pulp program in Alaska." It was time, he insisted, to utilize Alaska's timber.[29] By the late 1930s the Forest Service was proposing 50-year contracts to paper companies.

Similar perspectives were evident in a parallel effort to preserve wildlife habitat. Beginning in 1913, when President Taft created the Aleutian

Islands Reservation in an effort to regulate the harvest of sea mammals, the government set aside a series of wildlife refuges. Hunters, guides, and interest groups that depended on animal populations provided much of the political impetus for this activity. The Kenai Moose Range, established in 1941, was the 12th Alaska refuge.[30]

Another initiative had even greater potential. Since the 1880s Alaska had attracted a growing number of tourists, most of whom were wealthy adventurers like Harriman and his party. Many were members of elite hunting, wildlife, or mountaineering clubs, and they demanded the preservation of exceptional areas. Using the new Antiquities Act, President Taft in 1910 established Sitka National Monument, encompassing the old Russian community; in 1916 President Wilson authorized Old Kasaan National Monument, an abandoned Haida village with distinctive totem poles. The following year, Congress authorized Mount McKinley National Park, and the president created Katmai National Monument to preserve the site of a massive volcanic eruption on the Alaska Peninsula. In 1925 President Coolidge created Glacier Bay National Monument. By that time the Alaska parks accounted for 40 percent of the acreage in the entire national park system.[31]

For many years the Alaska parks existed mostly on paper. Congress provided no appropriations until 1916 and only minuscule amounts thereafter. Mount McKinley, the largest, had no superintendent until 1921. Hunting and trapping continued in the parks, and vandalism became a problem at the historic sites. By the 1950s the Old Kasaan site had deteriorated beyond repair.[32] As a result of haphazard management, only the most determined tourists found their way to Alaska parks. Mount McKinley had a total of 4,000 visitors in the 1920s, Katmai a mere 32.[33]

Despite those problems and the hostility of miners, loggers, and other local people, the parks had great political appeal. As early as 1908 the Forest Service proposed that the spectacular mountain area surrounding Mount St. Elias, north of Glacier Bay, become a national monument. In the late 1930s Alaska politicians and Park Service officials proposed an even larger Wrangell–St. Elias national park. In the meantime wildlife protection groups began to agitate for an Admiralty Island park to preserve the habitat of the brown bear population. Both campaigns failed, though they helped build support for a million-acre addition to the Glacier Bay monument.[34]

These activities also reflected the quickening tempo of government activity in Alaska after 1933 and the beginning of a pattern of dependence on public spending that would dominate Alaska history. What would such activities mean for Alaska's resources? In 1938 a group of government officials, representing agencies involved in managing those resources, attempted to reply. The Alaska National Resource Committee's statement, published as *Alaska—Its Resources and Development* in 1938, explicitly addressed two major questions: "Is there a national need for the immediate and rapid development of Alaska?" and "How may Alaska best be developed?"[35] Administrators prepared factual reports, and a committee of top officials wrote a powerful defense of federal stewardship. "Enlightened opinion" accepted federal ownership of Alaska lands. Restrictions on leasing reflected a realistic appraisal of the value of Alaska's resources.

> In the past there has been a feeling on the part of Alaskans that the Federal Government's policy [was] to lock up unnecessarily the natural resources. While available information indicates that Alaska has real development possibilities, it is not a 'vast storehouse of easily obtainable wealth awaiting only the opening of the door.'[36]

The report dismissed the assumption that Alaska could be compared to the Midwest or the Pacific Northwest. In fact, agriculture was impossible in most areas, and mining had little potential. Anticipating an argument that would become increasingly popular in future years, it also rejected the suggestion that Alaska's minerals were vital to national defense.

Assuming that some development should occur, the authors contrasted two approaches. One was a largely unfettered scramble for riches, like the gold rushes of the early twentieth century. This would produce a boom-and-bust phenomenon, create more quasi-ghost towns like Nome and Skagway, and leave Alaska ravaged and poor. The other approach involved the creation of a "well-rounded" economy with year-round jobs, permanent residents, and stable communities. This approach, which was consistent with a large federal role, was preferable. Yet "whether this Alaska is possible is by no means certain."[37]

Two of the specialist reports stand out because of their support for the well-rounded option. The first was "Forest Resources," largely written by B. Frank Heintzleman, the new regional forester. Heintzleman and his colleagues explained how a large-scale pulpwood and newsprint industry could emerge in Southeast Alaska. According to the summary statement, it was "the only major industry which seems to have definitely favorable prospects."[38] The second report, "Recreational Resources and Facilities," was similarly upbeat. In contrast to the meager opportunities for industry and agriculture, "this last frontier is an empire ... especially rich in recreational values." The report then proceeded to examine ways of stimulating tourism, such as building a highway from Seattle to Fairbanks. This was too much for one of the three authors, Robert Marshall of the Forest Service. In a ringing dissent Marshall condemned the highway proposal as incompatible with the preservation of wilderness. It would benefit only the idle rich who had time to drive 2,000 miles, attract irresponsible transients—"the people who now drift from one region to ... another in search of work"—increase the number of destructive forest fires, and endanger wildlife populations.[39]

Marshall also wrote an extended critique, which the committee included as an appendix. The goal of recreation planners "should not be development, the greatest possible returns or increasing the volume of tourist traffic." Alaska's "highest value lies in the pioneering conditions yet prevailing. ... In Alaska alone can the emotional values of the frontier be preserved." Rather than highways and tourist facilities, government officials should emphasize the creation of permanent wilderness regions, offlimits to even the low-impact activities his colleagues proposed. Because of Alaska's small population, no one would be hurt, no obvious opportunities forsaken, no expenses incurred. In addition to relatively small wilderness areas in central and Southeast Alaska, which his colleagues also endorsed, he proposed that all the land north of the Yukon River, except for a small area around Nome, be declared a permanent wilderness. "Let's keep Alaska largely a wilderness," he concluded.[40]

Alaskans had not been indifferent to the desirability of preserving sensitive areas (such as Katmai), but the notion of declaring large areas, even inhospitable areas like the mountains and tundra north of the Yukon, offlimits to economic activity was too much. Even to the authors of *Alaska—Its Resources and Development*, Marshall's proposals seemed irresponsible. His ideas had no immediate impact, however. Alaska boosters already had plenty to complain about in the report, and they disregarded the dissenting appendix.[41]

DEVELOPMENT THROUGH GOVERNMENT ACTIVISM

The coming of World War II soon overshadowed the plans of the late 1930s and introduced far-reaching changes. Alaska's proximity to the Pacific theater (dramatically illustrated by the Japanese occupation of two

Aleutian islands in 1942) enhanced its visibility and transformed its economy. Spending for bases, supplies, and salaries became the engine for a new boom and revived the get-rich-quick spirit of the gold rushes. It likewise provided momentum—demographic, economic, and ideological—for a statehood movement, which culminated in 1958–1959 with the creation of a state committed to development of Alaska's natural resources.

Presiding over this remarkable transition was one of the most colorful and influential figures in Alaska's history, Ernest Gruening. A New England newspaper editor and inveterate liberal crusader who became a top official of the Interior Department during the Roosevelt years, Gruening had little interest in or knowledge of the northern territory. By the late 1930s, however, he and his irascible boss, Interior Secretary Harold Ickes, had disagreed on several issues, and Gruening's position had become precarious. When the territorial governorship suddenly became available in 1939, Gruening found himself the new appointee. Initially dismayed at being demoted to the Interior Department's "Siberia," he soon embraced his new job with characteristic energy.[42] Taking advantage of the war boom, he enhanced the governor's power, adopted an activist program, and made himself the territory's best-known personality. By the early 1950s Gruening had joined hands with Alaska's traditional boosters.

When the new governor arrived in 1939, the Navy was building a base at Sitka and two more in the Aleutians. These were the first, limited steps in what would soon be a vast, haphazard, crisis-inspired program of Alaska activity that featured more failures than successes. The Alaska Highway from Edmonton, Alberta, to Dawson Creek, British Columbia, to Big Delta, Alaska was little more than a rutted woodland path. The Canol (Canadian Oil) pipeline from the Norman Wells field in Canada to the Alaska coast was almost unusable.[43] The Navy's exploratory activities in the giant Arctic Naval Petroleum Reserve Number 4, or "Pet 4," created in 1923 to ensure an adequate supply of fuel oil, simply confirmed what had been known for decades: there was probably oil along the Arctic coast. The military campaigns against the Japanese in the Aleutians were enormously costly. The Navy's expulsion of the Aleut from their homeland was one of the great scandals of the war.

All those activities brought people to Alaska. The territory's population rose from 73,000 in 1939 to 233,000 in 1943 (two-thirds of whom were soldiers) and 140,000 in 1945. Initially, it appeared that the war boom would be followed by a peacetime collapse, reminiscent of Alaska's earlier boom-and-bust cycles. But the Cold War and the Korean War inspired a new wave of spending that totaled more than a billion dollars in the 1950s.[44] During the Korean War years military employment (including civilian employees of the armed forces) totaled more than 40 percent of all Alaska workers. In 1954, the peak year, there were 49,000 such employees, or 47 percent of all Alaska workers. But even this number understates the total, since 10 percent of civilian employees were construction workers, many of whom were engaged in military projects. Another 40 percent were employees of federal, territorial, or local government agencies. In all, two-thirds of Alaska's workers were government employees, with the military playing the largest role.[45]

In the mid-1950s government employment accounted for 65 percent of total employment in the central and interior regions, which included Anchorage and Fairbanks; 62 percent in the north and west; and 29 percent in the southeast. For the territory as a whole, 60 percent of all workers were public employees.[46]

Military activity had an even greater impact on the distribution of Alaska's people. On the eve of World War II, Southeast Alaska was still the most populous region; Anchorage was a town of only 3,500. The military activity around Anchorage and Fairbanks introduced dramatic changes, and by 1950 Anchorage's population had grown to 35,000, Fairbanks' to 20,000. Juneau, the only other city of any consequence, had 9,000 residents. In the 1950s Fairbanks merchants reportedly scorned tourists in favor of soldiers and construction workers, who were less demanding.[47]

The changing character of Alaska's economy and society exposed the shortcomings of its government. When Gruening arrived, the executive and legislative branches operated much as they had in 1912: the appointed governor was almost powerless, the legislature was beholden to the salmon canning and mining industries, and the federal government preempted critical areas of decisionmaking, such as land use and game regulation. These arrangements had worked reasonably well as long as the territory was remote and sparsely populated. With the boom of the 1940s and 1950s, however, strains emerged. The growing population demanded better transportation, housing, and social services. The boom also exposed features of Alaska society, such as the de facto racial segregation of the Native population, that had attracted little attention in earlier years. Alaska's threadbare government seemed wholly inadequate.

Fresh from Washington and committed to activist, problem-solving government, Gruening found this situation unacceptable. For the next 12 years he battled to update and modernize the territorial government, largely by raising taxes on business and expanding public services. His opponents were representatives of the prewar establishment, notably "Judge" Winton C. Arnold, of the canners' trade association, and Austin E. "Cap" Lathrop, a Fairbanks entrepreneur who had demonstrated that it was possible to make a fortune in Alaska without government assistance. Gruening delighted in attacking these men and their corrupting influence on the legislature. To mobilize support, he appealed directly to the voters, worked with Republicans in the legislature, and maneuvered in Washington. In 1945 he won landmark civil rights legislation that banned discrimination in public buildings, including theaters and restaurants. His greatest victory came in 1949, when the legislature adopted his tax reform package.[48]

Gruening thought of himself as a populist mobilizing the people against monopolists and greedy interest groups. His self-image was not incorrect: his enemies were the monopolists who had long exploited their neighbors, and his identification with Alaska's Natives gave him credibility as a defender of the poor. Having taken on the conservatives, he had little choice but to appeal to the only other influential political entity, the boosters and promoters who had convinced themselves that only government under their aegis, with resources to bankroll their plans, could break the conservatives' hold and stand up to the federal agencies. By the mid-1940s Gruening was closely identified with them. He became the new Wickersham.[49]

Gruening's coalition soon became the dominant influence in Alaska politics. Apart from Gruening himself, it included congressional representative Anthony Diamond and the man who succeeded him in 1944, E.L. "Bob" Bartlett, the former territorial secretary. They worked with a loose-knit group of urban entrepreneurs, mostly Republicans, who subscribed to the Wickersham formula of government-assisted exploitation of the territory's natural resources. Most prominent was a group of Anchorage merchants and developers whose best-known representative, Robert B. Atwood, was publisher of the *Anchorage Daily Times*, the territory's most influential newspaper. Atwood had married Evangeline Rasmuson, whose father was president of the powerful Bank of Alaska. The Atwood and Rasmuson families would be at the center of the Anchorage business community for many years. By the early 1940s they were also close to Gruening.

In his conflict with the legislature, Gruening received help from a wholly unexpected source, the federal bureaucracy. When he first visited the territory, he found local miners and political leaders unstinting in their condemnation of the Interior Department. But World War II had revived the economy and demonstrated the value of government activism. Public administrators also gained new confidence in their potential as economic managers. Conflict with the Soviet Union added another element. If prosperity was the best advertisement for capitalism and democracy, and government activism was the best way to ensure prosperity, then it followed that government agencies had a responsibility to promote business activity. The anti–big business rhetoric of the New Deal years largely disappeared after 1945.[50]

Though the new perspective was not unique to Alaska, it had special significance there, given the location and large federal presence. In 1949 the Interior Department published a plan for Alaska that illustrated its new, more expansive conception of its responsibilities. The plan catalogued Alaska's problems: inadequate transportation, high living costs, inadequate housing, unresolved Native land claims, and "a very critical shortage of risk and development capital."[51] Private interests were incapable of addressing these problems:

> *Unless some large scale source of funds, administered with a thorough knowledge and appreciation of Alaska's needs and problems, is forthcoming, the task of settling and developing Alaska will be long and difficult. … The normal investment banker's point of view is not sufficiently broad or flexible enough to meet Alaska's development requirements.*

It concluded that "any government funds … must be administered with vision and business foresight."[52] Short-term needs included a cement industry, an expanded lumber industry, a pulp industry, and more "tourist and recreation facilities." Only when these needs had been addressed would it be possible to improve housing, schools, and the health of Alaska's Native population.[53]

Though the report itself had no demonstrable impact, it reflected the new cooperative spirit that had developed between federal administrators and Gruening and his allies; indeed, it could have been the boosters' blueprint for an Alaska state government. It also helps explain the single most significant nonmilitary development project of the postwar era.

A NEW TIMBER INDUSTRY

Since the 1910s, the managers of the Tongass National Forest had worked to create a timber industry in Southeast Alaska. Their rationale in the late

1940s was identical to their rationale in the late 1920s: it would promote economic growth and year-round employment, act as a counterweight to the declining fishing and mining industries, and promote community stability and civic consciousness. By the mid-1940s the foresters' prospects had improved. The domestic market for wood products was more favorable, and a vast export market—principally devastated Japan—had emerged. Finally, it seemed, their time had come.

In Alaska, the most notable champion of the wood pulp industry was B. Frank Heintzleman, still the forester of the agency's Alaska region and Gruening's eventual successor as territorial governor. A Yale graduate, Heintzleman typified the agency's elite leadership. For decades he was a leading figure in Juneau society, a patron of the arts, an avid supporter of the public library, and a leader of the Presbyterian church and the local Republican Party.[54]

As a member of the Alaska National Resource Committee and the author of a chapter in *Alaska—Its Resources and Development*, he had stood out. Alone among the Alaska administrators, he could identify a development that would create a "well-rounded" economy. "Fortunately," the report had intoned, "the pulp industry ... holds out [the prospect of] a year-round industry employing a quota of permanent employees while at the same time affording off-season employment to some of those now engaged in the fisheries."[55] By clear-cutting and reseeding, the Forest Service could supply a huge newsprint industry. "Every appropriate step will be taken to encourage the development of the pulp-timber and water power resources of Alaska."[56]

By the end of World War II, Heintzleman's ideas had won wide support in and out of the Forest Service. Since the 1920s he and his associates had been convinced that only long-term monopoly contracts would attract outside capital. In the 1930s they advertised the possibility of 50-year grants. In 1944, at the urging of Forest Service officials and timber industry officials, Congress passed the Sustained Yield Forest Management Act, which encouraged long-term contracts with timber companies.[57]

Because of the difficulty of building roads in the Tongass, Heintzleman and his assistants also specified clear-cutting as the preferred harvest technique. Despite its identification with the rapacious, unsystematic forestry of the nineteenth century, clear-cutting attracted renewed interest after World War II as a technique suitable to the "intensive management" that the postwar boom demanded.

In view of the later criticism of Forest Service policy, it is important to add that Heintzleman was not indifferent to other values. As Forest Service historian Lawrence Rakestraw observes,

> *During Heintzleman's administration there was much discussion of primitive areas, amenity values, and natural areas. Heintzleman had taken into detailed consideration matters of pollution, game management, and commercial fishing. A further consideration was preservation of scenery along steamboat lanes.*[58]

He consulted Forest Service experts on the suitability of his proposed mill sites and sponsored research on the relationship of logging to salmon reproduction. Of particular importance was the research of Raymond Taylor of the Alaska Forest Research Center. Between 1949 and 1953 Taylor and colleagues from the University of Washington and the U.S. Bureau of Fisheries conducted studies of the effects of logging on salmon streams. They concluded that logging had no adverse effects and that loggers and fishermen were compatible, not competing resource users.[59]

Buttressed with such information, Heintzleman sold his ideas to an increasingly receptive public and business community. Emphasizing themes that became staples of industry propaganda, he insisted that his plans would not be harmful to the forest. The wooded mountainsides that so impressed tourists were, in fact, overmature, decaying, diseased, and insect-infested forests. The only responsible option was to replace them with young, vigorous trees that would perpetuate the natural beauty and economic health of Southeast Alaska. This fanciful imagery, supposedly based on scientific research, had great appeal. Timber industry executives and workers cited it to emphasize the socially responsible nature of their work, but even more skeptical observers were disarmed. The liberal economist George W. Rogers, generally careful and well informed, casually described the forests of Southeast Alaska as "decadent" and "overmature."[60]

There remained, however, a seemingly tangential issue that threatened to sabotage Heintzleman's work as surely as economic depression had in the 1930s. That was the unresolved land claims of the Tlingit and Haida. Before the New Deal, no one had taken the claims very seriously. But Secretary Ickes and his liberal associates had revived the issue and provoked extended debates in and out of the government. By 1946 the claims had become a formidable concern and, to Heintzleman and his allies, a major obstacle. As a paper industry publication noted, "all negotiations between the Forest Service and pulp and paper operators ceased when

Mr. Ickes brought up the Indian question."[61] Heintzleman was furious. He attacked the Interior secretary for "introducing a new, wholly impractical, unnecessary and harmful element."[62]

What was to be done? In the short term the answer seemed to be legislation that would defer the claims and open the Tongass. Gruening and Bartlett insisted that Congress act before the wartime newsprint shortage eased sufficiently to temper the paper companies' enthusiasm for Alaska. The original bill included a provision awarding the Tlingit and Haida 10 percent of Forest Service proceeds in order to finance a suit against the federal government in the U.S. Court of Claims. But the salmon canners and the Washington state congressional delegation opposed any formal acknowledgment of Native claims, and the provision was deleted. In its final form the bill simply placed all receipts from timber sales in escrow until the claims issue was resolved. ANB leaders were appalled. As Alaska historian Stephen Haycox writes, "the Indians were removed from the process ... they were made dependent upon the Secretary of the Interior to protect their villages, on the Secretary of Agriculture to get a fair price for the timber, and on the courts of the United States to determine what, if anything, they were entitled to as compensation."[63] Congress passed the Tongass Timber Act in early summer 1947, and President Truman signed it on August 8. Heintzleman, Gruening, and other Alaska leaders breathed a collective sigh of relief.[64]

In 1948 Heintzleman awarded a 50-year contract to Puget Sound Pulp and Timber and to American Viscose Company, a manufacturer of rayon (not newsprint after all). They agreed to purchase 8.25 billion board feet of timber and to build a mill at Ward Cove, near Ketchikan. The actual contract was signed in 1951, and the mill, incorporated as Ketchikan Pulp Company, began operations in 1954.[65]

Other contracts followed in the 1950s. In 1953 a Japanese paper company, operating through a subsidiary, Alaska Lumber and Pulp, agreed to build a large sawmill and pulp mill in Sitka. The timber was to come from Baranof and Chichagof islands. The mills began operations in 1959. In the meantime, the Forest Service concluded a third agreement, with Pacific Northern Timber Company, for a pulp mill in Wrangell that was never built because of the company's deteriorating finances. A fourth contract, awarded in 1955 to Georgia Pacific for a Juneau-area newsprint mill, with timber from Admiralty and Douglas islands, also proved abortive. Despite these setbacks, the Forest Service plan did provide an element of diversification and a basis for the conviction that government-inspired economic growth was possible. It also provided an incentive for Natives to pursue their claims and a warning to those in Alaska and elsewhere who assumed that the Alaska wilderness was too large, too remote, and too rugged to be at risk.

STATEHOOD AND THE PROMISE OF DEVELOPMENT

By summer 1954, when Ketchikan Pulp Company began operations at Ward Cove, Alaska's changing character was apparent to even the most casual observers. It had more than three times its prewar population, a much larger economy based on government spending, and a more activist government than ever before. The territory's conservative political establishment was in decline, and federal bureaucrats were hardly distinguishable from local boosters. In retrospect it is easy to argue that most of these trends were fleeting and that the temporary alliance between Alaska's business community and the federal bureaucracy masked deeper conflicts. Yet in the mid-1950s, Alaska seemed to work. Contemporaries had reason to be optimistic about the future.

It was precisely at this time that a statehood movement first attracted a popular following. Statehood was not a new idea: James Wickersham had introduced an Alaska statehood bill in 1916, Anthony Dimond had sponsored another bill in 1943, and Bob Bartlett introduced bills in every session thereafter. Alaska voters had endorsed statehood in a 1948 referendum by a three-to-two margin, but that was before Gruening and his allies reformed the tax system and the Forest Service had demonstrated its commitment to economic development. The territory's new dynamism seemingly encouraged the movement for more fundamental change. Why?

The answer is complex and included a renewed commitment to political democracy and representative government in Alaska and other territories. But a more tangible stimulus operated consistently during the years from World War II to 1958, when President Eisenhower reluctantly signed a statehood bill, making Alaska the 49th state. The booster coalition—public officials allied with the territory's most aggressive entrepreneurs—persuaded a majority of Alaskans that booster control would bring greater prosperity than outsider control or any combination of local and federal efforts. At its core, the statehood movement was an expression of the long-standing desire to "unlock" Alaska's riches. Despite lip service to planned and sustainable development, statehood advocates were hostile to most conservation measures and to proposals, such as Marshall's, to leave large areas of Alaska untouched.

Several postwar developments made these ideas more salable than they had been in earlier years. Gruening's 1949 tax reforms had a huge impact. Not only did they provide territorial administrators with opportunities to show that they could provide the kinds of services expected of state government, but they also resolved, or seemed to resolve, the viability issue. Could so few people spread over such a large area create an effective political entity? The answer, by 1950 or 1951, seemed to be yes. As one historian explains, Gruening's tax reforms ensured the territory's solvency. "Now statehood could be legitimately pursued."[66]

At the same time the decline of the conservative coalition that had dominated the preceding quarter-century removed a major obstacle to statehood. Cap Lathrop died in 1950, and his influential paper, the *Fairbanks News-Miner*, soon joined the booster camp. C. W. "Bill" Snedden, the new owner, became an influential statehood advocate. After 1954, only the Juneau *Daily Alaska Empire* among the territory's major newspapers opposed statehood. Popular opposition, reflecting the influence of the Seattle-based canning industry, also remained strongest in the Southeast. But the Southeast's influence was waning as the fishing industry declined and as Anchorage and Fairbanks grew. In the 1950s lobbyist Bill Arnold and the canners became less active. Looking back at that period, Robert Weeden wrote that "non-resident businesses rapidly lost interest in Alaska. … They had opposed statehood earlier, but by the 1950's they didn't much care."[67]

The Republicans' waning popularity after 1954 also played into the hands of statehood backers. Because of the prominence of Gruening and Bartlett, most national observers believed Alaska would be a Democratic state. To Republicans, already on the defensive, the prospect of more Democratic senators was undesirable. They responded with obstructionist maneuvers until a deal involving statehood for Republican-leaning Hawaii as well as Alaska had emerged. President Eisenhower's reservations struck many Alaskans as partisan and unfair. Nebraska Senator Hugh Butler, the ranking Republican on the Public Lands Committee and the most vocal enemy of Alaska statehood, almost single-handedly transformed the statehood campaign from a small, elite movement into a popular cause.

For Gruening and his allies, statehood had implications apart from new business opportunities. Gruening made little secret of his desire to return to Washington as a U.S. senator and barely won his 1956 campaign for a

"Tennessee-plan" Senate seat (a shadow government designed to pressure Congress) and faced substantial opposition in later contests because of his broad interests and palpable ambition.[68] Bartlett was more circumspect (and popular) but no less ambitious. The other major figure to emerge from the statehood movement, William Egan, was a Valdez storekeeper and veteran of the territorial legislature who distinguished himself as the president of the 1955–1956 convention that drew up the state's constitution. Egan was a proponent of rapid development and state assistance to private enterprise. Personally, however, he was Gruening's opposite. Shy and uncomfortable in public, he seemed ill suited to a political career. But Egan loved politics and turned his personal limitations into political assets.[69] In 1956 he defeated Anchorage publisher Robert Atwood for the other Tennessee-plan Senate seat.

Gruening, Bartlett, and Egan had much company. Many delegates to the constitutional convention subsequently were elected to the state legislature, for example.[70] But there was a notable exception. In 1949, when the legislature had created the Alaska Statehood Committee to agitate for statehood, Gruening had appointed his friend Atwood to head it. Dashing and articulate, the Anchorage publisher became a familiar face throughout the territory. His campaign for a Senate seat was logical extension of his Statehood Committee work, and his loss to the unassuming Egan was crushing.

Despite their disadvantages, many Republicans were active in the statehood campaign. They included Atwood and Walter Hickel, an Anchorage real estate developer and Republican National Committee member who helped pressure Eisenhower to embrace the statehood cause. Even more influential was Bill Snedden, the Fairbanks publisher, who was a personal friend of Interior Secretary Fred A. Seaton. Snedden persuaded Seaton to add Theodore Stevens, the U.S. attorney in Anchorage, to his staff as an in-house lobbyist. According to historian Claus-M. Naske, Snedden also employed private detectives to collect scurrilous information on statehood opponents.[71] This story, perhaps apocryphal, nevertheless emphasizes the determination of the Alaska boosters.

The great coup of the statehood campaign was the constitutional convention of November 1955 to January 1956. Who could question the motives of delegates, cloistered in the frigid, apolitical confines of the University of Alaska for 75 grueling days of constitution making? Yet the results were hardly different from what would have emerged if Gruening and the Anchorage Chamber of Commerce had drawn up the document in a back room of the Westward Hotel. In his November 8 keynote address, Bartlett made sure that the delegates understood their charge.

"Fifty years from now," he began, Alaskans would "judge the product of this Convention not by the decisions taken upon issues like local government ... but rather by the decision taken upon the vital issue of resources policy." He warned of two critical dangers. "The first, and most obvious," was "exploitation under the thin disguise of development." In an obvious reference to the Alaska Syndicate and the Guggenheims, he charged that "the taking of Alaska's mineral resources without leaving some reasonable return for the support of Alaska government services and the use of all the people of Alaska" would constitute "a betrayal" of the state. The second danger was that "outside interests" would "attempt to acquire great areas of Alaska's public lands in order NOT to develop them." Alaskans, he argued "will not want and above all else do not need a resources policy which will prevent orderly development of the great treasures."[72]

Drafting the natural resources article was assigned to a committee consisting of two mining engineers, a miner, two fishermen, two merchants, a lawyer, and a homemaker. The result was a general statement calling for the state to make its lands "available for maximum use" in order to achieve "maximum benefit" for the people of Alaska. There were also long sections on mineral rights and fishing, which everyone assumed would be the state's economic foundation; a pledge to manage renewable resources "on the sustained yield principle"; and recognition of the desirability of state parks and other cultural sites. The convention later appended a separate "ordinance" calling for a referendum on fish traps, to be voted on at the same time as the constitution. Regardless of the details, there could be no mistake about the delegates' preoccupation. Atwood would later insist that "the purpose of statehood is development, that's in the state constitution."[73]

Whatever its strengths or weaknesses, the convention effectively silenced statehood opponents. The old conservative coalition collapsed; only one convention delegate, a Nome gold dredge owner, opposed statehood. A preliminary April 1956 referendum passed by a two-to-one margin (the only significant opposition coming from the southeast), and the final August 1958 referendum won by a seven-to-one margin. In the meantime, Secretary Seaton, trying to cut Republican losses, eased out Governor Heintzleman, who was identified with Republican skeptics.[74]

Still, there were dissenters, such as Jay Hammond, a U.S. Fish and Wildlife Service agent and guide from Naknek in southwestern Alaska. Hammond wrote letters to newspapers and to statehood advocates questioning the wisdom of their cause. They had been "statehoodwinked," he argued.[75] Hammond feared ambitious politicians and worried about the state's meager economic base, but he had an additional concern. As he later explained, the leaders of the statehood movement were "advocates of aggressive, no holds barred growth." They envisioned a future "at odds with what I thought was the best destiny for Alaska."[76]

Hammond's critique went to the heart of the statehood cause. To pay the added costs of state government, the state would have to increase tax revenues, preferably through increased economic activity. But it was perilous to assume that statehood alone would stimulate the economy. The only way to ensure greater activity would be to provide assistance either in the form of highways, airports, and other forms of infrastructure or in direct subsidies. The state would have to spend money to make money. This assumption had disturbing implications. First, it seemed to demand a commitment to unrestrained growth. Second, even with such a commitment, there would be a lag between the state investments and the tax receipts. If for any reason the expansion did not occur or was slower than expected, the state would have to raise taxes, which would discourage industry. Conceivably, the strategy could backfire and the state and its citizens would be poorer.

How could they guard against such a fate? The only immediate, practical answer was to maximize the opportunities available to entrepreneurs. Since nearly everyone equated opportunity with natural resources, a critical variable would be the amount of land the new state had at its disposal and where the land was located. Though this issue received little systematic attention during the statehood campaign, it was essential both to the campaign and to the larger question of Hammond's "best destiny for Alaska."

Since the eighteenth century, Congress had given new states part of the public domain lying within their boundaries to help finance schools, hospitals, prisons, and other services. By the late nineteenth century, the standard formula was 4 sections (of a total of 36) within each township, plus some additional land subject to negotiation. Florida had received the largest grant, 24 million acres, or 64 percent of the entire state. Among the states admitted after the Civil War, New Mexico had received the largest area, 13 million acres, or 16 percent of the total. Of the others, only Arizona and Utah received more than 10 percent. By this standard Alaskans could expect approximately 30 million acres from the 272 million acres of vacant, unappropriated lands.[77] This would be approximately 160 acres per capita—an enormous bonanza. Yet Alaska was not Iowa:

agriculture had little potential, and the best forests had already been claimed by the Forest Service. There were millions of acres of tundra and glaciers, and the northern third of Alaska was permanently frozen.

While Gruening, Atwood, and their allies talked about the desirability of representative government and self-determination, Bartlett addressed the less glamorous issue of the land grant. His first statehood bill had awarded the state "all vacant and unappropriated" land. Over the next decade, he had proposed various formulas, from four sections per township to 180 million unrestricted acres. In no case was the land clause crucial to the bill's success or failure, though Bartlett became more circumspect. He warned his allies not to appear too greedy, since Alaska's gain would be a loss for the rest of the country. On several occasions statehood opponents in Congress tried to increase the land grant to make the bill unpalatable.[78] Bartlett's campaign reached a turning point in 1950, when opponents, led by Arnold, attacked the statehood bill for including too little land—four sections per township. Arnold was so persuasive that statehood advocates dropped the traditional formula in favor of an acreage total: the state could select any of the territory's "vacant and unappropriated" land up to the limit. Thereafter the only issue was the number of acres. In this roundabout way, Arnold "made a significant contribution to Alaska statehood."[79]

As the statehood campaign bogged down in partisan wrangling, Bartlett was able to increase the total. The 1950 Senate bill gave the state 20 million acres; the 1953 House bill granted 40 million acres and was amended to give the state 100 million acres. For several years the 40 million and 100 million totals appeared in several bills. By 1955, however, 100 million acres seemed to be the consensus choice. In the final 1958 deliberations Congress came close to awarding Alaska a substantially larger total. Conservative objections produced a final compromise: 102 million acres plus a variety of smaller grants (such as 400,000 acres from the national forests) that raised the total to 104 million acres, or nearly 600 acres per capita.[80] The state had 25 years, starting in 1959, to make its selections. These remarkably generous provisions reflected the dynamics of the statehood campaign, Bartlett's skill as a legislator, and widespread ignorance of the details of the Alaska legislation.

In the end, the only groups that remained publicly skeptical were the national conservation organizations. Various conservation leaders, concerned about the future of Alaska's parks, wildlife, and undeveloped land, had expressed misgivings about statehood since the late 1940s. In the final

hearings, an official of the Wildlife Management Institute attacked the natural resources provisions of the proposed constitution. A. W. "Bud" Boddy,
head of the Alaska Sportsmen's Council, echoed these complaints.
Officials of the Wilderness Society were also wary, though they did not
officially oppose statehood.[81] Sensitive to the criticisms, Congress retained
federal control of fish and wildlife until the Secretary of the Interior found
the state fish and game department able to take over its responsibilities.

Statehood proponents, led by Egan, the newly elected governor, now
had what they wanted and needed, nearly one-third of Alaska and an invitation to select the most economically valuable lands. The no-holds-
barred growth that Hammond had feared became the order of the day.
New mining ventures were high on the boosters' agenda. Oil, long a
source of disappointment, also showed promise. In 1957 the Atlantic
Refining Company had struck oil along the Swanson River in the Kenai
Moose Range, 150 miles south of Anchorage. After conferring with prominent conservationists, Interior Secretary Seaton agreed to divide the Moose
Range, allowing drilling to continue. Alaska boosters had even greater
hopes for the Arctic coast. (Governor Heintzleman had sealed his fate
when he proposed a "small" state that excluded the Arctic.) Finally, boosters hoped to increase federal government spending. Defense expenditures
were declining, but there were other possibilities. With two senators and a
representative whose votes counted, Alaska would have greater clout in
Washington. Gruening, who had won his coveted Senate seat, told CBS
interviewers that his goal was to "build up" Alaska.[82]

A half-century after the Harriman expedition, Alaska was still relatively
poor and only marginally more accommodating to Native interests. Still,
many things had changed. The influence of outside corporate interests had
waned, and government had become more important. In addition to such
public enterprises as the government-owned railroad, continued high levels of defense spending and the accommodating plans of the Forest Service
made Alaska uniquely dependent on the federal government. While welcoming these activities (and continuing to complain about fisheries management and the "lockup" of lands in parks, refuges, and other federal
reserves), Alaska business and political leaders demanded more. In the
Alaska Statehood Act they obtained the right to select more than 100 million acres of Alaska land. Statehood was the first step in what would soon
become a wholesale reorganization of the Alaska landscape.

CHAPTER 2

CONSERVATION IN TRANSITION

Perhaps better than anyone else, Celia Hunter and Virginia Hill Wood embodied the positive qualities that outsiders often associated with Alaska. They had met as World War II Women Air Force Service Pilot flyers, better known as WASPs, and first visited Alaska in 1947. After several postwar jobs as pilots, they returned to Alaska and, with Hill's husband, Morton Wood, a former Mount McKinley Park ranger, established Camp Denali, a summer camp devoted to nature study and recreation, at Wonder Lake on the northern edge of Mount McKinley National Park. "We have operated on a very simple principle," Ginny Wood explained, "of just making our income balance our expenditures. ... Mostly we just rolled up our sleeves and built it. In bad years, we just reduced our standard of living accordingly."[1] During the winters they retreated to Fairbanks, where they bought land in the hills north of College, the community that had grown up around the University of Alaska, and built unpretentious log homes. During the winter they often traveled to College or downtown Fairbanks by snowshoe or dogsled. Soon "Dogpatch" (after the hillbilly community in the *Li'l Abner* cartoon strip) became a center of innovative, often heretical thinking about the Alaskan environment.

By the 1960s Camp Denali had become a well-known destination for conservation leaders and activists. In 1963 the Wilderness Society held its annual meeting there. A highlight of that gathering was the adoption of a resolution calling on the federal government to create wilderness parks in Alaska.[2] That resolution reflected several important developments of the postwar era: a growing sensitivity to the costs of the prosperity, a new appreciation of the value of undeveloped areas, and an understanding of the need for organized advocacy if those insights were to have any practical significance. In the years between World War II and the mid-1960s Alaska became a center of conservation activism, and Alaskan conservationists, fearful that statehood would lead to the problems that were increasingly evident in other states, organized to preserve Alaska's distinctive natural areas.

ORIGINS OF ENVIRONMENTALISM

At the end of World War II the American conservation movement was largely what it had been 30 years before, a tight-knit elite devoted to natural resource issues. The preeminent personality was Ira Gabrielson, former head of the U.S. Fish and Wildlife Service and president of the Wildlife Management Institute. Gruff, affable, and well informed, Gabrielson knew everyone and worked effectively with Congress and the federal bureaucracy. The creation of the Kenai Moose Range, the best known of the Alaska refuges, had been his greatest achievement and a measure of his political skill. For broad-based support he turned to organizations of hunters and fishermen like the Izaak Walton League and the National Wildlife Federation. Less important were the Audubon Society, just emerging as a conservation organization, and the Sierra Club, a California group devoted to preserving lands in the Sierra Nevada.[3]

Apart from Gabrielson, the most prominent individual conservationists were the leaders of the Wilderness Society. Founded in 1935 by Robert Marshall and a few like-minded enthusiasts, the society achieved prominence after 1946, when it named Olaus Murie, a wildlife expert who worked for the Fish and Wildlife Service, as executive director, and Howard Zahniser, another Fish and Wildlife veteran, as executive secretary. Murie had spent many years in Alaska and in Jackson Hole, Wyoming, where he continued to live. Zahniser became the society's Washington director. Other prominent Wilderness Society figures included Aldo Leopold, a University of Wisconsin professor of wildlife management and former Forest Service manager who had introduced the first "primitive" areas in national forests, and Sigurd Olson, a teacher and writer who had spearheaded the movement to preserve parts of the Superior National Forest in northern Minnesota as a wildlife sanctuary and wilderness recreation area.[4]

The evolution of the conservation movement would almost exactly parallel the Alaska statehood movement. From modest beginnings in the immediate postwar years, it emerged as a powerful political force, still devoted mostly to resource issues. In the 1960s more dramatic changes would occur, as new issues and sensitivities and a new, more diverse constituency began to transform conservation into environmentalism. Whereas conservation focused on specific resource issues and comfortably included industrialists and hobbyists who emphasized the efficient use of such resources, environmentalism was broader, idealistic, and often hostile to the practical concerns of utilitarian conservationists. Heralded in seminal works by Aldo Leopold and Rachel Carson, it emphasized the totality of human impacts, the value of ecosystems as well as specific resources, and the mounting dangers of industrial development.[5] Conservation and industrial growth were not separate and distinct; trade-offs were necessary.

The timing of this transition was largely a result of the changing economic and political environment of the postwar years. The revival of the economy produced more pollution and more kinds of pollution, including complex chemical residues and toxic wastes that were potentially more threatening than traditional pollutants. It also greatly increased the demand for wood, minerals, petroleum, and other raw materials. By the early 1950s that demand had translated into pressures to exploit resources in many de facto wilderness areas. Often, public officials were eager to help. After midcentury, government resource managers like B. Frank Heintzleman, the regional forester for Alaska, accommodated industry desires for increased access and greater output. To many conservationists, this was a betrayal of the legacy of "wise use" and expert judgment. By the end of the decade the divorce of the Forest Service and the leading conservation groups was nearly complete.[6]

Relations between the National Park Service (NPS) and the conservation movement also deteriorated. Conservationists had long criticized

NPS for emphasizing recreation by building lodges, restaurants, highways, and other tourist facilities at the expense of the natural environment. As visitation to popular parks increased in the postwar years, park managers combined plans for upgrading existing facilities with new development proposals. In 1952 NPS Director Conrad L. Wirth toured Alaska to gauge the potential for recreational opportunities. Twice he met with leaders of the Anchorage Chamber of Commerce to discuss the possibility of local groups' taking over the Mount McKinley hotel and developing other tourist facilities. A lodge at Wonder Lake was the focus of these discussions. A participant reported "considerable interest ... on the part of the local group."[7]

In 1956 Wirth announced an ambitious plan, called Mission 66, to expand parks and park facilities over the next decade. Wirth proposed to buy land and devote greater attention to nature education, but it was his call for additional roads, hotels, and other commercial facilities that attracted the greatest attention. Congress adopted most of the plan, and Mission 66 appropriations financed (among other things) lodges at Katmai and Glacier Bay and a paved road from the Mount McKinley station on the Alaska Railroad to the nearby park facilities. Alarmed at what else might be on the drawing board, Olaus Murie wrote to the regional NPS director.

> I suppose some kind of accommodation is planned for the vicinity of Mt. McKinley. Whatever is planned, it seems to me that the landscape planner should not attempt to rivet that highest mountain with a human-made structure. ... I do not believe that it benefits people to be able to lie in bed and view a natural phenomenon, be it Old Faithful or a grand mountain. ... Wonder Lake, as a beautiful foreground for the mountain, should be left alone and should not be cluttered with structures of any kind.[8]

Far more threatening than anything Wirth proposed was the alliance between the Interior Department's Bureau of Reclamation and western boosters that had emerged in the 1930s. Depression-era dam building had been a way to create jobs and encourage industrial activity. With the return of prosperity, the emphasis shifted from creating jobs to providing electricity and drinking water to growing western communities. Water was essential to economic development, and government controlled access to the area's rivers. Yet water projects had other effects, many unintended. Whole regions might be transformed in ways that were difficult to foresee.

The incident that best underlined these dangers dates from the late 1940s, when the Bureau of Reclamation announced a massive Colorado River project, involving 10 dams on tributaries of the river. One of the dams, on the Green River at Echo Park, Colorado, would be inside the boundaries of the Dinosaur National Monument, which featured large fossil beds. The proposed encroachment became a cause célèbre, the single most important conservation conflict of the 1950s.[9] Leading the opposition to the Echo Park dam were Zahniser and David Brower, the new executive secretary of the Sierra Club. In the course of the fight, which ended when Congress in 1956 finally deleted the dam from the Colorado River storage project, Brower honed the skills that would make him the best-known environmentalist of the 1960s—the "archdruid," in John McPhee's famous phrase.[10] In the process, he and his allies transformed the Sierra Club into a genuinely national organization with an all-embracing commitment to environmental protection.[11]

Other effects of this conflict had broader implications. First, it emphasized the inadequacy of existing administrative safeguards for wilderness areas in national forests and parks. If government officials could compromise a national monument, what hope was there for any wilderness area, especially those under the jurisdiction of the Forest Service and other multiple-use agencies? Second, it underlined the limited legal options available to environmentalists. In the words of historian Mark W. T. Harvey, the Echo Park battle "played out in an almost purely political arena."[12] In the ensuing years, environmental groups successfully pressured Congress for additional legal channels—a move with far-reaching implications for Alaska.

The first initiative was a bill to set aside permanent wilderness areas in the public domain. Zahniser drew up legislation to establish wilderness by federal statute, circulated it among conservationists, and persuaded Senator Hubert Humphrey (D-MN) and Representative John Saylor (R-PA) to introduce it in Congress. For the next eight years he worked indefatigably to mobilize the conservation organizations and create a groundswell of popular support. He had less success in Congress. Richard E. McArdle, the Forest Service chief, summarized the opponents' position when he testified that "the bill would strike at the heart of the multiple-use policy."[13] The Senate finally passed a wilderness bill in 1961, but Colorado Representative Wayne Aspinall, who chaired the House Interior Committee and championed the interests of miners and ranchers, stalled the legislation for years. Despairing of a solution, Zahniser and his allies agreed to major concessions: both houses of Congress would have to approve every wilderness measure, and mining claims in wilderness areas would remain valid for 20 years. Historian Steven Schulte concludes that Aspinall, not Zahniser, was the "ultimate shaper" of the Wilderness Act that President Johnson signed in September 1964.[14]

In the following years Congress passed a series of related measures. It sought to protect endangered species and wild and scenic rivers, for example, and in the National Environmental Policy Act of 1969 created far-reaching legal and administrative procedures that could be used to confront and conceivably thwart virtually any government initiative.

A final effect of the Echo Park fight also had broad implications. To halt the dam project, conservationists, led by Brower, had had to enlist the public. Over more than five years the various groups learned to work together, broaden their appeal beyond the conservation community, exploit the popular media, and translate public support into pressure for specific legislation. Brower (especially after Zahniser's death in 1964) emerged as one of the great publicists of that or probably any era. In the process the conservation organizations and the conservation movement were indelibly affected. Their leaders continued to pressure federal managers, much as Gabrielson had done, but they now had other powerful options, including the grass-roots campaign.

A WILDERNESS REFUGE FOR ALASKA

As the conservation movement grew and evolved, an obscure battle over the vast wilderness of northeastern Alaska illuminated the changes and the difficulties that lay ahead. The battle for the Arctic National Wildlife Range (ANWR) began in the early 1950s, became a national movement after 1956 (coincidental with the campaign for the Wilderness Act and the final phase of the statehood effort), and climaxed in 1960 with a last-minute conservationist victory. The Wilderness Society led the fight; wildlife was the focus. Although many Alaskans supported the campaign, the intense opposition of Alaska politicians revealed the central role of booster sentiment in the political culture of the new state.[15]

The northeastern corner of Alaska, bordered on the north by the Arctic Ocean and on the east by the Canadian border, was one of the most remote areas in North America. Since the end of Arctic whaling at the turn of the century, only a handful of outside visitors, hunters, prospectors, geologists, and wildlife experts had visited the region. Detailed maps of the area became available only in 1927. The winters were frigid, the land frozen and extremely rugged. The area included the highest mountains in the Brooks Range. Several hundred Natives living along the Arctic coast were the only human residents. However, the region was home to most Arctic mammals, in particular the large Porcupine caribou herd, which migrated each spring from the Canadian border to the Arctic coast, where calves were born. By the 1950s the herd had recovered from earlier depredations and numbered in the hundreds of thousands, making northeastern Alaska one of the great de facto wildlife sanctuaries in North America. The area had been withdrawn from the public domain in 1943 to facilitate military planning and remained off-limits to economic activity in the postwar years. Still, there were reasons for concern. The Navy's continuing search for oil in Pet 4, just to the west, and the aggressiveness of Alaska's political and business leaders created a sense of urgency, even if there was no specific threat. As Olaus Murie advised, "if we want a wilderness area up there we should do it *now*—or forget about it."[16]

In 1949 NPS Director Wirth had ordered a study of Alaska's recreational potential under planner George Collins. Over the next three years Collins visited Katmai, Mount McKinley, Glacier Bay, and several prospective park sites, but he was especially attracted to the Arctic. He later recalled that "by 1952 we had pretty well looked over Alaska except for the Arctic. That essentially was an awesome and impenetrable world. ... I kept pondering the means of approach."[17] He contacted officials of the U.S. Geological Survey and the Fish and Wildlife Service, who had responsibilities in the Arctic. His discussions with the Geological Survey's John Reed, an Alaska veteran, were particularly helpful.

> I met with John Reed in Washington. We had a lot of talks. I said: 'I want to get into the Arctic. ...' He said to me, 'If you stay east of Pet Four, there's nothing over there until you get to the MacKenzie Delta region in the Yukon. ... You'll be out of our hair; and that's where the finest relief, the highest mountains ... and the greatest landscapes are. ...[18]

With his study nearly completed, Collins was able to devote his attention to the Arctic. In 1951 he had arranged for NPS biologist Lowell Sumner to assist Fish and Wildlife officials in a survey of Arctic game that included the northeast. The following year he and Sumner camped for several weeks on the north and south sides of the Brooks Range. In 1953 he organized a larger expedition that operated on both sides of the U.S.-Canadian border.[19]

Collins and his associates were soon convinced of the area's value but weren't sure what to do about it. The almost inaccessible land did not make sense as a conventional national park, and the international border, which cut across the caribou routes, presented other problems. Collins recalled, "We didn't know what to call it. We used such terms as conservation reserve, or preserve, or conservation area. Generically, it was a park to us. ... We thought of it, in our hopes, as a great international park."[20] When Alaska politicians heard about the project and protested, Collins was less forthright. He wrote to the territorial governor, for example, that "we think of the country name as the Arctic International Wilderness—not as a park or monument."[21] Unsure of their next step, Collins and his associates turned to the conservation community for assistance. After the NPS Advisory Board noted Collins's work at its April 1952 meeting, the Sierra Club's board of directors passed a resolution endorsing an Arctic wilderness area.[22] In 1953 Collins and Sumner published an article describing it in the *Sierra Club Bulletin*.

The Wilderness Society took the next steps. In September 1953, as Collins and Sumner were completing their work, Olaus Murie visited Alaska and flew over the eastern Brooks Range with a representative of the U.S. Geological Survey. He "had a good look at the country" and was impressed. Aware that many Alaskans would strongly oppose any new federal initiatives, Murie decided on a low-key approach. He reported to Zahniser that "a lot of psychological progress will have to be made before enough Alaskans favor any further federal preserves, that is a phobia in Alaska."[23] Zahniser was initially skeptical. He had heard about the "psychological problem in setting aside wilderness in Alaska. It really is a perplexity. ... Will the wilderness disappear while we are waiting to be good psychologists ...?"[24]

Murie nevertheless persisted. To encourage "psychological progress," he asked the New York Zoological Society for $7,300 to enable him, his wife Margaret, and an archaeologist and a biologist, both from the University of Alaska, to spend summer 1954 in the Brooks Range.[25] Ostensibly their goal was research. Their real purpose was to publicize the area and to rally conservationist sentiment.

If Murie's plan had materialized, it is possible that an Arctic wilderness park would have emerged in the mid-1950s, well before the climax of the statehood campaign. Murie, however, contracted tuberculosis and spent the next year in a hospital. Even after his release he was unable to travel extensively. As a result, the ANWR campaign coincided with the final phase of the statehood effort, when local sensitivities were most acute.

The Muries rescheduled their Alaska trip for summer 1956. The new plan called for them to make a series of public appearances and then join two graduate students and Brina Kessel, a zoology professor at the University of Alaska, for 10 weeks at Lobo Lake on the Sheenjek River, just south of the Brooks Range. Murie explained that he wanted "to get an idea of the suitability of the area as a research center for the study of undisturbed biota, including wolves, as well as caribou, and mountain sheep and of course the vegetation."[26] Murie, the naturalist, was unquestionably sincere. But his larger goals were political. A major reason for choosing the Sheenjek was its accessibility to Fort Yukon, which had an airfield. A steady stream of invited guests would make any serious scientific work unlikely.

Murie started by cultivating local sentiment. He explained to Collins,

> ... I have adopted a go-easy method. I met with many people, from Fort Yukon to Juneau, and I can't remember a time when I came right out and said: 'Support this wilderness proposal.' I told them what our experience was, and I sincerely wanted them to make up their own minds.[27]

He agreed that "there should be no attempt to prohibit hunting or fishing."[28] And he conceded that prospecting would have to be permitted, as it was in other Alaska parks. The area would resemble the primitive areas in national forests. Several of Murie's confidants, such as Collins, continued to urge some type of cooperative plan with the Canadians.

Murie discreetly sought local supporters. His first target was the Tanana Valley Sportsmen's Association, a Fairbanks-area hunting and fishing club. When he attended a meeting in May, he found the members "much confused about the whole issue." One of Murie's allies recalled that "a lot of midnight oil" had been burned on the subject.[29] In keeping with his "go-easy method," Murie "sat and listened." He then explained "what a wilderness area is." He emphasized that hunting and fishing would not be banned, that "Indians and Eskimos would be free to hunt and trap." The "things that are kept out ... are roads and other developments."[30] By the end of the meeting he had won the association's endorsement. Reflecting on this and other experiences, he thought he detected "some mighty hopeful trends. I am trying to absorb the human motivations here. ... I want to get my feet on the ground on this new Alaska."[31]

The Sheenjek expedition was the highlight of the trip. Kessel and the graduate students devoted themselves to wildlife studies while the Muries entertained guests, ranging from local newspaper reporters to Supreme Court Justice William O. Douglas. It was an exhilarating experience. Surrounded by the majestic mountains and eager listeners, Olaus seemed to regain his old vitality. Margaret wrote in June that he "is feeling so well and is eager I have a time keeping up with him." It was "a real happy time, and just about Paradise."[32] They took hundreds of slide pictures and made several movies. Olaus planned a book and several magazine articles on their experiences.

After breaking camp in early August, the Muries spoke to groups in Anchorage, Fairbanks, and Juneau. The Fairbanks visit was especially successful. The Tanana Valley Sportsmen's Association voted Olaus an honorary life membership, and many individuals pledged support for the campaign. Murie was "greatly encouraged ... by the attitude of many Alaskan people."[33]

The following summer the Muries made another, more abbreviated trip to Alaska. Invitations from several Fairbanks groups and Margaret's college reunion (she had been the first woman to graduate from the University of Alaska) provided a pretext; the Conservation Foundation agreed to pay the bills. The Muries spent more than two weeks in Fairbanks and a few days each in Anchorage and Juneau. Local conservationists coordinated their activities. Clarence Rhode, the head of the Fish and Wildlife Service in Alaska, and Bud Boddy, for example, made their Juneau arrangements. Olaus showed films of the Sheenjek trip to civic groups and had numerous interviews with newspaper and television reporters; even Robert Atwood was cordial.[34] In Fairbanks, the sportsmen's association, the garden club, and the chamber of commerce called for an Arctic wildlife refuge.[35]

By fall 1957 Murie had made considerable "psychological progress." The "next step," he wrote, was to "see what Washington will do with this."[36] For that phase of the campaign he turned to Rhode, who served as his emissary to Ross Leffler, the assistant secretary of the Interior overseeing the Fish and Wildlife Service. When Leffler visited Alaska in summer 1957, Rhode served as his personal pilot, flying him over the Brooks Range and pointing out the Sheenjek. At Leffler's suggestion, Zahniser and Murie orchestrated a letter-writing campaign to Interior Secretary Fred Seaton. As Zahniser reported, letters "from Alaska especially are needed."[37] Here Murie's Alaska contacts proved invaluable. He enlisted James Lake of the Tanana Valley Sportsmen's Association to recruit letter writers in Fairbanks, and Bud Boddy to do the same in Juneau. The resulting avalanche of mail showed that many Alaskans supported the refuge.

In the meantime the Interior Department's wildlife experts worked out the administrative details. ANWR would extend from the Arctic shore to the southern foothills of the Brooks Range, a total of 9 million acres. The Canning River would be the western boundary. The Interior staff at first proposed to make ANWR a "primitive" area, the most restrictive classification. Warned that that would spark public opposition, they changed the designation to wildlife refuge, which would permit hunting, fishing, and trapping but no mining. There were more complaints. Most Interior officials apparently favored the most permissive type of area—a wildlife range, which would permit mining. The biologists, however, protested that mining would destroy wildlife habitat and antagonize the Canadians, who, they hoped, would create a similar reserve on their side of the border. Finally, they worked out a compromise: the order would permit underground mining but not private ownership of the surface, which would prevent miners from permanently occupying the land and using it for other purposes. Furthermore, Secretary Seaton would seek legislation to ensure that no later secretary of the Interior could unilaterally adopt a more permissive policy. The compromise did not affect gas and oil exploration, which would be permitted under a lease system.[38]

Leaders of the National Wildlife Federation, Audubon Society, Wildlife Management Institute, Izaak Walton League, and other conservation groups reluctantly agreed to the arrangement (as well as to the opening of the Kenai Moose Range, with various safeguards). But Murie complained that "we all thought it would be done in a more simple manner than that."[39]

By November 1957 Seaton was ready to act. A meeting of the department's advisory committee on fish and wildlife (which included Gabrielson, Olson, and Zahniser) provided the occasion. Leffler invited the Muries to discuss their summer on the Sheenjek. With Seaton in attendance, Olaus showed his slides and discussed their encounters with caribou and grizzlies. Five days later Seaton announced that he intended to reserve 9 million acres for an Arctic wildlife range.[40] A relieved Murie admitted that "the thing went through so much faster than we had hoped."[41]

Though impressive, Murie's persuasive powers were not the only reason for the secretary's announcement. When Seaton took office in 1957, the Eisenhower administration had a reputation for favoring industry over other interests. Seaton was committed to a more balanced and politically sensitive approach, but he faced a dilemma. The oil industry, a major political constituency, was eager to explore the Arctic coast and was demanding relaxation of the remaining World War II restrictions. But opening that area would look like another favor to industry unless he could find some offsetting gesture. ANWR was that additional element. In exchange for the wildlife range, Seaton persuaded the conservation groups not to oppose the opening of the rest of the Arctic coast. Ted Stevens, Seaton's assistant for Alaska, told a congressional committee that "we think we have gone as far as we can to meet the desires and needs of Alaskans, while at the same time carrying out our compromise with the conservation interests."[42]

There were also partisan considerations. Seaton knew that the leaders of the statehood movement, mostly Democrats, would strongly oppose his action because it added new federal restrictions. Given ANWR's many influential backers, it would divide Alaska politically and help carve out a Republican presence in the new state.

Interior Department attorneys prepared the legislation that was introduced in Congress in 1959. Ostensibly it addressed only the mining lease system. Everyone agreed that Seaton had the power to create a range with or without a ban on mining, and Seaton implied on several occasions that he would act unilaterally if Congress stalled. Yet he was cautious. Alaskans, on the verge of statehood, were concerned about federal restrictions that might hamstring their natural resource–based economy. Recent Defense Department withdrawals had angered many residents. Seaton wanted to avoid the appearance of arbitrariness; congressional approval would diffuse blame as well as credit. Stevens had another motive. As he explained to Bartlett, "we could establish the range and open it [to mining] if we wanted to. Some later Secretary [of the Interior] could close it. If this bill passes, no later Secretary could close it."[43]

Still, several obstacles remained. One was the rivalry among Interior Department agencies. By 1956 most conservationists had concluded that the Fish and Wildlife Service ought to administer the wildlife range. NPS officials initially concurred, but as the Interior Department bill went to Congress, rumors spread that NPS would lobby for control of the area. Such a change would antagonize Alaska hunting and fishing groups and undermine Murie's coalition. As a result, conservation leaders organized several meetings to address the rivalry. The most important of these were at the Sierra Club's biennial wilderness conference in San Francisco, in December 1957, and at the North American Wildlife Conference in St. Louis, in March 1958. David Brower recalled that he served as "ringleader" at these meetings.[44] According to historian Theodore Catton, the San Francisco meeting helped "crystallize" NPS interest in wilderness parks, even as it deferred to the Fish and Wildlife Service.[45]

By the time of the St. Louis meeting, the jurisdictional "quibbling" had been overshadowed by a rising chorus of opposition from Alaska. At first the criticism came largely from the mining industry, orchestrated by the Territorial Department of Mines and its aggressive head, Phil Holdsworth. In a March 1958 bulletin Holdsworth attacked the Seaton plan as a sham, arguing that a lease system would subject miners to so many bureaucratic obstacles that the area would be effectively closed to mining.[46] Conservationists dismissed Holdsworth as an extremist; they resolved "to keep quiet and not stir things up."[47] However, James Lake wrote from Fairbanks that the outburst "is only the forerunner of further opposition."[48] Shortly afterward the Anchorage Chamber of Commerce signaled its opposition in a formal vote. Within a few weeks boosters in most Alaskan cities had joined the opponents' ranks. Writing in disgust, Bud Boddy noted that "when things like this happen it makes one wonder. What would happen to Alaska if we had Statehood?"[49]

Within a few months, of course, they did have statehood and a state government firmly in booster hands. Governor William Egan lost no time in appointing Holdsworth commissioner of natural resources, and for the next two years, Holdsworth orchestrated opposition to ANWR. In his mind, the Seaton bill was proof of the federal conspiracy against the mining industry.[50] Even Senator Bartlett, a friend of the mining industry, was embarrassed by Holdsworth's intemperate statements.[51]

While distancing himself from Holdsworth, Bartlett made no secret of his opposition to ANWR. A member of the Senate Subcommittee on Merchant Marine and Fisheries, Bartlett used his position to delay congressional action, encourage opposition, and seek to persuade Seaton to drop the project. The prospect of a new Democratic national administration in 1961 also made delay expedient. Bartlett's tactics alienated virtually the entire conservation community, including the large group of Alaskans who had responded to Murie's campaign. By 1960 the battle lines between the Alaska politicians and the expanding conservation movement had been drawn.

The public hearings that Bartlett held on the Seaton bill, in Washington and then in Alaska, foreshadowed the conflicts that would increasingly dominate Alaskan public life. Ironically, it was Ernest Gruening, the self-proclaimed crusader and champion of liberal causes, who was most provocative. As the first witness on June 30, 1959, he insisted that he was a "fervent" conservationist, "an all-out conservationist," but he then proceeded to attack the leaders of the national conservation organizations, who were present, asserting, among other things, that they had conspired with the salmon canners to thwart Alaska statehood. In a notable statement he added, "I don't believe we should conserve moose for the sake of future moose. We preserve them so that future generations of human beings can see moose, and photograph moose, and hunt moose."[52] ANWR was an example of trying to "conserve species for the sake of the species." It "would be set aside not for the benefit of human beings, but to satisfy some theoretical conceptions of distant men unfamiliar with Alaska."[53]

Though he shared Gruening's biases, Bartlett was most upset by the partisan implications of the dispute, especially the understanding between Seaton and the conservation organizations that disregarded Alaska's elected leaders. The hearings made it clear that the conservation groups had agreed not to oppose the mining lease system, Seaton's intention to terminate the World War II withdrawal of more than 20 million acres just west of ANWR, or his plan to open Pet 4. Ted Stevens spelled out the understanding:

> We ... think that if the Wildlife Range were established ... the conservation interests ... would be more eager to help you and those interested in Alaska get such things as the naval petroleum reserve bill passed. ... Some of the very interests which are pressing for the establishment of this range have withstood or resisted the attempts to restore this ... area to public domain previously. We think this is a confidence-building factor.[54]

Bartlett was furious. He mercilessly grilled Harold "Pink" Gutermuth of the Wildlife Management Institute on the quid pro quo for ANWR. To the senator's charge that conservationists had used political "blackmail" to achieve their goal, Gutermuth replied that it "isn't a form of blackmail. ... I am just saying this, that you get people stirred up over one thing and that causes them to take a position on other things."[55]

Barlett received more bad news when his committee traveled to Alaska. His goal had been to provide a forum for opponents and dispute Murie's claims of Alaskans' support. To his consternation, only 53 of 142 witnesses who spoke at the hearings explicitly opposed ANWR, but 73 endorsed it.[56] Moreover, most of the anti-ANWR witnesses were unfamiliar with the actual proposal or, like Holdsworth, hostile to all conservation measures. Several University of Alaska mining and geology professors who argued against ANWR could not explain why, if the area was so valuable, there had been so little prior interest in it.

The pro-ANWR forces, in contrast, were well prepared and knowledgeable. Aided by the Wilderness Society and the Alaska Sportsmen's Council, they made impressive presentations. In Ketchikan, for example, Dixie Baade, a local activist, dominated the session.[57] Ten days later, in Fairbanks, the pro-ANWR group included representatives of the sportsmen's group, leaders of the garden clubs, and a large number of university professors, including Brina Kessel and Frederick Dean, the heads of the biology and wildlife management departments, respectively. The biologists carefully explained the needs of caribou and other Arctic wildlife. William O. Pruitt, a wildlife expert at the University of Alaska, insisted that 9 million acres, far from excessive, was "minimal."[58] By the end of the session they had thoroughly discredited Bartlett's contention that Interior Department planners capriciously sought to "lock up" the northeast corner of Alaska.

Celia Hunter and Ginny Wood, who also testified in the hearings, portrayed themselves as representatives of the business community. Hunter complained,

> ... in spite of the decline of importance of mining, and the increasing emphasis on tourism, the whole tone of our state administration is set by the mining interests. As a citizen I ask: What do the mining interests want? Apparently only the absence of any restraint whatsoever on their activities will satisfy them.[59]

Wood compared ANWR to Camp Denali, which she portrayed as the prototype of a new kind of tourism. Bartlett reluctantly conceded that her presentation was a "most fetching propaganda pitch."[60] He also acknowledged that his plan had backfired: rather than galvanizing opposition to ANWR, the hearings had generated greater support. His last hope was a more sympathetic Democratic president.

When the congressional session ended without Senate action, conservationists pressured Seaton to act unilaterally. Pink Gutermuth spoke for many others when he confronted the secretary: "Are you just sweet-talking us, or are we going to get this damned wildlife range proclaimed by the President?"[61] If any individual appeal had an effect, it was probably that of Sigurd Olson, who had become Seaton's closest contact in the conservation community. At Seaton's behest, Olson traveled extensively in Alaska during summer 1960, visiting parks and potential parks, including ANWR. He also made several trips to Ottawa to confer with Canadian officials about the possibility of an international wildlife sanctuary. These discussions seemed to be on the verge of success during fall 1960. Yet Olson warned that the Canadians expected the United States to take the first step.[62]

The larger question is why Seaton was so hesitant. He had succeeded in dividing the state and showing that the Democrats were insensitive to issues that many Alaskans took seriously, regardless of party affiliation. Governor Egan's belated offer to administer the area "in the interest of true conservation" was so insincere it did not warrant reply.[63] Bartlett acknowledged that he had been outmaneuvered when he labeled the eventual land order a "dirty Republican trick."[64] Seaton had repeatedly stated that he would act if Congress did not, and President Eisenhower had publicly endorsed the range in May.[65] Still there were reasons for a judicious delay, including a desire to prevent the Democrats from making the wildlife range an election issue. In early December, a month after John F. Kennedy defeated Richard Nixon, Seaton finally moved to create ANWR and two other wildlife ranges, including one at the mouth of the Kuskokwim River in western Alaska that would honor Clarence Rhode, who had died in an August 1958 plane crash. Altogether, the areas totaled more than 11 million acres. At the same time he revoked the World War II land order, making the area between Pet 4 and the Canning River (the eventual Prudhoe Bay oil field) available for leasing and state selection. Bartlett and Gruening asked the new secretary of the Interior, Stewart Udall, to reverse Seaton's ANWR order, though they understood that if he interceded, "every conservationist in the country would be up in arms, and storming."[66] After a respectable interlude, Udall declined.

A dozen years later, Alaska environmentalists appealed to Seaton for help in obtaining formal wilderness designation for ANWR.[67] His unwillingness to assist them underlined the narrowness of his commitment to ANWR and the importance of what had happened on the adjoining lands in the intervening years. Despite its remoteness, ANWR would become even more controversial after 1960.

THE ALASKA CONSERVATION SOCIETY

Seaton's action to create the Arctic National Wildlife Range seemingly had little immediate significance. Canadian officials proved more sensitive to miners' protests and did not set aside land on their side of the border for more than 20 years. The contraction of Alaska's mining industry made the U.S. mining controversy largely irrelevant, but in any event, ANWR existed mostly on paper. Bartlett and Gruening made sure that the Fish and Wildlife Service received no money to manage it. In 1969, after Bartlett had died and Gruening had been defeated, Congress provided the first meager appropriations. Yet until 1972 the staff consisted of just one man-ager—albeit a tenacious defender, Averill Thayer—plus an assistant and a part-time secretary.[68]

The ANWR battle did have one immediate effect, however. If the con-troversy temporarily divided the booster community, it mobilized the state's conservationists. Many were members of groups like the National Wildlife Federation, the Izaak Walton League, and the Wilderness Society, which had similar agendas but no specific plans for Alaska. The national conservation organizations were not oblivious to this deficiency. In 1955 the Wilderness Society proposed to create an Alaska conservation council to promote cooperation among members of different organizations. Murie originally hoped to preside over the formation of such a council during his 1956 visit.[69]

In April 1957 Ginny Wood captured the new sensitivity. She explained,

> We sit up here trying ... to preserve something of the Alaska that attracted us to it in the first place. Sometimes we feel that we are pretty much alone. ... Those who see the light or have some training or background in biology, botany, or ecology are usually connected with the military, the government, or the University and dare not enter controversial issues. We wonder if the time isn't ripe to form some sort of Alaskan Conservation organization (those that consider themselves such are mostly Sportsmen's Clubs first and fore-most). There must be many scattered about the Territory who are members of the Sierra Club, Wilderness Society, Audobon, Isaac Walton, Nat. Parks Assoc, Nature Conservancy etc., like ourselves, who had definate reactions and feelings about events taking place up here but have no way to channel it. There is a resentment against any Outside organization that pokes its nose in Alaskan affairs even when it is for Alaska's good. Outside commercial interests are welcomed as 'developers' of the Territory, but conservationists ... are looked upon as intruders. An organization that was strictly Alaskan might get fur-ther because of this.[70]

The Bartlett hearings were an opportunity to demonstrate the strength of conservationist sentiment. When they ended on October 31, 1959, leav-ing the fate of ANWR in doubt, the Fairbanks activists decided on a more organized, systematic approach. In February 1960 a dozen or more indi-viduals met at the Dogpatch cabin of John Thompson, a journalist who worked for the university's agricultural extension program and had spoken at the Fairbanks hearing. The group included Hunter, Ginny and Morton Wood, and many others who had testified. Thompson did not have enough chairs, so some of them sat on his bunk. They agreed that undesirable changes were imminent. "The Alaska of the wide open spaces, the dog team, the log cabin, and undiminished wildlife" was yielding to "the plow, the bulldozer, the oil derrick, and industry."[71] Yet neither the national organizations nor the Alaska sportsmen's groups seemed appropriate to address these challenges. What was needed was a new group, comprising Alaska conservationists (membership would be open to everyone, but only Alaska residents could vote), which would express the "definite reactions and feelings" of Alaskans and could not be dismissed as an "outside" group. They named the new organization the Alaska Conservation Society (ACS). Leslie Viereck, a research biologist at the university, was elected president, Hunter became secretary, and Thompson, treasurer. The board of directors also included William O. Pruitt; Dixie Baade, the Ketchikan activist; and Richard Cooley, a geographer who was studying Alaska's recreational potential. Ginny Wood became the newsletter editor and her cabin the ACS editorial office. The first issue of the ACS *News Bulletin* appeared in March.

ACS grew rapidly. Within three months it had expanded from 18 charter members, all Fairbanks-area residents, to 273 members, including 164 Alaskans and 109 who lived in other states (California led with 19, followed by New York with 16 and Oregon with 10). By the end of 1960 membership had grown to 400, with a slight majority of outsiders. Like most contemporary conservation groups, ACS was top-heavy with academics and government scientists, mostly biologists involved in wildlife research or management. Because many Dogpatch residents did not have telephones, they had weekly luncheon meetings in the university's biology department.[72]

Apart from Hunter and Wood, the individual most closely identified with ACS over its 20-year lifetime would be Robert Weeden, an Alaska Fish and Game biologist, Dogpatch resident, and wildlife expert. Weeden had earned graduate degrees at the University of Maine and the University of British Columbia. His dissertation research was on the ptarmigan. When a friend who headed the territory's game research program offered him a position, he accepted. Weeden's office was on the university campus, and his wife taught in the biology department. Though he had not testified at the Bartlett hearings, he was among those who crowded into Thompson's cabin. "We realized that huge issues would come up," he recalled. ACS would alert the public. It would "get the facts and speak clearly."[73] In late 1961 he joined the board and took over from Ginny Wood as editor of the *News Bulletin*.

ACS was soon absorbed in other battles. Even before the creation of ANWR, Alaska boosters had launched aggressive campaigns for massive public works projects that promised to transform Alaska. In the ensuing conflicts, ACS members demonstrated that getting the facts and speaking clearly could have an exhilarating effect.

Project Chariot had originated in the Eisenhower administration's effort to develop peaceful uses of nuclear energy.[74] The plan, in brief, was to set off nuclear explosions at a site on the northwestern coast of Alaska, chosen for its isolation, desolation, and distance from population centers. The rationale was muddled at best; the Atomic Energy Commission at first insisted that its purpose was to create a harbor but later described Project Chariot simply as an engineering experiment. Scholars have characterized it as an example of technological arrogance and bureaucratic excess. In any case, it was a prime example of the heavy-handed federal initiatives that Alaskans supposedly resented. Yet the state's newspapers and chambers of commerce immediately embraced the plan because it promised to bring federal dollars to Alaska. More ominously for Alaska conservationists, the new president of the University of Alaska, William Wood, enthusiastically endorsed the project. Like other boosters, Wood was mesmerized by the prospect of government money.

A critical feature of the project was a plan to conduct extensive biological research in the proposed blast area. Atomic Energy Commission leaders saw this as a way to guarantee the support of university officials and mollify skeptical scientists. The university's biology department was to receive more than $100,000. Leslie Viereck was hired specifically to do Chariot research, and William Pruitt was another prominent member of the team. In short, the university biologists, the core of ACS, were deeply involved in Project Chariot and in some cases professionally dependent on it. As the work proceeded and they became better aware of the likely results, they and the ACS faced a crisis of conscience.

By early 1961 the biologists were in full rebellion. Hardly a desolate wasteland, the target area was rich in flora and fauna, much of which would be obliterated by the blast or the radiation. Natives who hunted and fished in the blast zone would either be exposed to massive doses of radiation or have to give up their activities. When it became apparent that Atomic Energy Commission officials would not acknowledge these problems, the scientists opted for public exposure via the *News Bulletin*. The entire March 1961 issue was devoted to Chariot and included Viereck's letter of resignation from the project. A thousand extra copies were printed and sent to government leaders, scientists, and conservation groups outside Alaska. The Sierra Club *Bulletin* reprinted the entire issue several months later.

The repercussions were far-reaching. Widespread protests, focused on the dangers of atomic energy and representing a broadening of conservation activism, led to the cancellation of Project Chariot in early 1962. Whereas the ANWR campaign had emphasized traditional conservation issues, the Chariot protests broke new ground. Unlike their predecessors, the environmental activists of the 1960s rejected parochial interest group boundaries.[75]

In Alaska the effects were also dramatic. ACS gained instant credibility and influence—and enemies. Senator Bartlett complained bitterly to Egan that ACS activists were "third rate people ... the same people who so ardently support the Arctic Wildlife Range."[76] At the university, this hostility took more concrete form. President Wood ordered Brina Kessel to fire Viereck and Pruitt; she complied, creating the movement's first martyrs. In northwestern Alaska the impact of the Chariot controversy was no less important. Native reactions to the Atomic Energy Commission plan helped transform smoldering resentments into a renewed campaign for Native rights.

ACS continued to oppose nuclear testing in Alaska in the 1960s and early 1970s, though with less impressive results. The underground blasts, scheduled for remote Amchitka Island in the Aleutians, were planned behind a wall of official secrecy that made their likely effects difficult to evaluate. ACS leaders made little public effort to oppose the first test in 1965. When the second test was scheduled, in 1969, they were "reduced to wringing their hands in public," in the judgment of historian Dean W. Kohlhoff.[77] They were more outspoken in 1971, but public opposition to the final test was spearheaded by the national environmental organizations and by Alaska Governor William Egan and Senator Mike Gravel.

In the meantime ACS leaders confronted the most determined booster campaign to date. Since the 1940s the Army Corps of Engineers had identified more than 200 potential hydroelectric sites in Alaska. At the top of the list, in terms of size and potential, was Rampart Canyon on the Yukon River, 100 miles northeast of Fairbanks. In the mid-1950s the Corps proposed to build a massive dam that would create a 100-mile-long lake and generate twice as much electricity as any other U.S. hydroelectric facility. Alaska's boosters were impressed, and when Gruening arrived in Washington in 1959, he made Rampart his top priority. For two years he spent more time on it than on any other project. In 1960 he obtained an appropriation for a feasibility study; in 1961, after a tour of the area, he proclaimed that "we're going to get Rampart."[78] Gradually he became obsessed with the project, in part because he hoped the lake would be named after him.[79]

Alaska's boosters needed little persuasion to lend their support. By 1962 most Alaska politicians had endorsed the proposal, and the following year the mayors of Anchorage and Fairbanks organized a conference of supporters at Mount McKinley Park lodge that became the high point of the Rampart campaign. Governor Egan told the gathering that "we can win if we are completely united, as we were for the statehood effort itself. All geographical areas of Alaska, all economic and other interests in Alaska, must speak with one voice."[80] Gruening was less subtle. He decried "the infiltration" of the university and the state Department of Fish and Game by "fanatical conservationists" who would make it more difficult to convince Congress that Alaska spoke with a single voice.[81] Still, he was optimistic. He confessed to his diary that the meeting was a "most worthwhile gathering."[82] Supporters created a lobbying organization called Rampart (later Yukon) Power for America, raised funds, and persuaded Fairbanks publisher C. W. Snedden and University of Alaska President Wood to serve as president and vice president, respectively. Contributions from Anchorage and other communities financed a campaign to have Rampart included in the 1964 congressional rivers and harbors bill.

Rampart backers nevertheless faced two formidable obstacles. The first was the project itself. It would cost more than $1 billion and generate electricity for a nonexistent market. These unpleasant facts ensured a cool reception in Congress. The opposition of the Interior Department's Bureau of Reclamation and many Army Corps of Engineers professionals may well have doomed the project on economic grounds.[83]

The second problem was the emergence of an articulate dissenting voice within the state. In May 1961, in the ACS *News Bulletin* issue following the Chariot expose, Weeden attacked Rampart in a long essay that emphasized the adverse effects of dam building on the area's abundant waterfowl. In January 1962 the *News Bulletin* reprinted a newspaper article by Jay Hammond, Republican state senator, who questioned the economic rationale for Rampart as well as its impact on wildlife. Weeden called it

"one of the most thought-provoking essays yet to appear."[84] As the booster campaign intensified, ACS turned increasingly to Celia Hunter, an effective public speaker who was not dependent on the university or the state.
In September 1963, she responded to Gruening's attacks in a Fairbanks
television program. She emphasized the project's shaky economic rationale and potentially devastating ecological effects.[85] Gruening privately
conceded that her presentation was "skillful." It was based, he believed, on
internal Interior Department data, "showing further evidence of the leaks
within the Department."[86]

The most revealing public exchange occurred in April 1965, when a
Fairbanks television station arranged a debate between two Yukon Power
officers and Hunter and Terry Brady, ACS vice president. The first Yukon
Power speaker argued that Rampart would lift the local Native people out
of poverty and lead to a "huge population increase" in Alaska, creating a
market for electricity. He urged concern for "the human species first, wild
species second." Hunter came next. She argued that "Rampart is being sold
to the public on false grounds," attacked the assertion that it would cost
only $1.2 billion, and rejected the contention that there were no alternative
power sources. Citing Interior Department estimates that Rampart power
would be 25 percent to 150 percent more expensive than other electricity
sources, she argued that nuclear power, not hydropower, was the wave of
the future. The second Yukon Power speaker expressed surprise that Hunter
did not discuss threats to wildlife or plea for the ducks that nested in the
wetlands. He doubted that conservationists "really knew what they were
talking about when they deserted the field of wildlife conservation for economics." Brady was last. He discussed alternative energy sources for Alaska
and warned that Rampart would be the first of many dams that would
transform the northern third of the state.[87] Like Hunter, he insisted on
addressing the project's broader environmental impact. Apart from the
immediate significance of their remarks, Hunter and Brady had shown that
conservationists could no long be dismissed as sentimental animal-lovers.

By that time, the opposition to Rampart had become practically insur-
mountable. The hostility of the Fish and Wildlife Service, the Bureau of
Reclamation, Alaska Native groups—notably the 1,200 Athabascans who
would be forced out of their homes—and the conservation organizations
made it comparatively easy for Secretary Udall to turn down the dam proposal in 1967.

Apart from the boosters' defeat, the most interesting feature of the campaign was the suggestion of an emerging alliance between conservationists

and Alaska Natives. In both the Chariot and the Rampart fights, conservationists and Natives had argued for preservation of the natural landscape. Their position reflected a shared concern for wildlife and wildlife habitat as well as a more general sensitivity to the social and environmental costs of economic growth. Though there were apparently few actual contacts between conservationists and Natives, the *News Bulletin* published or reprinted many news stories from the *Tundra Times*, the Native paper.

Thanks largely to the Chariot and Rampart campaigns, ACS had outgrown its informal origins by the mid-1960s. ACS membership passed 600 in 1966 and 750 in 1968, and the circulation of the *News Bulletin* exceeded 1,000. To cope with the growing administrative burden, the board appointed Celia Hunter to serve as part-time executive secretary in late 1965 and amended the constitution to authorize local chapters. The first of these was the Kenai Peninsula chapter, formed in 1966. Will Troyer, a Fish and Wildlife employee who was the manager of the Kenai Moose Range, was instrumental in its creation.[88] The Anchorage (Cook Inlet) and Sitka chapters followed in 1968, and others at Kodiak, Fairbanks (Tanana-Yukon), Ketchikan (Tongass), Petersburg, and Seward were organized between 1968 and 1970. A Yukon Conservation Society, formed in 1966, worked informally with ACS. Only the largely Native communities of northern and western Alaska did not have active ACS groups by the end of the decade.

Amid these changes there was also continuity. Hunter, Wood, and Weeden continued to play central roles. In 1967 Weeden gave up the editorship of the *News Bulletin* to become ACS president; Wood succeeded him as editor. "This is essentially an incestuous organization," he later joked.[89] Other activists such as Dixie Baade, Jack Calvin, Troyer, and Calvin Fair, another Kenai resident, served for long periods. They and most ACS leaders had similar backgrounds. The *News Bulletin* published capsule biographies of candidates for ACS offices in the late 1960s and early 1970s. Of the 32 individuals who were featured, 25 were men and 7 were women. All but 1 or 2 were university graduates; half had graduate degrees, including 10 with PhDs. Three-quarters worked for public agencies, including the university and the Alaska Department of Fish and Game. Half had lived in Alaska before 1960; many of the younger people were University of Alaska graduates.

There was one subtle change, foreshadowed by the Chariot and Rampart battles. By the end of the decade the chapters often focused on issues that might have been on the agendas of similar groups in California or

Massachusetts. Tanana-Yukon, for example, helped develop a local air pollution ordinance and campaigned for a water and sewer bond issue.[90] Land
and resource issues remained overwhelmingly important, but the logic of
environmentalism made a narrow focus and limited agenda impossible.

PARK INITIATIVES

At the height of the Rampart battle, in early August 1965, the NPS Advisory
Board spent 10 days visiting sites in Alaska. Secretary Udall accompanied
the board for several days, as did NPS Director George Hartzog, his principal subordinates, and several members of the House Interior Committee.
Traveling by chartered plane, they visited the existing parks, went as far
north as Fort Yukon to see the area threatened by Rampart, and visited
sites the Park Service coveted, such as the Wood Tikchik region in southwestern Alaska. One of the most memorable incidents of the entire trip,
however, occurred in Anchorage, where the local chamber of commerce
organized a banquet, as it often did for visiting dignitaries. Assistant
Interior Secretary Stanley A. Cain recalled what happened when the chamber president introduced the after-dinner speaker, *Daily Times* publisher
Robert Atwood:

> [Atwood] spoke at some length in severe criticism of the Federal agencies operat-
> ing in Alaska. The burden of his theme was that Washington bureaucrats were
> shoving good Alaskan citizens around. ... It seemed to me that his tirade embar-
> rassed many people present, for they kept looking at their now empty plates. After
> objecting to any restrictions on the development and use of natural resources ... he
> sat down and the chairman said that closed the evening's program Someone spoke
> in his ear after which he got up and asked ... [Hartzog] if he wished to make any
> remarks. George spoke briefly and graciously while making it quite clear that the
> National Park Service intended to fulfill its national responsibilities in Alaska. No
> direct reference to Mr. Atwood's talk was necessary.[91]

Despite the role of NPS planners in the early stages of the ANWR campaign, the Park Service had played at best a modest role in Alaska. The old
complaint of federal indifference was probably closer to the truth than
Atwood's charge of "shoving good Alaska citizens around." The reasons for
this comparative neglect included the needs of better-established parks
and the preferences of former NPS Director Conrad Wirth. As late as 1964
NPS planner John Kauffman would label the Park Service "the Cheechak
[greenhorn] of all federal agencies" in Alaska.[92] At the time of the advisory

board's visit, there were still no tourist facilities at Katmai or Glacier Bay, and only a primitive lodge at Mount McKinley. After a dinner at Camp Denali, which included a discussion of the poor quality of the road to Wonder Lake, the bus returning members of the advisory board to the Mount McKinley Hotel broke down. Hunter and Wood had to rescue their distinguished guests.[93]

Important changes began with the appointment of Hartzog as NPS director in 1964. He recalled that he had "a simple credo for expanding the national Park System: take it now, warts and all." And "Alaska was ripe for the taking."[94] With the support of the president, Secretary Udall, and congressional leaders (even Wayne Aspinall on occasion), the park system expanded rapidly in the mid-1960s, adding eight parks and monuments, five national seashores, and dozens of other sites. In this setting, Alaska became irresistible. Hartzog appointed Assistant Director Theodor Swem to head the Alaska effort and created a committee under George Collins, now a parks consultant, to prepare an overview. Assisting Collins were Doris Leonard, a partner in his consulting firm (Leonard's husband, Richard, was an important figure in both the Sierra Club and the Wilderness Society); John Kauffman; NPS landscape architect Robert Luntey; and Sigurd Olson. Their report, "Operation Great Land," was completed in January 1965. Though never published, "Operation Great Land" was enormously influential. As historian Theodore Catton notes, its outstanding feature was its sense of urgency. Contrary to the prevailing view, which took Alaska's relative emptiness as an excuse for inaction, Collins and his associates insisted that NPS act before it was too late.[95]

Their thesis was that *"Alaska's scenery ... is worth a massive investment."*[96] NPS should move "from a minor to a major role. ... The time for 'iffy' excuses is past." Though cooperation with the state and the Canadians was desirable, "the Service should finally come into its own, with more money to spend, more jobs to fill." They proposed spending at least $150 million over 10 years and listed 39 Alaska sites or areas that deserved immediate attention.[97] Heading the list were the Brooks Range, the Wrangell–St. Elias Mountains, and several historic sites in Southeast Alaska. But they also included places that had received little attention, such as the Aleutian Islands, the Wood-Tikchik and Lake Clark regions of southwestern Alaska, and the Yukon Flats, the area that would have been inundated by the Rampart dam.

The Collins report led to a "great push forward."[98] In 1965 the Park Service established an Anchorage office to coordinate activity within the state. Two years later, Swem created a planning unit in Washington to win-now the Collins list and make specific, detailed proposals. Later that year Hartzog wrote to Alaska's new governor, Walter Hickel, outlining his intentions. He planned to ask Congress to enlarge Glacier Bay, Katmai, and Mount McKinley parks and build or improve tourist facilities in all three. His staff was studying other sites, including the Brooks Range and historic sites at Skagway and Sitka. In the future, NPS would devote more attention to interpretative and educational activities and designate a variety of his-toric and natural landmarks.[99]

Hartzog's plans proved premature, largely because of the resistance of Alaska's politicians and the turmoil that engulfed the Johnson administra-tion. Hickel's 1966 victory over Governor Egan represented the triumph of one booster faction over another; if anything, Hickel was even more com-mitted to resource-based development. He had little interest in parks and strongly opposed Hartzog's designs on the Wood-Tikchik area, which he hoped to sell for vacation homes and fishing camps. It eventually became a state park. Hickel refused to allow his staff to meet with NPS officials.[100] At the time he left Alaska in 1969 to become secretary of the Interior in the new Nixon administration, Wood-Tikchik was in limbo and relations between NPS and the state were strained.

Equally threatening were the effects of the Vietnam conflict. Although President Johnson supported Udall's and Hartzog's plans to expand the park system, the war crisis had paralyzed Congress. Hartzog had little real-istic possibility of congressional action on an Alaska parks bill before 1969, and the election of Richard Nixon and the appointment of Hickel created new obstacles. In the meantime the park planners continued their work.

One other possibility had arisen in late 1968. After Johnson announced his retirement, Secretary Udall suggested that he use his powers to create national monuments under the Antiquities Act of 1906 to give "a Christmas present to the nation." In August Udall and Hartzog discussed the proposal, and the parks director asked Swem to prepare a list for Udall's and the president's consideration. A few weeks later Udall made a similar request to other Interior agencies, the Sierra Club, and the Conservation Foundation. Swem's list, submitted on September 20, included extensions to Mount McKinley Park, plus the Wrangell–St. Elias Range, Lake Clark, the central Brooks Range, and St. Lawrence Island in the Bering Sea. Hartzog later added extensions to Katmai and the Wood-Tikchik area. Udall selected Mount McKinley, Katmai, the Brooks Range, and St. Lawrence Island for further consideration. (Wrangell–St. Elias and Lake Clark were dropped because the Bureau of Land Management had already taken preliminary steps to protect them and St. Lawrence Island because the Native community there had not been consulted.) During the following month NPS officials and Burton Silcock, the state Bureau of Land Management director, drew up precise boundaries for the three proposed monuments.[101]

Apparently the only competing proposals came from the Sierra Club. In early September Edgar Wayburn, the club's Alaska expert, proposed an expanded Mount McKinley Park, and on November 21, a Sierra Club delegation headed by Executive Director David Brower submitted a list of 27 possible monuments, mostly national forest lands in California, Washington, and Oregon. Udall complained that "he could not propose areas involving Forest Service lands without the support of the White House." Since he was still uncertain of Johnson's commitment, he told the delegation that Interior "was going ahead with several proposals that did not include national forest lands."[102] Since NPS had already devoted substantial time and resources to its proposal, this may have been a convenient excuse. In any event, none of the lands mentioned in the Sierra Club proposal appeared on the list Udall presented to Johnson on December 11.

At that meeting, Johnson asked Udall to discuss his proposals with congressional leaders, especially Representative Aspinall. Udall, however, refused to have anything to do with Aspinall.[103] He and the powerful Coloradoan had clashed repeatedly and by 1968 were openly hostile. Apart from their personal antagonism, Aspinall had become increasingly rigid in his defense of the status quo while Udall was pushing the Interior Department in the opposite direction. He sought to transform it into a conservation agency with its "purest conservation arm," NPS, as its vanguard. As the disarray within the Democratic Party and the Johnson administration became more acute, these distinctions became more critical.

Though Udall said that he did not care whether congressmen liked the proposed monuments or not, he did discuss them with Senator Henry Jackson (D-WA), the chairman of the Senate Interior Committee; Representative John Saylor, the leading Republican on the House committee; and other congressional leaders, including the Alaska delegation.[104] When Aspinall learned of these consultations, he was furious and threatened to withhold appropriations for the monuments and even lead a campaign to repeal the Antiquities Act. Johnson was taken aback. A battle with the crusty Aspinall was not the "Christmas present" he had envisioned. He was also concerned about Udall's loyalty. A John Kennedy appointee, the Interior secretary remained close to Robert Kennedy and had confessed during the bitter primary battles between Johnson and Kennedy that he might have to resign. As it became increasingly apparent that Udall had not followed orders, the Udall-Johnson relationship frayed even more. Udall later recalled that the president "raised hell with me ... he bawled me out good." At one point the secretary offered his resignation.[105]

Secretary-designate Hickel also may have been an influence. The prospect of a new development-oriented Interior secretary was an argument for immediate action. In his initial press conference on December 13, Hickel had repeated clichés about "locking up" natural resources and implied that he would adopt a different approach. Udall subsequently argued, "If you don't set aside these areas now, they never will be," but Johnson and his aides worried that Hickel would publicly attack the new monuments and create additional controversy.[106] Their fears were in fact groundless. Hickel soon realized that his statements had endangered his candidacy and became more circumspect—the first phase of what would be a remarkable, if temporary, transformation. In a meeting with Johnson on January 9, he did not object to the proposed monuments or to Udall's simultaneous effort to create additional wildlife refuges in Alaska.[107]

Some combination of those factors led Johnson to equivocate, postponing any decision on the monuments until his last days in office. Supposedly he had the proposals spread out on his bed while he dressed for the inauguration. Forced at last to decide, he signed orders for three monuments in Arizona and Utah and a fourth expanding Katmai by 94,000 acres. He refused to authorize the expansion of Mount McKinley by 2.2 million acres or the creation of a 4.1-million-acre Gates of the Arctic monument.[108] Johnson's actions meant that after four years of accelerated effort, the NPS campaign to "take" Alaska had added a meager 94,000 acres to the park system.

Hartzog, Swem, and their staffs were naturally disappointed. Their efforts had been ineffectual, and the future looked even more challenging. In retrospect, of course, their disappointment was premature, and Johnson's inaction was probably helpful. If the president had acted on their relatively modest requests, it is likely that the vastly more ambitious Alaska park plans that began to take shape two years later would have had less appeal. Given the splendor of Alaska and the public's growing awareness of its value and potential, Johnson's decisions worked to Hartzog's advantage. Six million acres of Alaska wilderness had been at stake in

1968. Nine years later, another president would review a new set of NPS proposals and choose to preserve more than 50 million acres of Alaska wilderness.

The years between 1950 and 1968 were thus years of preparation, testing, and, in some cases, frustration. No longer remote and obscure, Alaska had emerged as an important battleground in the contest between unregulated industrial growth and environmental protection. Because of its small population, vast size, and aesthetic appeal, Alaska assumed special importance to activists, who emphasized the desirability of additional parks and wildlife refuges and the concomitant need to curb the managerial powers of the federal natural resource agencies. From the perspective of 1968, their major achievements had been negative: they had thwarted the worst of the boosters' plans, but with the exception of ANWR—which could only be counted a partial victory—and the enlargement of Katmai, Alaska was no less vulnerable than it had been a dozen years before. And there was little doubt that the state, and perhaps the federal agencies, would pose other challenges. Indeed, as Hartzog and Swem were beginning to prepare their recommendations for additions to the park system, the pace of change suddenly accelerated, and the challenges that would confront park administrators and environmentalists suddenly became more obvious than ever before.

PART II

WILDERNESS POLITICS: ALASKA, 1960s–1976

And let us not forget the wilderness either. That is, after all,
the real calling card to me and my family. It is why, principally, we chose to live here …
                                        —Gordon B. Wright, 1971

Daddy, won't you take me to Port Protection Country,
down to Point Baker where paradise lay.
     I'm sorry, my son, you're too late in asking.
Ketchikan Pulp Co. done hauled it away.
                                        —Ketchikan Daily News, 1975

What is the Sierra Club, anyway?
A bunch of rich bastards in San Francisco who've made
their pile and don't want anyone else to make theirs.
They're saving the wilderness for themselves,
and damn everybody else.
                                        —Potter Wickware, 1979

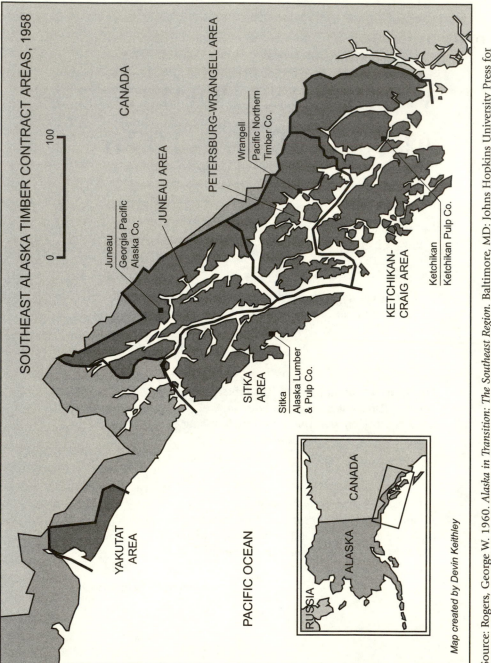

SOUTHEAST ALASKA TIMBER CONTRACT AREAS, 1958

0 100

CANADA

PETERSBURG-WRANGELL AREA

Wrangell
Pacific Northern
Timber Co.

Juneau
Georgia Pacific
Alaska Co.

JUNEAU AREA

KETCHIKAN-
CRAIG AREA

Ketchikan
Ketchikan Pulp Co.

SITKA
AREA

Sitka
Alaska Lumber
& Pulp Co.

YAKUTAT
AREA

PACIFIC OCEAN

RUSSIA

ALASKA

CANADA

Map created by Devin Keithley.

Source: Rogers, George W. 1960. *Alaska in Transition: The Southeast Region.* Baltimore, MD: Johns Hopkins University Press for Resources for the Future.

CHAPTER 3

ALASKA UPHEAVALS

In spring 1967 the Atlantic Richfield Company began to drill one last well on the Arctic coast. The site was recently selected state land about halfway between the eastern border of Pet 4 and the Canning River, the western border of the Arctic National Wildlife Range. Flat, windswept, desolate, a hundred miles from the nearest settlement, Prudhoe Bay had become a metaphor for Arctic oil exploration. Since the 1920s, geologists had insisted that the area was rich in hydrocarbons. After the Navy carried out extensive exploratory activities in the 1940s and early 1950s, oil companies moved in. By the late 1960s they had spent $150 million and had nothing to show for their efforts. British Petroleum, the leader, had given up. Atlantic Richfield had persisted without success. Prudhoe Bay State No. 1 would be Richfield's final effort.[1]

The Atlantic Richfield crew worked until May and then returned in November, after the surface had refrozen. By late December they had found large quantities of natural gas. Dealing with the gas delayed additional drilling until mid-January 1968. A test on February 18 showed gas under pressure and oil. "That was when we really began to get excited," recalled the crew leader.[2] Subsequent tests confirmed the significance of their find. Finally, on June 15, 1968, Atlantic Richfield publicly acknowledged that it had found the long-awaited Arctic field, ultimately the single most important North American field.

The reaction of Alaska's booster community can be gauged from its principal organ, the *Anchorage Daily Times*. At a New Year's party one of the geologists working at Prudhoe Bay had run into publisher Robert Atwood and was surprised to learn that he knew about the gas discovery. On February 16, the *Daily Times* ran a large headline: "Arctic Slope Well Strikes Oil." On May 18, still more than a month before Atlantic Richfield confirmed the discovery, the headline was even larger: "Arctic Oil Find Is Huge."[3]

The oil companies soon confirmed that judgment.[4] In October the companies with Prudhoe Bay leases formed a consortium, the Trans-Alaska Pipeline System, to create a transportation system for the oil. (This consortium would give way to a permanent successor, Alyeska Pipeline Service Company, in August 1970.) In February 1969, Trans-Alaska Pipeline executives announced that they would build an 800-mile pipeline to Valdez, on Prince William Sound, where tankers would collect the oil and transport it to refineries in Washington and California. In September, the oil companies again signaled their optimism by bidding a staggering $900 million for additional state leases near Prudhoe Bay. The simultaneous arrival of the Nixon administration and its new secretary of the Interior, Alaska Governor Walter Hickel, seemed to ensure a positive response to these events.

The Alaska announcements also had far-reaching implications for contemporary environmentalism. In November 1968 the Sierra Club had submitted a list of proposed national monuments to Interior Secretary Stewart Udall that did not include a single Alaska site. A few months later such an omission would have been unthinkable. The oil companies' plans would create a large industrial complex on the largely pristine Arctic coast. A pipeline would cross hundreds of miles of permafrost, dozens of rivers and wildlife migration routes, and several earthquake zones. The proposed oil terminal at the east end of Prince William Sound, one of the most beautiful of Alaska's inlets and a valuable resource to the fishing and tourism industries, raised other concerns. But the possibilities for catastrophic oil spills did not exhaust the list of threats. A highway parallel to the pipeline, the "Haul Road," would open a vast roadless area, creating the likelihood of additional industrial activities. Proponents often noted that the pipeline itself would disturb only a few thousand acres. In fact, as they acknowledged privately, it would open millions of acres of Alaska wilderness.

The effect was catalytic. The proposed oil field and pipeline galvanized the diverse elements of the environmental movement, accelerated the growth of an organized environmental presence in Alaska, and forced politicians to grapple with conflicting pressures for pollution prevention, parks and refuges, wilderness preservation, and social justice on one hand and economic growth, jobs, and domestic energy sources on the other. This chapter focuses on the events of 1968–1970 and the mobilization of forces, pro and con. Chapter 4 examines the national debate over the Alaska pipeline and the first phase of the negotiations that would forever alter the northern landscape.

A BELEAGUERED STATE

The boom that began in spring 1968 was all the more dramatic because of what had not happened in the preceding decade. Far from "unlocking" Alaska's riches, the efforts of the new state had exposed the hollowness of the boosters' claims. The fishing industry continued to decline, despite the creation of a reputable state fish and game department. A 1969 study by University of Alaska economists Arlon Tussing and Gregg Erickson concluded that Alaska mining companies were backward and uncompetitive. Thus, although Alaska was "as well-endowed with minerals as the rest of the nation, the overall circumstances of mining do not indicate the probability of an Alaska development boom."[5] The other mainstays were only marginally healthier. Timber industry production and employment in the southeast grew, thanks to the Forest Service, but the impact was limited to the region (and, of course, unrelated to the state's role). In the meantime, a decline in military expenditures and the Project Chariot nuclear experiment and Rampart dam debacles aggravated the state's economic woes.

While the boom failed to materialize, state expenditures rose dramatically. Preoccupied with federal restraints, the boosters had conveniently disregarded the magnitude of federal expenditures during the territorial period, especially for education, public health, and other social services. At the same time their rhetoric had raised expectations. The result was a persistent, deepening fiscal crisis. In 1959 the territory collected $23 million in tax revenues and spent more than $31 million, including almost $17 million for education.[6] By 1966 tax and license receipts had risen to $50 million but expenditures had climbed to $155 million. Federal subsidies totaled $77 million.[7] Far from freeing itself from federal interference, Alaska had become more dependent than ever.

The state had little success in addressing its problems. In 1961 the legislature raised a variety of consumption taxes—carefully avoiding any affront to potential business investors—and curbed nonessential expenditures. Topping the list of nonessentials were parks and recreational facilities. Air and water pollution, waste disposal, and other related environmental problems were likewise left to local government, which is to say, largely disregarded. Yet overall retrenchment proved impossible. The population continued to grow and the state began to confront the problems of rural Alaska, especially the Native-dominated north and west, where population growth, declining rural industries, and technological innovation curtailed traditional opportunities.

The state's deepening crisis exacerbated political tensions. A small but vocal group of secessionists sought to return northern Alaska to territorial status. The booster community divided over a proposal to move the capital to the Anchorage area. A devastating 1964 earthquake that destroyed Valdez and much of downtown Anchorage seemed to symbolize Alaska's troubled state.

Amid the gloom of the 1960s there was one bright spot, the state's gradual emergence as an oil producer. At the time of the Prudhoe Bay discovery Alaska wells were pumping more than 200,000 barrels per day and paying $50,000 a day in taxes and royalty fees to the state.[8] Virtually all of this oil came from the Kenai Peninsula and the adjacent waters of Cook Inlet. The Kenai discoveries had reassured contemporary boosters that their hopes were not entirely misplaced. They had also introduced a variety of environmental problems, including wildlife habitat destruction, water pollution, and the lobbying power of oil companies. The restrictions imposed by the Fish and Wildlife Service in the Moose Range and the cooperative approach of Standard Oil reassured many potential critics. By the 1960s, the area was often cited as an example of the compatibility of industry and wilderness values. But many conservationists remained skeptical. The same exploration teams that behaved responsibly in the Moose Range devastated adjoining state lands, where they were unregulated.[9]

The conservationists' greatest concern was the fragile wetlands and bays of Cook Inlet. By 1968 thirteen offshore drilling platforms were operating in the inlet, and oil spills from wells and tankers were a recurring problem.

From mid-1966 to the end of 1967 the Interior Department counted 75 incidents. The most serious one, in November 1967, killed more than 2,000 waterfowl.[10] The threat to fish and shellfish created a groundswell of local sentiment for more stringent controls on drilling, well operations, and transportation.

THE NATIVE CLAIMS STALEMATE

The Atlantic Richfield announcement of June 1968 proved to be just the first step in a prolonged process. The Prudhoe Bay pipeline did not win official approval until late 1973, and the first shipments did not leave Valdez until 1977, nine years after the original celebrations. The delay occurred despite the best efforts of the booster community. The most notorious example was the so-called Hickel Highway of 1968–1969, a winter road to Prudhoe Bay that the governor ordered in response to pressure from the state's truckers. Ill-conceived and poorly executed, the road cost twice as much as anticipated, had almost no impact on construction at Prudhoe Bay—the oil companies airlifted almost all their equipment and supplies—and left an ugly scar across hundreds of miles of tundra. But the state's business and political leaders and their oil industry allies soon discovered that they could no longer overlook groups with competing interests and perspectives. The ability of Natives and environmentalists to delay the pipeline project was a key to the sweeping land settlements that accompanied it.

From 1968 to the end of 1971 the principal obstacle was a problem that most white Alaskans had chosen to forget: the Natives' land claims. The boosters' policies had produced numerous clashes in the 1960s, as Native groups appealed state land selections. Confronted by state officials on the one hand and increasingly militant Native groups on the other, Secretary of the Interior Stewart Udall had imposed an informal freeze on land transactions in December 1966. Before leaving office in 1969, he had frozen all activity for an additional two years to encourage Congress to address the issue. To blunt opposition to his confirmation, Secretary-designate Hickel had reluctantly agreed to continue the freeze. The effect was to tie the fate of Prudhoe Bay, the Alaska economy, and the Alaska wilderness to the seemingly intractable Native claims issue.

The ensuing debates and legislative maneuvers, which ultimately led to the landmark Alaska Native Claims Settlement Act of 1971, are exhaustively detailed in the works of Mary Clay Berry, Donald Craig Mitchell, and others. The complex deliberations are important to the story of environmental mobilization because they illuminate the Natives' approach to environmental issues and thus the partnership potential of the two groups that were most critical of the boosters' plans. They also had a direct impact on the environmentalists' agenda by raising the possibility of a broader land settlement, one that would include parks and wilderness areas as well as pipeline corridors and subsistence regions.

If Alaskans generally were frustrated by their lack of economic progress, Alaska Natives had reason for even greater anxiety. Not only were they poor (the poorest Americans by some measures), but their situation appeared to be worsening. In contrast to the "healthy poverty" of earlier years, when most Natives had been geographically isolated and outside the market economy, the Natives of the 1960s suffered from an "unhealthy poverty."[11] Journalists who visited remote Native-dominated communities in the wake of the oil boom were struck by the prevalence of slum conditions. Bryan Cooper described Barrow, on the Arctic coast, as "a shanty town through which a hurricane had torn," a place where most adults were "either sleeping off hangovers or drinking themselves into new ones."[12] The director of the U.S. Office of Economic Opportunity found in Nome the "most abject poverty I've seen anywhere—including Africa, Latin America, India or anywhere else."[13] Alaskans had long known Bethel, near the mouth of the Kuskokwim River, as "sin city," but in the 1960s the town's per capita homicide rate exceeded that of any other American city.[14] The Federal Field Committee, an interagency research group authorized by Congress to survey Native life, reported alarming changes: between 1960 and 1966, the per capita homicide rate among Natives increased almost sevenfold; suicides tripled; and deaths from alcoholism more than doubled.[15]

Observers pointed to a variety of causes, some deep-seated, others transitory. The state's takeover of many federal activities and the nearly simultaneous introduction of radio and television, outboard motors, chain saws, and snowmobiles had profoundly disturbed nearly every aspect of rural life, leaving Natives in an uncomfortable limbo, with one foot in each of two strikingly different worlds.[16] Project Chariot and the proposed Rampart dam had been inescapable challenges to traditional lifestyles. State land selections and efforts by the Fish and Wildlife Service to enforce hunting regulations posed additional threats. Above all, there was the accelerating pace of oil exploration. Between 1962 and 1966 at least a dozen Native organizations coalesced to defend local and regional interests.[17]

Seeking greater political clout, representatives of these groups gathered in Anchorage in October 1966 to explore the possibility of a statewide coordinating body. The statement of the lands committee captured their mood. "The encroachment of an Alien civilization has reduced the customary use and enjoyment of our land and threatens the continuation of our culture," it complained. As a consequence, Natives should seek "full control and ownership" of lands that rightfully belonged to them in order to "develop such lands in an orderly manner." They wanted "agreements between effected Native groups and potential developers to permit continuing development of the land and its resources."[18] To achieve these goals, they created a new organization, the Alaska Federation of Natives (AFN), which quickly became the voice of Native Alaska in state and national politics.

At first AFN did not have a specific agenda. At the October 1966 meeting Native leaders were content to demand legislation authorizing a suit in the U.S. Court of Claims. They soon rejected that approach in favor of a more generous legislative solution. By 1967 they were demanding a combination of measures that would encourage market-oriented economic activities and preserve opportunities to live off the land: specifically, a large land grant (they favored at least 40 million and possibly 60 million acres), a cash award, and a stake in the state's economic development. These demands astounded the boosters, led by Hickel's successor, Governor Keith Miller, and resulted in a succession of bitter conflicts.

The disarray in Alaska was paralleled in Congress. The powerful heads of the pertinent Senate and House committees, Senator Henry Jackson and Representative Wayne Aspinall, opposed a large land grant and, in Aspinall's case, any meaningful concessions. Jackson's committee struggled with several bills, failed to win support for any of them, and adjourned. It resumed its deliberations in spring 1970 and eventually reported out a bill that the Senate passed in July. It awarded the Natives 10 million acres, $500 million, and an additional $500 million from anticipated mineral revenues. Since Aspinall refused to act, the bill's economic provisions (which most AFN leaders dismissed as grossly inadequate) were less important than an obscure provision, Section 23, which withdrew "all unreserved public lands" in Alaska and directed the secretary of the Interior to determine "which are suitable for inclusion as recreation, wilderness, or wildlife management areas" in national parks or wildlife refuges.[19] The secretary was to report to Congress within three years, and Congress was to act on his recommendations within two years.

Section 23 had grown out of the work of the Federal Field Committee. The committee's chair, Joseph Fitzgerald, and several staff members, notably University of Alaska economist Arlon Tussing and wildlife expert David Hickok, had argued for recognition of a conservation interest in Alaska's wildlands. They reminded the politicians and Native leaders that in the new era symbolized by Earth Day (April 20, 1970, while Jackson's staff was drafting the bill), any deal that did not take environmental issues into account was probably doomed. Tussing publicly called for a "grand bargain" that would reconcile the interests of different groups.[20] Hickok worked behind the scenes with Bill Van Ness, Jackson's top assistant and bill drafter.[21] The actual provision was modest and probably unworkable. It gave Congress too little time to act and explicitly permitted state selections during the study period. It would have encouraged competition between interest groups—the opposite of Tussing's "grand bargain." Nevertheless, it proved to be the most important legacy of the 1970 legislation. Harry Crandell, who had just left the Fish and Wildlife Service to become conservation director of the Wilderness Society, become aware of Section 23 through contacts with Hickok. He recalled in a private memoir that he went to Stewart Brandborg, the society's executive director, and "recommended that in the next Congress we try to turn the measure from an 'Indian claims' matter into a 'public lands opportunity.'"[22] By the time Congress adjourned, Crandell and his associates had a plan to mitigate some of the dangers of the proposed pipeline.

In the meantime, a more direct and immediate threat to the pipeline had emerged. In March 1970, a half-dozen Native villages along the proposed route that had earlier waived their claims to land in the pipeline corridor in exchange for a promise of jobs had second thoughts when the jobs failed to materialize. After Secretary Hickel (with the approval of Jackson and Aspinall) modified the freeze to permit work in the corridor, the villages asked U.S. District Judge George Hart to halt construction on lands they claimed. On April 1, Hart issued an injunction covering 20 miles of the proposed route. Many observers suspected that the Natives "are mostly looking for bargaining power with the oil industry; they may not stick with the case."[23] Whatever their motives, their attorneys contacted the major national environmental organizations, seeking allies.

The Natives' overtures spurred the environmental groups to act. They had become increasingly alarmed by reports that the oil companies, with the ill-disguised support of the state and the federal Bureau of Land Management, were working on the pipeline route.[24] On February 24, Edgar

Wayburn of the Sierra Club, Stewart Brandborg of the Wilderness Society, and Charles Callison of the Audubon Society complained to Hickel about such activity. They implied that they would sue if he did not restrain the oil companies.[25] Yet when Hickel disregarded their complaints, they hesitated, Art Davidson, the Alaska representative for Friends of the Earth (FOE), explained:

> *If FOE becomes a plaintiff no Alaska politicians will want to be associated with us. I'll probably become overnight the most despised man in Alaska. ... If we oppose the pipeline we are in a position of opposing the development of Arctic oil; that's a tough one. We might oppose the present plans with litigation to buy time for study ... A position of wanting the pipeline halted until all studies can be made will be much more acceptable to Alaskans than an argument opposing the pipeline period.[26]*

The Natives' injunction resolved this dilemma. Brandborg had already received covert legal advice about possible challenges from friends in the Interior Department. He then enlisted Friends of the Earth and the Environmental Defense Fund and charged that the government had violated the Mineral Leasing Act of 1920, which limited the width of pipeline right-of-ways, and had not met the requirements of the new National Environmental Policy Act, which required systematic assessments of environmental risks.[27] On April 13, James Moorman of the activist Center for Law and Social Policy, representing the environmental groups, persuaded Judge Hart to enjoin the Interior Department from authorizing the pipeline or the service road.

Shocked at this dramatic turn of events, Trans-Alaska Pipeline System executives became more cautious. When Governor Miller proposed to use his power to build the road, they rebuffed the state offer. In September, the president of Alyeska Pipeline Service Company, the new consortium, told the Anchorage Chamber of Commerce that a land deal had to precede the pipeline. The pipeline would be a sufficient challenge without added complications.[28]

Soon afterward, Alaska voters also signaled their desire for a settlement. In the November 1970 elections, Governor Miller lost to a rejuvenated William Egan, who had made peace with the Natives and promised to support their demands. Nick Begich, a Democrat who had made similar promises, won the state's congressional seat. With these changes, and President Nixon's replacement of Secretary Hickel (for reasons unrelated to Alaska) with Rogers C. B. Morton, a moderate who had no personal stake in Alaska, the likelihood of an agreement increased. Yet many problems remained. Fundamental disagreements remained on virtually all the major issues. In the meantime, the delays had encouraged the environmentalists to mobilize and voice their concerns.

ALASKA ENVIRONMENTALISM

By most objective measures the Alaska Conservation Society was well equipped to confront the challenges of the new era. It had an impressive list of achievements, an equally impressive leadership cadre, and a statewide membership. Through its affiliates it had demonstrated a willingness to embrace contentious local issues. Given the proliferation of such groups in the southeast, it was certain to be drawn into the growing conflict with the Forest Service. And it would soon play a vital role in the formation of regional centers, the distinguishing feature of the Alaska movement. Yet it quickly lost its preeminent role and by the end of the decade represented the most conservative wing of Alaska environmentalism.

The problem was both structural and psychological. The Alaska-only focus of ACS made less sense after Prudhoe Bay. The lack of a national presence was the factor that Alaskans who favored other groups over ACS most often mentioned. Many ACS members, however, continued to think of Alaska as *sui generis*. This perception may have reflected the influence of scientists whose research was based on Alaska's distinctive climate and geography. Whatever the exact reason, it made ACS members hesitate at critical moments, such as the Hickel Highway controversy. In that case they had privately fumed at Hickel but had been more circumspect in public. Bob Weeden explained that the Bureau of Land Management, under intense pressure from state officials, had asked ACS not to attack it for approving the road.[29] He privately protested to Hickel but received no reply.[30] Michael McCloskey of the Sierra Club recalled that ACS had a "staid, cautious way of doing business." ACS leaders "saw everything in terms of Alaska"; they didn't understand the new, broader perspective.[31]

ACS did have one national connection—a close but informal relationship with the Wilderness Society. In 1963 Celia Hunter and Ginny Wood hosted the society's annual meeting at Camp Denali and in the following years corresponded frequently with Brandborg and his director of field services, Clifton R. Merrit. When the Interior Department designated several sites in western Alaska as wilderness study areas, they worked together to mobilize favorable testimony and comment.[32] When Sitka activists organized a chapter of ACS specifically to work for the creation of a West Chichagof–Yakobi Island wilderness, near Sitka, Hunter referred them to Brandborg for technical information.[33] Hunter sat on the society's board and would serve as interim executive secretary in 1977–1978. Yet these contacts were informal and largely personal.

In any case, ACS's Alaska-only focus and preference for working within the local establishment meshed uneasily with the expanding perspectives and growing militancy of environmentalism. In Alaska, as in other states, there was a rush of new recruits, generally younger, less well established and less patient individuals, mostly recent arrivals. Most of them were university graduates, though fewer were scientists. Their interest reflected concerns about the impact of industrial development. Most of them had trained for the professions and services, not for mining, forestry, or other traditional goods-producing industries. As doctors, lawyers, teachers, or government bureaucrats, they had a personal interest in an expanding economy but little direct stake in the boosters' development plans. An economy based on tourism would be equally rewarding financially and infinitely more satisfying.

The environmentalist community of 1968 and afterward was also markedly more female. Brina Kessel and Margaret Murie had played notable roles in the campaign for the Arctic National Wildlife Range; Celia Hunter, Ginny Hill Wood, and Dixie Baade had been (and remained) influential members of ACS. They were, however, a distinct minority before 1968. At the first important gathering of the new era, a conference in Juneau in February 1969, 57 men and 13 women pondered the future of Alaska's wilderness areas. The 57 men included 20 Forest Service, Park Service, and Alaska Fish and Game officials.[34] Of the environmentalists, one-third were women, about the same proportion as in the ACS leadership. The proportions changed in the following years as more women became active. In Anchorage the leaders of the environmental movement would be predominantly women by 1972. In other communities women remained a minority of the total but assumed more assertive roles as officers, lobbyists, and publicists.

The new generation of activists saw themselves as participants in a national movement. The Sierra Club, the Wilderness Society, Friends of the Earth, and other national groups actively sought Alaska members. Alaska environmentalists sought affiliation with the national organizations to address national and international issues, have a voice in Washington, and maximize their local influence. A prime example was the Steller Society, a Juneau group organized in 1966 to oppose a proposed highway plan that compromised an important wildlife area. The Steller Society (named after an eighteenth-century explorer and naturalist) attracted local scientists and wildlife experts and logically should have become the Juneau chapter of ACS. Hunter and Weeden made several overtures, but the Juneau activists, led by Joe and Kay Greenough and Rich Gordon, held out.[35] Having succeeded in preserving the wetland, they turned their attention to the Forest Service's plans for the timber industry. Scientific analysis would play a role in this controversy, but so, too, would the ability to coerce Forest Service managers in Washington. At a climactic meeting at the Greenoughs' home in fall 1968, with Bob Weeden representing ACS and Anchorage activists Jerry and Mark Ganopole representing the new Alaska chapter of the Sierra Club, Steller Society members debated their future. They chose to become the Juneau group of the Sierra Club because of the club's national presence and political activism.[36]

In the meantime the Sierra Club had emerged as a different type of national organization. Under Executive Director David Brower it had played highly visible roles in the national campaigns to preserve Dinosaur National Monument and Grand Canyon National Park and had expanded both geographically and philosophically to become a national organization that could address a spectrum of environmental issues. At a time when old-line conservation organizations were broadening their focus and new specialized groups (epitomized at the national level by the research- and litigation-oriented Environmental Defense Fund and the Natural Resources Defense Council) were proliferating, the Sierra Club rode both waves successfully. Better than any other organization, it symbolized the rise of environmentalism.

In the fervid atmosphere of the late 1960s there were inevitable strains. Buoyed by his successes, the charismatic Brower became increasingly independent of the club's board and indifferent to day-to-day managerial problems. His relations with other prominent club personalities, notably President Edgar Wayburn and celebrated photographer Ansel Adams, soured to the point of confrontation. In a famous showdown in mid-1969, the board forced Brower's resignation. He and his followers then formed Friends of the Earth, committed to even broader goals and greater activism. The Sierra Club retained most of its members and momentum and under Brower's successor, Michael McCloskey, became stronger internally.[37]

In these critical years of growth and upheaval, which coincided with the Prudhoe Bay discovery and the emergence of the pipeline and Native claims controversies, individual Sierra Club leaders operating semi-independently developed special areas of interest, which in turn often defined the club's agenda. In summer 1967 Wayburn and his wife Peggy vacationed in Alaska, partly to gauge the potential for parks and wilderness areas. They were "dumbfounded by the magnificence" of what they saw.[38] Wayburn returned to San Francisco committed to adding Alaska to the list of club priorities. In the following years it became his "fiefdom."[39] He visited Alaska annually, publicized it in speeches and articles, and orchestrated the club's growing commitment to the preservation of Alaska's most notable natural areas; Peggy Wayburn wrote the Sierra Club's guide to Alaska.

During his 1967 vacation Wayburn also met with a small group of Anchorage-area members, most of them transplanted Californians. He encouraged them to form an Alaska chapter, noting that Alaska had more than 100 current members. Two couples, Jerry and Mark Ganopole, and Hans and Calle Van Der Laan, outdoor enthusiasts and long-time members, took the lead. In December they began a systematic campaign to organize an Alaska chapter. On May 28, 1968, two weeks before the official announcement of the Prudhoe Bay discoveries, 14 of the most enthusiastic members gathered at the Ganopoles' home to form a temporary executive committee and appoint officers. They submitted a petition with 78 names, well above the required minimum. On September 14, the Sierra Club board authorized an Alaska chapter.[40] All the executive committee members were from Anchorage except for Jack Calvin of Sitka.

In the meantime Wayburn had met Rich Gordon on a Sierra Club outing in Hawaii. A University of Wisconsin graduate who had come to Alaska to work for the Alaska Department of Fish and Game, Gordon soon became Wayburn's "eyes and ears" in Juneau. He played a major role in the Steller Society and in the organization of the Juneau group of the Sierra Club.[41] Besides Gordon, Donald Freedman, a physician who became the first chair; Richard Myren, a fisheries biologist; and Joe Greenough were elected to the executive committee. By the end of 1968 the Juneau group was ready to tackle regional issues.

The following summer Gordon B. Wright arrived in Fairbanks to teach music at the University of Alaska and to direct the local symphony. A Wisconsin graduate who had run a Madison bookstore and conducted a summer orchestra, Wright had been active in the Wisconsin Sierra Club

chapter and was a Brower partisan in the internecine conflicts of
1968–1969. Nevertheless, when Wayburn asked him to organize a
Fairbanks group, he responded positively. A few months later he reported
that "we have over 50 members in the area, with several very hard-work-
ing ones. While nothing specific has been established or accomplished we
have made the community aware that the Sierra Club does exist here." He
had recently spoken to the local Rotary about the club, "and while the
group was stony silent, they weren't particularly hostile."[42]

FOREST WARS

When Wayburn first committed the Sierra Club to Alaska, he had no specific action in mind. He wrote in January 1968 that Alaska was "a very long
range" project. The club was "not planning any immediate or dramatic
moves at this time."[43] The Prudhoe Bay discoveries soon forced him to
reconsider. Yet he was, in fact, doubly wrong. On the eve of the oil boom
a second major Alaska environmental controversy had emerged. The long-
standing effort of the Forest Service to create a timber and wood pulp
industry in Southeast Alaska raised many similar issues: the destruction of
the old-growth forest and the wildlife that depended on it; the elimination
of other possible uses for the logged areas; the aesthetic and ecological
devastation associated with clear-cutting; the pollution of the waters adjacent to the Ketchikan and Sitka mills; and above all, the scientific expertise and integrity of government managers. For most of the next decade the
two conflicts would follow parallel but independent paths.

By the late 1960s a vocal minority of Southeast Alaskans, ranging from
veteran conservationist Dixie Baade to Juneau Mayor Joe McLean, a new
Sierra Club member, were critical of Forest Service stewardship in the
Tongass. They had several specific concerns. They believed that Forest
Service managers, in their haste to accommodate the industry, had grossly
overestimated the amount of available wood. If they were right, the
foresters would have to expand the designated harvest areas before the 50-
year contracts expired. But even if they were wrong, the old-growth forest,
with the massive trees that were one of the area's most distinctive features,
was doomed. In the meantime, poorly drawn plans and lax oversight led
to large clear-cuts, soil erosion, stream sedimentation, and destruction of
salmon spawning areas. In Ketchikan and Sitka, the mills severely polluted the waters near the plants. Finally, Forest Service managers seemed

wholly indifferent to the need for wildlife habitat and recreational areas and positively hostile to proposals for preserving some areas as wilderness.[44] The foresters acknowledged that their goal was to convert the Tongass into a tree farm; environmentalists worried that, worse yet, they would create a denuded, blighted landscape.

Those complaints spurred a wave of organization in 1967–1968. The Steller Society was the first of the new groups, and the Sitka Conservation Society was the first to take permanent form. The Tongass Conservation Society began as a committee of the Southeast Alaska Mountaineering Association. The Sitka Sierra Club group and the Petersburg Conservation Society followed. Sierra Club partisans favored their group's national scope; others preferred the ACS approach. But many individuals were members of both organizations, and virtually all targeted the policies of the Tongass managers.

Initially, the Sitka Conservation Society had the greatest impact. Jack Calvin, a printer, guide, outdoor enthusiast, and ACS and Sierra Club member, was instrumental in its formation. Calvin had a consuming interest in preserving the coastal forest north of Sitka on Chichagof and Yakobi Islands, an area of dramatic mountains and giant trees. His infectious enthusiasm attracted others and gave the new society a compelling goal. As a colleague wrote in early 1968, they were "in the process of forming a chapter of the Alaska Conservation Society with the primary objective to secure wilderness classification for a portion of Chichagof Island."[45] Their West Chichagof–Yakobi Island wilderness plan would be a central concern of southeastern environmentalists for the next decade.

When the Wayburns came to Alaska in August 1968, Calvin took them and Brock Evans, the Sierra Club's Pacific Northwest representative, to the area. They traveled along the coast in Calvin's boat and hiked parts of the woods, where they encountered one of the large brown bears that inhabited the island.[46] The Wayburns then went to Juneau to talk to W. Howard Johnson, the regional forester, and his assistants. When they mentioned the desirability of wilderness areas, they received "the same old run-around." Johnson promised to identify appropriate areas by summer 1970, but his comments indicated that he favored "rock and ice," mountaintops and glaciers that had little economic potential. When Edgar Wayburn emphasized the need to preserve old-growth areas, one of the assistants became agitated, insisting that "the good Lord did not put trees here merely for people to look at." Johnson and his staff conceded that areas visible to cruise ships should be protected, but they were "still groping about the problem of scenic waterways and the degree to which logging should be curtailed." They dismissed Calvin's plan for West Chichagof–Yakobi as well as calls for the preservation of Admiralty Island.[47]

The mention of Admiralty Island raised what would become the second critical issue in the emerging confrontation. In 1965 the Forest Service had awarded a third 50-year contract totaling more than 1 million acres, including about half of Admiralty, to the Georgia Pacific Company. When Georgia Pacific backed out of the deal, the contract went to a second manufacturer and then, when it defaulted, to Champion International. In his meeting with the Wayburns, Johnson expressed his optimism about the Champion contract. It would be of particular value to Juneau, the nearest city. "I like to have the local community benefit," he told them.[48] Wayburn demurred, emphasizing the significance of Admiralty as wildlife habitat. In a later letter he repeated his concern over "the emphasis which is still being placed on timber management as the dominant use for the Alaskan National Forests."[49] Johnson replied that he and his staff had recently reviewed their plans for the Tongass. "You may be sure that our discussions revolved around many of the special interests of the Sierra Club." He added that cutover areas "will produce almost double the volume per acre now being cut when they are harvested" and that "the present removal is being done without any significant damage to the soil and other resources." His remarks suggested that he planned no concessions to the environmentalists' "special interests."[50]

In mid-September Johnson was even more explicit in near-identical letters to Celia Hunter and Sitka Conservation Society President Roger DuBrock, who had urged a delay in cutting West Chichagof and Yakobi Islands until Calvin's wilderness plan had received a thorough airing. Citing the 50-year contract with Alaska Pulp, Johnson insisted that the Forest Service "is firmly committed by a binding legal contract to authorize cutting of timber in this area. ... There is no other choice .... There is no leeway for us to make any other decision."[51] Hunter was alarmed:

> It sounds to us as tho this ... contract was dreamed up after the act, because at no time had it been mentioned by either the local forester or by W. H. Johnson, the regional forester, as a stumbling block to this particular selection. We are really concerned because if this is to be the tactic of the Forest Service, we haven't a prayer of getting any wilderness at all.[52]

DuBrock subsequently reviewed the provisions of the contract. He found that the Forest Service had not included West Chichagof–Yakobi in its five-year logging plan and that the contract included a loophole that allowed the Forest Service, at its discretion, to exclude specific areas. "Accordingly," he concluded, "we feel that the Forest Service assertion that its hands are tied by the contract is completely untrue and is indeed so great a distortion of the truth as to create serious questions as to the actual good faith of the Forest Service."[53] Later, the Sitka environmentalists won an admission from the president of Alaska Pulp and Lumber that the company did not care where its logs came from as long as the supply was adequate.

By the end of 1968 the cavalier behavior of the Forest Service managers had become a powerful catalyst throughout Southeast Alaska. In addition to stimulating local organization, it underlined the need for more drastic and comprehensive countermeasures. To a growing number of environmentalists, the answer was the 1964 Wilderness Act, which would curtail managerial discretion and preserve the status quo. That was what Jack Calvin and his fellow activists had in mind in proposing the West Chichagof–Yakobi wilderness. But a solution appropriate to the Sitka area might apply elsewhere as well. Formal wilderness designations—the most obvious embodiment of the preservationist thrust of environmentalism— had growing appeal as environmentalists grasped the implications of the oil boom.

What would soon become a systematic effort to utilize the Wilderness Act began inauspiciously in late 1968 when Bob Weeden proposed to the Alaska Sportsmen's Council that it and the Alaska Conservation Society sponsor a wilderness workshop—an "energizing session," he called it—to learn more about the Wilderness Act and what the federal agencies in Alaska were doing to implement it. The Wilderness Act had set aside as permanent wilderness 9 million acres of national forest lands (none in Alaska) and charged the Forest Service with identifying other lands that could be included in the new system. The Forest Service responded with a "considerable lack of enthusiasm."[54] To restrict the law's effects, the foresters devised a so-called "purity" principle, based on the legislation's reference to "primeval" lands. They argued that only land that had never been logged or otherwise disturbed was "primeval" and therefore eligible for consideration. This effort led to a series of lawsuits, and in 1974 Congress rejected the purity principle. In Alaska, however, this dispute had little significance; the Tongass and Chugach national forests had millions of undisturbed acres.

When the Sportsmen's Council declined to participate in Weeden's conference, scheduled for the weekend of February 15–16, 1969, Rich Gordon persuaded the Juneau group of the Sierra Club to cosponsor it. Weeden, as ACS president, and Bob Howe, the superintendent of Glacier Bay Park, agreed to be the official sponsors. Gordon did most of the work, and Sierra Club members hosted the visitors.[55] The Saturday sessions were designed to bring together Alaska activists and representatives of state and federal agencies. On Sunday the environmentalists would meet separately to decide what action to take. The "emphasis will not be on expressions of group views" but "on the training and energizing of people who have a deep love of wildland values."[56]

The conference attracted a large and impressive group. Among the 70 participants were representatives of the ACS chapters, the Sierra Club groups, the National Wildlife Federation, Alaska sportsmen's organizations, and the Southeast Alaska Mountaineering Association. Brock Evans; John L. Hall, assistant to the director of the Wilderness Society; and John Lammers, of the newly organized Yukon Conservation Society, also attended. Government representatives included Howard Johnson and a half-dozen members of his Forest Service staff, plus others from the National Park Service, the Bureau of Land Management, the Alaska Department of Fish and Game, and the state legislature. Bob Weeden's keynote address stressed the need for immediate action. Evans and Hall discussed procedures for creating wilderness areas. Jack Calvin urged support for the West Chichagof–Yakobi wilderness plan. Government officials reported on their activities. In keeping with the spirit of the meeting, Johnson announced that he would soon submit a wilderness plan for the Tongass.[57]

On Sunday the environmentalists created a new organization to promote the cause of wilderness. The Alaska Wilderness Council (AWC) would coordinate the activities of the local groups, provide technical assistance to the agencies, and lobby for wilderness legislation. Celia Hunter agreed to chair AWC, and Gordon, Mark Ganopole, and Dixie Baade, together with representatives of the local organizations, agreed to serve. The council's first assignment would be to review the proposals of the local groups and draw up specific plans, similar to the West Chichagof–Yakobi proposal. Within a month Gordon had revised the Gates of the Arctic plan that Udall had proposed to President Johnson.

Other collaborative efforts followed. In March 1969 the Sierra Club's 11th Biennial Wilderness Conference, in San Francisco, attracted a large contingent of Alaskans. Weeden spoke on Arctic wildlife and the dangers of oil exploration. Will Troyer, Richard Cooley, Celia Hunter, and Pete

Nelson, former head of the Alaska Department of Fish and Game, also made formal presentations. Mark Ganopole, Rich Gordon, and Art Davidson put together an impressive exhibit on the proposed Gates of the Arctic park. In all, more than 30 Alaskans participated.[58]

Ganopole, representing the Alaska Wilderness Council, also presented information on critical areas to the legislative committee considering the expansion of the state's meager park system. Several influential legislators—Jay Hammond and Lowell Thomas Jr. among the Republicans and Joe Josephson and Chancey Croft among the Democrats—were receptive. Effective lobbying by Ganopole, Weeden, Anchorage activist Sharon Cissna, and other environmentalists helped push the parks bills through the legislature. By the end of 1970 Alaska had a park system that included four of the largest state parks in the United States—Wood-Tikchik, Chugach, Denali, and Kachemak Bay.

The environmentalists' success was tempered, however, by the growing reticence of the sportsmen's groups. Many hunters and fishermen understood the need to preserve wildlife habitat but scorned broader environmental commitments; they remained old-style conservationists. Many of them also had professional or business interests that would benefit from a resource-based economic boom. Dixie Baade reported that she had tried to work with them. "I found it impossible. ... So far they have failed to stand up and be counted on a single crucial conservation issue in the state. ... They speak of conservation in the chamber-of-commerce approved fashion."[59]

Bud Boddy, of the Alaska Sportsmen's Council, had attended the February wilderness conference and agreed to serve on the AWC board but displayed little enthusiasm. The other activists began to view him with suspicion. One incident greatly increased their wariness. After Gordon and other members of the Sierra Club's Juneau group drew up a plan to preserve most of Admiralty Island, Gordon presented it to Boddy's organization. He recalled,

> I persuaded the Board of the Territorial Sportsmen ... to adopt a modified but meaningful version, and they drafted ... a detailed letter ... to all concerned. This letter was signed by their President, Bud Boddy. However, they then behind the scenes, decided (without action of their board) to hold off on it indefinitely.[60]

Gordon sent out the letter anyway and evoked "a lot of interest" but no additional activity. After 1969 Boddy and the sportsmen's organizations typically opposed proposals that called for new federal initiatives.

The environmentalists' relations with the Forest Service also deteriorated in spring and summer 1969. Johnson's statements at the wilderness conference had raised the possibility of more amicable relations, and his subsequent agreement to a private meeting with the executive committee of the Juneau Sierra Club reinforced the impression that he might be more flexible. There were rumors that he would offer more "rock and ice" in exchange for a free hand in cutting lowland wooded areas. The meeting at Donald Freedman's home, in July 1969, "was low key with no agenda. We mostly discussed mutual concerns," reported Rich Gordon, "notably the Indian land claims and the state selection program."[61] There were no offers, and the meeting ended with both sides far apart on the issue of wilderness legislation. Johnson complained in September that Wayburn "just doesn't want us to cut any timber."[62] His announcement shortly afterward of a plan to build a road up scenic and pristine Petersburg Creek and log adjacent areas sparked a local rebellion and the formation of another ACS chapter.[63]

As the situation grew more tense, the Champion contract loomed larger and larger. Sensing its vulnerability, the company hired a group of prominent scientists, including several University of Alaska professors, to study potential plant sites and recommend ways to minimize environmental damage. Company officials admitted that this was a "risky" strategy but believed it would alleviate public anxiety over potential water and air pollution. Their gamble seemingly succeeded. When the scientists recommended Berner's Bay, near Juneau, over a Sitka-area site, there was general rejoicing. "This is a fine Christmas present for Juneau," observed one official. Even Mayor McLean, known as "Sierra Joe" to industry supporters, expressed satisfaction. The mill, which would employ 600 by 1973, was the stimulus the community had been "looking forward to for, lo, these many years."[64]

In the meantime local environmentalists had concluded that their only recourse was legal action. With the assistance of Brock Evans, they began to prepare a lawsuit against the Forest Service, charging that the foresters had betrayed their multiple-use mandate. Money was a major stumbling block. The Alaskans had ample enthusiasm but little cash, and the Sierra Club, convulsed by the Brower controversy, was running large deficits. Those losses had already prevented it from joining other environmental groups in suing the Interior Department to halt the trans-Alaska oil pipeline.[65] Wayburn was torn; the club's financial plight demanded prudence and retrenchment, but the Alaska situation demanded immediate action. Although he had already agreed to help finance an Alaska "conservation representative," he concluded that the defense of Admiralty was so compelling that he could not avoid additional commitment.

Initially, the activists' goal was simply to publicize the threat to Admiralty. "In all honesty," Gordon noted, "I doubt that such a suit can block the contract." The publicity would nevertheless justify the expense and effort.[66] Jack Calvin agreed. "Naturally, we want to win, but even if we lose it will throw a man-size scare into the FS bureaucrats. Maybe the industry, too. Might even make the SOBs a little easier to deal with."[67]

The lawsuit, announced in February 1970, had a huge impact. Juneau, in the words of the local Sierra Club's Richard Myren, "went ballistic."[68] Virtually everyone who was not a club member attacked it. Most agreed with the Juneau Chamber of Commerce that it was a "crippling economic blow" to the city. Apart from business groups, the central labor council, the city council, and many prominent residents, including Bud Boddy of the Sportsmen's Council, expressed support for the Forest Service.[69] Mayor McLean, under intense pressure, publicly condemned the suit while defending the club. Mildred Banfield, a state representative, resigned her membership. Sanford Sagalkin, a prominent attorney and club member, was also critical. Their actions fed rumors that the club had split, that San Francisco had launched the suit over the objections of Juneau members, and that Forest Service employees were plotting to take over the Juneau group and repudiate the suit.[70] When the state legislature adopted a resolution asking the Sierra Club to withdraw the suit, an Anchorage representative complained that the language was too mild. "Just tell them to go to hell," he urged. "They have no business coming in here."[71] Few people would have questioned Gordon's observation that "the S. C. image up here is bad all the way around."[72]

The trial itself, which was delayed until November 1970, was anticlimactic. Warren Matthews, an Anchorage attorney and Sierra Club member, represented the plaintiffs. His lead witness was Gordon Robinson, a retired forester who often served as an expert witness in Sierra Club forestry cases. Robinson argued that the Forest Service was in effect a "single use" agency and that its preoccupation with logging had harmed the Tongass. Wayburn, Gordon, an Alaska Fish and Game biologist, and a California economist also testified for the club. At the end of the eight-day trial, the judge considered the charges and in a series of rulings, issued between March and May, dismissed all of them, in effect upholding the authority of the Forest Service.[73] Everyone assumed that the losing side would appeal, so the judge's decision was only a temporary setback. Indeed, by their own standards, the plaintiffs had won. The suit received wide publicity and forced Johnson and Champion to delay their plan to log Admiralty Island.

By the end of 1970, then, southeastern activists had temporarily slowed a government program that was incompatible with their vision of the region's future and had begun to define specific, positive goals. A Juneau booster acknowledged their achievements the following summer when the club formally appealed the 1970 decision. "Sierra Clubbers are not conservationists," he complained, "they are preservationists."[74]

ORGANIZATIONAL RESPONSES

The challenge in Southeast Alaska was obvious and unambiguous, and the environmentalists' goal—to pressure the Forest Service to live up to its ideals of multiple-use stewardship—was equally clear. The second, parallel battle, over the pipeline and indirectly over the state's future, was more complicated. How would environmentalists respond? The Chariot and Rampart campaigns had demonstrated the value of sophisticated communications. A decade of experiences with the Kenai and Cook Inlet oil fields suggested the kinds of problems that were likely to arise. Critical decisions would be made in Washington as well as Alaska. To influence those decisions, environmentalists would have to work together and mobilize popular support.

To promote cooperation, Alaska environmentalists were ready to appoint a full-time "conservation representative." George Marshall, Robert's younger brother, who was active in the Wilderness Society and the Sierra Club, may have been first to propose such a position.[75] By mid-1969 Wayburn and the officers of the Wilderness Society had discussed it several times. At a July meeting, the Wilderness Society's board drafted a plan for an "Alaska Field Effort." Stewart Brandborg of the Wilderness Society later met with Michael McCloskey of the Sierra Club in Washington to prepare "a comprehensive list of Alaska environmental needs and projects." They also consulted Weeden.[76] The "conservation representative" would lobby the legislature, coordinate the activities of the local groups, and speak for the Alaska environmental community. They agreed to employ John Hall, a former Forest Service employee who was currently Brandborg's assistant. A steering committee, made up of representatives of the Wilderness Society, Sierra Club, and ACS, would provide direction.

Hall's tenure proved exceedingly brief. Shortly after being named the conservation representative, Hall received an offer from the Forest Service to become its specialist on Alaska issues. To the environmentalists' surprise and chagrin, he accepted it. Gordon later confessed that he did not know "what to make of the man."[77] The debacle nevertheless had a positive outcome. As Bob Weeden's visibility had grown, his relations with his bosses at Alaska Fish and Game had become increasingly troubled. When the agency forced ACS and Sierra Club members to resign their leadership positions, he had had enough.[78] He held an adjunct position at the University of Alaska and was planning to take a teaching post in the future. In the meantime the Alaska groups needed a conservation representative. He agreed to fill the position and began his duties in September.

Weeden brought energy and skill to the job. He predicted, correctly, that "just letting everyone know what's going on in the field of resource use and management, and what's happening to environmental quality could keep me hopping."[79] An able public speaker, he appeared at numerous conferences and forums and was often featured in news accounts of those events. When the legislature was in session, he lived in the spare room of an artist friend's Juneau studio. Since he was the only environmental lobbyist, he had to attend numerous hearings and meetings. He was a "carpetbagger" to many politicians. Since he had only the most modest expense account, he could not participate in the capital's active social life. He looked back on his lobbying experiences as the least satisfying part of the job.[80]

Weeden also brought a judicious, academic perspective to his work. He was more cautious than many of his colleagues. On taking the position, he announced that he would be "helping conservationists get their homework done so that our opinions are based on sound and accurate knowledge of the facts"[81] He told a Canadian audience that he did not propose "turning Alaska into a permanent nature preserve" and predicted on another occasion that Alaska would continue to be "a supplier of raw and partly processed materials ... its economy based on exports of petroleum, hard-rock minerals, fish and forest products."[82] He hoped to delay the pipeline until thorough studies of the geology, flora, and fauna of the pipeline corridor had been completed and the industry was committed to the least disruptive approach.

Reflecting a faith in scientific research and planning, Weeden's ideas and prescriptions stood in bold contrast to the boosterism of the business community. They may well have expressed the views of most Alaskans outside the business community. They also struck a responsive chord among a small group of influential legislators, mostly Republicans, who were uneasy with government-business alliances favored by both political parties. Hammond, elected state Senate president in 1970, was their leader and most influential member, and Weeden found his door open.

The problem, of course, was that the boosters controlled the state government and through their new ally, the oil industry, wielded considerable influence in Washington. Weeden may have been the most thoughtful Alaskan, but his ideas were not likely to have any immediate impact. Wayburn and Brandborg were not happy. McCloskey recalled that Weeden "was not a good match in temperament or personality." His "academic perspective" prevented him from being an effective lobbyist.[83] Weeden did not disagree. In spring 1970 he accepted a faculty position at the University of Alaska in resource management. In his resignation letter he wrote that his "greatest contributions to Alaska in the long run" would arise from his "studies of resource and environmental situations, rather than from advocacy per se. … I may do more as a developer of ideas and information than as a salesman."[84] He also acknowledged that he "had to live there." Given the political climate, an aggressive lobbyist was destined to be a social pariah.[85]

The members of the steering committee assumed that they would be able to select a successor. Behind the scenes, however, problems had arisen. Some members of the Wilderness Society's board apparently had concluded that the Sierra Club had become the dominant influence and refused to authorize additional expenditures. Wayburn was "greatly upset." He learned of the conflict as he was about to leave for Alaska to recruit a new representative and was doubtful that the club could pay the entire cost.[86] Nevertheless, when he met leaders of the Alaska chapter in late July, he "assured them that Alaska's problems are of paramount importance to the Sierra Club.[87] He also emphasized that the club would persevere, regardless of what the Wilderness Society did. Ultimately he was able to raise enough money to make the conservation representative a Sierra Club staff member.

Initially the leading candidate was James Kowalsky, a young musician who had become interested in environmental issues as a graduate student at the University of Wisconsin and friend of Gordon Wright, the Fairbanks conductor and Sierra Club member. Later, as a professor at colleges in Kentucky and Minnesota, Kowalsky had become active in the Sierra Club. By 1970 he was eager to move to Alaska. He lobbied friends in the

Wilderness Society and the Sierra Club's Alaska chapter and won the endorsement of several influential Sierra Club members. Wayburn was less enthusiastic. He remembered Kowalsky as a fervent Brower supporter and worried that he would be viewed as an outsider, having visited Alaska for the first time in 1969.[88] Wayburn decided instead to hire Jack Hession, a University of Washington graduate student who had come to Alaska in 1968 to work at the University of Alaska's social science research institute, had returned in 1969, and was eager to stay. He began his new career in December.

Hession differed from Weeden in fundamental ways. In the first place, he was Wayburn's man; he did not depend on the Alaskans or a coalition of groups for his job or salary and was thus largely immune to local pressures. He was also an out-and-out preservationist and an aggressive lobbyist—in short, a booster's nightmare. In *Coming into the Country*, his prize-winning study of Alaska published in 1976, John McPhee tells of a Brooks Range camping trip with Hession and several Park Service planners. Halfway through the trip, Hession decided that he had to get back to the office. He set off alone in a leaky kayak to paddle 100 miles to the nearest airfield. Had he drowned or fallen victim to a hungry bear, McPhee observed, there would have been rejoicing throughout the state.[89]

Hession's selection had an unexpected bonus. Kowalsky decided to come to Alaska anyway. Arriving in 1971, he soon became a leader of the beleaguered Fairbanks environmental community and one of the state's best-known activists.

THE DYNAMICS OF ALASKA ENVIRONMENTALISM

Like contemporary movements devoted to civil rights, women's liberation, and peace, environmentalism appealed to a generation that was self-consciously rebellious, hostile to institutions, and antiauthoritarian.[90] Like other reform movements, it faced managerial challenges that could be overcome by the simple expedient of division and decentralization, though the process (like the creation of Friends of the Earth) was often messy and traumatic. The critical dynamic was intellectual and psychological. As people became sensitized to an issue, the risk of inaction or an "enemy" victory appeared worse than they had originally imagined. Established reform organizations often seemed indifferent to their concerns. A new organization, with a different focus, was often the result.

The Alaska environmental movement was a case study of this process. As Weeden noted in November 1969, "New conservation groups are springing up all over Alaska."[91] Virtually all activists had multiple memberships, though only a few could match Chuck Konigsberg of Anchorage, who boasted, "You name it, I belong to it."[92] Regardless of their associations, they faced two kinds of challenges. The first was the many threats associated with the Prudhoe Bay development. Apart from the pipeline per se, lease sales, oil revenues, and taxes (when and if the pipeline was completed) promised to make state money available for a variety of other schemes. No one doubted that the boosters had long wish lists and that many of these proposals would equal or exceed the pipeline in destructiveness. The second challenge arose from the state's enormous size. Fairbanks was more than 500 miles from Ketchikan. Each of the state's population centers had somewhat different concerns. ACS and the Sierra Club tried to address this problem by organizing local groups, but the tendency to define environmental issues exclusively in local or regional terms remained strong.

Given the obstacles, the formation of the Alaska Wilderness Council was an act of faith. Its ambitious agenda was feasible only because of Gordon, who brought boundless curiosity and knowledge to the organization, and Mark Ganopole, whose enthusiasm and administrative skill ensured that the effort did not bog down completely. Initially, the participating groups appointed individuals to report on the wilderness potential of Alaska's parks, wildlife refuges, and other public lands. Troyer, for example, recruited Art Davidson to report on Wood-Tikchik and Ganopole to report on Katmai. Bob Hall, from ACS, recruited Don Coolidge to report on Kodiak Island, Walt Parker to examine the Wrangell Mountains, and Dick Prasil to survey the Izembek wildlife refuge.[93] In June 1969 the council issued a list of proposed wilderness areas ranked by significance. The highest-rated group included Wood-Tikchik, Gates of the Arctic, West Chichagof–Yakobi, Keystone Canyon (near Valdez), and a section of the Kenai Moose Range.[94]

After that, the effort flagged. The indefatigable Gordon and a few Juneau colleagues devised a plan for Admiralty Island.[95] Dixie Baade examined parts of the Tongass, and Ganopole and other members of the Alaska chapter's parks committee studied south-central Alaska. The others were inactive. Bud Boddy informally withdrew as suspicions about him grew, and the ACS representatives (apart from Baade) contributed little.

As a result, the council's only significant public announcement after its initial report was a plan for Southeast Alaska, announced in March 1970.

It identified Admiralty Island, West Chichagof–Yakobi, central Prince of Wales Island, East Behm (a mountainous area east of Ketchikan), and Tracy Arm, south of Juneau, as prime candidates for wilderness legislation.[96] A sequel to the Sitka Conservation Society's West Chichagof–Yakobi proposal and the Champion lawsuit, filed a month earlier, it was also a blueprint for the emerging Tongass wilderness campaign.

The AWC plan persuaded Howard Johnson to propose another meeting in late April. Celia Hunter was initially hopeful, since Forest Service officials had refused earlier overtures. But obstacles quickly arose. Johnson wanted to meet in Anchorage, where he and his staff would be attending a conference, even though—as he well knew—the council's Tongass experts all lived in Southeast Alaska and, unlike the Forest Service delegation, would have to pay their own expenses. Baade believed that Johnson's goal was to isolate the most knowledgeable troublemakers. "The Forest Service is a master of the art of 'divide and conquer' and right now they are in a position to do just that," she wrote."[97] Other AWC members agreed, and the invitation was declined.

Johnson's invitation also caused the council to question its own mandate. AWC was supposed to provide expert information, not replace the local organizations or represent the environmental movement. Yet the reports of June 1969 and March 1970 implied some form of coordination and centralized decisionmaking. The discussions that occurred in the wake of Johnson's invitation did nothing to clarify the council's powers. As a result, the council floundered. By late 1970 it consisted largely of Mark Ganopole's Anchorage group, essentially the Sierra Club parks committee.[98] In March 1971 ACS withdrew its support, citing the "real weaknesses in organization." Celia Hunter suggested that the council "quietly slip into oblivion."[99]

If the Alaska Wilderness Council was not a long-term answer to the needs of Alaska environmentalists, it did force Alaska's environmental leaders to address obstacles to cooperation. In discussions of Johnson's invitation, Baade made a notable suggestion. "Because of distance, cost of travel and diversity of problems," she noted, "I feel it may be desirable to have regional groups to work on issues that are common to their own areas."[100] She was thinking specifically of organizations that would report to the council, but the idea of regional organizations persisted. In the following months three regional entities emerged to coordinate the work of local groups in each of Alaska's major population centers.

The first was a direct outgrowth of the council's Tongass proposals. On June 6–7, 1970, representatives of the Southeast Alaska groups gathered in

Sitka to devise a common strategy. The conferees included nine activists from Sitka, three from Ketchikan, and two from Petersburg, plus Rich Gordon and Brock Evans. Gordon reported that "after much discussion, it was agreed . . . that some form of semiformal arrangement was needed both to keep up communications with one another, and act as spokesman on area wide projects." They formed the Southeast Alaska Conservation Coordinating Committee (changed to Southeast Alaska Conservation Council, or SEACC, in 1971) to represent the Sitka Conservation Society, the Sitka and Juneau Sierra Club groups, the Tongass Conservation Society, the Southeast Alaska Mountaineering Association, and, tentatively, the Petersburg Conservation Society. The committee would include one representative from each group and would be "simply a tool to carry out area-wide functions on which all separate groups formally agree." In theory, at least, it was to "complement" the Alaska Wilderness Council by "providing a separate vehicle for coordination, action, and promotional functions." Dixie Baade was named the first "coordinator." She immediately called for a moratorium on logging until the Forest Service and the environmental groups studied each area on the AWC list.[101] As AWC declined, SEACC's rationale changed: by 1971 it had become "an action group."[102]

The second organization was an outgrowth of Jim Kowalsky's search for a job. By spring 1971 the Fairbanks Sierra Club group was reasonably active. Under Gordon Wright and James Anderson, his successor as chair, it campaigned against mining in Mount McKinley Park and monitored the pipeline controversies.[103] It was also beleaguered. The pipeline delays enraged the city's merchants and created an increasingly hostile environment. The presence of the better-known, more moderate and respectable ACS was also a complication, as was a growing suspicion among the members that the Alaska chapter of the Sierra Club had written off Fairbanks.[104] Wright concluded that the only hope for a significant presence was to find an energetic individual to confront the chamber of commerce and its allies. He favored an approach "where the rep gets close to the people" and persuades "every day Alaskans of the threats to the environment."[105] He had a specific candidate in mind.

Since Kowalsky had been a friend and defender of David Brower, it made sense to ask Friends of the Earth for assistance. FOE already had an Anchorage representative, Art Davidson, who was trying to establish an environmental center there. FOE officers were initially skeptical about hiring a second part-timer, but Wright's insistence that Fairbanks was not a backwater—"it is here that most of the work needs to be done"—and that

Kowalsky was the person for the job won Brower's support.[106] Kowalsky would supplement his FOE salary by playing in Wright's symphony and chamber orchestras.

The novel feature of the arrangement was Kowalsky's third assignment, as executive director of a new Fairbanks Environmental Center. The center was largely Wright's creation. It would be a place where people could go for information, meetings, and contacts with other environmentalists. It was also an answer to complaints about "outsiders" who were supposedly indifferent to local conditions. Most of all, like SEACC, it would bring together the various environmental organizations. As Wright recalled, "it didn't matter which hat you wore."[107] He raised the initial funds and persuaded J. A. Hunter, owner of a local insurance agency and representative of Defenders of Wildlife, to serve as president.[108] Hunter gave the center credibility as a community institution.

Kowalsky started in September 1971. Operating on a shoestring, he quickly made his mark as a passionate, uncompromising defender of wilderness values. He rented an old house and provided offices for the city's environmental organizations. With financial assistance from ACS and the Sierra Club Foundation, the center gradually lived up to its promise. The Sierra Club group had a less happy fate. With the center performing many of its functions, Wright decided to "let it go."[109] In 1972 he signaled his conversion to the new ecumenism by becoming editor of the ACS publication, now called the *Alaska Conservation Review*.

The third group also bore the imprint of a single individual. Charles Konigsberg had retired from the Air Force and moved to Alaska in 1968 to teach political science at Anchorage's Alaska Methodist University. He was attracted by the majesty of the Alaska wilderness but also by a vision of Alaska as a *tabula rasa*. Systemic planning would enable it to avoid the mistakes of older societies and devise superior institutions. He soon discovered that few of his neighbors shared his vision. On the contrary, most of them seemed interested only in recreating the comfortable and familiar institutions they had known elsewhere. He was appalled and frustrated. However, he soon found an outlet for his idealism in the Sierra Club and other environmental organizations. He sought to maximize their influence by organizing an Anchorage environmental center that would coordinate environmental activism throughout the state.[110]

During summer 1970 Art Davidson, with a modest grant from FOE and the assistance of local activist Barbara Winkley, had tried to create such a center. It was supposed to be the foundation for an Anchorage-area environmental council; in practice, it was a spartan office with a small library.[111] Its history is uncertain. Most of those active in the second, Konigsberg-inspired center were unaware of its existence. Davidson himself left his FOE position in 1972, when he took a state job.[112]

In early 1971 Konigsberg persuaded the ACS board to pledge $5,000 for a new center. His rationale was similar to Gordon Wright's:

> In Alaska, where the environmental situation has not yet approached the ecological crisis state, but where a development-psychosis ... rivals that of the gold-fever of old, the basic task is to 'keep it from happening here.' The basic human problem here is one of attitudes. If we can influence attitudes, the rest will follow. ... To deal with this situation we must begin by organizing more effectively ... to counter the development-psychosis.[113]

The new center would coordinate local efforts, publish environmental materials, and monitor the activities of government agencies. Konigsberg proposed a staff of four and an annual budget of $150,000.[114]

To inaugurate the new center, he obtained foundation support for a conference that brought together national and local activists. For two days in early December 1971, they discussed the center's potential. "At the end," recalls Helen Nienhauser, Stewart Brandborg of the Wilderness Society "gave us a fiery pep talk and said, 'start now. Sit down here before you leave this room and elect your first board.'" They elected Konigsberg president and Nienhauser and three other Anchorage activists as board members. Walt Parker, a civic leader, was already out of the room when Nienhauser "chased him down the hall and pleaded with him to come back." He too agreed to serve.[115] To emphasize the center's statewide focus, they added representatives from other communities, including Weeden, with Kowalsky as his alternate. A general meeting on December 28 ratified these decisions, and the center opened on January 1, 1972, with Jim Kross, a Sierra Club activist, as full-time executive secretary.[116]

By the end of 1970 the Prudhoe Bay discoveries, which were supposed to address Alaska's pressing economic problems, had merely introduced it to the turbulent mainstream of contemporary American society. Alaska's Natives had begun to organize in the 1960s to influence the state's land selections. The oil discoveries greatly increased their bargaining power and ensured that they would no longer be overlooked. Similarly, conservationists had mobilized to oppose irresponsible development plans. The pipeline controversy led to greater activism, additional organizations, and a larger role for the national organizations. After 1970 the focus of all these conflicts shifted to Washington, as Congress attempted to address the diverse demands of boosters, corporate leaders, Native groups, and environmentalists.

CHAPTER 4

CONGRESSIONAL RESPONSES

In August 1970, four months after Judge George Hart had enjoined the Interior Department from proceeding with the pipeline, two months after the native claims legislation had stalled in Congress, and three months prior to his dismissal, Secretary of the Interior Walter Hickel accompanied Jean Chrétien, the Canadian minister for Indian Affairs and Northern Development, on a tour of the North American Arctic. Hickel said he was "intrigued" by Canada's Arctic developments and wanted a "first-hand view." The two officials traveled more than 4,000 miles, starting at Baffin Island on the North Atlantic coast. "From there they puddle-jumped across the great expanse of the near-vacant North. They toured mining operations, drilling rigs and isolated communities." At Inuvik, near the mouth of the Mackenzie River, the center of Canadian oil exploration, they "inspected the tests Canadians are conducting with above-ground hot oil pipelines in permafrost terrain." Traveling west, they visited the Arctic National Wildlife Range (ANWR) and finally Prudhoe Bay.

There they examined "the oil drilling rigs and experiments being conducted to protect the tundra." Hickel professed to be impressed with the environmentally sensitive projects he observed. "It is a small step in terms of what is to come," he said, "but it is a giant step in the right direction."[1]

Hickel's report, like the news accounts of the junket, was most notable for what it did not say. Though Hickel and Chrétien visited several oil fields, discussed measures to prevent the degradation of sensitive terrain, and applauded showcase projects, they did not mention—at least officially—the possibility of a joint effort to transport oil from Alaska and the Northwest Territories to Edmonton, Alberta, where existing pipelines could carry it to the American Midwest. That omission spoke volumes about the Washington response to the Alaska upheavals, which began with the Hart injunction and continued with few interruptions until the end of 1973.

Despite growing influence and legislative victories on air and water pollution, environmentalists suffered surprising setbacks in their efforts to defend the Alaska wilderness. The essential problem was timing. Between 1970 and 1972 they rode a wave of public concern to unprecedented victories on Alaska issues as well as others.[2] But they soon confronted obstacles more intractable than the most aggressive Alaska boosters. An escalating energy crisis created a growing sense that the American public would have to chose between jobs, prosperity, and convenience on one hand and environmental protection on the other. In such a setting environmental legislation became difficult if not impossible. This sequence was apparent in the three Washington battles of the early 1970s that resulted from the Prudhoe Bay discoveries: the Native claims legislation, the oil pipeline authorization, and the Interior secretary's selection of potential park and refuge lands in Alaska, a result of the earlier Native claims act.

NATIVE CLAIMS AND ALASKA PARKS, 1970–1971

By summer 1970 resistance to a settlement of the Natives' land claims began to weaken. Most Alaska politicians were no more favorable than they had been in 1968, but they wanted to end the land freeze, and if one depended on the other, they were ready to deal. Environmentalists also favored a generous settlement. Bob Weeden probably spoke for most of them when he wrote that he was "not apprehensive about Native ownership of land because ... I see a strong bond between Natives and the land."

He was optimistic "about the Natives' sensible handling of their own natural resources."[3] At the same time, Weeden and his colleagues knew that a
settlement of the Natives' demands would lead to a new push for the
pipeline. By early 1971, Sierra Club and Wilderness Society lobbyists were
paying close attention to the Native claims legislation.

The most contentious issue of early 1971 was the Natives' demand for
at least 40 million acres. As late as fall 1970 most congressional leaders
and Alaska politicians rejected this number out of hand. Senator Henry
Jackson argued that such a large grant would divide Alaska into "a series of
large racial enclaves, ... tie up the economic development of Alaska, ...
affect conservation measures, national parks and forests, and hinder proper state and federal land-use planning."[4] As Native leaders became more
vocal and insistent (and at least perfunctorily raised their goal to 60 million acres), it became harder for Jackson, Representative Wayne Aspinall,
and other politicians to advocate lesser amounts. The turning point came
in March and April 1971, when the Nixon administration publicly
endorsed 40 million acres as an expression of the president's Indian self-
determination policy, announced the previous summer. Native lobbyists
played a large role in this change, and Donald Wright, president of the
Alaska Federation of Natives (AFN), applauded it.[5] Alaska's new senator,
Ted Stevens (appointed after Bob Bartlett's death in 1969), prepared
detailed maps showing that a 40-million-acre grant would not necessarily
compromise the boosters' plans. In the complex negotiations that
occurred over the following months, Oklahoma Senator Fred Harris and
Washington Representative Lloyd Meeds championed the AFN plan,
which called for a 60-million-acre grant. Aspinall continued to advocate a
grant of 10 million acres or less. The administration plan thus seemed like
a compromise rather than a bold innovation.

After April the focus of the debate shifted to the location of the land.
Should the settlement emphasize village lands, where residents lived,
hunted, and fished, or more economically valuable lands that could provide revenue, industrial opportunities, and jobs? In other words, were
Natives interested primarily in preserving their cultural heritage or in
acquiring wealth and political power? At the time most AFN leaders insisted on some economically valuable lands. In the words of AFN President
Wright, the "backbone" of the settlement was the proposal for regional
corporations "with broad business and investment powers." Such entities
would enable Natives to gain "economic leverage ... through proper
investment practices at the regional and statewide level."[6]

Because of AFN and its congressional allies, the Alaska Native Claims Settlement Act (ANCSA), passed in December 1971, awarded 22 million acres to initially 205 but ultimately 178 village corporations and 18 million acres to 12 regional corporations "with broad business and investment powers." A cash award of nearly $1 billion was to be distributed through the village and regional entities. From the beginning the regional corporations (and many of the village corporations as well) were dominated by so-called Brooks Brothers Natives, who favored development schemes. They also faced a variety of financial problems that created pressures to maximize short-term income. Many of these difficulties were the result of ANCSA's elaborate provisions, which resulted in years of litigation and mounting disillusionment.[7]

The law included other land provisions that were no less complicated and controversial. Edgar and Peggy Wayburn later described them as "incredibly complex and confusing."[8] That complexity was partly a measure of the environmentalists' success in adding an amendment calling for studies of new conservation units to the Native claims bills, on grounds that the American people had claims equivalent to those of the state and the Natives. This idea originated in Section 23, the Hickok–Van Ness plan, in the 1970 Senate bill. The parks proposal was debated and revised several times in 1971 and was not actually incorporated into the legislation until the final negotiations. But the Hickok–Van Ness plan had made environmentalists see the Native claims legislation in a new light. If, as historian Donald Craig Mitchell writes, "the men and women who did the conservation organizations' strategic thinking" had been "asleep at the switch" in 1969 and 1970, they quickly made up for lost time.[9] They lobbied vigorously and in the closing days of the congressional session organized an aggressive appeal to public opinion based on techniques honed in the years since the pioneering Echo Park campaign. They hoped this experience would be a prelude to a satisfactory resolution of the pipeline issue.

To make the best use of their lobbying resources, the environmental groups took their cue from David Hickok, who argued that "all those concerned with parks, wilderness and wildlife" would have to "get off their butts, forget their often unrealistic provincial feelings," and develop a "unified and compromised position."[10] During summer 1971 they created a new organization to coordinate their activities. The Alaska Coalition brought together organizations that focused on wildlife issues, including Audubon, Defenders of Wildlife, Trout Unlimited, the Wildlife Management Institute, and the National Wildlife Federation; activist organizations, including the Sierra Club, Friends of the Earth, and the Wilderness Society; and others with a more general focus, such as the League of Conservation Voters. The total varied between 9 and 12 over the following months. Mary Hazel Harris of Defenders of Wildlife was the first executive director.[11] The Wilderness Society and the Sierra Club, however, were the core, the "nerve center," and would do most of the day-to-day lobbying. The coalition's first important public act was to send a letter to President Nixon on September 30 complaining that "speculators and exploiters" were trying to hijack the Native claims legislation.[12]

In the meantime, National Park Service (NPS) Director George Hartzog had been working on an Alaska parks plan that he wanted to incorporate in the Native claims bill. Early in 1971 he had gone to Senator Jackson to discuss his park study proposal. Jackson referred him to Senator Alan Bible (D-NV), who would be in charge of the Senate bill. When Bible indicated that he planned to rely on the Alaska senators for advice, Hartzog became concerned that nothing would be done. In response, he suggested that Bible, his wife, and several friends visit Alaska as guests of the Park Service. When the senator agreed, Hartzog organized an extensive educational tour, which included sessions with Edgar Wayburn, Celia Hunter, Ginny Wood, and the NPS staff. Afterward, Hartzog spent several days at Bible's home in Nevada. "During that time," he recalled, Bible "told me to give him some draft language to accomplish what I wanted to do in Alaska."[13] Hartzog interpreted this invitation as an opportunity to present the plans his agency had developed from Operation Great Land, which totaled nearly 70 million acres. He may well have misjudged Bible's generosity. Though sympathetic to NPS, Bible also consulted other environmental lobbyists and Senate colleagues. His eventual amendment to the Senate bill, which became Section 17d(2) of ANCSA, provided for possible additions to each of the "four systems"—national parks, wildlife refuges, national forests, and wild and scenic rivers.[14]

Given Jackson's and Bible's support, the crucial deliberations occurred in the House of Representatives. For the previous decade the leading advocate of wilderness in the House had been John Saylor, a veteran Pennsylvania Republican. Although Saylor's environmental credentials were impeccable, he was a member of the minority party and something of a curmudgeon.[15] His proposal for an Alaska land planning commission was voted down overwhelmingly by the House Interior Committee, and the bill that emerged in September 1971 was largely the work of Interior Committee Chairman Aspinall. While rejecting Saylor's amendment, Aspinall and his colleagues did include a weaker measure, introduced by Representative John Kyl (R-AZ), which gave the secretary of the Interior authority to extend the freeze temporarily but specifically excluded land that the Natives or state desired or that the oil companies wanted for the pipeline. The secretary of the Interior could consider the remainder for possible parks.

To obtain a more satisfactory amendment on the House floor, the Alaska Coalition turned to Representative Morris Udall, a popular and influential Arizona Democrat. The tall, witty former basketball star had risen rapidly in liberal circles since claiming the congressional seat of his brother Stewart in 1961. As environmentalism became a political force, he had gradually superseded Saylor as the movement's legislative leader in the House. In this case, he joined Saylor in introducing an amendment to set aside a total of 100 million acres for study after the Native villages had made their selections but before any other selections. As Udall explained, "the State and Natives are dividing up public lands. ... Let's allow the American people a shot at some prime acres before they are all gone." He insisted that his amendment would have no effect on the pipeline.[16] Other members of the House were less certain. As Mary Clay Berry reported, "there was nothing in the amendment which specifically mentioned the pipeline and no one was sure of its effect on the project."[17] In short, the Udall-Saylor amendment added uncertainty to an already complicated situation. As anticipated, the Alaska politicians, oil companies, and unions opposed it. Alaska Representative Nick Begich was "cashing chips right and left," according to a close adviser, in an effort to defeat it.[18]

On this issue Begich also had the support of many Alaska Native leaders. A meeting in Bob Weeden's office at the University of Alaska on October 26, before the Senate vote, underlined the differences between them and the environmentalists. As Jim Kowalsky reported, two local AFN leaders "were seeking support" from the Alaska Conservation Society (ACS) for their position in the upcoming Senate vote "and asking that any amendments similar to the Udall-Saylor Amendment be opposed." They had just returned from Washington, where "they worked very hard to defeat the Udall-Saylor Amendment, as did, apparently, a large group of Natives from the AFN." Their opposition reflected a belief that the amendment "was an attempt to keep Native groups from having lands which would be economically most desirable." Weeden and Kowalsky were unable to change their minds. [19]

Despite the opposition, Udall and his allies attracted broad bipartisan support. Operating out of a room in the House office building, provided by wildlife champion John Dingell (D-MI), the Alaska Coalition urged members of environmental groups to deluge their representatives with letters and telegrams. A critical moment came when Representative Ron Dellums (D-CA), a civil rights leader who had cosponsored Udall-Saylor, wavered after some Alaska Native leaders attacked the amendment as a racist effort to sabotage the settlement. Lloyd Tupling, the Sierra Club lobbyist; Jack Hession, the club's Alaska representative; and Doug Scott, a Wilderness Society lobbyist, rushed to Dellums's office and convinced him that Aspinall had orchestrated the attacks. By threatening to introduce another amendment giving the Natives preferential selection, Dellums won admissions that Udall-Saylor would not interfere with the Natives' selection rights. He then reaffirmed his support for the amendment. At this news, Begich and Representative Meeds, who were spearheading the opposition, supposedly were crestfallen.[20] Udall satisfied other undecided representatives by accepting an amendment that explicitly excluded the pipeline route from the study area.

When the House finally voted, Udall-Saylor lost, 177 to 217. The result was a measure of what the *New York Times* described as "the power within both parties of oil lobbyists."[21] It also suggested that there was little sentiment in Congress for the kind of systematic research and planning that the environmentalists favored. Nevertheless, Alaska Coalition leaders were not discouraged. In the face of concerted opposition, they had gotten 45 percent of the vote and come within 21 votes of winning. The tally was close enough to ensure that Udall-Saylor would receive consideration by the House-Senate conference committee, assuming that Bible was successful in winning support for his bill.

After the dramatic confrontations in the House, the Senate deliberations were remarkably subdued. Bible introduced his version of Udall-Saylor. Stevens had already persuaded him to delete a provision Jackson had added earlier, giving the proposed land-use planning commission (an outgrowth of the Kyl amendment) veto power over Native and state selections. The Senate then approved the amended bill overwhelmingly.[22]

The conference committee, which included Udall, Saylor, and Bible, met during the first two weeks of December. The discussions focused on the village and regional corporation grants and the relations between Natives and the state—the issues that had dominated the debate since 1968. A conflict between Don Wright and Governor Egan, which led Wright to threaten to use "guns" as well as lawsuits, dominated media accounts.[23] In contrast, the environmentalists' demands created little excitement. Nearly everyone agreed that the act should include some form of the Kyl and Bible amendments.[24] Alaska Coalition leaders worried that the bill would be emasculated. When Stevens and Begich, also members of the conference committee, assured Anchorage newspaper reporters that the Bible amendment would be "completely different" and that nothing in the final bill would "slow down" state or Native land selections, their anxiety grew.[25] Yet their fears proved unfounded. Udall insisted that the final legislation include the House language, which explicitly spelled out the Interior secretary's responsibilities. He did agree to one change—reducing the acreage total from 100 million to 80 million.[26] In the final version, a revision of the Kyl amendment, providing for a limited freeze, became Section 17(d)1, and the Bible amendment became Section 17(d)2.

From the environmentalists' perspective, the central provisions of ANCSA were Section 11, which provided for the withdrawal of lands surrounding Native villages, excluding national park but not wildlife refuge lands; Section 17a, which created a joint federal-state land-use planning commission, with advisory powers; Section 17d(1), which declared a 90-day land freeze after passage of the act, during which the secretary of the Interior was to withdraw appropriate lands and "classify or reclassify" them; and Section 17d(2), which authorized the secretary to withdraw up to 80 million acres for possible additions to the four federal conservation systems. The secretary was to complete the 17d(2) withdrawals within nine months and provide periodic reports to Congress on them for two years. Congress would have five years to act on the secretary's recommendations. Neither 17d(1) nor 17d(2) was to interfere with the selection process spelled out in Section 11.[27]

There was another reason why these sections attracted so little contemporary attention. As Berry points out, "the language was ambiguous. ... The bill was hastily drafted so Congress could pass it before the Christmas recess."[28] Thus, it was possible for the Alaska politicians to view Sections 17(d)1 and 17(d)2 as harmless gestures and for Udall, Saylor, and Bible to see them as the triumph of national over parochial interests and the foundation of a far-reaching preservation effort. Although they appreciated the complexity and ambiguity of ANCSA, Alaska Coalition members were also pleased. They had worked together, helped obtain a generous settlement of the Natives' claims, and with allies in the Park Service persuaded Congress to think of Alaska as more than a repository of raw materials. On December 14, 1971, when Congress passed the landmark legislation, they were cautiously optimistic about their ability to influence the pipeline bill.

PIPELINE POLITICS

During spring 1970, while the land freeze and the Hart injunction were in effect, environmentalists received disturbing news of activity along the pipeline route. Bob Weeden reported that the oil companies were pushing ahead, regardless of what happened in Washington. He suggested that Ed Wayburn or Stewart Brandborg investigate. "There is a *very good story there, if someone wanted to do some researching.*"[29] The *Fairbanks News-Miner* later confirmed the reports.[30] In the meantime, Weeden and Celia Hunter also conducted their own investigation. Interrogating local Bureau of Land Management officials, they discovered that construction crews were exploiting agency regulations and reopening "old trails." In late April Hunter flew over the pipeline route. She noted a number of large construction camps and considerable activity. In many areas there were bulldozer tracks across the tundra far from any existing trail.[31] Responding to these reports, Wayburn wrote indignantly to Hickel: "While all the investigations and hearings have been going on, officials and contractors of [the Trans-Alaska Pipeline System (TAPS)] have been acting as if permission to proceed full-tilt was an accomplished fact, although such is not the case."[32]

In July Mike McCloskey made an extended inspection of the entire route, traveling with Bureau of Land Management officials. He reported that the route surveys were complete and preliminary work on the pipeline and road was progressing rapidly; the freeze and injunction seemingly had little effect. At Valdez, for example, "earth moving equipment is now at work there, and slash is being burned." North of Fairbanks "the tops of hills were shaved off ... for quarries for gravel. The BLM says these wrecked hilltops will provide good recreational vista points! (hah!)" At each of the camps "a major road leads off a few miles, up to 5 miles in some cases, to a major gravel pit or quarry." North of the Yukon River, the pipeline route and road "have already actually been cleared. A swath about 20 feet wide has been cleared with bull-dozers. ... This clearing has been done under the guise of seismic work."[33]

Clearly, the oil companies were confident that the pipeline would be built, and that it would be built to Valdez. What was the basis for this confidence? Their enormous resources were unquestionably a factor. Yet wealth alone might not have been decisive if the oil companies had not had other, less tangible resources. One of these was the support of the state. "The problem," Hunter bemoaned, "lies in the extreme sense of urgency evidenced" by Alaska's politicians, "who merely want to get the oil out of the ground. ... They have their eye on the money."[34] Federal government officials were no less biased. The Nixon administration was sympathetic, and Secretary Hickel's sentiments were well known. In the year after the injunction, Interior Department officials did their best to punish the plaintiffs. On at least one occasion they forced Wilderness Society attorneys to go to Alaska to review documents that were available in Washington.[35] Secretary Rogers C. B. Morton was more even-handed than Hickel, but he, too, assumed that the pipeline would be built. And on the issue of the Canadian alternative, he was as rigid as his predecessor.

Despite this support, the oil companies suffered a major setback in early 1971 when the Interior Department released a draft version of its environmental impact statement (EIS) for the pipeline, a requirement of the new National Environmental Policy Act (NEPA). The EIS was still a novel exercise, and Interior Department officials viewed it as a perfunctory bureaucratic hurdle. Their nonchalance made it a lightning rod for critics. Public hearings in Washington and Anchorage attracted more than 100 and 200 people, respectively. The sessions ran day and night and produced a record of more than 3,000 pages, with an additional 3,000 pages of appendixes and 1,000 pages of letters.[36] Most of the witnesses were critical. Leaders of the national and Alaska environmental organizations accused the Interior Department of whitewashing the project. The new Environmental Protection Agency, the Army Corps of Engineers, and even the Commerce Department submitted critical evaluations. Government scientists were more explicit in their private correspondence. U.S. Geological Survey scientists reported that "everywhere there is anger and resentment because research highly pertinent to the pipeline has been deliberately omitted."[37] The state's biologists had serious concerns about the pipeline's impact on caribou migrations, commercial fisheries, and wildlife habitat. Yet Governor Egan had forbidden Alaska Fish and Game employees to testify, so "a considerable amount of information damaging to the impact statement will not be presented."[38] These responses underlined the potential power of the EIS.

Secretary Morton, new to the job and less committed to the pipeline than his predecessors, quickly distanced himself from the draft EIS. He acknowledged that "many of the great problems" had not been solved and would require "a long, hard look."[39] He ordered his staff to do a better job. Their "long, hard look" would require more than a year, ensuring further delay.

The EIS debacle and a growing appreciation of the problems associated with the Valdez route led the oil companies to propose a variety of technical improvements (such as elevating the pipeline in permafrost areas) and

pipeline critics to consider the Canadian alternative more seriously. The
Canadian government contributed by proposing a Mackenzie Valley
pipeline of its own, and Canadian environmentalists, who had adamantly opposed a pipeline, began to rethink their opposition as they contem-
plated the likelihood of a tanker disaster along the British Columbia
coast.[40] Leaders of the Sierra Club and Wilderness Society still hoped to
thwart any pipeline, but chided by Weeden, Hunter, and other Alaskans
who appreciated the boosters' strength and determination, they began to
consider the Canadian route as a fallback position. Even some Alaska
politicians became interested. State Senators Jay Hammond and Bob
Palmer and Representative Clem Tillion, long-time defenders of the fishing industry, called for an investigation of the Canadian route because "it
has become obvious that the route selection was a political decision rather
than a technical one." Not only would a Canadian pipeline spare Alaska's
waters, it might even produce more revenue for the state.[41] By summer
1971 a loose coalition of environmentalists, Canadian authorities, dissi-
dent politicians, and midwestern politicians (who were concerned about
gasoline supplies) were promoting an all-land pipeline. Several routes to
the Mackenzie Valley were proposed; the one preferred by environmentalists would go south from Prudhoe Bay and east, below ANWR.

Secretary Morton responded by ordering his staff to consider the
Canadian route in the final EIS. He also pressured the oil companies to
confer with Canadian officials about a possible pipeline. A perfunctory
meeting was held in Ottawa in late March 1972.[42]

Two vigorous opponents remained, however. The first was the Egan
administration, which was determined not to lose any of its potential
income. The governor's foremost concern was the state's fiscal situation.
Total expenditures tripled in the early 1970s, and the $900 million oil
lease windfall of 1969 was quickly exhausted. Without new revenues huge
deficits were inevitable. A Valdez pipeline could be completed in three
years (given the extensive preparatory activities) and begin to pay off
before painful reductions became necessary.

The second opponent was the oil industry, which opposed any destination except Valdez. In late March 1972 British Petroleum's Alaska executives
invited Wilderness Society attorney James Marshall to discuss an out-of-
court settlement of the society's suit. Marshall recalled their conversation.

*I said I did not believe we would ever consent to a pipeline such as they proposed
or to the vast shipments from Valdez to the west coast, but I recognized that soon-*

er or later oil would be taken from the north slope and suggested that they make a study of the Canadian route. ... I got no reply on this latter point.[43]

Four months later H. Lee Watson of the Environmental Defense Fund attended a similar meeting. He wrote afterward that his "impression was the BP people were quite rigid in their point of view. ... Economics ruled out [the Canadian] route but they claim it would be just as bad for the environment as the Alaskan route anyway. ... The Canadian pipeline would also present political problems which do not exist with the Alaska pipeline."[44]

Although Egan's motivation was obvious, the reasoning of the petroleum executives is harder to explain. The most thorough contemporary study, by economist Charles J. Cicchetti of Resources for the Future, forcefully argued that the Canadian route would be more profitable, assuming that the Alaska oil was really destined for the U.S. market. Cicchetti believed that the oil companies hoped to sell the oil to Japan.[45] H. Lee Watson probably identified the other critical factor when he reported that the Canadian route would raise "political problems that do not exist with the Alaska pipeline." Given the severity of the opposition in the United States, the oil companies had little taste for additional conflict. In any case, they were as rigid as Egan. As Edward Patton, president of the oil industry consortium, now renamed the Alyeska Pipeline Service Company, told an Alaska legislative committee, "You ought to quit worrying about Canada."[46]

Another meeting during that period was equally revealing. In May 1971 Secretary Morton visited Alaska for the first time. He spent most of his time with politicians and booster groups but agreed to meet the Cordova District Fisherman's Union, an organization of Prince William Sound fishermen who opposed the Valdez terminal. When one of the Cordova leaders asked about the Canadian route, Morton replied that "what we get into here is a real, real problem" of the state's responsibility "to those whom it sold in good faith those leases." He added that "there's been no application, there's been nobody willing to put up the money to build the pipeline down through Canada."[47] The fishermen and most pipeline opponents concluded that on this point, Morton was no more receptive than Hickel. In an influential article published at the same time, Representative Les Aspin (D-WI), a leading proponent of a Canadian pipeline, predicted that the full EIS would not consider the Canadian route or support a delay in awarding the pipeline permit. The oil companies would get what they wanted unless public opposition "grows enormously."[48]

Public pressures did grow enormously, but not in the way that Aspin hoped. At a time when Congress and the Interior Department were at least entertaining the idea of systematically evaluating alternative routes, a growing energy shortage discouraged any move that was likely to result in additional delay. By 1971 domestic oil and gas production was falling short of rising domestic demand. The reasons included the prosperity of the 1960s and the absence of incentives for conservation. The Nixon administration's disastrous experiments with price controls, which dated from 1970, also exacerbated the problem. In the meantime environmental activism and environmental regulations slowed the construction of new refineries, power plants, and pipelines.[49] In 1972 the Organization of Petroleum Exporting Countries (OPEC) would become another factor. The domestic and international crises would soon merge to create the most formidable economic and political challenges of the decade.

In any other setting the release of the final EIS, on March 20, 1972, just as the post-ANCSA freeze was ending, might well have generated an irresistible movement for the Canadian route. Although Morton delighted in telling how many millions of dollars and thousands of hours his staff had expended on the massive report, it did not satisfy most critics. Forced to work quickly, government scientists had had to extrapolate from research that was only marginally pertinent. Their analyses indicated how little they or anyone knew about the likely effects of the pipeline and how many things could go wrong. Although they did not include a direct evaluation of the Canadian option, indirect references suggested that it would be less damaging. David Brew, who headed the effort, wanted to consider a Canadian oil and gas transportation system (everyone assumed that a gas pipeline would follow the Alaska highway to Canada), which he believed would almost certainly be preferable. His superiors rejected this request, though one of Morton's assistants later added a brief assessment designed, apparently, to show the courts that the department had considered every option.[50]

In the aftermath, interest in a Canadian pipeline increased. The *New York Times* and other leading newspapers endorsed the Canadian option, as did a dozen midwestern senators. Eighty-three members of the House and 23 senators called for hearings on the EIS, which was tantamount to endorsing the Canadian route. In late March the Canadian energy minister arrived in Washington to assure U.S. officials that the Canadian government would share recently completed environmental studies of the Mackenzie River valley. Shortly afterward, the Canadian government announced that it would build a Mackenzie River highway and would expedite a pipeline application.[51]

In the meantime the Environmental Defense Fund recruited experts to evaluate the EIS. Their comments, totaling 1,300 pages, became the basis of a "counter impact statement," released on May 4. It attacked the EIS for accepting "at face value the fundamental premises of the oil companies" and urged consideration of the Canadian route. On May 8 Morton asked various government scientists to read and comment on the charges. David Brew's reaction was telling. "Through systematic analysis," he concluded, the Canadian route "is clearly to be preferred on environmental grounds, and ... more analysis is needed to establish the ranking on an economic basis."[52] Still, after concluding that the opposing scientists had no new and damaging factual information, Morton announced on May 11 that he would grant a permit for a trans-Alaska pipeline. In the words of the Wilderness Society's attorneys, his decision confirmed that the Interior Department "has never, *and never will,* objectively consider whether a Canadian alternative would better serve the American public."[53]

One obstacle remained: the Hart injunction of 1970. After oral arguments on August 14–15, 1972, the judge ruled that the Interior Department had the power to grant exemptions to the 1920 Mineral Leasing Act and had fulfilled the requirements of NEPA. He acknowledged that an appeal would follow and predicted that the Supreme Court would ultimately have to resolve the case.[54] In early October the appeals court heard oral arguments and on February 9, 1973, ruled unanimously that Morton had violated the Mineral Leasing Act's limitations on the width of right-of-ways. It refused to rule on NEPA and suggested that the Interior Department seek congressional action if it wanted to proceed. On April 4, the Supreme Court refused to hear the government's appeal, letting the appellate decision stand. While the environmental groups celebrated and Governor Egan attacked the decision as "the worst possible opinion that could have come," Senator Stevens more realistically observed, "if the court has decided against it, we'll just have to change the law."[55]

After the "initial jubilation," recalled Brock Evans, now the head of the Sierra Club's Washington office, "we all realized that we were in for a serious battle ahead." In the ensuing conflict over pipeline legislation, which Evans described as "the longest and toughest and most sustained" he had experienced, several factors were decisive. First was the mounting energy crisis and the pipeline proponents' ability to exploit public anxieties. Evans reported that "the political climate of the Congress was ... so intense and angry on the whole question of energy vis-à-vis environment that we concluded quickly that we could not last ten seconds in anybody's office attempting to argue the point that the oil should stay in the ground."[56] Or as another observer reported, "Not a single senator took the position that Alaskan oil ought to remain untouched."[57] Second was the position of the Canadian government, which seemed to be less than enthusiastic about a Canadian pipeline. Many Canadian environmentalists remained unconvinced, and the Liberal government, which had lost its parliamentary majority in 1972, remained in power only because of an alliance with the New Democratic Party, which was hostile to U.S. interests. The resulting ambiguity was a godsend to the oil companies and their lobbyists. Senator John Melcher (D-MT), head of the Public Lands Subcommittee, which was considering the legislation, observed that the Canadians' statements do not "add up to a very firm position."[58]

Morton argued the administration's case in a letter to the Senate on April 4, 1973. He called for the immediate passage of right-of-way legislation. "It is also in our national interest ... that the Congress not force a delay ... while further consideration is given to a pipeline through Canada." He insisted that the environmental advantages of the Canadian route were negligible and promised restrictions that would make the Valdez pipeline earthquake proof. "Moreover, we are insisting that operation of the maritime leg be safer than any other maritime oil transport system now in operation." In the meantime the Canadian government had made several demands that would dilute the oil companies' power and profits. "They are unacceptable from the point of view of our national interests," Morton wrote, "when we have the alternative of a pipeline through Alaska that will be built by American labor and will deliver its full capacity of American-owned oil to our markets." Morton added that "Canadian native claims would probably have to be resolved, a process that took years in the United States."[59]

The ensuing congressional debates took an unexpected and ominous turn. Morton noted in his April 4 letter that two steps were required to begin construction of the Valdez pipeline: Congress had to resolve the right-of-way issue, and the courts had "to determine that the environmental impact statement complied with the requirements of the National Environmental Policy Act." The House and Senate Interior committees quickly approved bills that overturned the appeals court decision and granted the broader corridor that the oil companies demanded. They added a provision authorizing immediate construction of the pipeline. Supporters of the Canadian route responded with an amendment (called Mondale-Bayh in the Senate and Udall in the House) that authorized a one-year study of the Canadian route before Congress voted. Given the pressure to do something about the energy crisis, the amendments had little chance of success. The real issue was the adequacy of the environmental impact statement.

Morton's assurances notwithstanding, the EIS was the Achilles heel of the government's case. Despite the time and money devoted to it, many issues were unanswered, and alternative approaches, such as the Canadian route, had received no systematic consideration. Led by the Environmental Defense Fund, environmentalists had assembled an impressive group of dissenting scientists, including several Interior Department employees who agreed, if subpoenaed, to detail their misgivings.[60] It was not unrealistic to imagine that a judge would force more delays or even rule that the Interior Department had failed to show that a pipeline could be built and operated without unacceptable damage.

On the verge of victory, the Alaska politicians increasingly focused on this potential nightmare. Senator Stevens recalled, "I had a group of people come over to my house in Maryland, and we spent several evenings going over what could be done. I was convinced ... that Congress had the power to close the courts to these demands."[61] His answer was an amendment to the right-of-way bill rubber-stamping the 1972 EIS and prohibiting court challenges. This tactic raised other issues, including the status of NEPA. If Congress circumvented the new law at the first sign of trouble, was there any hope of meaningful assessments of environmental risks? Senator Jackson, NEPA's author, was sensitive to this complaint and opposed the amendment. Yet he, too, was frustrated by the delays and at one point promised to introduce his own override bill if construction had not started by 1974.

The other effect of the amendment was to expose and exacerbate the conflict between Stevens and Mike Gravel, the other Alaska senator. Though both men were closely identified with the booster community and the pipeline, they were long-time rivals and antagonists. They also viewed their jobs and careers differently. After initially antagonizing colleagues with his abrasive manner, Stevens had become part of the Senate establishment; by 1973 he was Senator Jackson's "fair-haired boy."[62] Gravel, on the other hand, had little patience with the horse-trading that characterized the legislative process. Though he had won his seat by defeating Gruening in the 1968 Democratic primary, he was in many respects a younger version of him. A booster at home, he was a liberal in Washington, best known for opposing the Vietnam War. He was also eager to embrace popular causes. He had to run for reelection in 1974 and was looking for ways to bolster his appeal. When Stevens explained his proposed amendment, Gravel replied that "it was going to be his amendment."[63] Stevens seethed but deferred to his colleague, since Gravel's support was essential to winning Democratic votes.

The first crucial vote occurred on July 13, when the Senate defeated the Mondale-Bayh amendment by 29 to 61. Only a handful of liberal senators (including five Republicans) supported Mondale-Bayh, which also circumvented NEPA by requiring a congressional vote on the Canadian route after the year-long study. Environmentalists later discovered that the State Department had deliberately misrepresented the position of the Canadian government, prompting Senator Melcher to complain about "inept, inexcusable delays" and sabotage. Yet Senator Walter Mondale (D-MN), the sponsor, conceded that the margin of defeat was too great to overcome.[64]

The more important vote, on the Stevens-Gravel amendment, came on July 17. Many senators who had opposed the Canadian option were equally troubled by this measure. A vigorous lobbying effort spearheaded by the Sierra Club and the Wilderness Society targeted senators from California, Hawaii, and Nevada, all of whom had voted against Mondale-Bayh. Stevens expected the environmentalists to win as late as July 16.[65] The initial vote was 49 to 48 in favor of the amendment, but California Senator Alan Cranston, who had been detained, arrived in time to vote against it, tying the vote. Vice President Spiro Agnew then broke the tie with an affirmative vote. Pipeline supporters were especially pleased that Senator Bible voted for the amendment. Stevens believed that Bible's sympathy for Alaska's economic problems was the key.[66]

There were also critical defections among eastern Republicans. Since the bill was portrayed in the eastern press as a boon to Alaska and California at the expense of the Northeast, their behavior was a gauge of the growing concern over fuel shortages—and the shortcomings of the environmentalists' campaign. Both Pennsylvania senators (Scott and Schweiker), one Connecticut senator (Weicker), and one Massachusetts senator (Brooke) voted for the amendment. Most perplexing was the yes vote of Brooke, who had supported Mondale-Bayh.

After the House rejected the Udall amendment by a large margin, Republican Representative John Dellenback of Oregon proposed to delete the NEPA override. A frustrated Udall charged that "a lot of those who helped to write the National Environmental Policy Act into law are preparing to gut it."[67] Nevertheless, the Dellenback amendment failed, 198 to 221, and the House later passed the bill with the override.

The environmentalists' only remaining option was to challenge the constitutionality of the act. David Brower and others wanted to make such a case, but Environmental Defense Fund lawyers argued that a suit had little chance of success and would likely provoke a strong negative public reaction.[68] The Wilderness Society and Friends of the Earth then turned to the American Civil Liberties Union but received no encouragement.[69] Morton issued the pipeline permit on January 23, 1974.

The authorization of the pipeline—albeit with more regulations and safeguards than had been foreseen in 1968 or 1969—was the environmental movement's most serious political setback in at least a decade. It had "immense symbolic importance."[70] National environmental leaders tried to put the best face on the debacle. It "is only one aspect of the formidable conservation war we are fighting in all of Alaska," Wayburn wrote.[71] Brock Evans concurred: "We lost a big battle; but not the whole war."[72] Jack Hession was more realistic. "The oil pipeline is a battle that was fought and essentially lost."[73] He blamed industry lobbying, the devious policies of the Nixon administration, and public anxieties over energy supplies and prices.

Wayburn recalled only one possible miscalculation: "had we been willing to compromise our hard position beginning in March of this year, we might have rescued the NEPA portion of the decision." Like most people, Wayburn and other environmentalists had misjudged the severity of the energy crisis and its escalating effect on public and congressional opinion.[74] From his post in Washington, Evans was more critical. After the ANCSA battle the Alaska Coalition had recast itself as the Alaska Public Interest Coalition, with more than 20 affiliated organizations. But the core groups, the Sierra Club, Wilderness Society, and Friends of the Earth, "were just about the only organizations who did any work whatsoever at the critical place—on Capitol Hill—until after the Senate vote. ... We pleaded with other organizations to help, but very little came through, until the shock of the anti-NEPA vote began to register."[75] Linda Billings, Evans's assistant, was also critical of the Sierra Club effort against the Trans-Alaska Pipeline System:

> I did not get the impression that the Sierra Club chapter and group leaders were to a large extent convinced as to the urgency of the TAPS campaign, nor was the general public. They were not as responsive to the pleas for mail, and they were not as eager for information as we have seen on other issues such as Grand Canyon. ... Alaska was a long way from them, and they had pressing fights right in their back yards.[76]

The campaign's shortcomings were nowhere more apparent than in Alaska, where the many new environmental organizations might have undercut the boosters' support for the Valdez pipeline. Yet Hession and Hunter were the only Alaskans who played prominent roles in the campaign that preceded the pipeline authorization. The problem, then, was not simply inadequate lobbying; it was also the informal character and organization of the coalition. Given the power of the oil companies, the determination of the boosters, and the rising anxiety of consumers over energy supplies, only a genuine grass-roots effort, reaching into every part of the country, was likely to produce a favorable outcome.

SECTION 17 OF ANCSA

In the meantime the selection of potential Alaska parks, wildlife refuges, and national forests had proven equally controversial and, from the environmentalist perspective, hardly less disappointing. Sections 17d(1) and 17d(2) had acknowledged a national interest in Alaska lands comparable to the state and Native interests. Yet the fine print was ambiguous. In its final form the law seemed to authorize the secretary of the Interior to set aside various lands, including 80 million acres of potential parks and wildlife refuges, before the Native regional corporations or the state authorities made their final selections. This was not stated explicitly, however, and Alaska's congressional representatives insisted that state selections could precede the secretary's withdrawal of 80 million acres. The law also failed to distinguish between the various federal conservation agencies, despite the central role of the National Park Service in the drafting process. Environmentalists had gotten the Forest Service excluded from the final Senate bill, but the conference committee had reinserted it.[77] As a result ANCSA set off a bureaucratic turf war. At one point the Forest Service proposed 79 million acres for multiple-use management.[78] Hartzog, among others, was outraged.[79]

The upshot was that a potential land rush turned into a genuine rush of monumental proportions. By spring 1972 nearly 200 million acres of public land had been claimed by one entity or another. The most obvious losers were planners like Richard Cooley and Arlon Tussing, who favored a systematic process based on the public interest.[80] Though Section 17a of ANCSA had created a joint federal-state planning commission, it had only advisory powers and was not taken seriously outside Alaska. The winner, at least in the short term, was Secretary Morton, whose powers were magnified and who, ironically in view of his simultaneous role as the administration's pipeline champion, became the environmentalists' ally.

On December 21, 1971, Assistant Interior Secretary Nathaniel Reed wrote to the heads of NPS and the Fish and Wildlife Service to inform them of their "mind-boggling" mandate during the three-month freeze. He called on them "to meet regularly to delineate areas which must be preserved." Their goal was to "pick out the vital land masses." They faced the "greatest challenge and opportunity" of their lives.[81]

NPS officials, led by Assistant Director Ted Swem, had anticipated this charge. In numerous reports and memos they had refined a long list of historic, archaeological, and "natural" sites, as well as possible collaborative ventures with the Canadian and Soviet governments.[82] They had relied on Alaska environmentalists for much of their detailed information. In early April 1971, for example, Richard Stenmark, one of the NPS planners, had sent Fred Dean, the head of the wildlife management department at the University of Alaska and a long-time ACS activist, a map of the Brooks Range showing various boundaries for a Gates of the Arctic park. He had marked several boundary options, including those from Rich Gordon's 1969 proposal, and the current Alaska Wilderness Council plan. "A combination of the Alaska Wilderness Council and the Gordon proposals appears to be the most attractive," he suggested.[83] A month later, Ernest J. Borgman, the head of the Alaska planning group, sent another map with slight changes.[84] By mid-December the NPS effort had produced a comprehensive list of proposed parks, national monuments, recreation areas, and historical and archaeological landmarks.

It had also produced a consensus about what areas were most valuable. At the top of everyone's list were the Brooks Range west of ANWR, the Wrangell and St. Elias mountains in south-central Alaska, an expanded Mount McKinley Park, and the Lake Clark region, a mountainous area between Mount McKinley and Katmai. Sitka and Skagway, in Southeast Alaska, headed the list of historic sites. NPS planners also wanted to expand ANWR and make it a wilderness area. The Park Service recommendations included a total of 10 proposed parks and monuments and 2 recreational areas. The priority list would remain almost unchanged through the legislative battles of the next nine years.

In the weeks following the passage of ANCSA, however, it was not clear which, if any, of these lands would be available. As Hession reported after the December 23 meeting of the Alaska chapter's Parks and Wilderness Committee,

> *I suggested that Sec. 17d is ambiguous on the question of State selection within the 90 day freeze. General response was that State pre-emptive selections ... are a distinct possibility. Dave Hickok suggested that the State might try blanket selection of remaining 78.5 million acres in an attempt to block national interest withdrawls. ... It could then withdraw certain selections and select elsewhere. Discussion ensued as to whether Interior Department would allow such a ploy by the State. Answer not known.*[85]

They did agree that Morton had to complete the national-interest selections before mid-March, when the 90-day freeze ended. After that, in Hession's words, "Morton would be racing the State on a first-come, first-served basis."[86]

By the end of the year, the Sierra Club had organized a campaign to pressure Morton to act quickly and to include the priority areas in his selections. The club (with assistance from the Wilderness Society, Trout Unlimited, and Audubon) proposed to spend $29,000 on ads in the *New York Times, Washington Post, San Francisco Chronicle, National Observer*, and *Christian Science Monitor*, urging readers to send letters and telegrams to the secretary. In January delegations of environmental leaders were to call on Morton and his assistants. If these techniques did not have the desired effect, the club would consider legal action.[87]

Ten days later Representatives Udall and Saylor sent Morton a letter drafted by the Wilderness Society's Harry Crandell. Besides emphasizing the importance of immediate action, they argued that Morton could use his authority under Section 17d(1) to impose order on the land selection process and ensure that the national interest prevailed over the ambitions of the state and the regional corporations.[88]

On January 21 and 24, Governor Egan did what the activists had anticipated, filing for the state's remaining 77 million acres. He insisted that the 90-day freeze did not apply to the state. "While this may come as a surprise to some lay observers," he explained, "it was not lost on the members of Congress most intimately involved." If conflicts resulted from these selections, the Joint Federal-State Land Use Planning Commission could "consider land exchanges" or other ways of achieving an "optimum pattern." However, if Morton selected the same land, the state would sue.[89] The state selections were concentrated in the central Brooks Range, the Wrangell Mountains, and other areas that NPS and the Alaska environmentalists had targeted. "The intention," wrote a Wilderness Society official, "seems to be to block Interior from significant new park and wildlife range withdrawals."[90]

Egan's provocative action produced an equally vigorous reaction. McCloskey rewrote the Sierra Club's newspaper ads to give them a sharper edge: "A giant land grab, the likes of which the world has never known, is now underway ... the state government of Alaska has already jumped the gun."[91] At his urging, former Interior Secretary Stewart Udall wrote a syndicated newspaper column directed specifically at Morton. "Ignore the 'small thinkers' in your department," Udall urged.[92] On February 22, Environmental Defense Fund attorneys hand-delivered a message promising a lawsuit if Morton did not reject the state's preemptive selections.[93]

The threats were probably unnecessary. By late January the efforts of NPS and the Fish and Wildlife Service were well advanced. Ted Swem had submitted a preliminary report, calling for 42 million acres of new park land and 86,000 acres of historic and archaeological sites. The Fish and Wildlife Service proposed adding 54 million acres in 22 units. The agencies also proposed additions to the wild and scenic rivers system totaling 10 million acres.[94] Their proposals were circulated within the Interior Department over the next month.

The most important revisions resulted from the continuing work of the Alaska Wilderness Council, now effectively reduced to Mark Ganopole's Anchorage committee. Despite her uncertain mandate, Ganopole frantically recruited volunteers to prepare detailed recommendations. Her group became the "Maps on the Floor" Committee. In a January interview, she captured the atmosphere of early 1972:

> We have the potential for a damn fine thing. [But] we're not getting anywhere because we don't have the people. ... There's a place for ... the short term worker, the long term worker. We need anybody. I like to gather the people with knowledge together with the people who don't have any. ... We could easily use 50 people right now. We could set up committees, establish goals, and off they go. I'm called chairman, but I don't run nothing. People can move at their own speed and on their own initiative.[95]

She had eight regular helpers, all severely taxed. They "worked like hell, day and night—families were ignored." About a dozen others participated sporadically. The committee also sought out individuals with expert knowledge, such as guides, hunters, and even miners. The total may have been as high as 200.[96] Of particular importance were NPS and Fish and

Wildlife Service professionals like Will Troyer and Bailey Breedlove. Rich Gordon attended a half-dozen meetings and interviewed a number of state and federal conservation officials.

With Ganopole's prodding, the Maps on the Floor Committee completed its work on schedule and mailed its recommendations in early February. Walt Parker later hand-delivered a copy to Morton. Ganopole also went to Washington to confer with Sierra Club lobbyists. She stressed the need to work with Native representatives.[97] A delegation from the national environmental groups met with Morton on February 28, just before the Interior Department staff was to submit its final recommendations. As a result Assistant Secretary Nathaniel Reed added 13 million acres to his d(1) proposals. The additions, notably the Noatak River region west of Gates of the Arctic and an area south of the Yukon River, proved to be wise choices. They ultimately became important parts of the Noatak and the Yukon Charley national preserves.[98]

Reed's recommendations, which he submitted to Morton on March 2, 1972, were a compilation of NPS, Fish and Wildlife Service, and environmentalists' proposals. He listed 68 million acres under the secretary's d(1) authority and 80 million under his (d)2 authority. Morton reduced the d(1) withdrawals to 45 million acres before announcing his decisions on March 15. He also reserved 59 million acres for Native village selections, 40 million acres for regional corporations' selections, and 1 million acres for a pipeline corridor, and he approved 35 million acres (of the 77 million that Egan had demanded in late January) for state selection.

In reaction the environmental groups praised the secretary, while most Alaska politicians were critical. Senator Gravel characterized Morton's action as a "misuse of authority." State Attorney General John Havelock described it as a "135 million acre rip-off." Alaska House Speaker Gene Guess, a Democrat and frequent supporter of conservation measures who was preparing to run against Stevens, attacked Morton's order as "a premeditated assault on Alaska's sovereignty to manage its own destiny."[99] Stevens himself urged restraint, noting that the decisions were not final and that the governor's threatened lawsuit could paralyze the entire process.[100] Under ANCSA Morton had until September 1972 to make his final d(1) and d(2) withdrawals. He would then have another year, until December 1973, to prepare detailed proposals for Congress to consider.

During the following months, which were also the critical months of the pipeline battle and the 1972 election campaigns, the contending groups attempted to influence Morton. The environmentalists relied on

Assistant Secretary Reed, who summarized his position when he told McCloskey that the Republicans "cannot go into the fall election having granted [a] pipeline permit to oil companies unless conservationists get their eighty million acres."[101] The Alaska politicians and their supporters counted on the lawsuit Governor Egan filed in April 1972, after Morton announced his withdrawals. Most observers believed that it would be thrown out of court or result in a new land freeze, but it was potentially a time bomb. Conceivably it could embarrass the Nixon administration, antagonize the Natives, and make Morton and his staff seem ineffectual. Egan was widely suspected of using it as a lever to force Morton to embrace the new Joint Federal-State Land Use Planning Commission.

In this politically charged atmosphere, the commission inevitably became a political football. Egan hoped to use it to exchange potential park lands for other lands the state coveted, including those in existing national parks and wildlife refuges. He proceeded to pack the state contingent with political loyalists, including Commissioner of Natural Resources Charles Herbert, an outspoken defender of the mining industry. In March Herbert compared Morton's d(2) withdrawals to Pearl Harbor. "We're in an awful battle ...," he explained.[102] None of the other state appointees had any background in land use planning. The Interior Department appointees were more varied. They included Joseph Fitzgerald, the former head of the Federal Field Committee and a current Atlantic Richfield executive; James Sullivan, the mayor of Anchorage; Harry Carter, a Native leader; Celia Hunter; and Richard Cooley, now a professor of environmental studies at the University of California. The first federal cochairman was Jack Horton, the former deputy undersecretary of the Interior, who had won the environmentalists' enmity in the pipeline battle. He was soon succeeded by Alaska Bureau of Land Management head Burton Silcock, a more accommodating individual who was jealous of NPS and the Fish and Wildlife Service. Since the state appointees presumably would vote as a bloc, the only question was whether Hunter and Cooley could sway the other federal appointees.

Although Morton recognized the commission's weaknesses, he found it impossible to disregard it completely. By appearing to pay attention to its recommendations, he hoped to appease the Alaskans without overly antagonizing the environmental groups. Reed told McCloskey that Morton wanted to make the "commission's work the battleground for much of the forthcoming debate." He sought "to win 80 percent of the battle in commission."[103]

Morton and Reed were inevitably disappointed. The commission did not meet until July 31, 1972, and then rubber-stamped the governor's demands. When Cooley moved to ban new mining claims on d(1) lands, the best he could manage was a tie vote, with Hunter, Fitzgerald, and Carter supporting the motion. This was the environmentalists' only "victory."

Hession, who attended the session as an observer, came away frustrated and angry. Hunter and Cooley "were overly accommodating to the state ... and did not vigorously defend the national conservation interest." The other members of the commission were as bad as he had anticipated. Fitzgerald indicated that "his order of preference was Natives, state, federal." Carter believed the d(2) withdrawals were contrary to Native interests. Sullivan endorsed every state proposal. They all deferred to Herbert.[104]

Having completed their initial review, four members of the commission went to Washington on August 16 to report to Morton. Their general comments on the d(1) and d(2) withdrawals were highly critical and may have helped persuade Morton to make some concessions. Their specific comments signaled, in effect, what the governor really wanted. Behind-the-scenes negotiations between state and federal attorneys over the state lawsuit intensified during the last two weeks of August.

Washington representatives of the national environmental groups became increasingly concerned as rumors of an out-of-court deal spread. Wayburn made a special trip to Juneau in late July to confer with Morton, who was visiting the d(2) areas, and Stewart Brandborg arranged a meeting between Morton and leaders of 17 environmental groups for August 11. Amid pleasantries, several of Morton's comments provided clues to his thinking. At one point he listed his objectives as preserving "values that are in the national interest," satisfying the Natives' claims, and creating manageable administrative units. And, he added, "we want to end up with Alaska as a viable state." He elaborated:

> One of the things where we could lose the long battle, or we could lose the war, is if we fail to provide the state with a reasonable way to go ... and if there is a real problem of the state being able to develop its resources to the degree that it should, the Congress is going to begin to move toward more opportunity for state selection. ... We have got to make sure that land is just not the cull. They have got to have something that will make the state go.[105]

In late August, the Wilderness Society's Harry Crandell obtained a copy of a still-secret memorandum of understanding—an out-of-court settlement of the state's lawsuit that largely followed the Land Use Planning Commission's proposals. In the memorandum Morton agreed to surrender certain areas that the state sought for their mining potential (notably an area south of Mount McKinley Park, the southern foothills of Gates of the Arctic, and certain lands in the central Alaska Range); in return the state relinquished its claims to the other contested areas. Crandell prepared a protest telegram for George Marshall, the society's president.[106]

At the same time James Moorman, director of the new Sierra Club Legal Defense Fund, weighed the environmentalists' options. Although most observers believed that Egan would lose if the case went to court, Moorman was less confident:

> ... there is a serious risk that Alaska could win its lawsuit. I believe the State judge could rule in their favor, and the wrong panel in the Ninth Circuit could uphold the district court judge and the Supreme Court would refuse to review the matter.

He proposed that the chapter "protest vigorously ... to force more concessions from Alaska but not to blow up the settlement." A suit attacking features of the agreement could be considered later.[107]

These deliberations explained the environmentalists' response to the settlement, announced on September 5, 1972. The Alaska chapter and ACS condemned it as a "cozy back room deal." Wayburn called on Congress to repudiate it, and the Washington representatives of six environmental groups attacked it. Yet none of them called for legal action.[108] Privately, they were relieved. As Moorman had warned, the state could have won much more. In the future it would have little political leverage. Egan's self-serving statement that the settlement was "a victory for the state all the way through" was at best a half-truth.[109] Moreover, the Interior Department did not immediately transfer the lands to the state. In theory, at least, they would still be available for inclusion in parks that Congress (as opposed to the secretary) defined.

On September 13, 1972, Morton announced his "final" d(2) selections. They totaled 78.4 million acres and reflected minor concessions to critics, but their significance was uncertain.[110] The secretary was not obligated to adhere precisely to these decisions in preparing his final recommendations to Congress (due in December 1973) or even to limit his requests to 80 million acres. Morton ultimately asked for 83 million acres, and the environmental coalition responded with a bill calling for 119 million acres of parks and refuges.

Over the next 14 months three groups attempted to influence Morton's recommendations. The first was the Land Use Planning Commission, now the de facto voice of the Egan administration. In April and May 1973 the commission held hearings in 31 Alaska communities and in San Francisco, Seattle, Denver, and Washington, D.C. Everyone understood that this burst of activity was largely window-dressing for the governor's agenda. On one occasion, when a subcommittee proposed to reconsider some of the land that the state had obtained in the September settlement, Natural Resources Commissioner Herbert threatened to resign. The others quickly backed down.[111] Many of his own allies viewed Herbert as an anachronism and an embarrassment. Yet in the commission deliberations his only effective rival was Joseph Josephson, a new Egan appointee who hoped to use his commission experience as a springboard to elective office.

Because of the commission's obvious bias, many environmentalists viewed the hearings as a waste of time. Hession bemoaned the lack of vigorous national park advocates at the Anchorage hearings.[112] The Wilderness Society had only limited success in organizing Denver environmentalists for the hearing there. Those who did testify sensed the hostility of most of the commissioners. George Marshall complained, "There seemed to be some questions asked for the purpose of trying to get witnesses to show their ignorance of Alaska." He thought that Carter, the AFN leader, was the "brightest" of the critics, though even he was "definitely Alaska for the Alaskans."[113] Hunter and Cooley, increasingly isolated, began to prepare minority reports.

The second group attempting to change the outcome was the environmentalists. Ganopole initially announced that the Maps on the Floor Committee would submit detailed proposals to the Land Use Planning Commission, but as the commission's bias became more obvious, she shifted her attention to the parks legislation that the Sierra Club and Wilderness Society were planning. In late 1972 she recruited teams to focus on specific regions, in effect reconstituting the Wilderness Council. Barbara Winkley agreed to head the southern Alaska team, Walt Parker the central Alaska team, and Jack Hession the Arctic team.[114] Rich Gordon reported to Wayburn in early March 1973,

Jack, Mark and I have been working hard on the 80 million acre studies. Thanks to Mark's charm and oomph, quite a number of agency people have briefly joined in our discussions. We also set up a meeting in Fairbanks after the ACS board meeting, to discuss concepts, and to try to set up working groups up there. Jim

Kowalski agreed to coordinate the work on that end. My general impression is that there is generally quite close agreement on concepts and area priorities.[115]

Would their proposals have any effect on Morton? They became increasingly concerned as infighting between the Park Service and the Forest Service intensified and Morton's commitment to the Park Service seemed to waver. Gordon had long talks with Barney Coster, the head of the Forest Service's Alaska planning group. Though amiable and sympathetic, Coster was under pressure to make the strongest possible case for new national forests.[116] By fall 1973 the leaders of the national groups had decided that they could not rely on Morton. On September 23 representatives of the Sierra Club, Wilderness Society, Friends of the Earth, and the Alaskans met to devise a single proposal. (One outgrowth of that meeting was a decision to include Admiralty Island, which was not among the 17d(2) lands, as a wildlife refuge.) From this point the environmentalists largely operated independently. Wayburn had already published an article in the Sierra Club *Bulletin* calling for 85 million acres of parks and wildlife refuges.[117] In November they submitted a (d)2 bill to Senator Jackson in an effort to counter the impact of what they assumed would be an unsatisfactory Interior Department report.

The third group was the federal agencies. In early 1973 Ted Swem's Alaska Planning Group (comprising representatives of NPS, the Fish and Wildlife Service, and the Bureau of Outdoor Recreation, which administered the wild and scenic rivers system) proposed several administrative innovations, including a Noatak ecological reserve, which NPS and Fish and Wildlife Service would jointly operate, and a Nunamiut-Koyukon national wildlands in the central Brooks Range, which NPS would jointly manage with the Arctic Slope Regional Corporation, the new Native entity. It also recommended more than 200 research projects on the flora, fauna, and geology of likely park areas. By early July Swem had identified 85 million acres of potential wilderness, including 49 million acres in parks and 32 million acres in wildlife refuges.[118] In the fall the Alaska Planning Group supervised the drafting of environmental impact statements for each of the more than two dozen units it proposed.

In the meantime the Forest Service and Bureau of Land Management were working on competing plans. Coster's Forest Service group proposed seven new national forests and additions to the Tongass and Chugach forests, totaling 42 million acres. The Bureau of Land Management urged a "fifth" system—in addition to the national parks, wildlife refuges, national forests, and wild and scenic rivers—with itself as the fifth agency.[119] During August and September the heads of the various agencies debated the precise mix of policies and administrative authorities for Morton's report to Congress.

At this point Morton's role became crucial. By summer 1973 he seemed ready to award something to all of the contending bureaucrats, including the Forest Service and Bureau of Land Management managers. His defenders insisted that his goal was to command the broadest possible support for his proposals. A more plausible explanation is that he had lost a behind-the-scenes conflict with Agriculture Secretary Earl Butz, who championed the Forest Service. Journalist Jack Sheperd reported "rumors of secret agreements that cut deeply into potential national parks and wildlife refuges."[120] On several occasions Morton had said that he expected Congress to take the full five years allotted by ANCSA and to rewrite much of the legislation. Given the bureaucratic squabbling and the growing disarray within the Nixon administration, he may well have decided that a more determined fight was foolish. In any case, his December 17 announcement marked a dramatic retreat from his earlier position. The NPS was now allotted only 32.6 million acres. (It had been slated to receive only 29 million in mid-November.) The Forest Service received 18.8 million acres in three new national forests. The Bureau of Land Management and the Fish and Wildlife Service were to jointly manage two units, the Noatak and the Iliamna national preserves.[121]

The Interior Department's procedures for notifying the contending interest groups compounded its problems. An assistant secretary briefed Senator Stevens on November 8, McCloskey and Wayburn several days later, Governor Egan on November 27, and Senator Gravel and Representative Don Young (a Republican who had succeeded Begich, killed in an airplane crash) on November 29. Stevens was hostile and vituperative, charging that Morton had capitulated to the environmental groups. Ted Swem, who participated in the briefing, reported that "many of his statements were so irrational that no attempt was made to reply."[122] The transcript notes that many of the senator's questions were "unanswerable."[123] Egan and Gravel were also angry, mostly because of what they interpreted as personal slights. The earlier meeting with Sierra Club officials, duly reported in the Anchorage newspapers, particularly rankled. Swem reported that Gravel "was very critical of the Department for not briefing him as well as the Governor at the same time Senator Stevens was briefed and prior to the briefing of the conservationists."[124]

All of those charges and complaints were repeated when Morton made his official announcements in mid-December. Alaska boosters could hardly contain themselves. "The state seemed to explode," reported the *Anchorage Daily News*.[125] The most extreme of the booster attacks came from now-retired Ernest Gruening, who attacked "conservation extremists" who were "in total disregard of the interests of the people of Alaska" and who sought to transform the state "into a combination of wilderness and zoo."[126] Implicit in his statement was the assumption that wilderness and zoos were unimportant, probably frivolous, and certainly not in the "interests of the people of Alaska."

The environmentalists were only slightly less critical. After his briefing Wayburn criticized Morton for disregarding the advice of his professional staff and announced that the Sierra Club "will do our utmost to reverse major parts of the plan."[127] Robert Cahn, an influential reporter for the *Christian Science Monitor*, charged that Morton had capitulated to the Agriculture Department.[128] These comments reflected the shortcomings of Morton's recommendations but also the frustrations of nearly four years of nonstop activity that had produced little except a vague and unsatisfactory plan for Alaska parks. Despite its supposed popularity, the environmental movement had relatively little to show for its efforts and even less reason to expect the Congress to act on Morton's proposals anytime soon.

It was appropriate that the last phase of these deliberations coincided with the outbreak of a new Arab-Israeli war, the beginning of the OPEC oil embargo against the United States and other Israeli allies, and the advent of the "energy crisis" of 1973–1974. Energy shortages and rising gasoline and fuel oil prices, more than any other factor, altered the political balance as Washington grappled with the pipeline issue. Until mid-1972 environmentalists seemed to have the upper hand, and it would not have been unreasonable to forecast a Canadian pipeline as well as a host of new parks and wildlife refuges. By the end of 1973 the oil industry was victorious and the park and refuge proposal faced an uncertain future. The next three years of pipeline building and boom conditions in Alaska saw unprecedented assaults on the Alaska wilderness as well as new efforts to preserve what remained.

CHAPTER 5

SOUTHEAST ALASKA AND THE WILDERNESS MOVEMENT

Dixie Baade arrived in Ketchikan in the late 1940s when her husband Bob, a biologist, took a job with the territorial fish and game department. She fell in love with the rugged mountains and glaciers, the dense forests and fog-shrouded islands. To her surprise, she soon became an unwilling participant in the USDA Forest Service's plan to create a more diversified economy in Southeast Alaska. By 1973 she was thoroughly disenchanted:

> *Ketchikan presently has a basically transient population with little or no interest in the future of the community. The loggers are almost entirely seasonal. … Mill workers on a year-round basis wait to retire or transfer. The person who had planned on staying here finds the situation increasingly discouraging. There has been a marked increase in the cost of just living here. … At the same time we find a steady deterioration in the quality of living conditions. The influx of people who simply do not care about esthetic values has led to a proliferation of trash everywhere. There is trash and filth on the city streets, along the waterways, the highways and on the beaches. The development of the timber industry has caused seri-*

ous air, water and noise pollution. It has meant the destruction of beautiful areas where one once went for relaxation.[1]

By that time Baade had become a leader of the emerging environmental movement in Southeast Alaska. She had helped form the conservation committee of the Southeast Alaska Mountaineering Association, which evolved into the Tongass Conservation Society, a local branch of the Alaska Conservation Society (ACS). She was also active in the Sierra Club, the Alaska Wilderness Council, and the Southeast Alaska Conservation Council (SEACC). By the early 1970s she had become the most outspoken local opponent of the Forest Service and its policies. Friends scorned her. Her husband's position was jeopardized. She wrote, "… the timber industry is playing for keeps and the stakes are the whole of southeast Alaska."[2]

Baade's scathing comments had long rankled her neighbors, but her association with the Sierra Club's legal offensive of the early 1970s made her persona non grata. The Champion lawsuit temporarily thwarted the plan for a third Alaska mill. Two years later, in conjunction with the Natural Resources Defense Council and several western conservation organizations, the club sued the Forest Service over the perfunctory environmental impact statements it had prepared for logging plans in roadless areas. A Washington, D.C., district court judge issued a temporary restraining order in July 1972 and an injunction in August. A trial was scheduled for December, but on November 28, the chief of the Forest Service conceded the case and ordered detailed environmental impact statements for all logging contracts involving roadless areas.[3] Though the lawsuit did not affect the 50-year Alaska contracts, it effectively halted other logging contracts in the Tongass and Chugach national forests. Planned harvests totaling 94 million board feet in fiscal 1973 and 110 million board feet in fiscal 1974 were suspended. These were relatively small operations that environmentalists were not particularly interested in stopping. However, they were critical to the rapidly dwindling number of locally owned timber companies. John J. Schnabel, owner of the most prominent of the independents, located in Haines, complained to Jack Hession that "this town is dependent on us and the closure of the Forest Service sale program has destroyed us."[4]

Ketchikan business leaders soon organized a counterattack. A full-page ad in the *Ketchikan Daily News* on November 10, 1972, announced that "the Sierra Club's lawsuit … is immediately against us, THE PEOPLE OF ALASKA." It quoted Governor Egan extensively on the dire effects of the injunction.[5] Five days later, when Hession spoke to the Alaska Sports and Wildlife Club in Ketchikan, he was heckled and booed. Baade reported that the meeting "degenerated into a near riot with shouting, swearing, and a complete lack of order." Richard Wilson, the local Forest Service official, joined in the verbal attack. Senator Mike Gravel, who was present, helped protect Hession.[6] This incident was unusual only because of the publicity it attracted. Brock Evans reported that his files were "full of similar evidence of incredible hostility toward the wilderness in any form in Southeast Alaska ... it's very rough country indeed."[7]

Those experiences, together with the apparent collusion of local and federal officials, explain the particular thrust of the environmental movement there. Facing intense and ever more intolerant opposition, environmentalists became more aggressive as well. Increasingly they opposed *all* managerial discretion. The West Chichagof–Yakobi wilderness plan of 1968 became the model for a broader campaign to preserve the most ecologically and aesthetically valuable areas of the Tongass. The Southeast Alaska wilderness campaign would be a notable example of the broader environmentalist critique of public resource managers and their supposed expertise and political neutrality.

CHAMPION REVISITED

The forestry battles of the early 1970s took place against a background of conflicting political and legal pressures. Congress had passed a series of sweeping regulatory measures, many of which, like the National Environmental Policy Act (NEPA), immediately came under attack for increasing business costs and adding novel categories of "social" regulation. At the same time, the slowing of the economic boom of the 1960s and the emergence of inflation as a political issue, especially during the energy crisis of 1973–1974 and the severe recession of 1974–1975, created pressures for a more business-friendly government. These contradictory trends in public policy were palpable in the debates over the Alaska pipeline. They were no less evident in the parallel conflicts over forestry policy. The Nixon administration was caught in the middle. While endorsing politically popular measures such as NEPA, it simultaneously worked to increase the supply of lumber and other wood products, both to placate the industry and to hold down construction costs. Faced with contradictory pressures, Forest

Service managers, already under attack for their secrecy and unresponsiveness, became more defensive.

One result was a series of legal confrontations between environmentalists and Forest Service managers. The 1970 and 1972 suits were early irritants. Another suit over the Forest Service's plans to log Afognak Island, in the Chugach National Forest, increased tensions. A fourth suit over logging on Prince of Wales Island had far-reaching implications for national forest management. Together with administrative appeals and the ongoing debate over wilderness planning, these disputes polarized relations between the Forest Service and Southeast Alaska environmentalists. The time when the Forest Service would willingly participate in a conference of environmentalists (as it had in 1969) became a distant memory.

In 1971 the Sierra Club Legal Defense Fund appealed Judge James Plummer's Champion decision, which had dismissed the environmentalists' case. James Moorman, representing the environmentalists, was optimistic. His principal complaint was that the 50-year contract called for such extensive logging that it precluded other uses of the national forest and thus violated the agency's multiple-use mandate. That argument received unexpected support in early 1973 from Champion's own experts. A company-sponsored investigation, by A. Starker Leopold and Reginald H. Barrett of the University of California at Berkeley, concluded that the logging would have a devastating impact on wildlife. To lessen the adverse effect, Leopold and Barrett proposed a more gradual approach, based on a 100-year rather than 50-year schedule. The company at first refused to release the report because of its likely impact on the suit. Many local people feared the Leopold-Barrett recommendations would make the contract unprofitable.[8] The appeals court cited the study in ordering the case back to Plummer's court for a new trial.

The second trial began in late September 1974. For several days Moorman and the Forest Service attorney sparred over the admission of new evidence. Finally Plummer sided with Moorman and admitted testimony from Barrett, together with documents showing that some Forest Service officials opposed logging on Admiralty Island.[9] Moorman reported that Barrett was "an excellent witness" and that the Forest Service personnel, including former Regional Forester W. Howard Johnson, "were not very impressive." The judge seemed to agree, suggesting that the government supply other witnesses. Moorman believed that Plummer would still rule against them but that the new evidence greatly increased the chances of a successful appeal. He added prophetically that Plummer "will take his time." The judge was known to be in poor health; rumors circulated that he might die before issuing a decision.[10]

While Plummer deliberated, two additional developments altered the situation. The first was the 1974 election defeat of Governor Egan by former state Senator Jay Hammond. Pledging to balance economic and environmental interests, Hammond had attracted many Alaska academics and intellectuals, some of whom he brought into his administration. One of the new governor's first acts was to ask University of Alaska economist George W. Rogers to mediate the Champion conflict. Rogers had several conferences with leaders of the Sierra Club, the Sitka Conservation Society, and the Forest Service, all of whom gave lip service to his endeavor, but was unable to make any headway before a second development dramatically complicated the situation.[11] In early 1975 Sealaska, the Native regional corporation in Southeast Alaska, formed an alliance of southeastern village corporations and the region's two urban Native corporations, Shee Atika (Sitka) and Goldbelt (Juneau), for the purpose of logging the Tongass forestlands they were scheduled to receive under the Alaska Native Claims Settlement Act. The plan suggested that the conflict between subsistence and profits, at least in Southeast Alaska, had been settled decisively in favor of the latter. Environmentalists were particularly alarmed at the announcement that the Sitka and Juneau corporations planned to select prime timberlands on the west side of Admiralty Island, adjoining the Native village of Angoon in the Champion lease area. Environmentalists envisioned a new nightmare: if the Forest Service won the Champion suit, the company would cut the trees; if the environmentalists won, the Natives would cut the trees (perhaps using the same contractors).

Hession led the effort to save Admiralty. His goal was to persuade the Sitka and Juneau corporations to select other lands off Admiralty and to persuade the Angoon Natives to commit their lands to subsistence.[12] At first he had little success. He reported in July 1975 that the Sitka and Juneau leaders "told me they were not interested whatsoever in a compromise with us."[13] To his chagrin he discovered that many Native leaders were indistinguishable from white boosters. But there were other possibilities. The Interior Department and indirectly the Forest Service had to approve the land transfers, which created possibilities for delays and negotiations. Ultimately a series of suits and countersuits persuaded Goldbelt to look elsewhere.

Equally important were the tensions that had developed between Angoon and the outside groups. From the beginning the Angoon residents were wary of the logging plan; the money they received would be meager compensation for the destruction of the forest. Angoon elders listened to the Sealaska proposal and rejected it. The opposition of a respected elder—communicated in a taped Tlingit-language message sent to each of the other village elders—was particularly influential.[14] The Angoon leaders also began to work with the environmental groups. A prominent elder, Edward Gambel, recalled that "we were accused of going to bed with the Sierra Club. The Sierra Club had been trying to protect Admiralty Island for fifty years. It just happened that we were advocating the same thing."[15] Gambel's nephew, Sterling Bolima, who had recently returned from Seattle to work for the village corporation, became the intermediary. A canoe trip to Angoon in summer 1975 by Wayburn, Moorman, and Sandy Sagalkin, the new assistant attorney general, cemented the relationship,[16] and Bolima became the environmentalists' most important Native ally in the Southeast.

By fall 1975 the conflict between the Native groups had become part of the larger struggle over Admiralty. Angoon sued the secretary of the Interior to stop the urban Native corporations from obtaining the Admiralty lands. The Sierra Club filed a similar suit, and Shee Atika and Goldbelt countersued. In early 1976 the three suits were consolidated over the objections of the urban corporations. The litigation, coupled with attacks on clear-cutting in the southern Tongass and low pulp prices, were too much for Champion, which had been waiting impatiently since 1968. In March 1976 the company asked to be released from its 50-year contract. Forest Service officials, who had observed the continuing legal snarl with growing irritation, were furious and even considered legal action against Champion.[17] Regional Forester Charles Yates complained bitterly that it would take years to find a replacement for Champion. Sealaska's offer to take over the lease did not impress him.[18]

The Sierra Club won additional victories in the following months. Goldbelt agreed to accept forest lands off Admiralty, and Angoon committed itself to preserving its local lands. By 1978 Shee Atika was the only holdout. Its executive director had been involved in an earlier conflict with the Sierra Club in the Pacific Northwest and was uncompromisingly hostile. He was reported to have concluded secret deals with Alaska Pulp.[19] In any case, the conflict would continue for another decade, even after most of Admiralty Island had been preserved as a national monument.

The strategy honed in the Admiralty fight—holding the Forest Service to the letter of the law, mobilizing public opinion, and hoping that delays would ultimately sabotage the logging plans—also proved effective in opposing a harvest plan for Afognak Island in the Chugach National Forest. That sale also dated from 1968 and included virtually every tree on the rugged extension of Kodiak Island. Low prices led to delays, however, and in 1973 the Chugach managers renegotiated the contract to reduce the total cut. Still, the new plan would likely devastate the island's bear and deer populations and lead to extensive erosion of the island's thin volcanic soils.

The local community, consisting largely of fishermen, became alarmed. The Kodiak-Aleutian chapter of ACS spearheaded the opposition and had little trouble finding allies, including the area's legislators and the Alaska Department of Fish and Game. Hession arranged for Gordon Robinson, the Sierra Club's forestry expert, to evaluate the logging plan, and the club joined the ACS suit in 1974. Ultimately, public opposition and the lawsuit persuaded the timber company to abandon the project.[20] However, the regional Native corporation, Koniag, and the local village corporations quickly filled the void. They were, in the words of one activist, "very much anti-conservationist" and planned to log the islands as soon as they obtained title.[21]

The Afognak conflict underlined two features of the forestry conflicts of the 1970s. The first was the continuing preoccupation of the Forest Service with large-scale logging. Though the Chugach National Forest had relatively little commercially valuable timber and Forest Service managers there devoted more attention to recreation than their counterparts in the Tongass, the Afognak sale revealed their emphasis on logging. The second feature was the inherent conflict between logging and fishing. In Ketchikan and Juneau the prospect of additional jobs and profits had galvanized local residents against the Sierra Club. On Kodiak Island, where logging posed a threat to the economic status quo, most people opposed the Forest Service plan. The fishing community would prove to be the environmentalists' one reliable interest group ally.

THE CLEAR-CUT CONTROVERSY

Ten days after Hession's ill-fated November 1972 appearance at the Alaska Sports and Wildlife Club meeting in Ketchikan, a letter appeared in the *Ketchikan Daily News*. The authors were Darlene Larson and Alan and Sandra Stein, residents of Point Baker and Port Protection, two small fishing communities at the northern tip of Prince of Wales Island, the largest and most accessible of the coastal islands in the southern Tongass and part of the Ketchikan Pulp Company's 50-year contract area. Larson and the Steins wrote,

> We are anxious to prevent industrial and lumber demands ... from destroying a life style that has existed in harmony with nature for over a hundred years. ... The people who live here, do so under interesting circumstances ... the setting is highly esthetic, with their homes being simple structures constructed of surrounding materials, such as logs and shakes. The people are almost all fiercely independent and highly individualistic due to the fact that they live by their own hands—mainly by fishing.[22]

The previous summer, a contingent of Forest Service employees had surveyed the land and made plans for the roads, camps, and offshore log dumps that would accompany the logging. Clear-cutting would continue for a decade, until the local forests had been exhausted. Residents were appalled.

Two days later Dixie Baade replied in a private letter. She summarized Hession's recent experience in Ketchikan and a meeting with Senator Gravel. "We have been trying to get help from Congress in slowing down (at least) this steady onslaught of the chain saws," she explained. "It seems to me your letter may help ... particularly in regard to the impact this terrible large-scale clearcutting has on an entire way of life in southeast Alaska."[23]

This exchange marked the beginning of one of the least promising environmental battles of the decade. It featured the Forest Service and its allies on one side, and a handful of fishermen and their environmentalist allies on the other. Ten years earlier the Forest Service probably would not have worried about local residents, but as Baade and other environmentalists mobilized resistance to logging, more and more seemingly apolitical bystanders like the Point Baker–Port Protection protesters became involved.

Two individuals played critical roles in the protest. The first was Baade, who encouraged it, identified with the protesters' complaints and aspirations, opened doors for them, and made sure that their cause was not lost in the welter of forestry lawsuits. The second was Alan Stein, a recent arrival on Prince of Wales. A former Students for a Democratic Society activist at the University of Wisconsin, Stein had moved to Alaska with his wife and children as the student movement fell apart. The Steins settled at

Point Baker, an isolated village of about 30 people (Port Protection, with another 30 people, was two miles away) without electricity or telephones and a half-day boat ride from the nearest town. Like his neighbors, Stein fished for a living and built his own home. Ostensibly, he had forsaken politics for the rustic lifestyle of Point Baker. Then the Forest Service arrived, and Stein discovered that far from escaping modern capitalism, he had built his forest home directly in its path. At community meetings in August 1972 and February 1973, Forest Service managers explained their plans and solicited residents' reactions. As Regional Forester Richard Wilson explained to the Port Protection residents in early 1973, "You will have logging camps, log dumps, and roads. There will be a community of about 100 people, with families. That much is sure, but we can keep a road out of your communities." His listeners were not happy. "We want to keep this area the way it has been. This is a fishing community," one man protested. "Logging is coming. What we want to know is how far we can keep it back," added another. Stein then attacked the plan in its entirety and threatened a lawsuit. As a reporter noted, "frustration was openly evident at the meetings."[24]

With Baade's help, Stein and his neighbors had little trouble enlisting allies. In December Hession reported that he was following the conflict and that the Sierra Club Legal Defense Fund was pressuring the Forest Service to prepare an environmental impact statement for the area.[25] By early 1973 the Point Baker–Port Protection dispute increasingly resembled the Afognak Island conflict. In both cases local people spearheaded the protests and mobilized support by emphasizing the conflict between a policy that was supposed to boost the local economy and the likely effects of large-scale logging on fishing, the dominant local industry.

Yet the two cases soon diverged. By the time the Forest Service released its environmental impact statement in late 1973, the local opposition was in disarray and the future of the protest uncertain. Several obstacles had emerged in the intervening months. First, the Forest Service was at least superficially responsive. Wilson agreed not to extend logging roads into the coastal communities and, over the protests of Ketchikan Pulp managers, moved the proposed camp and log dump (an offshore storage facility that typically polluted the water and precluded other activities) away from the settled area. Later, when the company proposed buying the store at Port Protection, apparently to create a company town, he vetoed the purchase. Reminding company officials of their pledge to minimize their impact, he explained that "the amount of timber available ... depends on living up to these commitments to not impact the Point Baker–Port Protection communities."[26]

Second, the Point Baker–Port Protection residents were not as united as Baade had assumed. Their individualism made concerted activity difficult, and the outspoken Stein became a polarizing force. Opposition to him centered in Port Protection. When he argued in a letter to the *Ketchikan Daily News* that the logging plan was simply the first step in a larger Forest Service plan to build a highway system through Southeast Alaska, 21 Port Protection residents wrote to the paper disavowing his leadership.[27] Although they objected only to his self-appointed role as spokesperson, their complaints were troubling. If the protestors could not agree among themselves, what hope could they have of influencing the Forest Service?

The most serious problem, however, was the intense competition for attention and resources in the environmentalist camp. The many other lawsuits of 1970–1971 were already taxing the groups' resources. In June 1973 Hession suggested that ACS and the Tongass and Sitka conservation societies take the lead in a Point Baker–Port Protection lawsuit. Though the Sierra Club Legal Defense Fund would help, the Sierra Club itself would remain in the background because of the Champion suit.[28] Putting this plan into effect proved difficult. Baade wrote that "if financing could be assured, I think everyone would like to go ahead," but the ACS groups were strapped for funds and the $10,000 they would need was a huge obstacle.[29] Baade tried and failed to persuade the United Fishermen of Alaska to provide financial assistance.[30]

Yet the case did not die. Stein and a handful of neighbors, organized as the Point Baker Association, scraped together $2,000 and recruited Richard Folta, a Haines attorney active in the new Lynn Canal Conservation Society. Folta agreed to take the case pro bono, though he knew that his involvement would sour his relations with the Haines business community. Hession continued to help behind the scenes, and Gordon Robinson visited Point Baker to assist with an appeal to the Forest Service's environmental impact statement. The Tongass Conservation Society joined the Point Baker group in the suit.[31]

They originally expected to attack the Forest Service's plan to create a log-sorting yard and dump near Port Protection, but Wilson's flexibility foiled that strategy. Baade complained that "we have not yet had just the right bay or tideland … that we would want to make an issue of."[32] As the Point Baker activists studied the environmental impact statement, however, they realized that they had a far better target. They understood the importance of salmon streams and took it for granted that anything that disrupted them, such as clear-cutting, would reduce the fish population. Yet the scientific basis for that assumption was uncertain; earlier Forest Service studies had concluded that the fish losses were minimal and temporary. At precisely that time, however, Richard Myren, a U.S. Marine Fisheries scientist and Juneau Sierra Club activist, was completing a study that attacked the earlier studies on methodological grounds. Tree removal might well have a devastating impact on salmon reproduction, as the anecdotal evidence indicated. With Myren's help the activists made the destruction of salmon streams a central argument of their critique.[33]

They soon discovered other deficiencies in the environmental impact statement. Interviewing state and federal biologists, they discovered that the scientists had not been adequately prepared or given enough time to do their work, and agency managers had disregarded their reports. The biologists believed their investigations had been pointless gestures; the Forest Service had already decided to log the area.[34]

Having exhausted the Forest Service appeals process by the end of 1974, Folta filed a lawsuit (Zieske v. Butz) in February 1975. He charged the Forest Service with violating federal and state water pollution statutes and its own 1897 Organic Act, which prohibited clear-cutting. This remarkable assertion grew out of a 1973 West Virginia federal circuit court decision, upheld by an appeals court in August 1974. The West Virginia decisions halted clear-cutting in the Monongahela National Forest and marked the first successful legal attack on a major feature of Forest Service policy. The agency and its industry supporters were aghast.[35]

Zieske v. Butz was tried in December. Folta did not expect a favorable decision from Judge James Von der Heydt, who had refused to grant a temporary injunction and was considered hostile to environmental suits.[36] To his surprise Von der Heydt embraced the Monongahela decision. Though the judge limited his ruling to the area around Point Baker, the implications for other areas of the Tongass were obvious. Furthermore, if the Forest Service appealed and lost, the clear-cutting ban would apply to the entire Pacific Northwest. The industry was temporarily paralyzed.[37] Alaska politicians joined elected officials from other states in demanding legislation to overturn the decision.

Thus, the protests of a handful of settlers on Prince of Wales Island contributed to an emerging state and national debate over Forest Service policy. The impact on the northern tip of Prince of Wales Island was less favorable. Von der Heydt's decision did not affect road building, camp building, and other nonlogging activities. The judge also dismissed the environmentalists' other charges, including their assertion that logging destroyed salmon streams. Folta prepared an appeal, but he was unable to win financial backing from the Alaska groups or the national organizations. He acknowledged that "we would have a very difficult time overturning the Court's decision on appeal."38 Ultimately, the Point Baker–Port Protection activists were unable to prevent the resumption of large-scale clear-cutting, and as the forest around Point Baker and Point Protection was logged, many of them moved away.

WILDERNESS BATTLES

Although the battles between the Forest Service and environmental groups continued through the 1970s, environmentalists sensed the weakness of their position. Since nearly every available tree would be required to meet the commitments to Ketchikan and Alaska Pulp, a purely defensive response would only delay the inevitable. Through collusive bidding and other illegal competitive maneuvers, the companies had eliminated most of the independent timber companies and by 1976 had monopolized timber sales outside the 50-year contract areas. They appeared to be becoming stronger.[39] What could be done?

By now the conventional answer was to utilize the Wilderness Act to declare the most notable areas of the Tongass and Chugach national forests off-limits to the loggers. The 1970s had seen a dramatic increase in the number of designated wilderness areas in national forests and parks, especially in western states, and an ongoing campaign for additional wilderness, spearheaded by the national environmental organizations.[40] The West Chichagof–Yakobi and Admiralty wilderness plans pointed the way for Alaska activists. The problem was that only Congress could create wilderness areas, and Congress rarely acted without the cooperation of the state's senators.

In late 1971 Congress had authorized the first Alaska wilderness areas, all small, remote parts of wildlife refuges. It omitted Glacier Bay and Katmai national monuments because of mining claims and local opposition. Governor Egan had told reporters that he had "higher hopes" for those areas.[41] Proposals for wilderness areas in the Tongass would likely encounter vigorous opposition from boosters and Forest Service managers, who had "higher hopes" for those areas as well. In Southeast Alaska, as Bob Weeden explained, the movement for wilderness was "a counterweight to timber sales."[42]

As cutting spread into areas that had distinctive recreational or aesthetic values or were critical to local subsistence activities, the wilderness campaign escalated and became more confrontational. The environmentalists had won a temporary victory in 1971, when Regional Forester Charles Yates announced that logging on West Chicagof and Yakobi Islands would be postponed for five years while the Forest Service reevaluated the area.[43] Yet Yates was careful not to imply that the delay might lead to a change of policy. Ranger Hank Hays, assigned to oversee the study, was "a pleasant person" who had little authority.[44] After a meeting in early 1973, Rich Gordon reported that Hays had referred to environmental organizations as "the enemy."[45] Gordon Robinson noted rumors that Hays "is being forced to take positions in favor of the timber industry."[46] No one believed that the eventual decision would be any different from the one that had been expected in 1971.

A second "victory" came in January 1973, when Yates made a long-awaited announcement of new wilderness study areas as part of the larger roadless area review and evaluation process.[47] He named six, including Tracy Arm, south of Juneau, and Granite Fiords, east of Ketchikan. Together they totaled 2.5 million acres, mostly rock and ice with little industrial potential. The one exception was Petersburg Creek, a river valley near the town of Petersburg, whose preservation was the raison d'être of the new Petersburg Conservation Society. Otherwise, the omissions, which included West Chichagof–Yakobi and Admiralty Islands, were the most notable feature of the announcement. Mark Ganopole attacked the selections as unrepresentative. The Sierra Club castigated Yates's choices as "inadequate and misleading" and urged activists to submit their own proposals to Forest Service Chief John McGuire.[48]

Southeastern environmentalists had already agreed on a dozen priority areas in the Tongass and Chugach forests. Their list included Granite Fiords and Tracy Arm, though they wanted larger areas than Yates proposed—the larger East Behm Canal region or the still larger "Misty Fiords" area instead of just Granite Fiords, for example. Also on the list were West Chichagof–Yakobi and Admiralty Islands, Afognak Island, the forested parts of southern Baranof Island, and the eastern side of the Kenai Moose Range.[49] In response to the Sierra Club call, they agreed to prepare a detailed proposal by mid-April, the Forest Service deadline.

The Forest Service's new Tongass land use plan, released in January 1975, was the agency's unofficial response. In preparation since 1971, it was an outline of the foresters' long-term plans and inevitably reflected the impact of the protests, counterproposals, and lawsuits of the intervening years. As a result it and an accompanying draft environmental impact statement attracted wide interest.[50] In large measure the documents reaffirmed the status quo. The plan left no doubt that the West Chichagof–Yakobi study would recommend new logging, that the Forest Service continued to view Admiralty Island as a source of timber, and that the environmentalists' wilderness proposals would not receive serious consideration. James Moorman described the plan as "an attempt to launder environmental assessment and wilderness consideration … out of their future management decision."[51] SEACC castigated it as "grossly distorted in favor of utilization values."[52] A leading activist concluded that it reflected "that same dichotomy of vast management authority and astounding incompetence."[53]

For environmentalists, the land use plan was the last straw. Though they hoped to stop clear-cutting and other destructive activities, they became more certain that the only long-term solution was the Wilderness Act. Meeting in Sitka in early March, they created their own "maps on the floor" committee and identified 45 critical areas of the Tongass. They were careful, even conservative, proposing only nine "instant" wilderness areas. (The list included four of the Forest Service's study areas, plus West Chichagof and Yakobi Islands and the Sweetwater-Honker Divide, one of the few undisturbed sections of Prince of Wales Island.) They also proposed one wild and scenic river and 17 "roadless recreation" regions, a designation they hoped would circumvent the Forest Service's continuing insistence that official wilderness areas bear no evidence of human activity. They included Admiralty Island and East Behm Canal in this category. Finally, they listed 18 "watersheds"—areas adjacent to lakes and rivers that would be off-limits to loggers in accord with a "water edge policy" designed to protect critical wildlife habitat and recreational zones.[54]

To emphasize the seriousness of their commitment to the 45 areas, they launched a "wildlands" study to provide up-to-date data on each area. To head it, Jack Hession suggested Pete Brabeck, a Coloradoan who had participated in a similar survey there as a university student. Brabeck did the initial work and then recruited two friends, Ted Whitesell and Gordon Rodda, who had also worked on the Colorado project. Edgar Wayburn provided $1,500, and local contributors added another $500 to cover their expenses. Whitesell and Rodda worked through summer 1975, visiting Juneau, Sitka, Petersburg, and Ketchikan. They concluded that "no quick and dirty survey could profess thoroughness." In September Rodda returned to Colorado, but Whitesell remained to finish the work. By December he had prepared detailed reports on six areas and less complete reports on the others. The reports would allow environmentalists "to respond on short notice to any challenge with voluminous factual documentation." He also persuaded SEACC to employ another Colorado veteran, Mary Ellen Cuthbertson, to continue the project.[55]

By that time, many of the 45 wildlands were under siege. Preparing for a new cycle of logging, the Forest Service issued environmental impact statements on West Chichagof and Yakobi Islands and other areas. SEACC leaders responded angrily, but there was little they could do.

At this point Judge Von der Heydt's just-released *Zieske v. Butz* decision became an influence. The clear-cutting ban did not directly affect any of the 45 areas, but it raised doubts about the legality of clear-cutting in Southeast Alaska and discouraged timber producers from making new commitments. Environmentalists rejoiced. Ted Whitesell recalled that he "knew almost immediately" that his "life would have to change."[56] He decided to stay, and Hession hired him as his assistant for Southeast Alaska.

The new round of logging plans and the prospect of congressional action also had a profound impact on SEACC. Since its formation in 1970, the organization had been a loose-knit coalition of community protest groups. Its strength lay in its ability to respond to specific threats. Since regional foresters could adjust plans to local circumstances, this structure made sense. Yet Monongahela and *Zieske v. Butz* raised the possibility of fundamental changes in Forest Service policy. If SEACC were to capitalize on that possibility, it would have to act quickly and decisively.

On February 7, 1976, 50 representatives of southeastern environmental groups met in Juneau to reorganize SEACC. They decided to create a more centralized organization, capable of dealing with the Forest Service in Washington as well as in Southeast Alaska. A committee drew up by-laws; Dick Folta agreed to handle the legal details, and Kay Greenough and Ron Hawk volunteered to serve as co-executive directors. Greenough had been a founding member of the Steller Society and the Juneau group of the Sierra Club but had left Alaska after her marriage failed. She returned shortly before the Juneau meeting, and local activist Cliff Lobaugh urged her to attend.[57] Hawk was a young engineer who had worked for the state.

Drawn to the environmental movement, he was eager for a more active role.[58] Like Greenough, he sensed the potential for dramatic change. In April SEACC representatives gathered again and approved the reorganization. A year earlier SEACC had been almost moribund. Now it had a "staff" of Greenough, Hawk, Whitesell, and Cuthbertson.

Its first challenge was the congressional battle over clear-cutting. Timber interests, AFL-CIO, and most western politicians supported a bill introduced by Senator Hubert Humphrey (D-MN) that simply removed the clear-cutting ban. A competing bill, drafted by James Moorman of the Sierra Club Legal Defense Fund, after consultations with Gordon Robinson and other environmentalists, was introduced by Senator Jennings Randolph (D-WV). It limited the size of clear-cuts, protected stream banks, and imposed other restrictions on forest managers. With Democrats divided, the Randolph bill had little chance. The real issue was the environmentalists' ability to force Congress to add some of Randolph's restrictions to the Humphrey bill. Humphrey himself favored revision, and the timber industry's champion, Senator Mark Hatfield (R-OR), was not inflexible. Alaska Governor Hammond favored a two-year waiver of the Monongahela decision while Congress devised a permanent solution that included restrictions on clear-cutting, protection for stream banks, and some wilderness designations. Congressional leaders, however, were wary of temporary measures. They turned instead to Senator Gravel, who supported the Humphrey bill but was sensitive to criticism of the Forest Service. Gravel called for stream protection and a genuine commitment to multiple use. Together with Hammond, he urged a study of the Tongass by a blue-ribbon panel whose recommendations would bind the Forest Service.

Whitesell, Hawk, and Greenough all spent several weeks in Washington during the congressional session. They worked with a coalition of environmental organizations called Save Our National Forests that was promoting the Randolph bill. Together with Alan Stein, Jack Calvin, and Celia Hunter, they testified at the Senate hearings and "made a definite impression" with their stories of Forest Service negligence. They found the House Agriculture Committee less receptive. Nevertheless, Whitesell and Stein testified, recounting their experiences and impressions.[59] The Alaskans also lobbied individual senators and representatives and complained to Forest Service officials about the behavior of the Tongass managers.

Their immediate goal was to persuade Gravel to back a specific Tongass amendment. By May the Senate negotiators agreed that the Tongass required special treatment. Gravel then asked SEACC, Alaska Pulp, and Sealaska to develop a compromise measure that would circumvent the Forest Service. Whitesell and Alaska Pulp's attorney met several times and found that they had common interests. Whitesell wrote to Wayburn,

> As far-fetched as it may sound, a compromise bill may not be totally out of the question. The reason is that SEACC has raised the threat of numerous suits over timber plans and the industry wants to see if they can get rid of these legal hassles. ... Industry representatives therefore seek a bill which would give us most of the areas we are determined to fight for (as study areas) in return for a legislative guarantee ... that we will settle for what we get in this bill.[60]

Gravel organized public meetings in July to elicit comment on a "once and for all" examination of the 45 areas. Although many supporters spoke in favor of the compromise, some industry representatives were unyielding. Ketchikan Pulp managers organized a crowd that took over the Ketchikan hearing and accused Gravel of capitulating to environmentalists. The Juneau Chamber of Commerce was also hostile.[61] A chastened Gravel quickly distanced himself from the proposed amendment. A month later the Senate Agriculture Committee held hearings in Alaska on the Humphrey bill. SEACC activists appeared at every session and received respectful hearings. Even in Ketchikan, a "moderate tone" prevailed.[62]

Yet these hearings, like Gravel's, had no apparent effect on the legislation. In September the Senate passed a strengthened Humphrey bill with no specific Tongass provisions. The House passed a bill that merely repealed the clear-cutting ban. The conference committee split the difference, adding restrictions from the Senate bill, including a vague reference to renegotiating the 50-year contracts but no Tongass provisions and no wilderness.[63] Most environmental groups opposed the final legislation, as did the timber industry. The National Forest Management Act imposed mild restrictions on clear-cutting, provided modest safeguards for wildlife habitat, and required additional planning. While registering the rise of public dissatisfaction with the Forest Service, it did not significantly alter the agency's managerial prerogatives.

Having failed in Washington, SEACC leaders devoted fall and winter 1976 to appeals against numerous Forest Service logging plans. At first they were hopeful that the new regional forester, John Sandor, would be more flexible and sympathetic. Ron Hawk explained to Sandor that SEACC members "do not trust the Forest Service. ... Time and again we feel that we have been deceived." Criticism of Forest Service policy was

"either misinterpreted or deliberately misused ... to condemn us for interference."[64] Once again, however, SEACC leaders were disappointed.
Sandor postponed any action on West Chichagof–Yakobi until he could
review the staff reports, but in the end he simply reaffirmed the earlier
decision to log about half the area and permit mining in the other,
reserved part. He was no more receptive to the other appeals.

SEACC activists soon found themselves overwhelmed. The avalanche of
environmental impact statements was so great that they were "in an
impossible situation." SEACC had barely enough money to "get the
appeals going. Legal proceedings would be impossible for us."[65] They
hoped for assistance from the national organizations, but the Sierra Club
and the Wilderness Society, on the eve of a renewed campaign for additions to the federal conservation systems under Section 17d(2) of the
Alaska Native Claims Settlement Act, were wary of more lawsuits.[66]
Nevertheless, Moorman did pursue the West Chicagof–Yakobi appeal. He
interviewed Sandor, whom he found "very stiff and cold ... actually less
sympathetic than was Yates," his predecessor.[67]

By September 1976 the Forest Service had partially logged 6 of the 45
areas and was preparing to clear-cut 14 others. Despite all the protests,
appeals, threats, and negotiations, very little had changed since Jack
Hession had been mobbed in Ketchikan and Dixie Baade had mobilized
support for the Point Baker fishermen. Commenting on an updated version of the Tongass land use plan, released in August 1976, Jack Calvin
provided a fitting epitaph for this chapter in the history of Southeast
Alaska. The Forest Service, he wrote,

> ... is learning the language of conservation while continuing its obsessive policy of
> destroying old-growth forest. It talks of multiple use while betraying ... a terrible
> lack of sympathy for or understanding of all forest functions except the production
> of cellulose. While acknowledging the demands for preserving selected parts of the
> forest it continues to fight to the bitter end against wilderness (except for its own
> treeless selections) and all other withdrawals from its insatiable cutting plans.[68]

The events of 1972–1976 were depressingly consistent with the outcome of the oil pipeline controversy and the deliberations over potential
park and wildlife refuge sites. Like Congress, the Forest Service was indifferent if not hostile to the environmentalists' campaign for the Alaskan
wilderness, insisting that Alaska was primarily a repository of exploitable
natural resources. Yet the environmentalists were not as isolated as they
imagined. Alaskans might find it hard to resist the boosters' promise of

easy riches, but they, like most Americans, were increasingly sensitive to the social and environmental costs of industrial growth. By the mid-1970s many of them, including many who had no interest in environmental activism per se, were ready to join the environmentalists in attacking unbridled growth.

CHAPTER 6

OIL AGE DISCONTENTS

In early 1974 Alyeska Pipeline Service Company lawyers negotiated a far-reaching labor agreement with the international unions whose members would build the Alaska oil pipeline. They offered generous wages and comfortable living conditions in exchange for a no-strike pledge. With the national economy in recession and unemployment rising, the agreement was a coup for the unions. Accordingly, in March a delegation of satisfied leaders presented the contract to their local organizations in Anchorage. Soon after they began their presentation, Jesse Carr, secretary-treasurer of Teamsters Local 959, interrupted. "This is a bucket of shit. ... I don't know what in hell you're all standing here saying this stuff for, because it's lousy. ... I'm not signing it. And nobody in the International is going to sign it for me."[1] No additional discussion was necessary. The contract was renegotiated to include even more generous overtime rates and a "safety" clause that effectively negated the no-strike pledge.

Jesse Carr was arguably the most colorful figure to emerge from the Alaska pipeline melodrama. His career had been a rags-to-riches story. Moving to Alaska in the late 1940s, he found a job as a truck driver and became a Teamsters organizer. An aggressive negotiator, he soon dominated the local union. In the 1950s he won a statewide jurisdiction for Local 959 and began to organize outside the transportation sector. Recognizing the potential of the new state government, he became an ally of Governor William Egan. By the end of the 1960s he represented 10,000 Alaska workers and had become the state's foremost labor leader. In the process he cut many corners. Charged in federal indictments with embezzlement and extortion, he escaped conviction but acquired a reputation for unsavory behavior.[2]

In the meantime the pipeline project was the opportunity of a lifetime. Carr not only won generous wages and benefits for his members but extended his reach to thousands of nonpipeline workers. In one notable incident, Fairbanks school principals besieged his office, demanding to be organized. By the mid-1970s Carr's Teamsters represented 80 occupations and one-third of Alaska's workers. In the words of one observer, they had become "the most politically powerful group in Alaska."[3]

A pragmatist in his dealings with employers and politicians, Carr had little use for environmentalists. He hired many outgoing Egan administration officials in 1975 and called the new governor, Jay Hammond, a "son of a bitch."[4] Any legislator who was overly sensitive to environmental problems could expect a Teamsters-inspired challenge in the next election.

For a few years in the 1970s Carr was a potent, flamboyant symbol of Alaska boosterism and the social strains that accompanied the pipeline project. His ubiquitous presence prompted many Alaskans to ask themselves whether the booster approach, with its cozy insider deals and alliances, truly served the interests of the state and its citizens. Their rebellion against the excesses of the pipeline era temporarily redefined Alaska's environmental community and created opportunities that had not existed earlier.

The most serious dislocations were recorded in the census data. Alaska's population rose from 330,000 in 1973 to 413,000 in 1977, and then declined to 400,000 in 1979–1980. The total included 4,000 migrants from other states in 1972–1973, 10,000 in 1973–1974, 34,000 in 1974–1975, and 23,000 in 1975–1976. Then, as the pipeline neared completion, the flow reversed. In 1976–1977, 4000 people left the state, followed by 4,000 the following year and 10,000 in 1978–1979.[5]

Population growth was highly concentrated in the towns along the pipeline route. Fairbanks attracted about one-third of the newcomers, growing from 46,000 in 1973 to 63,000 in 1975.[6] Rents and property values skyrocketed, traffic congestion became a severe problem (particularly in the winter, when the intense cold turned exhaust fumes into ice fog), and the traditional business center became an area of seedy bars and brawls. Crime, divorce, and delinquency rose alarmingly, and old-timers bemoaned the rip-off atmosphere.[7] Valdez and the smaller towns along the pipeline route experienced similar upheavals.

Compounding those problems was the behavior of the business community. Most Fairbanks merchants sought to "maximize their profits by minimizing their expenditures for such things as taxes and capital investments."[8] Their shortsightedness encouraged the rise of new shopping centers on the city's periphery and the eventual collapse of downtown retailing. Alaska's business leaders had argued that their promotional schemes would benefit everyone. But when the boom finally arrived, it created opportunities for exploitation that favored insiders at the expense of other citizens. Another source of unhappiness was, ironically, the shallowness of the boom. Alyeska executives had predicted expenditures of $1 million per day in the Fairbanks area alone. In reality, their spending averaged about $800,000 per day, including taxes and wages that were not disbursed locally. A more realistic total for Fairbanks was $500,000, and the actual figure may have been closer to $200,000.[9] The impact outside the immediate construction area was even more muted.[10]

Yet it was the indirect effects of the pipeline that really mattered. The construction boom would last three years, but oil would flow through the pipeline for decades. The state now had a long-term revenue source. Would it follow the example of the Fairbanks merchants or the advice of University of Alaska social scientists who advocated planning to improve the quality of life?[11] The behavior of the legislature provided an early answer.

The state had begun to anticipate the bonanza in 1969, when the Prudhoe Bay leases had brought in an unexpected $900 million. Although that was a one-time payment, it suggested the possibilities that would arise with additional lease sales, royalties, and taxes. And as Bob Weeden would observe in 1978, "the tap of government growth, once turned on, couldn't be turned off."[12] In 1960 the state's operating budget was $28 million, 98 percent of which came from taxes; in 1978, the budget was $800 million, only 39 percent of which came from tax collections.[13] Government employment rose by more than 15,000 in the 1970s. Per capita state expenditures rose to more than $2,000 per person, twice as high as state expenditures in New York or California.[14]

Dissatisfaction was apparent almost from the beginning of the boom. A prominent banker's dismissal of the social costs—"We'll just have to hold our noses and live through it"—added to the anxiety level.[15] In Fairbanks, a new Social Concerns Committee of the Fairbanks Council of Churches began to criticize the booster approach. Though relatively little of this criticism focused on environmental issues, it did emphasize a growing unease about Alaska's future. Environmentalists discovered a surprising number of allies.

THE ENVIRONMENTAL MOVEMENT MATURES

However disastrous the pipeline may have been for Alaska's environment, it was a boon to Alaska's environmental movement. Alaska Conservation Society (ACS) membership peaked at about 1,100 in the mid-1970s, the Sierra Club chapter grew to about 600, and Friends of the Earth to about 200, and the organizations achieved greater public visibility and acceptance. In 1972 and 1973, as the pipeline debates dragged on, the state legislature adopted a resolution asking the governor to sue the Sierra Club for $1 billion. The Associated Contractors printed 10,000 bumper stickers with the slogan "Sierra Go Home." Jack Hession warned of "an atmosphere of panic and hate" similar to the anti-Native hysteria that preceded passage of the Alaska Native Claims Settlement Act.[16] But the beginning of pipeline construction shifted the focus. Apart from a few insiders, no one was entirely happy with the ensuing boom. To many people, the environmentalists' warnings and complaints suddenly made sense.

During the mid-1970s Fairbanks environmentalists operated in the eye of the hurricane. The informal alliance of Alyeska, the chamber of commerce, and the Teamsters kept them on the defensive, despite the city's mounting problems. At one point the mayor described environmentalists as "anti-God, anti-man, and anti-mind."[17] ACS temporarily lost its best-known local members when Bob Weeden joined the new Hammond administration and Celia Hunter became president and then interim executive director of the Wilderness Society. The local Sierra Club group collapsed, leaving the burden of local activism squarely on the shoulders of Jim Kowalsky and the Fairbanks Environmental Center.[18]

Kowalsky managed to recruit several local business executives for his board, demonstrating that the Fairbanks establishment was not monolithic.[19] Nevertheless, he faced a continuous struggle. A $3,000 grant from ACS in early 1972 was a godsend. Kowalsky took himself off the payroll and hired an assistant at $400 per month to manage the center's day-to-day operations. He sublet rooms in the old Seventh Avenue house to other groups, enabling the center to maintain an office, library, and meeting room for $40 per month.[20] But local contributions were still inadequate. By the end of 1973 Kowalsky was back on the payroll (at $200 per month), with a part-time administrative assistant. The center's 1974 budget projected expenditures of $11,000 and revenues of only $7,300. Kowalsky confessed that "we are quite badly in need."[21]

The pipeline boom probably saved the center. Memberships and revenues increased in 1974 as the costs of the boom became more apparent, and the center hired Stan and Pat Senner, veteran Friends of the Earth activists, as office managers. Freed of administrative responsibilities, Kowalsky became a whirlwind of activity: he wrote a weekly column for the *News-Miner*, made regular radio broadcasts, spoke at countless public meetings, and generally was a thorn in the side of the local business community.[22] By mid-1976, when he resigned to work full-time for Friends of the Earth, the center was an established community institution.[23] Kowalsky recalled that it was "an attempt to sneak conservation in the back door ... when reactions to outside conservation efforts in Alaska brought negative and volitile responses. ... [However] the lines have blurred somewhat since Texas [i.e., the pipeline workers] had occupied Alaska."[24]

The Alaska Center for the Environment in Anchorage had a markedly different history. It operated in a less frenetic environment, had a larger base to draw upon, and had larger ambitions. The initial budget provided for an executive director at $1,000 per month, a secretary at $700 per month, and total expenditures of $60,000 per year.[25] ACS contributed $5,000, the Sierra Club Foundation $4,500, the Wilderness Society $2,000, and local donors pledged nearly $3,000. Jim Kross, a local activist, became executive director. Its headquarters on Sixth Avenue included a library and meeting rooms.

Yet many issues remained unresolved. "Jim Kross is still seeking guidance as to how his time is to be allocated," the board reported in February 1972. One concern was the balance between local and statewide problems. Kross felt "he should be spending his time on larger issues," but Bob Weeden and others objected that that would duplicate the work of ACS and the Sierra Club. A related question was the center's political role. Kross proposed to be active but preserve the organization's nonpartisan, tax-exempt character.[26]

Directly or indirectly, the board addressed both questions by embracing an innovative publishing venture. Wary of the high costs of printing and mailing a newsletter, it appointed a committee to investigate "the possibility of distributing the newsletter via the *Anchorage Daily News*."[27] The lesser of the two Anchorage papers, the *Daily News* was eager to compete with Robert Atwood's *Daily Times*. For $350 per issue it offered to add a special section, prepared by the center, that would go to all 15,000 *Daily News* subscribers. This was the origin of the monthly *Northern Light*, a lively and provocative survey of Alaska environmental issues.

The decision to publish the *Northern Light* meant that the center had to find authors and editors and, above all, a steady income. By May 1972 most of the grant money had been spent, and contributions were averaging only about $200 a month. Local activist Pete Martin issued a warning: the center "is facing financial difficulties and may not be able to continue into the summer unless additional sources of money can be obtained."[28] Kross's suggested solution only exacerbated the crisis. He proposed to do contract research while volunteers ran the center and prepared the *Northern Light*. Despite the severity of the center's financial problems, many members believed this solution was inconsistent with their mission. Relations between Kross and the board deteriorated. A major clash occurred in late August, when he insisted on pursuing his strategy and President Chuck Kongisberg publicly reprimanded him.[29] Kross resigned in October, and the center became an all-volunteer operation.

For the next year the center's future remained uncertain. Konigsberg was succeeded by Helen Nienhauser, who worked as a full-time volunteer, often accompanied by her young children. By the end of April 1973, "totally burned out," she resigned.[30] A six-member executive committee succeeded her. Odette Foster agreed to manage the office until a permanent replacement was found. Additional help came from an unexpected source. Nienhauser had been trying to recruit summer interns from Richard Cooley's environmental studies program at the University of California at Santa Cruz. Her efforts seemingly had failed when Peter Scholes, a Santa Cruz student who was traveling independently in Alaska, unexpectedly appeared. He was quickly enlisted. Sharon Cissna, a member of the executive committee, "found him temporary lodging and the executive committee will figure out where we go from here."[31]

In the meantime the leadership issue remained. Nienhauser recalled that she "was almost ready to throw in the towel but Odette and ... Sharon Cissna were not."[32] They organized an August retreat for board members and volunteers. Out of these discussions emerged a new structure. Rather than a single director, they created a shared executive. Five volunteer direc tors would each be responsible for one day per week. Each director would keep a detailed log of activities for the next day's director. Together, they formed a coordinating committee to set policy. The board also decided that each of its members had to volunteer in some capacity. Those who were unable or unwilling to participate were asked to resign. Nearly half of the board members left.

The new organization reinvigorated the Anchorage center. With lower costs and a corps of activist volunteers, it was able to offer additional services. Its Wednesday "sack lunch" attracted large groups. Lectures, slide shows, and workshops augmented day-to-day educational activities. The center attracted summer interns from Santa Cruz and other institutions. Scholes returned during summer 1974 and remained for six months. His successor, Dee Frankfourth, spent spring 1975 in Juneau, monitoring the legislature. Many center volunteers were active in Jay Hammond's 1974 gubernatorial campaign. By that time some board members worried that the center had "grown to the point that it is turning off or turning away volunteers who would contribute time and talent ... if they felt ACE had any meaningful direction."[33]

Meanwhile, an annual fund drive stabilized the center's finances. The 1973 drive, headed by Walt Parker, raised $5,000. The 1974 campaign, chaired by Joe Josephson, raised $16,000. The 1975 goal was $27,000, enough to hire a professional director. Chancey Croft, the Democratic state Senate leader, agreed to serve as honorary chair. With the help of a concert by folksinger Peter Seeger, the center raised $20,000, a considerable achievement but still not enough to pay a full-time salary and publish the *Northern Light*. What should it do? Robert Atwood provided the answer. Atwood's printing company now put out both Anchorage newspapers, and he suddenly doubled the cost of the *Northern Light*, making it prohibitively expensive. The center's reluctant decision to scrap the *Northern Light* reduced its budget by $5,000, enabling it to hire a full-time executive director, Paul Lowe.

The center's volunteers provide a snapshot of grass-roots environmentalism in the mid-1970s. Fourteen of 17 who were profiled in various issues of the *Northern Light* were women. Most were in their 20s and 30s

(Millie Johns, a "longtime homesteader," was the notable exception), college graduates, recent arrivals, and leaders of activist organizations. Helen
Nienhauser had graduated from Brown University and moved to Alaska in
1959. By the early 1970s she had written a hiker's guide to south-central
Alaska and headed a local abortion rights organization. Sharon Cissna
arrived in 1967 after graduating from the University of Washington. A
founder of the Sierra Club chapter, she also headed the citizens' committee that pressured the legislature to create a state park system. Peg Tileston
graduated from Earlham College and moved to Alaska in 1972 with her
husband, who was a planner with the Bureau of Land Management. She
organized a campaign to combat booster dominance of the local media
and served as secretary of the Anchorage Parks and Recreation Council.[34]
The others had similar backgrounds and avocations. Lanie Fleischer headed the Parks and Recreation Council, Odette Foster edited the Sierra Club
newsletter, Mary Pat Brudie was an officer of the local League of Women
Voters chapter, Joanne Merrick was active in a mountain rescue organization, and Barbara Caraway volunteered at a free clinic. Among the men,
Bob Childers had worked for Jack Hession on the Afognak logging suit,
David Chell was a freelance filmmaker, and Jim Summer taught at a local
high school.[35]

Despite its dramatic growth, environmentalism still attracted the kinds
of people who had founded the Alaska Conservation Society a decade and
a half earlier. Educated, idealistic, influenced by contemporary social
movements, they would have been comfortable at a meeting of the Sierra
Club in San Francisco or the Appalachian Mountain Club in Boston. The
one notable change since the 1960s, the growing prominence of women,
was suggestive of the broader changes in gender roles that were also a hallmark of the era. But the women's backgrounds were similar to those of
their male colleagues, and they were able to make substantial commitments to the Alaska Center for the Environment because they were full-
time homemakers and mothers (though the rapid turnover in their ranks
reflected the lure of full-time jobs). The more significant difference from
the early 1960s was their broadened perspective. Like their predecessors,
these activists opposed destructive development schemes, but they were
interested in a wide range of other environmental causes as well. If traditional conservationists had been too narrowly focused, the environmentalists of the 1970s risked losing "meaningful direction."[36]

The other new organizations of the 1970s had many similarities. In 1974
residents of several small communities near Mount McKinley Park organ-

ized to oppose mining and other threats. The Denali Citizens Council represented a cross-section of local people, though its board of directors included only one "businessman and homesteader"; the others were scientists, photographers, and writers.[37] Trustees for Alaska, an Anchorage-based organization of attorneys, also dated from 1974. Organized with the assistance of the Natural Resources Defense Council, it divided the burden of suits and appeals with the local branch of the Sierra Club Legal Defense Fund.[38] The first Native environmental organization, Nunam Kitlutsisti ("Protector of the Land" in the Yupik language), appeared in 1973. The Association of Village Council Presidents in the Yukon-Kuskokwim area sought to preserve subsistence opportunities and traditional lifestyles. When Calista, the area's regional corporation, signed a drilling agreement with Shell Oil, the village leaders became alarmed about possible oil spills and habitat destruction. Under Harold Sparck and David Friday (and with modest financial assistance from the Wilderness Society), Nunam Kitlutsisti publicized environmental dangers in the area.[39]

To Alaska and national environmental leaders, the organization of Nunam Kitlutsisti briefly revived the dream of an environmentalist-Native coalition based on a shared preservationist ethic. By 1975 there were encouraging developments among Kodiak Island and North Slope Natives as well; Mike McCloskey predicted the emergence of "similar groups" in each of the Native regions.[40] But the environmentalists were disappointed. The Native communities were sharply divided between traditionalists and advocates of moneymaking projects and often unable to act.[41] Jack Hession summarized the limits of Native-environmentalist cooperation:

An assertion often heard among Alaska conservationists is that Alaska Natives are our natural political allies. ... Actual political experience has been that we work with the Natives on some issues ... but oppose them on others.[42]

A notable example of this on-again, off-again relationship was a plan for a Nunamiut national park in the central Brooks Range. The plan grew out of collaboration between the Arctic Slope Native Association, the Nunamiut Village Corporation (the Inupiat community at Anaktuvuk Pass, in the Brooks Range), and David Hickok's planning group at the University of Alaska. The Nunamiut were concerned about preserving traditional lifestyles; Arctic Slope Native Association leaders worried about state encroachment on their lands, particularly after the 1973 out-of-court settlement opened several areas of the southern Brooks Range to state selection; and Hickok was interested in wilderness preservation. In April 1973 the president of the association called for a Gates of the Arctic park with joint Native–Park Service management. Subsequent negotiations with Park Service planner John Kauffman led to a proposal for a two-section park on either side of a cooperatively managed Nunamiut national wildlands, embracing Anaktuvuk Pass and the surrounding area. Interior Secretary Rogers C. B. Morton approved the plan, but the Office of Management and Budget vetoed it. A bill introduced by Senator Henry Jackson died in committee. By that time Kauffman and his Park Service colleagues had had second thoughts about the plan, prompted by suspicions that Native leaders saw the wildlands as a way to enhance their own development plans.[43]

OIL AGE POLITICS

In 1973 Governor William Egan had formidable credentials as an anti-environmentalist. He relentlessly promoted the pipeline, attacked the Section 17d(2) withdrawals in the Alaska Native Claims Settlement Act, packed the Land Use Planning Commission with political allies, opposed wilderness legislation, and supported the Tongass logging plans. He was also personally hostile to environmentalists. After his 1974 defeat, activist Ginny Harris rejoiced that the environmental groups would no longer have to worry about the state "trying to pull a sneaky every time we turn around."[44] Yet for all his shortcomings, Egan was not a creation of the chamber of commerce. He had begun his career as a shopkeeper in Valdez, where the Guggenheims and the Alaska Syndicate were as unpopular as the federal government. He had entered politics as a protégé of Ernest Gruening and Bob Bartlett and shared their suspicions of big business. In 1971 he proposed state ownership of the pipeline in order to keep an eye on the oil companies. That idea proved too ambitious for the legislature, but it did suggest that Egan's brand of boosterism was not synonymous with capitulation to the oil industry.

By 1973, however, Egan was in trouble. Government employment and expenses were rising, and Egan's ties to organized labor made wage or spending cuts virtually impossible. His only choice was to increase revenues, which may explain his behavior during the following months. In a series of convoluted negotiations with the legislature and the oil companies, he seemingly betrayed his own principles by selling out to the oil industry.[45] And then he and his Department of Natural Resources commissioner, Charles Herbert, made an even more critical blunder.

Fishing, traditionally Alaska's first or second industry, sustained many small communities around Bristol Bay, the Aleutian Islands, the Kenai Peninsula, and Southeast Alaska. One of the most productive of these areas was Kachemak Bay, near the southern tip of the Kenai Peninsula. A center of the shrimp and crab industries, Kachemak Bay was threatened. The Cook Inlet oil fields were 75 miles north, and the Nixon and Ford administrations planned oil leases in the Gulf of Alaska to the south. The many small spills that had occurred since the 1950s in the relatively placid waters of Cook Inlet were worrying; a major spill in the turbulent Gulf of Alaska would be a nightmare. Fishermen operating out of Homer, Seldovia, and other southern Kenai communities were naturally anxious. Their anxieties turned to anger when the Egan administration unexpectedly announced in November 1973 that it would sell leases in the bay itself.

Such an announcement was certain to generate opposition, but Egan and Herbert created a firestorm. The state issued a public notice only two weeks before the sale and made no announcement at all in Homer, the largest Kachemak Bay community. It made only a perfunctory effort to obtain information about the bay from the Alaska Fish and Game Department.[46] Worst of all, Herbert refused to hold a public hearing on the lease proposal after 308 Homer and Seldovia residents petitioned him. Egan insisted that the lease sale itself was unimportant and that a public hearing would be held if there were an actual proposal to drill. His lands administrator would promise only that the state would "minimize damage" to the bay.[47] A protest organization, Citizens for a Better Community, emerged from the petition effort. Headed by ACS member Frank Tupper, it threatened legal action. The sale, on December 13, raised $25 million and exacerbated the political uproar.

Egan's political enemies eagerly exploited the situation. Walter Hickel, the favorite for the 1974 Republican gubernatorial nomination, visited Homer in February, attacked the Kachemak Bay leases, and reminded voters of his vigorous action as secretary of the Interior during the infamous 1969 Santa Barbara oil spill.[48] Another group of Republicans had a greater impact, however. Its local leader was state Senator Robert Palmer of Homer, who represented the Kenai communities. Palmer and his House counterpart, Representative Clem Tillion, were long-time defenders of the fishing industry. Their concern about habitat changes made them de facto conservationists, though they were uncomfortable with the label.[49] And since towns like Homer would be overwhelmed by a nearby oil boom, their concerns were not confined to the fate of the industry. On economic development issues they were closer to the Sierra Club than to the rest of the Republican Party.

Moreover, they had a leader of growing stature and visibility. Jay Hammond of Naknek, a fishing village on Bristol Bay, was colorful and charismatic, sufficiently iconoclastic to appeal to Alaskans' sense of individualism (he was the first prominent Alaska politician to wear a beard), and sufficiently conservative to reassure them. As an employee of the U.S. Fish and Wildlife Service in the 1950s, he had become a critic of the government's wildlife management policies. He had had reservations about statehood. As a member of the legislature in the 1960s, he had been a champion of the fishing industry and an opponent of booster schemes like the Rampart Dam. As Senate president, he had the temerity to propose a study of the costs and benefits of a Canadian pipeline. He had befriended Bob Weeden and had written articles for the *Alaska Conservation Review*. By the early 1970s he had moved beyond the pragmatism of Palmer and Tillion to argue that development ought to pay for itself. On environmental issues he was drawn to the Alaska-centered perspectives of ACS.[50]

The political implications of the lease issue were readily apparent when Palmer held a public hearing in Homer on February 23, 1974. Various elected officials and 170 local residents attended. Most of the speakers attacked the Egan administration. The most impressive of them, Jim Rearden, a former state biologist, discussed the bay's importance to the fishing industry. At a subsequent committee hearing in Juneau, Palmer and his colleagues forced the Fish and Game commissioner to acknowledge that he had played no role in the lease decision.[51] Palmer subsequently introduced a bill requiring the state to hold public hearings when requested (it passed unanimously) and another that would name the bay a "critical habitat," a designation that increased the regulatory authority of the Fish and Game Department. When the critical habitat bill reached the House, Tillion organized a bipartisan coalition that threatened to unseat the House speaker, an oil industry champion, if he prevented a vote. The bill passed overwhelmingly.[52]

The political stakes rose on May 18, when the Army Corps of Engineers held a public hearing in Homer on Shell Oil's request for an exploratory drilling permit. The reassuring statements of the company's biologists did little to placate the angry crowd. Opponents, including fishery and cannery representatives, Alaska Fish and Game officials, environmentalists, "housewives, and business men," called for delays and an environmental impact statement. Palmer condemned the state's contention that an environmental impact statement was not necessary.[53]

By that time Kachemak Bay had become an election issue and a symbol of the potential costs of the oil boom. Hammond had entered the Republican gubernatorial primary as an outsider and critic of the boom. Though Hickel also condemned the Kachemak Bay leases, his booster reputation (not to mention enthusiastic endorsements by Robert Atwood and Jesse Carr) left little doubt about his loyalties. Hammond, in contrast, attracted voters who were critical of the booster approach. Bob Weeden, Walt Parker, and Chuck Konigsberg were advisers, and most environmentalists added their endorsements. In the primary many Democrats crossed over. Hammond won by 7,000 votes.

In the general election Hammond portrayed himself as a moderate who would resist special interest pressures. "Most Alaskans," he argued, "desire that our resources neither be locked up nor ripped off." He wanted the new wealth to benefit "all Alaskans, not simply the fortunate few."[54] Egan tried to rally Democrats and pipeline workers, but Kachemak Bay haunted him. He campaigned briefly in Homer, apologizing for acting "wildly and recklessly."[55] When the votes were counted, liberal Democrats had made dramatic gains in the legislature, winning control of the House, but the gubernatorial contest was a virtual tie: after two recounts Hammond emerged as the winner by fewer than 100 votes.

Hammond's remarkable victory was a breakthrough for Alaska environmentalists. At the February 1975 annual meeting of ACS, Celia Hunter and Bob Weeden chaired a session on their organization's history and prospects. Their conclusion: "ACS is no longer the 'Loyal Opposition' (as far as state politics go). ... ACS is now in a position to influence not 'if' things will happen, but 'how.'"[56] Hammond appointed ACS president Ernst Mueller, a scientist who had worked for the U.S. Environmental Protection Agency, to head the state Department of Environmental Conservation; Walt Parker to head the Department of Highways; and Weeden to preside over a new policy planning office. Sandy Sagalkin was named assistant attorney general. Other ACS members filled lesser posts. Bob Palmer became the governor's chief of staff. Weeden recruited Konigsberg and Rich Gordon to serve as his assistants.

Still, Hammond faced many obstacles. The narrowness of his victory and the profligacy of the legislature limited his options. Atwood and Carr were unrelenting in their attacks. As Jim Kowalsky reported,

Jay has a very uphill battle to keep his ship of state afloat. Alaska is nearly broke. ... Just last Tuesday the Republicans met and told him to shape up ... 'Shape up' means to get rid of Bob Weeden as his chief planner, and other environmentally oriented cabinet members surrounding him and advising him ... Jay is probably in the toughest spot any governor could be, given his feeling for the land.[57]

Kachemak Bay was the easiest problem to address. With public opinion aroused, a vital industry at stake, and Egan a convenient scapegoat, the leases became an obvious target. When Army Corps officials ruled on the basis of an abbreviated environmental impact statement that exploratory drilling could proceed, Citizens for a Better Community and a group of Homer fishermen formed the Kachemak Bay Defense Fund to raise money for a lawsuit. In late November they hired Warren Matthews's law firm and planned a national fund-raising campaign.[58] When a judge dismissed the suit in May 1975, Matthews appealed to the state supreme court and Hammond promised that if the appeal failed, he would propose legislation to buy back the leases. As Frank Tupper explained, Kachemak Bay had become "a rallying point ... among those who feel an obligation to protect existing viable lifestyles and economies."[59]

Assuming that the supreme court would reject the suit, Hammond sponsored a bill in January 1976 to create a Kachemak Bay marine sanctuary and buy back the leases. In their haste to outlaw drilling, the governor's legal staff included language in the bill that seemed to give the state control over all activity in the bay, provoking the Homer Chamber of Commerce to complain about draconian regulations. The attorney general hastily organized a public meeting in Homer. After the crowd voted overwhelmingly to support termination of the leases, he urged them to write to their legislators "so they don't think I'm crazy when I come back and tell them what happened."[60] Later, when the city's merchants became more aggressive, the fishermen responded with a boycott of local businesses.[61]

A wholly unexpected development ultimately tipped the balance decisively in favor of the fishermen and environmentalists. Anticipating approval by the court, the oil companies had moved a large floating oil drilling rig, the *George Ferris*, off Homer in early 1976. Damaged during the move, the rig required extensive repairs. By the time they were completed, the *Ferris* had become hopelessly mired in the mud at the bottom of the bay and had to be dislodged with explosive charges. In the words of the *Homer Weekly News*, "technological inadequacy, lack of study, and lack of knowledge about local conditions" had wrecked the rig.[62] A delighted Frank Tupper announced that "the best testimony we had was given by the oil industry in Kachemak Bay."[63] Speaking at a fund-raising dinner for the Kachemak Bay Defense Fund, Governor Hammond labeled the event the *"George Ferris* Memorial Dinner."[64] Opposition to the bill collapsed. The final legislation provided for a one-year moratorium on drilling and gave the governor the power to acquire the leases through eminent domain. The state bought back the leases in the late 1970s.

Hammond's next target was the Forest Service. As Weeden wrote in October 1975, "one of the principal objectives of the Hammond Administration has been to place the State in a role of an active and permanent watchdog over Forest Service programs." Its long-term goal was more ambitious: to become "a full partner in the formulation of land use plans."[65] When the Forest Service released its 1975 Tongass land use plan, the governor's assistant circulated it among state agencies and received responses that were as hostile as the environmentalists' critiques. He then wrote to Regional Forester Charles Yates, saying that the plan "must be refocused and rewritten." The "overly great emphasis" on timber production would prevent the emergence of a diversified economy. "The impression remains that a Forest-wide decision has already been made to harvest lumber on a priority basis, with other values considered only if practicable." This bias would lead to an "irretrievable loss of the mature forest ecosystem." In addition, "formal Wilderness designation is treated far more restrictively than Congress intended or than other agencies allow."[66] Although this was a private communication, an Alaska Fish and Game employee appeared at a meeting of the Tongass Conservation Society on April 9, read his department's critical evaluation of the land use plan, and distributed copies to reporters. Yates could hardly contain himself. The state, he growled, had created an "intolerable situation."[67]

Judge Von der Heydt's decision in *Zieske v. Butz*, released in December 1975, provided another opening. Hammond called for a two-year waiver of the clear-cutting ban coupled with an extensive study of Forest Service policies and protection for "several environmentally critical areas." As noted earlier, his proposals generated little enthusiasm in Washington. Natural Resources Commissioner Guy Martin defended them at congressional hearings, and Alaska's senators dutifully supported them, but most interest groups favored immediate action, and the Forest Service opposed any investigation it could not control. Hammond's attempt to find a middle ground did not please the loggers or the environmentalists, who blamed him, among others, for the eventual resumption of clear-cutting. Leaders of the Southeast Alaska Conservation Council (SEACC) were angered that neither he nor Martin included any of the 45 SEACC areas in the government's list of environmentally critical areas.

OTHER CHALLENGES

As Hammond learned in his battle with the Forest Service, it was one thing to articulate the frustrations of ordinary Alaskans, and something else to devise effective antidotes. Nearly every issue involved diverse interest groups and required action by Congress as well as the state. Several little-known conflicts of the mid-1970s illustrated these complexities. Most arose, predictably, from the oil boom.

The effort to monitor Alyeska and ensure compliance with the law, was, in the words of two skeptical students of the boom, "a disaster."[68] Journalist Robert Douglas Mead summarized the problem: "Alyeska did not take very seriously the conditions imposed on it."[69] The company's de facto policy was to disregard anything that proved inconvenient and rely on its public relations staff to deflect criticism. That approach surprised no one who had followed the pipeline deliberations. In an August 1973 memo, later published as an unsigned editorial in the *Alaska Conservation Review*, Bob Weeden expressed his concern over the state and federal regulatory efforts. He contrasted their meager resources with the oil companies' determination to make up for lost time. The Interior Department teams assembled in 1969 and 1970 to work on pipeline issues had been disbanded, and the state agencies "are in even worse shape." The Alaska Department of Environmental Conservation was "almost completely unprepared." And since the "political atmosphere" in Washington and Juneau was not "conducive to stringent environmental protection," the handful of available regulators would be subject to "tremendous" pressures. As a partial solution, Weeden proposed that the environmental movement assemble its own team of expert monitors. He estimated that the cost would be $75,000—at a time when all Alaska environmental organizations were spending about one-quarter of that amount annually.[70]

Although Weeden's idea was far too ambitious for the Alaskans, a group of national organizations, organized as the Arctic Environmental Council, did attempt to monitor pipeline construction. Officially sponsored by the Arctic Institute, the council included a spectrum of organizations and had at least the nominal support of Alyeska. The Sierra Club participated, but Friends of the Earth and the Wilderness Society remained aloof. George

Alderson of Friends of the Earth concluded that the council was in reality an effort to avoid the kind of surveillance that Weeden had envisioned; he declined to participate.[71] The wisdom of his decision was soon apparent. Council representatives made several trips to Alaska but never had enough money to undertake meaningful inspections or publish their reports. Some of the participants, including the chairman, Fred G. Armstrong of the Aspen Institute, made enthusiastic comments that were widely circulated in Alaska and elsewhere. An increasingly uncomfortable Brock Evans, representing the Sierra Club, argued that some effort was better than nothing, but he faced growing criticism. One incident was indicative of the council's dilemma. When Evans criticized certain Alyeska activities to Sierra Club members, Alyeska managers reprimanded him for violating the chain of command.[72] The most effective member of the council was probably University of Alaska wildlife expert David Klein, who documented numerous shortcomings in the Alyeska effort. Klein became increasingly frustrated and resigned from the council in 1976.

Several journalists and environmentalists also made individual inspection trips. Mead, for example, traveled widely up and down the pipeline route, and Peter Scholes of the Alaska Center for the Environment, Pat Senner of the Fairbanks Environmental Center, and Gail Mayo of ACS spent three days with state officials examining the northern section. These efforts were brief, however, and wholly dependent on the goodwill of Alyeska.

What of the federal and state surveillance efforts? For all practical purposes the federal effort was nonexistent. The head of the Interior Department's Alaska Pipeline Office, Andrew P. Rollins, proved remarkably unobtrusive. Journalists later disclosed that he had accepted gifts and favors from Alyeska subcontractors.[73] In contrast, Chuck Champion, the state pipeline coordinator, took his job seriously and forced numerous changes. But he and his meager staff were unable to prevent many environmental violations that "are now largely irreversible and in some cases self-perpetuating."[74] Champion became best known for exposing Alyeska's inefficiencies and cost overruns. Ayeska managers demanded his dismissal, but Hammond refused.

Gil Zemansky was less fortunate. A sanitary engineer on leave from the University of Alaska, he was assigned to oversee sanitation at the construction camps. When he discovered and publicized flagrant violations of state regulations, he became a pariah. Alyeska executives barred him from staying overnight at the camps or purchasing fuel at company airfields.

Commissioner Ernst Mueller, his boss, at first supported him. But Alyeska increased the pressure on Hammond and Mueller, and Zemansky soon found himself back at the university. His articles for the *Northern Light* and other environmental publications were among the most effective critiques of the pipeline project.[75]

If the pipeline produced a multitude of localized disasters, two other federal government responses to the energy crisis had broader but no less ominous implications. The first was a plan to accelerate offshore oil drilling around Alaska's treacherous coasts. This initiative pitted the Nixon and Ford administrations against their own environmental agencies. The Hammond administration, rightly alarmed, sued to prevent lease sales in the Gulf of Alaska. But the governor then proposed offshore lease sales adjacent to the Prudhoe Bay fields, an area as precarious as the Gulf of Alaska. Even more perplexing was Hammond's 1977 decision not to oppose federal lease sales in lower Cook Inlet adjacent to Kachemak Bay. The area was subject to frequent storms, and the consequences of a major spill would have been as disastrous as a spill in the bay itself. Suits by environmentalists, fishermen, and Native groups eventually forced the Interior Department to postpone the sales and reduce the size of the lease area.[76]

The second initiative was a proposed natural gas pipeline from Prudhoe Bay. As early as 1972 Jim Kowalsky had foreseen a double disaster: an oil pipeline to Valdez and a gas pipeline across the Arctic National Wildlife Range (ANWR).[77] A large contingent in Congress (including most of the midwestern senators and representatives who had agitated for the Canadian oil pipeline route) favored a proposal by Arctic Gas, a U.S.-Canadian consortium, for a line across ANWR to the Mackenzie Valley, where other lines would carry the gas south and east, ultimately to the Midwest. An alternative route, proposed by El Paso Alaska, another consortium, would follow the oil pipeline to Valdez, where the gas would be liquified and shipped to California. To counter the political influence of Arctic Gas, El Paso enlisted Alaska boosters. The all-Alaska route had inherent appeal, and the prospect of more than 20,000 construction jobs (versus about 12,000 for the Arctic Gas project) ensured the support of Jesse Carr. The Hammond administration endorsed the El Paso plan.

Environmental groups faced a dilemma. The Arctic Gas plan compromised ANWR, while the El Paso plan increased the danger to Prince William Sound. Alaska environmentalists were quick to point out that Arctic Gas did not have to cross ANWR. An underwater pipeline from Prudhoe Bay, or an overland pipeline that followed the oil pipeline to

Fairbanks and then paralleled the Alaska Highway to Canada, would eliminate the most obnoxious feature of its proposal.[78] Arctic Gas rejected these possibilities, insisting that either would make the project too costly; executives believed they would win approval for their cheaper approach.[79] Environmentalists then turned to El Paso in an effort to find a minimally satisfactory plan. Yet their concerns about Prince William Sound (not to mention the California terminal site) made the El Paso plan equally unacceptable.[80]

A breakthrough occurred in 1976 when a new consortium, Alcan Pipeline, proposed a line that would follow the oil pipeline to Fairbanks and then the Alaska Highway to Edmonton. Environmentalists strongly supported this proposal. Although the Federal Power Commission endorsed both the Arctic Gas and the Alcan proposals in 1977, Arctic Gas was unable to proceed because of unresolved Canadian Native land claims, and Alcan executives were discouraged by inflated construction costs and declining gas prices. There would be no gas pipeline in the 1980s or the 1990s.[81]

The most significant feature of the controversy was the environmentalists' influence on the decisionmaking process. Local and national environmental groups worked together to defend ANWR and delay a decision until the gas companies agreed to an acceptable route. In 1974 the Sierra Club, Wilderness Society, and Audubon Society agreed to share expenses for legal representation at the Federal Power Commission hearings, the initial battleground. As the hearings continued and costs mounted, the Sierra Club Legal Defense Fund assumed more of the burden. An appeal to the Alaska Conservation Society for 10 percent of the total cost was rebuffed because of the society's many commitments and flagging resources. In the end the national organizations, with modest ACS assistance, sustained the campaign to the end of 1977.[82]

A simultaneous effort to ban mining claims in national parks inspired another cooperative effort. Mount McKinley and Glacier Bay were two of six national parks that permitted mining claims. Celia Hunter and Ginny Wood had long publicized the ill effects of the small mining enterprises operating in the Kantishna hills, on the northern edge of Mount McKinley Park, and the Denali Citizens Council continued their work. Though miners caused widespread damage to the area's streams, none of the mines were a long-term danger to the park.[83] The threat to Glacier Bay was more serious. Newmont Mining, a large international corporation, proposed to develop a huge nickel mine and a town of 2,000 residents on the western border of the park. Newmont's appeals mobilized the booster community.

Senator Lee Metcalf (D-MT) and Representative Morris Udall introduced bills in 1975 to prohibit additional claims in parks. A congressional ban on new claims would not directly affect the Newmont project, but it would prevent the mine from expanding and subject it to greater regulation. As the Metcalf and Udall bills neared passage, the mining industry campaigned for amendments to limit their applicability. In the Senate, the environmentalists easily prevailed. An amendment by Senators Ted Stevens and Mike Gravel to exclude the westernmost area of Glacier Bay failed by a vote of 33 to 53, and the Metcalf bill passed, 70 to 16. The more critical battle was in the House, where the Interior Committee was sharply divided. Representative Don Young succeeded in excluding the western edge of Glacier Bay by a vote of 22 to 19. At the same time Egan appointees to the Land Use Planning Commission persuaded the commission to support the exclusion, and Newmont lobbyists won a similar endorsement from the Alaska legislature. Their goal was to persuade the House to retain the Young Amendment, forcing a conference committee to reconcile the bills.

Alaska environmentalists, led by Hession, Ron Hawk, Rich Gordon, and ACS lobbyist Sharon Lobaugh led the opposition. A letter-writing campaign demonstrated that many Alaskans opposed the Newmont plan.[84] The Juneau Sierra Club group sent out thousands of appeals to activists in other states. This activity helped persuade the House to reject the Young amendment in favor of another amendment, sponsored by Representative John Seiberling (D-OH), that preserved the Senate bill and ultimately led Newmont to back away from the project. It was a small but encouraging test of strength.[85]

HIATUS

During spring 1974 Senator Gravel devoted much of his time to his upcoming reelection campaign. One issue he planned to address was the Section 17d(2) withdrawals under the Alaska Native Claims Settlement Act, which Congress was supposed to act on by the end of 1978. In February, his staff and Democratic activists Joe Josephson and Guy Martin met to devise a strategy. They concluded that Gravel ought to distance himself from Morton's 17d(2) bill and introduce his own measure. He should propose "only a limited amount of acreage, perhaps 50 million, as opposed to the 80 million limit," since "a great many persons are unhappy about the excessive amount requested by the Secretary." Gravel's bill should also permit "the extraction of minerals," subsistence and sport hunting, and the creation of transportation corridors. The Senator should keep in mind:

> ... that reaction to Morton's plan has been strong, that most people feel the withdrawal is too large, that few people understand the action, and that there is a strong emotional factor. Considering that it is a complex issue, it may never be well understood by Alaskans. But whatever the ultimate resolution of the d-2 lands is, your position should be one that is as conservative as possible.

Handled properly, they concluded, "you could have a lot of fun with it."[86]

Between December 1973, when Morton submitted his d(2) legislation, and November 1976, when the election of Jimmy Carter upset the Washington status quo, politicians had "a lot of fun" with the d(2) issue. Alaska officials competed to appear "as conservative as possible." In May 1975, Representative Young introduced a d(2) bill that set aside 13 million acres for parks, 28 million acres for national forests, and 27 million acres for other multiple-use classifications. Apparently concluding that it was impossible to be more conservative than Young, Gravel did not bother to introduce his own bill. In the meantime, the Interior Department continued to push Morton's 1973 proposals, and a new Alaska Coalition bill, introduced by Senator Jackson and Representative Udall at the coalition's request, called for 106 million acres of parks and refuges. None of these measures, however, received serious consideration.

Although congressional liberals gained seats in the 1974 elections, the House and Senate Interior committees hardly changed. James Haley (D-FL) succeeded Wayne Aspinall (defeated in the 1972 primary) as chairman of the House committee but was cut from the same prodevelopment cloth. Henry Jackson's Senate committee was no more energetic. After several false starts, it did nothing in 1975. "Back of all this," Edgar Wayburn bemoaned, "is a lack of any demand from constituents."[87] In early 1976 two Senate Interior Committee staffers traveled to Alaska to discuss 17d(2) legislation with local groups. They "tossed very cold water on hopes for Senate action this year, even hearings." Only Jackson and three or four others were even aware of the issue; the rest were "uninformed and perhaps uninterested at this stage."[88] Apart from the committee members, many senators and representatives had unhappy memories of the bruising

Alaska battles of 1970–1973. If the senators "got the impression that they were in for an endless round of Washington and field hearings, it would be very difficult to get them to take up the issue."[89] Nor could environmentalists expect help from the White House. President Ford had little interest in parks and became more receptive only in late 1976 as his reelection campaign stumbled toward defeat.

Still, two developments from this period influenced the 17d(2) legislation that did eventually emerge. The first was Governor Hammond's effort to devise a 17d(2) plan that balanced his environmental concerns with Alaska political realities. The second and more important development was a renewed effort by Alaska and national environmentalists based on the work of the Maps on the Floor Committee of 1972–1973. The new campaign would reflect bitter memories of Morton's final 17d(2) decisions, as well as a sense that the Alaska politicians, probably including Hammond, would have "a lot of fun" with the issue but would never support legislation that included large national park or wilderness components. This time, the environmentalists would take the offensive and keep it.[90]

Hammond's approach reflected his interest in natural resource planning and a desire to maximize Alaska influence in the planning process. As a candidate, he had emphasized the desirability of "greater state input in planning and managing" federal lands.[91] Shortly after his inauguration he had had a cordial meeting with Edgar Wayburn, who later reported that the governor "would like to see some type of Federal-State-[Native] Regional Corporation cooperation."[92] To flesh out his ideas, Hammond asked Bob Weeden to head a task force of state officials with responsibilities for natural resources. To assist him, Weeden appointed a committee of technical experts that included Rich Gordon (who since 1973 had been working as a writer-editor and wildlife resource expert for the National Park Service); Robert LeResche, a Fish and Game biologist who would later become commissioner of Natural Resources; and Sandy Sagalkin, the assistant attorney general. Natural Resources Commissioner Guy Martin summarized their assignment when he observed that "the State is in a position to put together a broader-based and more creative approach than Interior could do."[93]

During the following months Weeden and his staff did most of the work. Drawing on Gordon's vast knowledge and the expertise of the others—including Ben Shaine, a Santa Cruz student whom Weeden added to the advisory committee—they put together an innovative plan. In May Weeden reported that the state's 17d(2) bill would ask for three things:

First, a series of 'core' park and refuge lands, amounting to about the same acreage [65 million] as in Morton's bill; second, a large area of national lands in which prime values will be identified—mainly wildlife and other surface values—but whose management agency designation will be left for later determination; third, a permanent joint commission with strong advisory powers. We may also propose a federal Alaska Land Classification Board, to be linked with a similar state board, with classification authority in prime use and [Bureau of Land Management] lands.[94]

Working out the details proved to be a challenge, and the final proposal, scheduled for August, wasn't ready until October. To reconcile conflicting interests within the administration, Weeden and Hammond had to make damaging concessions. Led by its probusiness members, including Economic Development Commissioner Langhorne "Tony" Motley and Highways Commissioner Parker, the task force rejected Weeden's plan in favor of an alternative that combined minuscule additions to the four federal conservation systems—national parks, wildlife refuges, national forests, and wild and scenic rivers—with a large multiple-use area under federal-state jurisdiction.[95] Sagalkin warned Wayburn that environmentalists would be disappointed with the final proposal.[96] The eventual bill proposed only 17 million acres of national parks and only 37 million acres for all four systems. It also proposed a fifth system—62 million acres of Alaska "resource lands" to be managed by a federal-state Alaska land commission, based on "prime uses." Hammond explained that "Federal lands would not be frozen into a rigid system" and suggested that the resource lands might include state and even private lands, but his emphasis was unambiguous. "What it boils down to is that Alaskans would have a proper voice in the management of federal lands."[97]

What had happened? The conflicts between Hammond's environmental and economic development advisers were part of the problem. The governor's limited political clout was also a factor. His efforts to persuade Young and Stevens to back a consensus approach based on his plan convinced even the most forgiving environmentalists that he had succumbed to parochial pressures. The National Park Service staff's devastating critiques of his plan reinforced their skepticism.[98] Seiberling, who would be a pivotal figure in the congressional debates over 17d(2), characterized Hammond's proposal as "the Russian approach: what is ours is ours; what is yours is negotiable."[99]

More than anything else, Hammond's 17d(2) plan soured his relations with Alaska and national environmentalists. At public hearings represen-

tatives of most environmental groups either criticized it outright or complained about its complexity. At the Anchorage hearing, for example, Peg
Tileston demanded more information. "This issue is much too complex
and too vital to Alaska's future to be treated in this manner," she complained.[100] Privately, the chief lobbyist of Friends of the Earth was more
explicit: "We must do all we can to scuttle the 5th system."[101] When a
delegation of environmentalists visited Weeden in February 1976, he
pleaded for understanding. "He asked us," reported Jim Kowalsky, "to seek
support for his proposal from outside conservationists." Several participants bristled at this request; others asked whether he expected public
support or merely tolerance of "behind the scenes in-committee compromises." At the end of this unhappy encounter Celia Hunter "urged that we
not beat the Gov. over the head in criticism."[102]

Even if Hammond had been more accommodating, the environmentalists' determination to chart their own course would have been a serious
obstacle to cooperation. Their experiences with Morton had demonstrated
the importance of a clearly stated position and aggressive lobbying. By the
time Hammond announced his plan, they had already committed themselves to a more ambitious proposal.

That process began in late 1974, when ACS issued a call to local and
national environmental groups to meet in Fairbanks at the conclusion of
the society's annual meeting. The Sierra Club Foundation and the
Wilderness Society agreed to help pay transportation costs.[103] As a result,
24 individuals gathered at the St. Matthew's Episcopal Church rectory on
February 19, 1975, for what would later be recalled as the first Alaska envi-
ronmental summit meeting. The group included long-time activists like
Celia Hunter and Rich Gordon, younger professionals like Hession and
Kowalsky, and comparative newcomers like Helen Nienhauser and Peter
Scholes. Brock Evans of the Sierra Club, Harry Crandell of the Wilderness
Society, and Charles Callison and Eugene Knoder of the Audubon Society
represented the national organizations. Stan Senner represented the
Fairbanks Environmental Council; Everett Drashmer the Denali Citizens
Council; and David Friday, Nunam Kitlutsisti. Dick Bishop, president, and
Tina Stonorov, executive director, headed the ACS delegation.[104]

The first day's discussion focused on potentially divisive issues. Hunter
and Kowalsky reported on the "Status of Rural People, Native and Non-
Native," and David Klein followed with a discussion of "Subsistence and
Sport Hunting." Other topics included mining, conflicts between 17d(2)
and Native lands, and "Joint Management Possibilities." The national and

state lobbyists reported on "the mood in Washington and Juneau." The second day was devoted to boundaries and management systems.[105] Gordon had already distributed an updated version of the Alaska Coalition bill, now totaling 120 million acres.

The result, in Brock Evans's words, was "an extremely productive meeting, and a good educational experience for all concerned."[106] The single most "productive" feature was an agreement to support legislation that approximated the Alaska Coalition bill. Hession had worried that "ACS may take a very conservative position ... as a result of the influence of former ACS leaders taken into the Hammond administration."[107] Since the Weeden task force was just beginning its deliberations, the ACS representatives might have insisted on delay. Instead, as Evans noted, "local conservationists, in particular the ACS people, benefited by the exposure to the realities of environmental politics." They conceded that "we must give our friends something to bargain with."[108]

The second achievement was a series of agreements on sensitive issues. The ACS representatives initially called for opening some 17d(2) areas to mining. The national representatives objected: "The time to compromise, if we must, is when our friends on the Interior committee are sitting down at the Mark-Up Session with opponents—who surely will want all areas opened up." After an extended discussion, the group agreed to omit all references to mining. It also agreed to support subsistence hunting in principle but to let Congress grapple with the details. Sport hunting was another potentially divisive issue. The national representatives conceded the need to open some areas through preserves, which the Park Service had already embraced in some situations. The group also decided not to include Pet 4 lands in the legislation and to support a single omnibus bill.

On boundaries, there were several disagreements. Led by Bishop, the ACS representatives proposed to reduce the northern addition to Mount McKinley Park to preserve sport hunting in that area. The fact that Bishop owned land there offended some participants. Others were more sympathetic, acknowledging the importance of hunting to many Alaskans. Gordon recalled that Bishop "was extremely helpful in harmonizing the overall Alaskan positions."[109] The meeting also divided on a related issue, the appropriate boundaries for park and preserve areas in the Wrangell Mountains. As one observer noted, "There didn't appear to be any proper place to put a boundary which would both preserve sports hunting, and yet have an adequate national park." Another disagreement arose over lands on the south side of Mount McKinley that Morton had earmarked for state selection in 1972. Despite objections by the national representatives, the group voted 10 to 8 not to insist that these lands be included in the expanded park.

After two long days Evans was pleased. The summit had produced a "good basic consensus upon which to build our ultimate legislative thrust." Even the supposedly parochial ACS representatives had been conciliatory and helpful. "Everybody I talked to," Evans noted, "agreed that the ACS people came much farther in adopting a national outlook than anybody thought they would, including themselves."[110]

Having resolved most of their own differences, the environmentalists still had to persuade Congress to act. Several House members, including Seiberling, traveled to Alaska in summer 1975, and the Senate Interior Committee had brief, desultory hearings later in the year, but there were no immediate results. Wayburn's many 1975 and 1976 letters to congressional leaders record the environmentalists' growing frustration. At one point he conceded that "if we can get it through by the Fall of 1978, we'll be doing very well."[111]

Senator Jackson provided the only real encouragement. Members of his Interior Committee staff had a long session with Kowalsky, Hession, Hunter, and Bob Childers on February 23, 1976. They confirmed that the committee was unlikely to consider the 17d(2) issue in 1976 but insisted that Jackson was committed to action in 1977. Moreover, he "was strong on retention of federal ownership." The Interior Committee "would never legislate state management of federal land." The governor's fifth system was unacceptable. Otherwise, Jackson and the other senators wanted to preserve their options. Yet one point was clear: if the environmentalists wanted "to get anything decent," they "*must* make this a national campaign," persuade the Congress that "this is a one-time shot," and let legislators know that Morton's 83-million-acre withdrawal "is the bare minimum."[112]

With this behind-the-scenes encouragement, environmentalists began to prepare a grass-roots campaign aimed at the new Congress. The national organizations would take the lead and try to show that Californians and Ohioans cared as much as people who happened to live in Alaska. A second, related goal was to show that Alaskans themselves were divided and that their elected officials were at odds with a large and articulate minority. To make this point, Alaska environmentalists would have to work together. The 1975 Fairbanks summit had been a major step toward that goal. To sustain that spirit, Hunter and Kowalsky organized a second summit for spring 1976. "We need to see where we are, where we want to go and we need to figure out [how] to organize the various groups…," Hunter told the ACS annual meeting in April.[113]

Jim Kowalsky did most of the preliminary work for the 1976 summit. "This is a national issue…," he wrote, "but the initial thrust should come from Alaskans." First, however, they would have to answer basic questions: "What exactly do we want to happen and what should our proposal ask for?" One possible addition was non-d(2) lands in Southeast Alaska, such as Admiralty Island, West Chichagof–Yakobi, Misty Fiords, and parts of the Copper River delta, between the Tongass and Chugach national forests. "We are uncertain … whether to include these areas."[114] In terms of the conference itself, he foresaw a three-stage process. On Saturday morning, representatives of the national organizations would emphasize the need for a concerted national campaign. In the afternoon, the Alaskans would decide "what are the roles of Alaskans and national groups." On Sunday they would try to develop specific proposals and decide whether to include the Tongass lands and possibly Pet 4. Attendees were to bring their own food and sleeping bags, plus a dish for a potluck dinner Saturday night.[115]

Officially sponsored by ACS, the Fairbanks Environmental Center, and the Denali Citizens Council, the summit met on May 15–16 at the Mount McKinley Park hotel. Nearly a hundred people attended, including most of those present at the Fairbanks summit, a large Native contingent, and SEACC representatives Ted Whitesell and Rich Gordon. Hession, Kowalsky, Knoder, and Hunter represented the national organizations. Pam Rich, who had worked briefly at the Fairbanks Environmental Center and joined the Friends of the Earth national staff as its Alaska specialist, also played a prominent role.

They reviewed a variety of substantive issues, such as hunting and "instant" wilderness. The Natives were insistent on subsistence rights, implying to Hession that they would oppose the legislation "unless their interests are accommodated."[116] There were also disagreements over whether to include Pet 4 in the legislation. New ACS President Larry Mayo added another discordant note when he announced that the society would consider all the d(2) bills, including the state's proposed legislation. Yet everyone agreed on the need for immediate political action. "Each group must have a say but we should all agree to disagree on some points."[117] Hession, Mayo, Gordon, and others volunteered to prepare position papers on contentious issues for a later meeting.

There was little disagreement over the inclusion of several Tongass wilderness areas in the legislation. Most national leaders, fearful of overreaching, were hesitant to make the d(2) campaign into an Alaska wilderness campaign. Including Tongass and Chugach lands would increase the hostility of Alaska's senators and draw the Forest Service and the aggressive southeastern boosters into the fight. On the other hand, the d(2) legislation presented an unparalleled opportunity to resolve a host of problems. The apparent unwillingness of Congress to impose significant restrictions on the Forest Service (the outline of the National Forest Management Act was clear, though it would not be adopted until fall) raised the prospect of endless lawsuits and the gradual destruction of the forest. But the most compelling reason for including the SEACC wilderness areas was SEACC's success in publicizing its efforts. By 1976 Alaska environmentalists were well aware of the Tongass wilderness campaign. They were not willing to write off the southeastern activists just because of the d(2) focus of the legislation or the likely opposition of the state's senators and the Forest Service. In late April SEACC leaders had agreed to ask the Mount McKinley conferees to include at least five major southeastern wilderness areas in the d(2) bill.[118] The conference participants concurred; Hunter recalled a "very strong feeling" that the Southeast had to be included. Yet they agreed that the national organizations would make the final decision.[119]

Hunter opened the Sunday morning session by insisting that "we need to get into the mechanics of this: we need to go home knowing what people will do and what will happen and we need a timeframe. ... The most important thing is to get the campaign off dead center." They agreed to form an Alaska steering committee to coordinate activities and work with the national organizations. "The environmental centers are the focal points and so would serve as places for the members of the steering committee." Hunter, who was spending most of her time in Washington as president of the Wilderness Society, agreed to serve temporarily as state coordinator. Dee Frankfourth, recently elevated from intern to staff member at the Alaska Center for the Environment, would be her full-time assistant. Stan and Pat Senner of the Fairbanks Environmental Center also agreed to assist. An advisory board of 18, representing the various groups, was to guide them. The new organization would revive the name Alaska Coalition. Gordon, whose knowledge of the Alaska wilderness was unsurpassed, was named the coalition's "philosopher."[120]

By May 16 Alaska environmentalists were committed to a national campaign. On this issue, at least, they had broken with Hammond, his supporters, and others who emphasized local over national interests. Their decision ensured that they would play a prominent role in the subsequent d(2) campaign and contribute materially to its outcome.

The second summit was thus the climax to several notable developments. At one level it was a response to the painful experiences of 1971–1973, when the ad hoc campaigns of the national groups had failed to exploit the pipeline construction delays to win approval of the Canadian route or obtain a satisfactory national commitment to national parks and wilderness areas in Alaska. The decisions of May 15–16 also reflected the stresses and tensions of the economic boom and the growing conviction among a large minority of Alaskans that environmental protection was no longer an unaffordable luxury. They underlined the triumph of the environmentalist perspective: natural resource preservation ought to be guided by the resources at hand and not by the original d(2) decisions of Washington bureaucrats. Finally, as Brock Evans and others noted, they expressed a conviction that whatever the differences between the various groups, the proposed legislative campaign represented the last best opportunity to derive something of permanent value from the state's windfall.

PART III

THE ANILCA CAMPAIGN: ALASKA AND WASHINGTON, 1977–1980

"Who's the guy who wants to lock up Alaska?" a man inquired.
Udall stepped out of the milling crowd.
"I am," the Arizona Democrat said. "And John Seiberling
too. You'll have to hang us both together."
After the hearing, ... the man who wanted to meet the
fellow "who's gonna lock up Alaska" ... came forward.
"Hey Udall," he shouted, "you should run for president."
                                                —*Alaska Advocate*, 1977

I am just back from Alaska ... The present situation is a festering
wound ripe for demagogs.
                                                —Nathaniel P. Reed, 1979

CHAPTER 7

CONGRESS DELIBERATES

I n *Coming into the Country*, John McPhee devoted a chapter to John Kauffman and other National Park Service staffers who were planning the proposed Gates of the Arctic National Park. While noting the dedication of Kauffman and his colleagues, McPhee also recorded their sense of anxiety. After all, there was no assurance that Gates of the Arctic, or any other park, refuge, or national forest, would actually materialize. Referring to Section 17d(2) of the Alaska Native Claims Settlement Act (ANCSA), he wrote, "All the paragraph provided, however, was that eighty million acres could be temporarily set aside and studied. There was no guarantee of preservation to follow."[1] By 1976 Kauffman had good reason to worry. Congress was no closer to acting than it had been in 1973. If 1978 passed without action, the d(2) withdrawals would end and the opportunity to preserve parts of the Alaska wilderness would be lost, perhaps forever. The legacy of the most dramatic decade in Alaska history would be the oil pipeline, a likely gas pipeline, the development-minded Native regional corporations, a booster-dominated state, and the ascendancy of the multiple-use agencies, the Forest Service and the Bureau of Land Management, in the two-thirds of Alaska that was still federally owned. Much of Alaska would remain undeveloped, but only because no one had thought of a way to make money from it.

Of course, that scenario disregards the increasingly self-confident and assertive environmental movement, which by spring 1976 was ready to make the d(2) proposals the centerpiece of an aggressive political program. By the conclusion of the second "summit," environmentalists were united on the need for a revived Alaska Coalition and a national effort. Their subsequent campaign would be a landmark in the annals of political activism.[2] Ultimately it would produce the most significant victory in the contemporary campaign for parks, wildlife, and natural areas. But the margin of victory would be small. The decisive factor would be the support of large numbers of people who had no first-hand knowledge of Alaska. Almost as important would be the contributions of Alaska personalities and institutions, ranging from technical advice to almost daily reminders that the boosters and their allies did not speak for all Alaskans.

PRELUDE

A preview of the coming struggle occurred in mid-February 1977, when Governor Jay Hammond, Senators Ted Stevens and Mike Gravel, and Representative Don Young held two days of private hearings, supposedly to devise a consensus position on d(2) issues. The 16-hour event, which Dee Frankfourth castigated as a "back-room, card-dealing operation," included one 90-minute session with Alaska's environmental leaders.[3] Given the environmentalists' frayed relationship with the governor and antagonistic relations with the congressional delegation, only a united, forceful presentation was likely to have any effect. Regardless of the outcome, however, the hearing would be a useful test of the revived Alaska Coalition.

The most obvious obstacle to unity was residual support for Hammond from the Alaska Conservation Society (ACS), reiterated in several policy statements released after the Mount McKinley Park summit. Meeting on February 3 at the home of David and Mark (formerly Ganopole) Hickok, who had recently married, Sierra Club leaders worried that the apparent conflict might be used to discredit them.[4] As in the past, they turned to

Celia Hunter for assistance. Pam Rich and other lobbyists conferred with Hunter in Washington, where she was attending to Wilderness Society business. Rich reported, "I met with her after the others did. Then she spent a night at my place so we had lots of time for talking. I think she's getting stronger and understands more clearly what's going on here."[5]

Hunter returned to Alaska for an emergency Anchorage "minisummit" on February 7, called to prepare for the hearing, and emphasized the need for unity. She, Jim Kowalsky, Rich Gordon, Peg Tileston, and Larry Mayo were nominated for the four-member panel. Mayo, ACS president, lost because "other coalition members felt some uncertainty as to whether Mayo would be able to fully espouse the coalition's position, and voted accordingly."[6] Gordon drafted a statement emphasizing their agreement on the objectives of a d(2) bill. With minor revisions they adopted it and sent it to the governor. "More than anything," Frankfourth wrote, the minisummit enabled coalition leaders to "verbalize together our reasoning and justification" for the forthcoming bill.[7] Sierra Club leaders reported with relief that despite "rough edges, the Coalition is alive and well."[8]

On February 15 and 16, a procession of interest groups, ranging from the Alaska Chamber of Commerce to the Alaska Coalition, paraded before the state's elected leaders. Each group read a brief statement and answered questions. As Gordon and Tileston reported, "it was clearly a political forum, with the Governor/delegation lecturing more and listening very little."[9] Apart from the environmentalists, the other groups opposed any meaningful d(2) bill. The Natives emphasized subsistence activities; the Izaak Walton League representatives discussed sport hunting. The others defended their particular interests. The officials were no more united. Hammond and Stevens favored a "fifth system" of lands to be managed by a federal-state commission, Young's position "was harder to discern," and Gravel was vague and noncommittal.[10]

The environmentalists' session was equally revealing. Young was characteristically blunt and antagonistic. Stevens asked unanticipated, somewhat bizarre questions about the relationship between d(2) lands and the Clean Air Act. When Gravel rambled on about a fifth system, though not necessarily the governor's fifth system, Hunter, still a member of the Land Use Planning Commission, responded that federal-state commissions (such as the one Hammond envisioned) tended to be highly political and hostile to wilderness values. Hammond, who in Kowalsky's words "seemed short with us, generally crabby," referred to ACS position papers and asked "whether the coalition had fallen apart. ... Celia deftly skirted the issue, essentially saying that the Coalition was alive and well."[11] She assured the governor that ACS fully supported the coalition and that "we know the existing management system best."[12]

What had been accomplished? The hearings had shown that there was neither an Alaskan consensus nor any realistic prospect of one. Stevens subsequently introduced a "consensus" bill that called for five new parks totaling 10 million acres and a federal-state fifth system that would man-age 56 million acres of federal land.[13] Hammond and Young endorsed it, but no one else took it seriously. By April Hammond acknowledged that it would have to be drastically revised.[14] Gravel went his own way; his behavior reflected both his idiosyncratic approach and the divisions with-in the booster community.

The disarray in the politicians' ranks did not stop Alaska's industrialists, led by the miners and timber companies, from creating Citizens for the Management of Alaskan Lands (CMAL) to oppose the environmentalists. Headed by Hammond's first Commerce commissioner, Langhorne "Tony" Motley, the organization received support from several local governments and from such outside groups as the American Mining Congress. "It is going to take lots of money," Motley reported.[15] (He did not mention that his fee, reportedly $500 per day, would be CMAL's largest expense.) Anchorage busi-nessman Bill Sheffield agreed to head a local fund-raising effort.

In the months that followed, the environmentalists' unity and determi-nation and the boosters' divisions would both be critical variables in what became a prolonged and increasingly divisive campaign. The February ses-sion was meaningful after all.

H.R. 39

The bill that so riled the Alaskans in February 1977 was the result of extended deliberations that had begun with the Alaska summits and con-cluded in November 1976. It originated with the Maps on the Floor Committee of the early 1970s, the Park Service planners, and the 1975 and 1976 summits, but the bill itself, like the campaign to promote it, was the product of a series of meetings between representatives of the national environmental organizations.

In mid-July 1976 Michael McCloskey and Brant Calkin of the Sierra Club, Celia Hunter and George Davis of the Wilderness Society, David Brower of Friends of the Earth, and Vim Wright of the Audubon Society met in Denver to initiate the process. They assigned Jack Hession and Rich Gordon to complete the revisions agreed upon at the May summit and enlist the Native organizations.[16] In the meantime their lobbyists were to identify crucial congressional districts and devise an educational campaign. After a long discussion at Pam Rich's Washington home on August 6, the lobbyists agreed that "the kind of commitment, workload and commitment of resources that we have done before large floor fights—such as the Alaskan Native Claims Settlement Act—is needed at the beginning. ..."[17] A second meeting of the national officers and representatives, on September 17 at Audubon headquarters in New York, focused on publicity and advertising, as did a third meeting, on October 25 in Washington. By the end of October the Washington staffs had prepared mailings and activist lists and set up a "boilerroom" at Friends of the Earth headquarters to direct the effort.[18] Finally, the groups' Alaska experts met on November 8—Hession recalled it as a "big summit"—and put the finishing touches on the campaign. They refined boundaries and developed mutually acceptable compromises on such issues as subsistence and sport hunting. Reflecting the improved political climate, due to the election of Jimmy Carter, they decided to seek as much "instant" wilderness as possible and to include the most prominent Tongass areas.[19] Mike McCloskey and Chuck Clusen, Brock Evans's assistant in the Sierra Club's Washington office, did the actual drafting. Representative Morris Udall and Senator Lee Metcalf (D-MT) agreed to introduce the bill, called the Alaska National Interest Lands Conservation Act.

In its initial form H.R. 39 reflected a theme that representatives of the national organizations had emphasized at the Mount McKinley summit: Ask for what you want. It set aside 115 million acres, comprising 10 new national parks, preserves, and monuments totaling 64 million acres; additions to Mount McKinley National Park and to Katmai and Glacier Bay national monuments totaling 8 million acres; nine new and two enlarged wildlife refuges (including a doubling of the Arctic National Wildlife Range, ANWR) totaling 46 million acres; 23 wild and scenic rivers with 4 million acres of adjacent land; and additions to the Tongass and Chugach national forests totaling 1.6 million acres. The bill disregarded Interior Secretary Rogers C. B. Morton's boundaries: some of the lands were in the original d(1) areas and some had been included in the 1972 out-of-court settlement. Other features included the designation of some parklands as preserves, open to sport hunting; the creation of "subsistence management zones" to accommodate Natives and other rural residents; and 145 million acres of instant wilderness, including virtually all the new park and refuge lands and 5 million acres in the Tongass and Chugach national forests. The national forest wilderness areas included West Chichagof–Yakobi, Admiralty Island, the nearby Yakutat forelands, and Misty Fiords. The proposed Wrangell–St. Elias National Park and the expanded ANWR (now renamed the Arctic National Wildlife Refuge) were adjacent to new or proposed Canadian parks and would fulfill a long-time dream of park planners.

The bill was highly complex and became more so in the following months as supporters and opponents added amendments. The critical features, however, were the total acreage allotted to national parks, wildlife refuges, wild and scenic rivers, and national forests—the four federal administrative systems; the distribution of lands between the "pure" conservation agencies and the multiple-use Forest Service (and any fifth system, including stewardship by the Bureau of Land Management, that might emerge); and the amount of instant wilderness. There were many other provisions—those dealing with subsistence activities and Native and state land selection, for example—that were only indirectly related to the environmentalists' goals. The following account emphasizes the issues that were most critical to proponents and opponents of the legislation in the late 1970s.

From the beginning, the most controversial feature of the Udall bill was its call for millions of acres of instant wilderness. The addition of so much wilderness would revolutionize the wilderness preservation system and encourage additional congressional action on the nearly 60 million acres of roadless national forest land outside Alaska. Alaska boosters viewed wilderness as anathema, and other critics, ranging from the governor to Forest Service bureaucrats, equated it with "single use" and limited managerial discretion. Still other Alaskans, concentrated in the Southeast, worried about the "meat and potatoes" issue—the possibility of job losses and business failures. That concern, coupled with the role of the Forest Service, made the comparatively modest Tongass withdrawals (half of which were included in the Forest Service's wilderness study areas) one of the most bitterly contested features of the bill.

The Forest Service left no doubt about its position. Its new Tongass land-use plan earmarked for cutting half of the 45 areas selected by the Southeast Alaska Conservation Council (SEACC), 12 before 1981. Forest Service managers may have deliberately targeted land included in the Udall bill. In early 1977, for example, they joined the Alaska Highway

Department in announcing a plan to bridge the Dangerous River, which would open the Yakutat forelands, one of the proposed wilderness areas. They also released an environmental impact statement for a road that would cross the proposed Misty Fiords wilderness to a mining claim owned by U.S. Borax Company. John Sandor, the regional forester, publicly attacked Udall, indicating that his rationale for the southeastern wilderness areas was "not really square."[20]

With these exceptions the first phase of the congressional battle was surprisingly positive. After a lobbying trip to Washington in early 1977, Ron Hawk was unexpectedly upbeat. He reported that Representative Young "is acting the most receptively and nicely that he ever has towards conservationists. ... he is finally feeling some pressure to respond to our requests." Senator Stevens was also surprisingly friendly. Both men pledged not to oppose a wilderness study of West Chichagof–Yakobi. When the House Interior Committee's Public Lands Subcommittee held a hearing on a proposed Endangered American Wilderness Act, which initially included the West Chichagof–Yakobi wilderness, Young held the map while Hawk described SEACC's plan. Not to be outdone, Gravel told Hawk that the consensus d(2) bill would "have something in it for SE."[21]

The Alaska Coalition was also the beneficiary of two fortuitous political changes. The first was the election of Carter, who had an impressive environmental record as governor of Georgia and had attracted the support of many activists.[22] His choice for secretary of the Interior, Cecil Andrus, governor of Idaho, was also an advocate of environmental protection. At the same time, changes in the leadership of the House of Representatives dramatically affected the coalition's prospects. For many years the Interior Committee had been the fiefdom of Wayne Aspinall and James Haley. But Aspinall had been defeated in 1972 and Haley retired in 1976, leaving the chairmanship to Harold Johnson (D-CA), and when Johnson decided to head the Public Works Committee instead, to Morris Udall. Though the committee's membership remained sharply divided, Udall's position tipped the balance in the environmentalists' favor. In prior sessions Don Young and other opponents of Alaska legislation had been able to persuade Haley to assign Alaska bills to the Public Lands Subcommittee, whose most influential members had little interest in parks. To outflank them, Udall created a special subcommittee on Alaska lands and named his friend John Seiberling to head it.

Since his election in 1970, Seiberling, a Democrat from Ohio, had been increasingly attracted to parks and public lands issues. Scion of a promi-

nent family, he had fond memories of summers at the family's private
island retreat. Those early experiences had awakened an interest in conservation that broadened in the 1960s. As a member of Congress he was
largely responsible for the creation of the Cuyahoga Valley National
Recreation Area in his own district, and he worked to expand the national
park system. In 1975, as a member of the Parks Subcommittee, he visited
many of the proposed Alaska parks and was awed by the area's splendor.
In 1976 he played a decisive role in banning mining claims in national
parks. By early 1977 he was eager to use his new position to push H.R. 39.

Shortly after the appointment of the Alaska Lands Subcommittee, he
had a long session with Ron Hawk, Chuck Johnstone of the Sitka
Conservation Society, and Sterling Bolima, the Angoon lobbyist. They discussed the Tongass situation in general and the threats to Admiralty Island.
Hawk reported that the Ohioan "was really impressed with the magnitude
of our problems ... and is willing to really do more to help us."[23]
Seiberling urged them to add other SEACC wilderness areas to the Udall
bill. Shortly afterward he introduced a bill to create an Admiralty Island
Preserve, administered by the Park Service, that would protect the Angoon
community from logging. Mary Ellen Cuthbertson reported that "things
are really happening!"[24] Jack Calvin believed that the Forest Service and
the loggers were "running scared."[25] Governor Hammond unhappily
reported that Seiberling was "very confident, very assured."[26]

That confidence was based on an assumption that the Alaska
Coalition's national grass-roots campaign would ensure serious consideration of H.R. 39. It presumably would be a "cheap vote," one that almost
everyone outside Alaska could embrace. The danger was that support
would be so shallow that the bill might be sabotaged in committee or
overlooked in the rush to address other issues. A campaign reaching into
every congressional district would be the most effective antidote to those
dangers.

The Sierra Club took the lead. Wayburn's operation had become an official task force in 1974 and by 1976 was aggressively building contacts in
every state. He boasted that his mailing list had increased from 650 to
"about 1,000" and that the club's 50 state chapters and 200 local groups
had Alaska coordinators.[27] His budget for 1977 would be at least
$30,000.[28] As the campaign became more extended and difficult, the
Sierra Club assumed a larger role in Washington as well. Yet Wayburn also
understood the delicacy of his position. He did not attend either of the
Alaska summits. His task force often met in Alaska but remained in the

background. The panel that represented the environmental community at the February hearing included Tileston and Gordon, who were active in the Alaska chapter but were better known for other associations.

Wayburn's reticence also reflected the weakened state of the Wilderness Society and Friends of the Earth. In the mid-1970s the Wilderness Society was torn by internal strife unrelated to Alaska (though not without impact: in the ensuing reorganization Celia Hunter became interim executive director, and Harry Crandell, the legislative director, left to join the staff of the House Public Lands Subcommittee and then became chief of staff of Seiberling's subcommittee). For several critical years the Wilderness Society's lobbying effort was ineffectual. As interim executive director (1977–1978), Hunter spent much of her time in Washington but could not replace the departed Stewart Brandborg and his aggressive staff. Friends of the Earth had always operated on a shoestring, and its fortunes did not improve. After Pam Rich resigned to follow her husband to Montana, its role in the Alaska Coalition gradually diminished.

There were also organizational growing pains. Over the winter of 1976–1977, for example, Dee Frankfourth and her colleagues at the Alaska Center for the Environment had prepared a brochure for the forthcoming campaign. They devoted lavish attention to the text but failed to check the list of coalition members. After 500,000 copies had been printed, they discovered that they had omitted the Brooks Range Trust, a small Alaska organization that had provided much-needed operating funds, but had mistakenly included Nunam Kitlutsisti, which was not a member. Both groups were unhappy. The former's officers felt unappreciated, and Harold Sparck, the latter's leader, reported that he was "shell shocked" by his neighbors' complaints at being associated with "such a radical coalition." He had no choice but to disavow the coalition and "lie low."[29]

On most issues coalition leaders fared somewhat better. Hunter kept ACS focused on the goal of wilderness preservation, arguing that "we can and do get together on the things that matter, and argue endlessly on those that don't."[30] Kowalsky served as unofficial emissary to the Native communities and was able to assuage their concerns about the "radical coalition." The environmentalists' support for subsistence hunting in parks and wildlife refuges (and the absence of explicit guarantees in the consensus bill) led some villages to endorse the Udall bill.[31]

A meeting of coalition leaders at the Sierra Club office in Washington on April 23 provides a snapshot of the campaign at its inception. Twenty-one participants represented ACS, the Fairbanks Environmental Center, the Wilderness Society, the Audubon Society, the National Parks and Conservation Association, Friends of the Earth, the Sierra Club, and the Alaska Trollers, a recent addition from the southeastern fishing community. Nine were Alaskans. Others, such as Rich, Peter Scholes, Gene Knoder, and Wayburn were veterans of Alaska environmental politics. Three were current coalition staff members. The wide-ranging discussion covered subsistence, cooperative land management, and preparations for hearings on the Udall bill. The coalition had $1,883 in the bank and $850 in outstanding bills. One coalition employee, Cathy Smith, was partly paid by the Friends of the Earth Foundation; a second, Gordon, was supported by ACS. The third would leave in April. At the end of the meeting Pam Rich happily announced that the Garden Clubs of America had endorsed the Udall bill and would send representatives to the forthcoming Atlanta hearing.[31]

In the following months the coalition gradually assumed more permanent form. Rich's departure led to the emergence of Chuck Clusen as the coalition's dominant figure. A veteran Sierra Club staffer, Clusen bore much of the responsibility for the coalition's cohesion in the following years. Taking over an ill-defined job and a heterogeneous constituency, he centralized authority over critical functions (relations with the White House and the Congress in particular) and maintained generally amicable relations among the member groups. His de facto second in command was Doug Scott, the Sierra Club representative for the Northwest. Clusen and Scott had been roommates at the University of Michigan and were close friends, though their styles differed. Clusen became famous for his coolness under fire, Scott for his energy and aggressiveness. Clusen devised strategy and coordinated relations with organization leaders while Scott and his assistant, Scholes, headed the lobbying team, and Jack Hession was in charge of research. They had able and cooperative colleagues. Cathy Smith served as treasurer, and the Sierra Club's John McComb ran the coalition's computer operation, a first for a reform campaign. Altogether, the staff ranged from 20 to 30, most of whom remained on the payrolls of their original organizations. In addition, countless volunteers from all parts of the country spent days or weeks in Washington. When Congress was in session, a half-dozen or more Alaska activists were likely to be there.

Although the Alaska Coalition was relatively well financed, it was sustained primarily by the youthful vigor of activists who had come of age in the 1960s. A graduate student who researched the coalition operation described them as young, mostly in their 20s, university graduates, veterans of local and national political campaigns, and above all, "incurable environmental idealists," devotees of what they often described as the Earth Day perspective.[33] Alaska was a metaphor for beleaguered Nature, under attack from the rapacious forces of modern technology and international capitalism. The emergence of Carter, Udall, and Seiberling gave them an opportunity to strike back. They began by mobilizing other like-minded individuals around the country.

THE SEIBERLING HEARINGS

The first test of the environmentalists' strategy came in spring and summer 1977, when Seiberling's subcommittee held extended hearings on the Udall bill. To emphasize the national character of the issue, Seiberling scheduled sessions in various locations: altogether, there were seven days of hearings in Washington; one day each in Chicago, Atlanta, Denver, Seattle, Sitka, Juneau, Ketchikan, Anchorage, and Fairbanks; and 20 days of community meetings in small, often remote Alaska locations. The Sierra Club took the lead in organizing testimony at each of the major urban sites. State and congressional district coordinators recruited activists and provided them with information. Briefing sessions helped them prepare for the hearing.[34] At the Washington hearings, 53 of 76 witnesses supported H.R. 39. Similar preparations in Atlanta, Chicago, Denver, and Seattle ensured that the hearings were well attended, lively, and overwhelmingly favorable to the Udall bill. Tony Motley of CMAL reported that it was "a stacked deck, both in the structuring of the House hearings and in the excellent job the sponsoring organizations have done throughout the country." His "most dominant and recurring impression … [was] how militant, well organized, absolutely dedicated on all fronts" the environmentalists were.[35] He later recalled that the hearings "were basically pep rallies for the environmentalists. We were just getting killed."[36]

In Chicago, for example, 220 people testified, the vast majority for the bill. At least 50 others had to leave before they had an opportunity to speak. Some brought written statements from friends or relatives. Because of the large crowd, Seiberling and Representative Bruce Vento (D-MN) conducted simultaneous sessions in separate rooms. Cathy Smith of the Alaska Coalition reported,

Because we were able to organize the hearing schedule, we were able to get all of the out-of-staters on in the morning, and the Chicago people in the afternoon. Everyone appeared in panels of between 5 and 10 persons. Incidentally, we did all the panelling the night before the hearing—something to be avoided in the future.[37]

Bill Horn, from Representative Young's staff, asked each witness about his or her group affiliation in an effort to show that they were (in Smith's words) "coralled into doing it by the Sierra Club." Though Seiberling told them they didn't have to reply, they "continued to volunteer it. ... People are generally proud of the alliance and we found it difficult to convince them not to mention it." By the afternoon they "started asking questions of Seiberling and particularly of Young's staffer. This was *extremely* effective."[38]

The first important clashes occurred on June 18 in Seattle, where 1,200 people signed up to testify. Approximately 1,000 attended the hearing, including Sierra Club members from Oregon, Idaho, California, and Alaska. Opponents included local construction workers, oil and mining industry representatives, and the governor of Washington. Young himself attended, attacked the bill, and tried to intimidate supporters. Several times he rose and left the room as environmentalists were introduced.[39] The most dramatic moment occurred when Jim Whittaker, a famous mountaineer and the manager of a large store devoted to outdoor recreation, testified in favor of the bill. Young tried to portray rock climbers as spoiled children and Whittaker as a hypocrite. "Let's not kid ourselves. Your pocketbook is involved," he snapped. Whittaker replied, "We're looking down the road a bit. You haven't climbed high enough. Sorry." The audience applauded enthusiastically.[40]

Seiberling's plan called for two trips to Alaska. The subcommittee was to spend July 1–10 in the Southeast and August 6–21 in the interior. It scheduled conventional hearings for Sitka (July 5), Juneau (July 7), Ketchikan (July 9), Anchorage (August 12), and Fairbanks (August 20). The other days were devoted to meetings with residents in the proposed park areas. The schedule reflected Seiberling's growing fascination with Alaska and his and Udall's desire to test the political climate. Harry Crandell, who was in charge of the preparations, worked closely with Ron Hawk to ensure that the members saw the worst of the Tongass clear-cuts.

Alaska environmentalists believed they could show that Alaskans were sharply divided. Cuthbertson wrote optimistically that "we must put on a show of support at these hearings that will simply overwhelm both the committee and our opposition."[41] SEACC and the Wilderness Society, with assistance from the other groups, held a three-day "wilderness workshop" in Sitka to discuss the bill. Shorter sessions followed in Juneau, Haines, Sitka, Ketchikan, Petersburg, and Juneau.[42] In the meantime, the Juneau and Sitka Sierra Club groups organized participants in their respective areas, while Wayburn's task force recruited and prepared witnesses for the Anchorage and Fairbanks hearings. Ketchikan remained a problem. The president of the Tongass Conservation Society had recently been fired and driven out of town, and other members were frightened. The Sierra Club had no members who were willing to testify.[43]

The opponents also organized. In each town with a chamber of commerce, Seiberling and his colleagues faced concerted opposition. Some of the small towns, like Pelican, a fishing village adjacent to the proposed West Chichagof–Yakobi wilderness, were overwhelmingly supportive; others were divided, with critics emphasizing specific features of the bill they did not like.[44] Seiberling received a preview of what awaited him in the larger communities on July 4 in Petersburg. In an informal meeting at Sandy's Café, he confronted a large, raucous group. Though Petersburg was a fishing town, only one fisherman was present. The crowd voted 36 to 6 in favor of more mining and 40 to 2 for logging.[45]

When the subcommittee members arrived in Sitka, they encountered a noisy mob. Demonstrators outside the auditorium carried signs reading "Make our forests grow, plant a Sierra Clubber."[46] A chainsaw demonstration by Alaska Pulp employees reinforced the implied threat.[47] The chamber of commerce asked merchants to close during the hearing; those who refused received threatening phone calls. Rumors that "500 hippies" were en route alarmed many residents. The nearly 1,000 people in the hall gave Representative Young a "lengthy round of applause" and booed Jack Calvin. Seiberling refuted some of the more wildly inaccurate predictions of possible job losses and economic decline. He asked, "How are we to protect the land from huge outside corporations?"[48]

The next day Alaska Pulp managers gathered to congratulate themselves on their showing. One executive noted that the Republican staffers "were very impressed with the fact that we could close down the businesses in the town and get that sort of a turnout." He was not concerned about the testimony of Sitka Conservation Society members. However, he was "disturbed about … the fact that two of our own people testified against us. … At the proper time I plan to call these people and their department heads into this room and question them how they got so smart."[49]

In Juneau supporters and opponents testified in approximately equal numbers. The crowd of 500 "was far less hostile than in Sitka," and most witnesses "seemed content to politely voice their positions and then leave."[50] Representatives of the chamber of commerce and timber industry led the opposition. Robert LeResche, Hammond's new Natural Resources commissioner, endorsed the Stevens consensus bill and proposed a national recreation area for Admiralty Island. Seiberling attacked the opposition's tactics. "My impression is the people of Alaska have been sold a bill of goods by vested corporate interests," he observed.[51] But he also suggested that the bill might be amended to permit mineral exploration in some wilderness areas, and when Representative Teno Roncalio (D-WY) predicted that the total area would be reduced to 90 million acres or less, Seiberling did not contradict him.[52]

The Ketchikan hearing was a more subdued replay of the Sitka hearing. The chamber of commerce urged merchants to close their stores, and union members picketed outside the hall. Seven hundred people crowded the auditorium; when Young called on opponents to rise and "stretch," a large majority stood. Local politicians expressed their concerns about possible job losses; state Senator Robert Ziegler caused a sensation when he accused environmentalists of "despicable" tactics. Ron Hawk, representing SEACC, argued that a revision of the 50-year Forest Service contracts would save both wilderness and mill jobs. More than 30 environmentalists, including some from Wrangell and Petersburg, followed him. One man stood up, removed his shirt and seemed to be reaching for his belt. Young whispered: "We're going to have a streaker!" But the man only shouted "Alaska, yippee!" and ran out.[53] Others were less bold. A contingent of local fishermen refused to testify because of the "hostile climate." Later that evening the leader of the pulp workers union called Seiberling to apologize for the demonstrations. He, too, had been intimidated.[54]

The Southeast Alaska sessions produced several revelations. In a July 19 meeting with the subcommittee, Regional Forester Sandor conceded that H.R. 39 would have no adverse effect on local employment but warned against any additional wilderness designations.[55] Some local environmentalists interpreted his statement as evidence that Forest Service executives had reconciled themselves to the Udall bill. Others viewed it as confirmation that the Forest Service planned to log the other SEACC areas. In Ketchikan Seiberling indicated that the U.S. Borax mine site would "probably" be excluded from the proposed Misty Fiords wilderness. This alarmed SEACC leaders, who were preparing a suit to stop the Forest

Service from approving the mine road. They were also upset by a newspaper account of Seiberling's speculations. He had said that if the Tongass areas were deleted from the bill, the local economy would be paralyzed while Congress considered new wilderness proposals. But the *Southeast Alaska Empire* garbled the statement and "generated a great deal of concern in the conservation community."[56]

The subcommittee's second trip, in August, produced more demonstrations of the environmentalists' organizational skills. Meeting on July 16–17, the Alaska task force of the Sierra Club "set a goal [of] obtaining at least a 50-50 showing in Anchorage, and even better for Fairbanks." Hession emphasized that "Alaska conservationists must testify in record numbers at the most important public hearings ever held in Alaska."[57] Representatives of Sierra Club groups in those cities promised to contact every member and produce a record turnout.[58]

The Anchorage hearing, on August 12, brought forth "an outpouring of distrust and bitterness, lofty visions and idealism."[59] Seven hundred people attended the opening session, and nearly 300 waited through the day to testify, including a large group wearing shirts that read "Me Too d(2)." The president of the local Kiwanis displayed a giant cabbage to illustrate the state's agricultural potential; a folk singer dedicated a song to Representative Udall. Another man announced that "the Sierra Club is here in force. They're coached and they're salaried." Most of those who spoke, however, repeated the now familiar slogans of CMAL or the environmental groups. At the end of the day Seiberling announced that 136 witnesses had favored the bill and "only" 131 had opposed it. This score embarrassed the *Anchorage Daily Times*, which had attacked Seiberling before the hearing for suggesting that the numbers would not be important. Later, at a cocktail party, Seiberling read aloud a *Daily Times* editorial comparing him to the biblical Goliath. "Can you believe this?" he asked, shaking his head. "Can you even believe it?"[60] Senator Stevens was visibly upset at news the environmentalists had triumphed at Anchorage. "Most of those people testifying were not Alaskans," he charged. "They were up here for the summer."[61]

Three hundred people testified at Fairbanks on August 20. The morning session featured public officials, including the governor, who proposed to include 50 million acres of state land and an equal amount of federal land in his fifth system. George Matz of the Fairbanks Environmental Center noted that "both sides seemed to like what he said."[62] The mayor and local legislators were critical of H.R. 39.[63] In the afternoon Seiberling, Udall, and two other committee members held separate sessions. The most common objections were that the bill would undermine the state's land selection process and make large areas inaccessible. However, the majority of witnesses—Matz estimated 60 percent—were supportive. Some of the most effective presentations were by individuals who described how the bill would affect them. Seiberling promised that it would be revised to ensure access to wilderness areas, preserve the state's role in fish and game management, and expedite the transfer of public lands to Native groups.[64]

The Seiberling hearings were a milestone in the Alaska campaign. They publicized Alaska's spectacular scenery, demonstrated the effectiveness of the Alaska Coalition, and exposed the divisions in Alaska society. After August it was possible to argue that half or more of all Alaskans favored the preservation of large areas in an undeveloped state. In January Seiberling had been the only Democratic member of the House Interior Committee who had actually visited Alaska. By August most members of Congress were at least aware of Alaska's mountains and wildlife.

The hearings also helped identify the weaknesses in the Udall bill. The wilderness provisions in particular had become lightning rods for criticism. In June Udall had privately anticipated these complaints:

> There is a real genuine fear about doing too much to lock up lands when we don't know the facts. We should be careful of making irreversible mistakes and should lean toward mechanisms which point the land toward its ultimate use, but maybe have mechanisms to unlock or maybe mechanisms to review before the final decision is made.[65]

The Alaska hearings confirmed this view. "I believe we reached for too much instant wilderness," he told reporters on August 19. "We may eventually have as much wilderness as I proposed, but I don't think it ought to be wilderness now." He added that "We're flexible, we're flexible on this thing. ... The flexibility is on boundaries, acreages, and wording to protect established uses."[66]

Udall's allies were also ready to make adjustments. Seiberling brought Byron Mallott, president of the Alaska Federation of Natives, to Washington to discuss the bill's subsistence provisions, and he met with officials of the U.S. Geological Survey and the Bureau of Mines to review Alaska's "mineral potential."[67] At the July meeting of the Sierra Club task force, the Alaskans listed changes they believed "must be considered in formulating the final content of the Udall bill," including stronger provisions on subsistence hunting, "possible limited mineral entry," snow mobile travel in wilderness areas, and other revisions that would defuse local complaints.[68] At the conclusion of the hearings Bill Horn, Young's staff assistant, also drew up a list of desirable changes. His list included a plan for cooperative land management and a method for expediting state land selections; otherwise it was practically identical to the Sierra Club list.[69]

THE HOUSE DEBATES

In late November 1977 Governor Hammond surprised many environmentalists by announcing that the state wanted the d(2) legislation to include the remaining 33 million acres it was entitled to under the Statehood Act. The lands he listed included several million acres of Udall's proposed parks as well as parts of Pet 4 and the Arctic National Wildlife Range.[70] Though Natural Resources Commissioner LeResche acknowledged that the governor's request was a negotiating tactic, environmentalists were perplexed and angry. Bob Weeden, now back at the university, agreed to investigate. He wrote to LeResche: "Knowing how vigorously" the state had worked "to persuade the federal government of the unique values of the [Arctic National Wildlife] Range during the past two years," it was "gratifying" that the state would use its selection rights to create "a state-owned Wilderness ... despite the recalcitrance of foot-dragging feds."[71] Four months passed. Finally, LeResche replied that Weeden's interpretation was not quite right: the state wanted the ANWR lands because of their potential as an oil field. Weeden replied caustically that Hammond was "now bending over backwards to please development-oriented groups. ... I feel very confused about what basic principles and motives are being followed."[72]

That episode was an appropriate introduction to the congressional campaign in the following months. Apart from demonstrating the popularity of the preservationist perspective, the Seiberling hearings had emphasized the narrowness of the boosters' objections. Seiberling and Udall had insisted that H.R. 39 was not a threat to the state's economy. Indeed, by encouraging tourism, the state's second fastest growing industry, it was likely to have a positive impact.[73] They had also indicated their willingness to consider modifications in response to legitimate complaints. An outside observer might have predicted the early passage of a compromise bill. In fact, the conflict escalated as boosters poured more (mostly public) money into their campaign and became more strident in their criticism.

Why? First, although parks and refuges would not reduce (and might well stimulate) overall business activity, they might hurt specific interests. The best example was the mining industry, which was still politically influential. Udall and the environmentalists had deliberately excluded the most promising mineralized areas, but they balked at excluding less promising areas with notable scenic or ecological values. The growing battle over the U.S. Borax site in the southern Tongass was an illustration. With fewer opportunities on federal land, miners would have to turn to state or private lands, where they would have to pay royalties rather than the minuscule fees levied by the federal government.[74]

A second reason for the intensity of the congressional battles of 1977–1978 was the convergence of the d(2) conflict and the larger contest over environmental regulation. Would environmental regulations hamstring the economy and lower American living standards? Or would they create "cleaner" economic opportunities and enhance the quality of life? Most people and interest groups thought they knew. Development interests were strongest in rural areas and in western states, and environmental groups were more formidable in urban areas and in the Northeast and the Pacific Coast. One new and potentially decisive factor was the Carter administration. The president had appointed environmental activists and sympathizers to a number of posts. He also ordered Interior Secretary Cecil B. Andrus to shake up the bureaucracy and emphasize land stewardship, including the preservation of Alaska's roadless areas. At his confirmation hearing Andrus had announced that an Alaska lands bill would be the new administration's top priority. A year later, Mike McCloskey concluded that the Carter administration had been "amazingly good."[75]

As Udall and Seiberling began their revisions, the administration's position became important, perhaps decisive. In April Andrus had appeared before the Seiberling subcommittee and pledged support for an Alaska bill. He rejected the Morton bill and pledged to make a thorough study of H.R. 39. Shortly thereafter, he revived the Alaska planning group, named holdover appointee Curtis "Buff" Bohlen to head it, and ordered Bohlen and his staff to review the Morton proposals and H.R. 39. Andrus's obvious preference for the Udall bill was a blow to the Bureau of Land Management and the Forest Service. The National Park Service staff quickly reviewed H.R. 39 and submitted its recommendations for parks and park boundaries; the Fish and Wildlife Service undertook a similar review.

By mid-September the staff recommendations were ready.[76]

In the meantime Andrus and his staff confronted the Alaska politicians. In early July Bohlen visited Alaska and spent several days with the governor's staff and the Land Use Planning Commission. Andrus arrived the following week for a fishing trip with Hammond, followed by a session with the commission. Hession reported that "they worked him over pretty hard on the need for 'cooperative management.'" Andrus subsequently praised the "concept" of cooperative management but rejected Hammond's fifth system. His statements were apparently a "bone" to "pacify the locals."[77]

Andrus also faced opposition from the U.S. Department of Energy, which strongly opposed wilderness status for ANWR. Andrus was unimpressed. "If in fact the area does have high oil and gas potential, then we are saying ... let it be the last place that America develops if we need it."[78] Carter agreed with him.

The Interior Department's September proposal called for 91 million acres of parks and refuges (including 42 million acres of national parks, 45 million acres of wildlife refuges, and 2.5 million acres of national forests), 41 million acres of instant wilderness (mostly in existing units), federal-state management of subsistence zones, and a cooperative planning commission with advisory powers.[79] The major deviations from the Udall bill were in the park proposals: Andrus called for an 8.2-million-acre Gates of the Arctic park, versus 13.6 million acres in the Udall bill; a 3- million-acre Lake Clark park, versus 7.5 million acres; a 12.1-million-acre Wrangell park, versus 14 million acres; and so on. There were exceptions: Andrus proposed to increase ANWR by 8.9 million acres, versus Udall's 8.4 million. Altogether, Andrus reduced Udall's national park acreage by 22 million acres and his refuge acreage by 5 million acres. Still, his total was 10 million acres more than Morton's.[80]

Assured of administration support, Seiberling and his staff spent the following weeks revising H.R. 39. Their new bill added 104 million acres to the four systems (45 million to parks, 53 million to refuges, 2.7 million to wild and scenic rivers, and 5.8 million to national forests) and designated 82 million acres of wilderness. Park and refuge boundaries were redrawn to exclude mineral claims and increase sport hunting. A new subsistence provision loosened federal controls. The Interior Department was authorized to conclude cooperative agreements with state, local, and Native authorities, and an advisory coordinating council was to recommend cooperative management zones.[81] Seiberling proposed to start the markup process in early November.

At this point, however, he encountered unexpected opposition. He had anticipated Republican efforts to weaken the bill but not the active hostility of several Democrats. The leader of this faction, Lloyd Meeds (D-WA), was a supporter of parks and wilderness areas in Washington and an author of ANCSA. But he had won reelection by only a handful of votes in 1976, apparently because he had devoted too little attention to local timber interests. He was also rumored to be mending fences in an effort to secure a federal judgeship. But there was another, more ominous dimension to his role. Doug Scott specified:

> ... *it is extremely unlikely that he is charting his course without considerable coordination with Washington's junior Senator [Henry Jackson].* It is simply inconceivable, given long-established patterns within the Washington State delegation, to think that his course is independent! *Thus, the real worry of Lloyd's behavior is its possible signal of what to expect in the Senate.*[82]

Meeds's role—and by implication Jackson's—was partly a reflection of the old colonial relationship between the Pacific Northwest and Alaska. Washington industrialists had long opposed anything that would restrict their access to Alaska's resources, and the Seattle Chamber of Commerce had recently voted to spend $60,000 to oppose H.R. 39. Most of the money went to one of Jackson's former staffers, who became the chamber's Alaska lobbyist.[83] Seattle-area unions had a more immediate interest: many Alaska timber and construction workers were Washington residents who returned to their homes in the winter. They accounted for Ketchikan's fearsome reputation, for example. Their presence had long been a major complaint of those who wanted stable, permanent communities and an end to Alaska's colonial status. Many of the transients were Meeds's constituents.

The other Interior Committee Democrats who sided with Meeds— James Santini of Nevada, Austin J. Murphy of Pennsylvania, and Matthew F. McHugh of New York—all had strong ties to organized labor. Although the Alaska Coalition ultimately enlisted the United Auto Workers, the United Mine Workers, and several smaller unions, the AFL-CIO officially opposed H.R. 39, and several AFL-CIO organizations, together with the Teamsters, actively opposed H.R. 39.[84]

The emergence of the Meeds faction coincided with the appearance of strains in the Alaska Coalition. One problem was Brock Evans, the veteran

Sierra Club lobbyist who was accustomed to running his own operation and did not welcome Pam Rich, Chuck Clusen, or other staff members who considered themselves his equals. A "great restlessness" developed between them.[85] After Clusen became chairman of the coalition, the men agreed to work separately. Evans concentrated on other issues.

Clusen also had detractors. His relationship with Wayburn was initially ill defined and prickly. He was close to Scott but not to Peter Scholes, who moved to Washington in 1977 as part of the Wilderness Society's contribution to the staff. Volunteers complained of Clusen's aloofness. When Mike Holloway, vice-chair of the Sierra Club's Alaska chapter, arrived in Washington in September, he found the atmosphere at the Sierra Club office unexpectedly chilly. He sensed that the "professionals were tolerating a 'visitor'" and soon moved to the Friends of the Earth office, which he found more welcoming.[86] A group from Ketchikan had similar experiences. A consultant later concluded that poor communication between the Washington staff and the visiting activists was the most serious deficiency of the Alaska Coalition effort. It often took the form of "curt and negative replies to inquiries" and was particularly noticeable "when there was considerable pressure and a crisis was occurring."[87]

By early 1978 many of these problems had been resolved. Staff functions had been clarified and staff members were more comfortable in their jobs. Apart from Clusen, Scott, Scholes, and Smith, Steve Young of Audubon coordinated the grass-roots organizations, and Dee Frankfourth was responsible for the Alaska volunteers. Celia Hunter, Rich Gordon, Ron Hawk, and Jack Hession all spent long periods in Washington. Volunteers from other states visited for briefer periods. In early February the staff conducted a colloquium for 100 Alaska coordinators.[88]

In the meantime, Meeds and his allies were providing Seiberling, Udall, and the coalition with a painful preview of what lay ahead. A one-week briefing by the subcommittee staff became a prolonged ordeal as Young, Meeds, and others raised questions about virtually every provision of the 178-page bill. The *Fairbanks News-Miner* described their tactic as a "mini-filibuster."[89] Meeds also announced that he would propose his own alternative to H.R. 39. It would allot "uncontroversial" lands to parks and refuges and set aside everything else for study. He told a press conference that H.R. 39 "would tie up huge tracts of land without adequate study to determine their potential mineral wealth." His staff told hometown newspapers that it would restrict commerce between Puget Sound and Alaska.[90] By the time Meeds had agreed to begin the markup, the Thanksgiving recess was approaching. Seiberling adjourned the subcommittee until January.

When the subcommittee reconvened on January 17, 1978, Meeds offered a substitute for H.R. 39. The vote on January 18, 7 to 10 in opposition, set the pattern for the markup process. Seiberling won by holding all the Democrats except Meeds and Santini; the five Republicans supported Meeds. Meeds then proposed amendments to virtually every provision of the Udall bill. He sought to reduce the size of parks and refuges, increase the size of preserves, and delete wilderness. The committee accepted many of his amendments with little discussion. The more extreme proposals, such as making all of Wrangell–St. Elias a preserve, lost by 7 to 10. In some cases Meeds was able to attract wavering Democrats. On the Gates of the Arctic boundaries, for example, he won one vote 10 to 7 (Murphy, McHugh, and Corrada [D–Puerto Rico] defecting) and then lost on a slightly different amendment 7 to 9. After Meeds's proposal to delete part of the southern addition to Mount McKinley Park failed, 7 to 9, he angrily left the session. Two days later the Democrats gathered for a "rapprochement," but Meeds demanded the elimination of all wilderness areas, including the Tongass, and they "agreed to continue to disagree." Altogether Meeds proposed 24 amendments, 16 of which were adopted. They reduced the total acreage to about 100 million acres. Seiberling believed that this "probably represented a consensus all parties would accept."[91]

Young then introduced additional amendments—89 in all, 85 of which were adopted. The most important of his proposals authorized commercial fishing and fish hatcheries in wilderness areas. Most observers considered this a bid for the fishermen, most of whom supported H.R. 39. After a long and contentious discussion, Seiberling and his allies insisted that such activities were already permissible and defeated the amendment 5 to 9.

The subcommittee considered two additional substantive changes during the final phase of the markup process. Seiberling proposed to give the state authority to regulate subsistence hunting and fishing on federal lands. It was adopted. Meeds, who had rejoined the subcommittee, also offered an ambitious amendment—to authorize the secretary of the Interior to approve mining in parks and refuges, subject to congressional veto. Seiberling countered with a substitute, which created a variety of regulatory obstacles to mining. During the "heated debate" that followed, Seiberling cited Senator Jackson's opposition to current mining laws and suggested that Meeds follow his lead. Meeds replied, "That's just what I'm doing. Jackson told me to get the Hell over here and change this bill!" Representative Vento then proposed a modified version of the Seiberling amendment, which Seiberling accepted. The ensuing vote was 9 to 8 in favor of the Vento-Seiberling amendment.[92] The subcommittee then adopted the bill (with Young dissenting) and sent it to the full committee on February 7.

The Interior Committee markup, from February 28 to March 15, was largely a replay of the subcommittee deliberations. A proenvironment minority, including Representatives Philip Burton (D-CA) and Paul Tsongas (D-MA), worked to strengthen the bill, while several Republicans wavered, and two undecided Democrats, including Representative Murphy, took "a walk" and did not attend. Representative McHugh, the other wavering Democrat, resigned from the committee during the markup; his replacement, Robert Kastenmeier (D-WI), was a Udall loyalist. As a result, Udall and Seiberling were able to command a narrow majority throughout the proceedings.

The first test occurred between February 28 and March 1, when Seiberling and Meeds engaged in an extended debate over Meeds's proposal to substitute what he called a "compromise" bill for the subcommittee's "no growth, no development" bill. Meeds proposed 92 million to 95 million acres for the four systems but eliminated most of the wilderness and included enough loopholes to make most of the land de facto multiple use. Udall led the counterattack. Congress had treated the state and the Natives with remarkable generosity, he argued. It should have set aside parks and refuges first, given land to the Natives second, and then taken care of the state. But this sequence was "unfortunately reversed," giving the state and the Natives the best land, plus access to the land that the Bureau of Land Management would continue to administer. "This is some lockup!" he charged. It was time to restore balance. Meeds's charge of "no growth" was really a confession of "no facts; no common sense."[93] After considerable parliamentary wrangling, the committee defeated the Meeds alternative 20 to 23.

In the following days Udall, Seiberling, and their allies fought off major revisions. Young lost decisively when he tried to bring up amendments that the subcommittee had already rejected. At one point Representative John Krebs (D-CA) observed that he had lived in Jerusalem for many years, but "the Jerusalem hagglers could take lessons from Young."[94] Young and Meeds were often successful, however, when they proposed more appealing changes. Their principal target was the Tongass wilderness areas. Bill

Horn had produced a report, widely circulated, contending that H.R. 39 would raise logging costs and lead to job losses. His data and analysis were questionable, but his charges worried many committee members. Citing the threat to Tongass millworkers, Meeds proposed to reduce overall wilderness acreage to 33 million and place 60 million acres under study. Without this change the bill was "a prescription for disaster, would aggravate organized labor, and would not survive a floor fight in the House."[95] To counter this move, Representative Bob Eckhardt (D-TX) proposed to delete 5 million acres, including the entire Misty Fiords wilderness. Udall and Seiberling reluctantly supported Eckhardt's amendment in order to defeat Meeds. An angry Meeds described it as an "abortion." In any case, the Eckhardt amendment won the votes of two wavering Democrats, and the Meeds amendment lost 20 to 24.[96]

Seiberling also felt compelled to compromise on ANWR because of recent U.S. Geological Survey reports of oil deposits along the Arctic coast. He proposed to make the entire area a wilderness but to authorize the Interior Department to study the coastal region. The Republicans wanted to exclude the coastal area altogether. Seiberling quoted a prominent oil executive who had said that years of study would be necessary "before any investment was appropriate." In the meantime "it made no sense to take the area out of wilderness status." The Republican amendment lost 16 to 23; Seiberling's proposal won 21 to 19 and survived a move to reconsider by one vote, 21 to 22.

Young did succeed in deleting 450,000 acres (Rich Gordon estimated it was actually 800,000 acres) from ANWR's southern border. His amendment precipitated a long debate over state land selection rights. Seiberling finally agreed to the reduction if Young promised not to propose other boundary changes. Young agreed.

The committee approved the revised bill on March 21 by a vote of 32 to 12. It added 98 million acres to the four systems, including 43 million acres to parks, 51 million acres to wildlife refuges, 1.7 million acres to wild and scenic rivers, and 3.3 million acres to the Tongass and Chugach national forests. Seventy-five million acres would be wilderness.[97]

The bill then went to the Merchant Marine Committee, which had jurisdiction over wildlife refuges. Representative Robert Leggett (D-CA), who chaired the Subcommittee on Fisheries and Wildlife, had agreed to consider the legislation only after Udall had finished.[98] The prospect of more delays—Young was also a member of this subcommittee—prompted Leggett and Buff Bohlen, who now headed the committee's staff, to negotiate. The subcommittee would reduce the wilderness acreage and Young would not delay the legislation.[99] Leggett also wanted to enlarge several refuges and stop the ANWR oil study. To placate state officials and the Land Use Planning Commission, he agreed to support a cooperative wildlife study area in southwestern Alaska.[100]

The committee's markup session on April 27 reflected those arrangements. It made Pet 4 a wildlife refuge; reduced wilderness acreage, and created a Bristol Bay cooperative management area (but not a fifth system). There were two major disputes. Representative John Breaux (D-LA) proposed a study of caribou and oil drilling; if the study found no incompatibility, drilling in ANWR could proceed. Leggett and David Bonior (D-MI) opposed Breaux's amendment, citing the president's objections. It lost. The second dispute was over a proposal to delete 600,000 acres from the Yukon Flats refuge, part of the agreement with Young. Leggett insisted on upholding the deal.[101] The committee's actions increased the total refuge acreage to 77 million and reduced total wilderness by 8 million. Harry Crandell worried that "H.R. 39 could no longer be portrayed as a compromise, carefully drawn measure. Floor credibility no longer assured."[102]

In mid-March Alaska Coalition leaders drew up a plan for the final stage of the House campaign, the floor fight. They proposed "a lobbying effort beyond the scope of any we've previously been a part of."[103] Twenty full-time lobbyists, a research committee, and a media committee were to conduct a "professional, tightly coordinated operation aimed at ensuring the success of 'The Land Conservation Vote of the Century.'" Sandy Turner, an experienced political organizer, joined the staff to coordinate the work of the constituent organizations. Eight coordinators in Washington were to keep in touch with state coordinators. Phone banks and mass mailings provided additional contacts.[104] Their goal was simple: "not to win [but] to win Big."[105]

Each lobbyist would be responsible for 15 to 18 representatives. At the end of the day, they would report back to Doug Scott or Peter Scholes. From late afternoon until late in the evening, staff members and volunteers would work the phones, lining up hometown supporters or experts who could influence particular lawmakers. Scott recalled the scene at the Sierra Club office during the days leading up to the vote:

> Lobbyists were phoning in up-to-the minute appraisals of how each representative would vote. These triggered calls to volunteer leaders ... Every night we updated assessments, planned intensified lobbying of the most critical representatives, and readied lobbying instructions and hand-out materials for the following day.[106]

By early May they had detailed reports on every representative. Most Democrats from the Northeast and from urban districts generally were "safe." Many Republicans from the Northeast were also supportive. The challenge facing coalition lobbyists was suggested by Ohio's half-dozen Republicans who represented rural areas and small towns. One was "wobbling," another was "hopeless," others "were at least interested." The hidebound Clarence Brown was apparently beyond redemption. "Write off fucker," the report advised.[107]

Seiberling and Leggett drafted a revised bill, which they presented to the House on May 17. It created 10 new national parks (7 with preserve units) totaling 43 million acres, added new and expanded wildlife refuges totaling 77 million acres, designated 25 wild and scenic rivers, and made additions to the Tongass and Chugach national forests totaling 2.7 million acres; 68 million acres would be wilderness. The bill also permitted subsistence activities, authorized sport hunting in preserves, and created a Bristol Bay cooperative management program.[108]

Three critical votes preceded the final vote. A Young amendment to delete 4.5 million acres lost 141 to 251. A Meeds amendment to reduce total wilderness acreage to 33 million acres and eliminate the Tongass areas lost 119 to 240. And Young's proposal to send the entire bill back to committee lost 67 to 242. The final vote, on May 19, was 277 to 67—the "Big" victory that coalition leaders had sought. The bill commanded large majorities among eastern and midwestern representatives. Massachusetts, New Jersey, and Pennsylvania together provided one-third of the victory margin on the Young amendment and one-quarter of the margin on the Meeds amendment. Southern and western representatives divided evenly except on the final vote, when many Young and Meeds supporters switched sides. Yet the regional totals obscure important distinctions, especially in the West. California and Colorado, for example, were strongly supportive while the other western states backed Young and Meeds. The Washington delegation was the most strongly negative of all, providing six votes for the Young and Meeds amendments and only one for Udall.

The House votes of mid-May 1978 reflected the growth of environmentalism and the coalition's aggressive lobbying. Environmental sensitivity was strongest among Democrats, easterners, and urban dwellers, weakest among rural residents and those identified with extractive industries, especially Alaska's extractive industries. The best example of these divisions was the contrast between California (strongly supportive of the Udall bill) and the surrounding, lightly populated states (mildly to strongly hostile).

The House votes were not the "cheap" votes that many observers had antic-ipated. The CMAL campaign had mobilized trade associations, chambers of commerce, and labor unions. Yet the Alaska Coalition maintained the momentum it had generated during the 1977 hearings. It now had its big victory. But only six months remained before the d(2) withdrawals expired, and the Senate had yet to take any meaningful action. On May 19 there was still no assurance that the Alaska campaign would produce tan-gible results.

THE SENATE CAMPAIGN

With the successful House vote the focus of the Alaskan campaign shifted to the Senate and particularly to the Senate Energy (formerly Interior) Committee. The Senate was typically less responsive to public opinion, and a disproportionate number of Energy Committee members were from lightly populated western states, where development interests dominated both parties. Several western senators regularly gave proxy votes to Chairman Jackson and did not attend the committee meetings. Doug Scott recalled that he and his colleagues were "outsiders there"; they "did not have the same influence" they had in the House.[109] They took some com-fort in the knowledge that CMAL, the trade associations, and the unions also had less leverage.

The key to the Senate debate was Jackson, who had long dominated the Energy Committee. In theory, Jackson's role gave the environmental-ists an advantage: he had played a leading role in shaping the environ-mental legislation of the previous decade, including the National Environmental Policy Act, and was a recipient of the Sierra Club's highest award. He had also introduced the environmentalists' Alaska bills in the 1970s, and his staff had encouraged them to make a concerted, once-and-for-all campaign in 1977. Yet Jackson was suddenly reticent. Though committed to legislation, he was wary of the coalition campaign. He was, as his friend Cecil Andrus recalled, "shaped by the World War II experi-ence. ... Jackson saw the need for conservation—but also oil reserves and minerals that the country might need in an emergency."[110] A variety of political pressures reinforced these concerns. Jackson resented Carter and was unwilling to rubber-stamp his "number one" environmental meas-ure. He was also keenly aware that many Seattle business leaders opposed H.R. 39.

Jackson's position left the campaign bereft of Senate leadership. Lee Metcalf had agreed to introduce the coalition bill, but ill health (he died later in 1977) prevented him from playing an active role. Coalition leaders hoped to recruit Frank Church (D-ID), but he declined because of other issues. They settled on John Durkin (D-NH), a junior senator. Durkin spent a week in Alaska in May 1977, fishing with Dixie Baade, meeting the SEACC staff, and conferring with environmentalists in Anchorage and Fairbanks.[111] He also attracted 10 cosponsors. But he did not have the standing of Jackson or Church. The lack of a powerful sponsor meant that Alaska's senators would have greater influence on the legislation.

Since succeeding Ernest Gruening in 1969, Mike Gravel had acquired a reputation as a flamboyant and loquacious outsider. A former real estate developer, he was an archetypal booster who championed showy public works projects. His pet scheme was a giant enclosed recreational facility near Mount McKinley. In April 1978, he proposed a "magnetic levitation" train that would run between Anchorage and the domed city.[112] Terms like "lightweight," "show horse," and "opportunist" often appeared in accounts of his activities.

On d(2), Gravel was unyielding. He refused to endorse the governor's fifth system and advocated a plan that was even more favorable to the state. After reviewing Gravel's proposal in early 1978, Harry Crandell wrote that "if Senator Gravel wasn't serious ... this proposal would be a joke. But he is."[113] Barring acceptance of such a plan, Gravel was clear about his intention to prevent any legislation from passing the Senate. Critics assumed that he wanted to keep the issue alive for his 1980 reelection campaign.

In contrast, Ted Stevens had become an insider who had "won the respect and affection of his colleagues."[114] Largely indifferent to ideology, he was an accomplished wheeler-dealer. He was also close to Jackson. Critics labeled him the third senator from Washington. Yet there was another side to Stevens, one that was most visible in Alaska. After a meeting in early 1978, an angry environmentalist wrote that the senator was "a feisty little man—a man who gives the impression of meeting up with the business end of a porcupine, with all quills at the ready."[115] Stevens rarely passed up an opportunity to demonize environmentalists as the "effete rich" who sought to make Alaska "their private playground."[116] They were "people from down south or those who lived here for two months and call themselves Alaskans."[117]

By the late 1970s environmentalists were accustomed to Stevens's demagoguery. Some were outraged. "How does one counter accusations that
Jim Kowalsky is a well-paid minion of the enemies of Alaska except with
utter dismay," asked one observer. Most of them, however, refused to take
Stevens's jibes seriously. Tina Stonorov attended a meeting the senator had
with representatives of the Fairbanks Chamber of Commerce in June
1978. She recalled afterward,

> ... it was a situation of the big time person with connections coming to town to
> explain all the good he is doing. ... I decided that I would attend simply to be pres-
> ent as a thorn in everyone's side and not let them down: after all the greenies are
> everywhere and ever present—right? ... The Fairbanksans present know nothing
> about d-2, DC, national movement, etc. etc. etc. it was really brought home that
> they are completely out of touch ... Stevens took advantage of all their shortcom-
> ings ... giving long simple minded replies that obscured every issue totally, mixed
> issues up and blamed everything—every ill of society on environmentalists. It was
> actually kind of wonderful how he did it—he should have been an actor.[118]

Despite his bluster, Stevens was circumspect about what he would actually do. On several occasions he opposed delays because environmental
sentiment would only grow stronger. He apparently believed he could
engineer a booster-friendly law that would quiet the environmentalists.
"The key," he indicated, "is whether any federal land is to be opened to
economic interests—timber, mining, tourism or any development."[119]

But he too faced obstacles. One was disarray in the boosters' ranks,
reflected in Walter Hickel's long-anticipated challenge to Hammond in the
1978 Republican primary. Equally troubling was a state proposal, called
the Beirne Initiative, that would give away a million acres of state land to
"homesteaders." Although Hammond condemned the initiative, most
Alaska politicians applauded it, and the voters initially agreed. To outsiders, it was an indication of how ill-equipped the state was to manage its
own lands, much less federal lands as part of a fifth system. Another fias-
co involved the state-sponsored Steering Council for Alaska Lands, created
to educate the country on the d(2) issue. Based on the illusory "consensus"
position, the council proved unwieldy and unmanageable. After spending
hundreds of thousands of dollars on consultants, a film that pleased no
one, and a public opinion poll that was supposed to document opposition
to the Udall bill but actually showed widespread support, the council collapsed in disarray.[120]

Still more serious was the rapidly escalating conflict between Gravel
and Stevens. Long antagonistic, their relations deteriorated rapidly in the

1970s. Gravel refused to endorse the consensus bill, attacked Stevens's proposals, and called several of his statements ridiculous. Stevens said Gravel's criticism made him so angry that he couldn't sleep, and he got up "in the middle of the night to make a list of Gravel's actions on the d-2 issue."[121]

The most important point on that list was undoubtedly Gravel's promise to filibuster any bill that emerged from Jackson's committee. Apart from defeating the legislation, his goal was to portray Stevens as "soft" on d(2). Stevens "was prepared to sell out too much."[122] Gravel's accusations might complicate Stevens's 1978 reelection campaign, but they were also likely to drive uncommitted senators into the Durkin camp.

Alaska Coalition leaders were unsure what to make of these developments. They generally agreed with Tina Stonorov that "Gravel has gone MAD!" and viewed Stevens as a devious schemer.[123] One of Seiberling's staff assistants analyzed a letter from Stevens, listing objections to the House bill. The aide concluded that it was "a farrago of rhetoric with a quite limited number of specific points. ... I wonder whether there is any point in directly addressing Stevens ... he will not be either impressed or reasonable regardless of facts or responsible presentations."[124]

In mid-June 1978, as the Senate Energy Committee began to mark up the Alaska legislation, Clusen, Wayburn, and McCloskey assessed their prospects. Clusen concluded that "mass confusion" among the Alaskans had created an "upbeat" mood among environmentalists.

This scattering of various Alaska political leaders across the landscape ... may prove to be the most important factor in enabling us to get a bill on the floor. ... There may be a situation here which we may exploit to our advantage. ... Since it is a known fact that Gravel would like nothing better than to make a fool out of Stevens and vice versa, we may be able to ... play one against the other and similarly with the Governor.[125]

Other developments, however, were less favorable. Jackson had told Wayburn that he was pessimistic about the bill's prospects, a statement that Clusen, at least, interpreted as a bid for "significant concessions to the Alaska senators." Jackson was "clearly maximizing his maneuvering room." The Interior Department was also a question mark. Clusen and other coalition leaders were concerned about Andrus's relationship with Hammond, who was seeking help for his reelection campaign. "This raises the possibility of Andrus making concessions. ... to help out his good friend, Jay Hammond. ... Quite frankly, we've had great difficulty throughout this campaign in getting the Interior Department to get all its machinery moving smoothly."[125] In view of these dangers, Clusen made an appointment with Stuart Eizenstat, Carter's chief domestic affairs adviser. He wanted to "press the idea of the President threatening strong land freezes if this bill does not pass" and to establish a "direct relationship with the White House lobbyists."[127]

Several days later Clusen, Scott, Scholes, and representatives of the national organizations met Eizenstat and members of his staff. For a half-hour they discussed "what should be done if the bill is not enacted this year." Clusen urged that the president "use the strongest of withdrawal authorities, i.e. the Antiquities Act, to designate all of the areas in the House-passed bill as National Monuments." Eizenstat, though noncommittal, was "quite interested" in "withdrawal options." The environmentalists then spent an hour with Bob Thompson, Carter's Senate lobbyist. Thompson believed the bill was dead. Coalition leaders insisted that a "strong bill" was still possible but emphasized that they "would prefer to come back next year than to have some rigged deal ... which gutted significant parts of the House-passed bill." As they discussed strategies and options, Thompson "seemed to gain enthusiasm," realizing that "it is an easy issue for many senators to vote for and one for which Carter could gain much credit." They agreed to meet again in a few weeks.[128]

In the meantime Senator Jackson made no secret of his disdain for the House bill. He announced that the Energy Committee could focus on "policy issues" and then proceeded to offer his own proposals on each issue.[129] Coalition lobbyists believed that six members of the committee were likely to support the coalition's position. Three others were approachable. Five were certain opponents, and Jackson controlled the other two votes. In effect, he could give the environmentalists a solid majority or ensure their defeat.[130] He had also invited the Alaska senators to attend as nonvoting participants. Stevens accepted, but Gravel declined; for several days he used procedural appeals to prevent the committee from meeting.

The best illustration of Jackson's approach was an early effort to open ANWR to gas and oil exploration. The Udall bill had doubled the size of ANWR and designated the northern two-thirds as wilderness. Opponents, however, refused to concede defeat. The failure of exploratory activities in Pet 4 (officially renamed National Petroleum Reserve Alaska in 1976), west of Prudhoe Bay, created additional pressures to go east into ANWR. A Geological Survey report, judiciously released in spring 1978, trumpeted the potential of the ANWR coast. As a result, Seiberling and Udall had agreed to additional geological studies. Jackson sought to settle the issue once and for all.

On July 18 he proposed an eight-year study of the entire Arctic coast to identify oil and gas deposits. Six committee members, including most of the Republicans, supported his plan; Durkin and Howard Metzenbaum (D-OH) opposed it. Durkin countered with a proposal to make the whole area wilderness. Jackson dismissed Durkin's alternative and called for a vote on his plan. The vote, delayed until July 24, was 12 to 7 in favor of the study. Durkin and Metzenbaum then tried to limit the size of the study area. This proposal lost 9 to 10, with one Republican and one additional Democrat joining the Durkin faction. Dale Bumpers (D-AR), who had disappointed coalition leaders by supporting Jackson, then proposed a ban on actual drilling unless Congress specifically authorized it. Jackson agreed to this change. The committee adopted the amended measure 12 to 7.[131]

That series of votes set the pattern for the committee's deliberations. Jackson used his bipartisan coalition to dominate the proceedings. By the end of August his staff was introducing new material so rapidly that no one knew exactly what was happening. Tony Motley observed that after one session "seven people on the same side of the issue could not agree on what had taken place." The senators had "trouble agreeing on what they've agreed on."[132] Crandell wrote that "in all my years of legislative activity I have never before seen a committee work on such an important piece of legislation when the level of knowledge (or interest) has been so low."[133]

In the face of that onslaught, Durkin had little influence. After numerous clashes with Stevens, Jackson asked them to meet privately to resolve their differences. Several fruitless sessions later, Durkin ended the meetings, refusing to deal "with that untrustworthy s.o.b."[134] The continuing conflicts gradually discouraged Durkin's followers; after mid-August, he usually represented the environmentalist position alone. By September, when the committee turned to the Tongass, Jackson, Durkin, and Stevens were typically the only participants. Jackson and his staff made the decisions, subject to Stevens's haggling. What had promised to be a dramatic confrontation between environmental and antienvironmental interests proved wholly one-sided.

The result was a bill that differed significantly from H.R. 39. It included all the units in the House bill but reduced the total acreage to 93 million; raised the national forest total to 8 million acres, including almost 6 million in a new Porcupine National Forest on land the House bill had earmarked for ANWR and the Yukon Flats Wildlife Refuge; and created five

Bureau of Land Management "conservation" areas, totaling another 8 million acres. The national park system would receive only 42 million acres, half in the form of preserves. Gates of the Arctic was divided into five separate units; ANWR was carved up between three management agencies.[135] The bill created 38 million acres of wilderness, mostly in national parks. It added 6 million acres to ANWR (versus 10 million in H.R. 39) and no wilderness (versus 14 million acres in H.R. 39). The secretary of the Interior was to conduct an eight-year study of the oil and gas potential of the Arctic coast.

Jackson's influence was most obvious in the Tongass sections. Over Stevens's vociferous objections, he insisted on keeping Misty Fiords intact—he told his staff "to hell with Borax"—but then placed part of it, together with part of Admiralty Island, into a "reserve" or "pulp bank" that could be opened with congressional approval if timber shortages threatened local employment. The bill also required the Tongass managers to make available at least 520 million board feet of timber per year and authorized an annual fund of $10 million to aid in achieving this objective.[136]

On October 5 the committee voted to approve the bill. Jackson requested and was given virtually unrestricted authority to draft a compromise measure.[137] Jackson could have had no illusions about the task before him. A week earlier, in response to the Senate committee's ANWR vote, Chuck Clusen, Cynthia Wilson (Andrus's representative), and Harry Crandell had met to prepare a response. They agreed on what was unacceptable: mining in parks or wilderness areas, designated transportation corridors, exclusion of ANWR or Tongass lands, less than 90 million total acres or less than 50 million acres of wilderness, and a fifth system.[138] Udall and Seiberling wrote to Jackson on August 1, listing "those matters ... the House views as basic." The letter quoted Andrus's statement that 93 million total acres was "the absolute 'bottom line'" and emphasized the importance of wilderness, though it did not include a specific total.[139] The letter arrived during an Energy Committee session. Jackson read it, handed it back to his aide and "made no audible comment."[140] After the committee released its final report, the administration and the coalition predictably declared it unacceptable.

For months there had been widespread speculation about what would happen at this point. Most observers believed that the president would act unilaterally if Congress did not pass an Alaska bill. In late September, Andrus promised new parks, refuges, and wilderness study areas regardless of what Congress did.[141] Stevens also predicted that Carter would use the

Antiquities Act to set aside much of the park and refuge land covered in H.R. 39.[142] With this threat in the background, congressional leaders searched for a way to break the impasse. Too little time remained for a formal conference committee, and Gravel, who described the Senate bill as "a terrible mish mash," was unyielding.[143] Only some quick, informal arrangement that produced a bill close to the Senate version would have any chance of passage. That is apparently what Stevens had in mind. At a press conference in late September, he was reported to be "confident— even cocky" that he could conclude a deal with Udall "to accept the Senate bill."[144]

On October 11 Jackson arranged a meeting of Durkin, Stevens, Udall, and Seiberling to explore the possibilities. At the same time Stevens sent telegrams to various groups in Alaska, asking them to pressure Gravel: "I am telling Alaskans: if they want that bill, convince Gravel to help me."[145]Gravel sent out his own telegrams asking for advice. The following day he announced that most of the messages he had received—he specifically mentioned CMAL and the Steering Council for Alaska Lands—had urged cooperation and that, as a result, he was withdrawing his filibuster threat.[146]

With that apparent concession the negotiations took on a new urgency. Andrus interrupted a vacation to participate, and Gravel attended as well. By the evening of October 13 they had reached agreement on a number of issues. The senators agreed to eliminate the Porcupine National Forest and designate most of ANWR (but not the Arctic coast or the southern foothills) as wilderness. Crandell reported that "the Senate version of all other proposed areas (Parks, Wildlife Refuges, SE Alaska) was adopted, with only minor modifications."[147] Jackson and Udall ordered their staffs to draw up new legislation. As the meeting was breaking up for the evening, Udall seemed optimistic. "Let's get it resolved and go to the floor with it," he urged. At that point Gravel, who had been silent, interrupted: "Just a minute," he said. "I've got a few things I want to raise." He demanded seven designated transportation corridors and a ban on use of the Antiquities Act—all anathema to the environmentalists. The other participants were furious. Gravel insisted that he would be reasonable and Jackson instructed the staff to consider his demands.[148]

During the night the staff prepared a new ad hoc bill. It raised the total acreage to 95 million and wilderness to 51 million acres and included several provisions designed to placate Gravel. The Alaska Coalition staff also prepared revisions, which Clusen presented to Udall early the following morning.[149]

When the lawmakers met at 9:00 on October 14, the last day of the congressional session, the debate continued. No one was pleased with the tentative agreement, and the House negotiators, buttressed by the coalition's critique, were increasingly wary. Whether an actual deal would have materialized is unclear, but that question soon became moot. When Gravel learned that his transportation corridors would be subject to veto by the Interior secretary, he protested, promising to filibuster anything less than mandated corridors. In a later public statement he emphasized his unhappiness with the Alaska Coalition proposals on the Tongass and ANWR. They were "near proof that the environmental community seeks ... to prevent economic activity on state, native, private and non-appropriated federal lands."[150] Whatever his exact concern, his objections made any agreement impossible, and the meeting broke up.

As the negotiators were leaving, Andrus suggested that they extend the d(2) deadline. He had already prepared a bill for a one-year extension. Everyone seemed to agree, and Stevens and Seiberling refined the language. Udall attached it to another House bill later that day and it passed. The Senate did not consider the extension until 5:30 a.m. on the morning of October 15, at the end of a hectic night-long session. After bitter exchanges with Stevens and Durkin, Gravel declared that he would not approve the extension and began a filibuster, dooming that bill as well.

In this fashion the campaign for Alaska lands, involving thousands of individuals, million of dollars, and the fate of 100 million acres of Alaska wilderness, came to an ignominious end. Surprisingly few tears were shed. Gravel opposed the Senate bill, and even Stevens declined to support it. Alaska Coalition leaders were equally disgruntled. Clusen recalled that "we were not unhappy" with the outcome.[151] When reporters later asked Stevens about the administration's threats to use the Antiquities Act in lieu of legislation, he replied that any withdrawals would cause "substantial difficulties" and complicate the work of the next Congress.[152] As usual, Gravel did not share his concerns. He had earlier urged Alaskans not to worry about the expiration of the d(2) withdrawals. "The only thing that's going to expire is a memo from the Congress of 1971 to the Congress of 1978 to look at this and maybe do something."[153]The events of 1977–1978 demonstrated the popularity of environmental causes, the cohesion of the Alaska Coalition, and, at the same time, the ability of a relative handful of representatives and senators (Meeds and his followers, as well as Jackson, Stevens, and especially Gravel) to force significant concessions and even defeat popular measures. The contrasts with the events of 1972–1973 also stand out. H.R. 39 evoked more emotion and enthusiasm than the earlier attempt to dictate the pipeline route. Environmentalists were better prepared to sustain the campaign and had, in Udall, Andrus, and Carter, greater influence. As Clusen insisted, there was every reason to believe they could push through a bill in 1979 that was as strong as the bill Gravel had sabotaged—or perhaps even stronger.

CHAPTER 8

BIRTH OF ANILCA

Life in interior Alaska, according to Ginny Hill Wood, revolves around three seasonal events: Freeze-up, Break-up, and Crack-up. The first two are part of Nature's cycle; Crack-up, on the other hand, is a human phenomenon. Typically occurring in late winter, after months of darkness and subzero temperatures, it

> ... manifests itself by marriages and other relationships breaking up, flaring tempers, suddenly selling out and splitting for the Lower 48, quitting jobs or school, or maybe just cutting your hair short or shaving your beard.[1]

In 1979 Crack-up came early and took different forms. The tensions of the boom years, the pressures of the divisive campaign for the proposed Alaska National Interest Lands Conservation Act (ANILCA), and the demagoguery of two gubernatorial elections (the Republican primary contest between Governor Jay Hammond and Walter Hickel, which resulted in a dead heat, resolved in Hammond's favor by the courts, followed by an unsuccessful Hickel write-in effort) were too much. The result was a "fracturing" of the "fabric of Alaska's relationships, political and social."[2]

Crack-up was soon apparent in the debates over Alaska's potential park and refuge lands. The completion of the oil pipeline had eased the crisis in state finances and clarified the state's economic future. In theory it should have made Alaska's business and political establishment more relaxed and tolerant, more receptive to what economist Arlon Tussing had called a "grand bargain" with environmentalists. The pending expiration of the Section 17d(2) withdrawals under the Alaska Native Claims Settlement Act was an additional reason for compromise and resolution. In fact the state's new prosperity only encouraged greater resistance and more extreme assertions of states' rights. These perverse effects meant that Alaska's politicians would again play a disruptive role in the deliberations of Congress.

Apart from those pressures, the continuing national economic malaise ensured that the renewed debate would not be a simple replay of the events of 1977–1978. The energy crisis and recession of 1973–1975, coupled with deeper problems suggested by a persistent decline in productivity, resulted in what economist W. Carl Biven has labeled "the decade of the Great Inflations."[3] By 1978 it appeared that the economic outlook might be improving. But a spiraling political crisis in Iran in 1979–1980 led to a new round of oil price rises that reverberated through the economy. The second energy crisis and the subsequent recession, even more severe than that of 1973–1975, increasingly absorbed the attention of Congress and the Carter administration. Like the political climate of Alaska, the economic problems of the late 1970s added uncertainty to the environmentalists' campaign for passage of ANILCA.

ALASKA, 1978–1979

In Alaska the fracturing Wood observed was most apparent at the top of the political system. Senator Mike Gravel's performance at the meetings of the ad hoc congressional committee not only sabotaged the legislation but also transformed his rivalry with Ted Stevens into "mutual loathing."[4] Stevens could barely contain himself. "What he was thinking of when he killed the bill God knows and I'm not even sure if God could fathom his thinking," he told one interviewer. He suggested that Gravel seek "psychiatric help."[5] Gravel counterattacked by openly supporting Stevens's lightly regarded

Democratic opponent in the 1978 senatorial contest. Gravel-financed ads portrayed Stevens as weak and irresolute: "If we want both our Senators to fight their hardest on the D-2 issue, then either we change Ted's mind, or we replace him. ... Toughen up or we'll get rid of you."[6]

A month after the election, which Stevens won handily, the rivalry became implacable. On December 4, 1978, Stevens attended Hammond's inauguration in Juneau, then flew by private jet to Anchorage for a meeting with officials of Citizens for the Management of Alaskan Lands (CMAL). Stevens's wife Ann, Tony Motley, and two Alaska business executives accompanied him. As the plane was landing, a severe wind gust flipped it over and broke it into pieces. Only Stevens and Motley survived. Reasoning that the CMAL meeting would not have been necessary if a d(2) bill had passed in 1978, Stevens blamed Gravel for his wife's death. He refused to accept Gravel's condolences and began to recruit candidates to challenge his colleague in 1980.[7]

A parallel conflict between Hammond and Cecil B. Andrus further complicated the situation. As late as summer 1977, Alaska Coalition leaders had worried about the close ties between the governor and the Interior secretary. But the Andrus-Hammond friendship became increasingly strained as the Alaska politicians positioned themselves as champions of state power. Alaska Coalition analysts considered Hammond's plan for federal-state resource management a sophisticated expression of the states' rights position, but it satisfied few boosters. As the governor's political future became increasingly problematic, he abandoned this "fifth system" for more conventional demands.

In 1977 Representative Morris Udall had agreed to include a provision in his bill facilitating state land selections if the state agreed to stay away from the proposed parks. This bargain entailed no sacrifice by the state, since it had already acquired the lands (such as Prudhoe Bay) with the greatest economic potential, and the Alaska Coalition drafters had deliberately excluded other lands coveted by the mining and oil industries. The redrafting of H.R. 39 in fall 1977 subtracted even more. According to several reputable analysts, the divorce was now virtually complete. The only possible exceptions were the Tongass and the Arctic National Wildlife Refuge (ANWR), and they were questionable. As Matthew Berman, a University of Texas researcher, pointed out, the Tongass wilderness provisions would result in savings, not costs. "Commercial timber management in the Tongass," he concluded, "is a hidden jobs-subsidy program, a federal welfare program." Similarly, the ANWR coast was an uncertain gamble.[8] But such analyses were no more popular than Hammond's fifth system. Given the prevailing political climate, it was difficult for any ambitious politician to settle for only 95 percent of Alaska's commercially exploitable natural resources.

Two days after the end of the congressional session, Stevens requested a meeting with President Carter. Because of the senator's "reasonable attitude and willingness to compromise," Carter's staff urged the president to see him as soon as possible. They discussed the legislation, and Stevens made an "emotional appeal to hold off on executive action, pending congressional action in 1979.[9] Two months later, after Carter had acted to preserve much of the d(2) lands, Stevens charged that the president had violated a "clear understanding" that he would not include the Tongass lands. He had destroyed the "keystone" of the likely legislation. Carter's aides were incredulous and insisted that the president had made no commitment.[10] Andrus, who was present at the meeting, was no less surprised. He later described Stevens as one of the "orneriest" men he had ever met.[11]

Shortly afterward the governor became involved. On October 30 the Interior Department released a draft environmental impact statement on the d(2) lands, a prelude to presidential action. Five days later the Hammond administration asked the federal district court for an injunction to prevent the president from using the Antiquities Act to set aside Alaska lands. Most observers saw this action as an election-eve stunt. Two weeks later, safely reelected, the governor proposed to "defer" the suit in return for the president's promise not to use the Antiquities Act. Bob LeResche, his natural resources commissioner, also indicated that the state would not select lands that were included in the d(2) legislation. The following day, however, LeResche filed for 9 million to 11 million acres in the proposed park areas. As Jack Hession noted, the total wasn't great, but the selections were "diabolically located" to create "massive damage."[12] This was a more serious provocation than the lawsuit. It could only be interpreted as an effort to sabotage the d(2) legislation by creating unmanageable state inholdings. It also violated Hammond's professed commitment to cooperative land management. Two days later Andrus suggested that Hammond withdraw the controversial selections and he would consider the settlement offer. Hammond refused, effectively ending the negotiations. Andrus felt betrayed.[13] At a later meeting with Hammond, he severely criticized the governor for "going back on his word."[14]

Many observers were amazed at what Jack Hession described as Hammond's "incredible" action. "Had the Governor not gone into court, and not filed for the d-2 lands," he wrote, "there would have been no compulsion or justification for the Antiquities Act application." Thanks to Gravel and Hammond, he concluded, "conservationists go into the next Congress with an enormously strengthened position."[15]

Three weeks later the state steering council reviewed these events. Hammond's explanation is recorded in the council's minutes:

> [The governor] thought he had a deal with Andrus. Hammond agreed not to push the state selections that are in conflict with a D-2 bill. ... In return Andrus wouldn't use the Antiquity Act. ... Hammond had told LeReash [sic] to suspend the applications on those 9 million acres. But LeReash didn't do it. ... Hammond was acting very upset with Andrus. He said Andrus backed out of the deal, and he was glad that LeReash hadn't gotten around to canceling those State Selections. But, I think Hammond blames LeReash for the mess. ... I think Hammond blames LeReash for screwing up the deal ... Hammond also blamed LeReash for messing up the personal relationship he had with Andrus.[16]

After Hammond left the meeting, LeResche, "obviously more relaxed," presented his side of the story. In a meeting with Andrus's aides he

> made a presentation on State Selection. Cynthia Wilson flat told him they weren't getting anything. At this time, he just left. That discussion was why he didn't cancel the State Selections in conflict. ... He said that he had a discussion with Stevens and that Stevens wanted continuing litigation to force action in Congress.[17]

Whatever the exact explanation, the state's actions added to the mounting pressure on Carter to use the Antiquities Act, the strongest option available to him. The Alaska Coalition submitted a long rationale, arguing that the preservation of the Alaska sites would make Carter "the greatest conservation President rivaled by none."[18] It also drafted and circulated letters to Carter signed by 130 representatives and 18 senators calling for Antiquities Act withdrawals. Also calling for the "strongest action possible" were 18 Alaska environmental organizations. A group of prominent Republicans, including Rogers Morton, Laurence Rockefeller, and Nathaniel Reed, added their endorsement.[19]

Hammond's failure to withdraw the controversial selections and the environmentalists' campaign set the stage for Carter's decision. On November 17, 1978, the president reviewed his options. James Moorman, now assistant attorney general, argued in favor of a settlement with the state, citing the uncertainty of litigation and the adverse effects of a possible injunction. Andrus led the opposition. Fed up with the Alaskans, he urged rejection on political grounds. A settlement would undermine support in Congress and discourage the environmentalists. Conversely, an executive order would demonstrate presidential leadership. Stuart Eizenstat, Carter's chief domestic adviser, summarized the debate. "On balance, this is a tough and close call." However, the "political factors are all on the side of Interior since acceptance of the settlement will look like we succumbed to pre-emptive State action and were unwilling to tough it out." He favored Andrus's position.[20]

In his autobiography Andrus recalls these events differently. He supposedly raised the possibility of using the Antiquities Act on an unprecedented scale. "Can I do that?" the president asked. "You have the authority, sir," Andrus responded. "Let's do it!" Carter reportedly replied.[21] Although this account oversimplifies the process, it probably captures the spirit of the occasion. The secretary's role was crucial. He was responsible for preparing the administration's response to the congressional stalemate. If he had trusted the Alaska politicians, he might well have recommended a more conciliatory course. In fact he was the most insistent of Carter's advisers. Given Andrus's position, it is hard to imagine Carter's choosing not to use the Antiquities Act. On November 18 Carter formally rejected the settlement.

On November 21 the U.S. District Court in Anchorage heard the state's request for an injunction against the Antiquities Act. Afterward, Moorman, who represented Carter, was unexpectedly optimistic. They had "wiped the State out."[22] Two days later the judge rejected Hammond's request for an injunction.

On November 28 Andrus and Agriculture Secretary Bob Bergland submitted their recommendations to Carter. They had temporarily withdrawn all the lands included in the House bill and called for Carter to proclaim national monuments encompassing the proposed national park lands, several important wildlife refuges, Admiralty Island, and Misty Fiords. Bergland's recommendations for Admiralty and Misty Fiords were particularly important, since the Forest Service had lobbied against the Tongass measures.[23]

On December 1 Carter created 17 new national monuments, covering 56 million acres. Anticipating charges of "overreaching," he did not include all the lands covered in the House and Senate bills but directed Andrus to use other laws to create wildlife refuges encompassing an additional 40 million acres.[24] The Antiquities Act did not provide for wilderness designations, and Congress would have to appropriate money to maintain the monuments. Still, Carter's action was a dramatic response to the congressional deadlock and the expiration of the d(2) withdrawals. Hammond lamented that "Alaska's worst fears have been realized."[25]

Carter's action greatly accelerated the crack-up of 1978–1979. Encouraged by the *Anchorage Daily Times* and the legislature, a variety of bizarre protests followed. A group of sportsmen's organizations calling itself the "REAL Alaska Coalition" organized a rowdy assault on Mount McKinley Park—the "Great Denali Trespass"—that resulted in the death of a protester who drove his snowmobile into an airplane. Another group, Alaskans United, tried to organize a citywide strike in Anchorage. A Fairbanks man camped outside the local post office for 11 days. Supposedly he shook 15,000 hands during his frigid vigil.[26] Hostile bumper stickers, fiery protest meetings, and threats of secession became routine. When Congress reconvened in January 1979, planeloads of outraged boosters descended on Washington. Their boorish behavior—Tony Motley christened them "propeller heads"—did little to inspire confidence in the state or its leaders. Hammond recalled that "those who whipped Alaskan emotions into a White heat" were more responsible for the final legislation than the environmentalists.[27]

Hammond and other critics of the d(2) legislation may have taken perverse comfort in the knowledge that the strains of the congressional battle were also taking their toll on Alaska's environmentalists. In the Southeast the Udall bill had initially had an exhilarating effect. Ted Whitesell periodically worked for the Alaska Coalition, and a steady procession of Southeast Alaska Conservation Council (SEACC) members lobbied Congress in 1977 and 1978. As its prospects brightened, SEACC's staff also increased: Ron Hawk and Kay Greenough continued to run the Juneau office; Paul Peyton, a former Alaska Pulp engineer who would soon join the coalition staff, set up a Sitka office; and Leonard Steinberg, a biologist with the U.S. Fish and Wildlife Service, ran a similar operation in Ketchikan. Mary Ellen Cuthbertson of the Sierra Club continued to work on the wilderness studies.

But the news was not entirely positive. The Sitka and Ketchikan hearings underlined the depth of local opposition to the Tongass wilderness provisions. The omission of Misty Fiords from the House bill was a blow, and Senator Henry Jackson's "pulp bank" suggested that the final legislation might deviate significantly from H.R. 39. In addition, Stevens seemed to be increasingly preoccupied with the Tongass, raising the possibility that the Tongass wilderness areas might be jettisoned in the horse-trading that preceded final congressional action.

The necessity of dealing with the Forest Service simultaneously added to the strain. SEACC and the Sierra Club Legal Defense Fund sued to stop the agency from approving the road to U.S. Borax Company's Misty Fiords mine site. SEACC leaders were equally concerned about a new Tongass management plan, which called for logging more of their proposed wilderness areas.[28] Forest Service hostility to H.R. 39, its ill-disguised assistance to Representatives Don Young and Lloyd Meeds and CMAL, and its opposition to the Carter land withdrawals left little doubt about its intentions.

In fall 1978 Leonard Steinberg prepared a pessimistic assessment of SEACC's prospects. He concluded that the council had failed utterly to influence the Forest Service planning process. In May it had revised its wilderness plan downward to 39 areas and called for immediate wilderness designations for only 12. Yet in the preliminary draft of its new management plan, the Forest Service called for logging 18 of the 39 areas. Of 14 areas that had been cited in either the House or the Senate bill, it proposed to log 11. "If adopted in anything close to its current form," Steinberg concluded, the land use plan "will be the straw that will break SEACC's back." Since administrative appeals and litigation had failed, the organization's only hope was that Congress would increase the number of Tongass areas in the final legislation.[29]

All of those issues came to a head at SEACC's annual meeting. Sixty people gathered in Sitka on September 29 to hear reports on Washington developments by Ron Hawk and Paul Peyton. The next day most of them went by boat to a nearby Forest Service cabin, where they camped, walked the beach, and continued their discussions. Dividing into three groups, they pondered various financial and organizational challenges. The atmosphere was generally buoyant and optimistic. When they reconvened, however, the mood quickly changed. Hawk "confirmed his previous decision to resign," and Greenough indicated that she, too, would soon leave. The endless struggle with the Forest Service had worn them down, and their preoccupation with the Tongass had soured their relations with Chuck Clusen and Doug Scott. They had become "emotionally involved" and had lost "perspective." "Almost everyone at the meeting was stunned."[30] The resignations, coupled with the loss of Cuthbertson shortly afterward (due to Sierra Club cost cutting), raised new questions about the future of SEACC. After some discussion, the Juneau Sierra Club group proposed that SEACC hire a new executive director and an office manager. Steinberg, the only member of the new staff who remained in Alaska, took the post on an interim basis and later became executive director.[31]

H.R. 39 REDUX

There were good reasons to believe that Congress would act on the Alaska legislation in 1979 and that the results would be more generous than the arrangement that had so provoked Gravel in October. As Udall noted, "a lot of time was wasted and it's not going to happen again." If Gravel tried another filibuster, "it will be a 29-month filibuster and I want tickets for the front row."[32] Meeds's retirement also weakened the opposition in the House. Above all, Carter's actions had changed the dynamics of the battle. The monuments had become the starting point for the new Congress. Udall and his allies would work for more but accept nothing less. Mike Harvey, counsel to the Senate Energy Committee, summarized the prevailing view when he predicted that Alaskans would not "get the same deal they got at the end of the session. ... It was late and everybody wanted a bill. It'll never be that way again."[33]

Another plus was the state of the Alaska Coalition. The Seiberling hearings and the House vote on H.R. 39 had proven its ability to mobilize supporters. Friends and opponents alike were impressed. Brock Evans reported early in 1979, "the Alaska Coalition functions very smoothly on an ad hoc informal basis from day-to-day, and the various individuals within it have worked out a very effective way of working together."[34] Cathy Smith was now cochairman with responsibility for administrative matters, freeing Clusen to devote more time to politics. Scott, Peter Scholes, and Steve Young shared the lobbying effort; Rita Molyneaux of the Wilderness Society headed the media staff. Tony Cook was in charge of grass-roots contacts; Jack Hession headed research; Dee Frankfourth had responsibility for Alaska contacts, including the large number of activists who traveled to Washington. John McComb was in charge of finances and the computer operation. The Sierra Club and the Wilderness Society continued to pay most of the bills. By 1979, for example, the Wilderness Society had three full-time staff members assigned to the coalition (Scholes, Stan Senner, and Denise Schlener) and paid the salaries of two other full-time employees (Dee Frankfourth and her sister Vicky). Molyneaux devoted 50 percent of her time to the coalition, and several others—a secretary, two writers, field representatives—were involved periodically. Travel, printing, and mailing raised the total contribution to $142,000.[35]

The Alaska Coalition's greatest asset, however, was its huge cadre of dedicated volunteers. By 1979 some of them, such as Daniel Tandy of New Jersey and Carolyn Carr of Alabama, had become highly visible political organizers. Most of the others played more limited but hardly less important roles. Two examples are revealing. Penny Starr, one of the most active of the Ohio volunteers, made Senator John Glenn (D-OH) her personal project. Despite a generally liberal voting record and overwhelming constituent support for H.R. 39, the cautious senator refused to commit himself. Starr badgered him for more than a year, growing increasingly impatient with his evasive comments. At a meeting in early 1979 she reminded him that he had a mediocre record on conservation issues and suggested that he "shape up" if he wanted to be reelected. "He got very indignant and upset," she reported.[36] She believed that Glenn refused to commit himself because Ohio "big shots seem to be weighing in on the other side."[37] Without her efforts the senator might well have been swayed by those big shots.

Tennessee volunteers had similar problems with James Sasser (D-TN), who resisted coalition entreaties for a year and a half. Although Sasser pledged to support the Alaska bill in early 1978, numerous meetings over the following months left the impression that he would "go whichever way the wind shifts."[38] Tennessee activists enlisted a variety of friends and colleagues to pressure him, but nothing seemed to work. Finally a laudatory editorial in a Nashville newspaper tipped the balance.

By early 1979 coalition lobbyists had prepared an evaluation of the new Congress. In the House they counted 140 cosponsors and "safe" supporters; 186 "swing" members, including most of the newly elected representatives; 31 whom they called "Not Totally Lost"; and 79 "Dirty Thirty and Bad Guys." More detailed assessments of Interior Committee members included lists of individuals or groups likely to influence them.[39] Similar reports on the senators followed. In March another colloquium introduced dozens of activists to the data.

Yet there were also less favorable trends. The midterm elections had produced a large turnover in Congress and a substantial increase in Republican members. Five cosponsors of the Durkin bill had retired or been defeated, and only two or three of their successors expressed comparable interest. The House Interior Committee lost four Democrats and gained one Republican. Of the 140 Representatives who cosponsored the new Udall bill, only 14 were Republicans; of 18 Senate cosponsors, only one was a Republican.

The opposition lobby was also more formidable. In 1978 the CMAL budget had been five times the coalition budget; in 1979 it would be at least seven times as great. Contributors included most of Alaska's leading businesses, headed by the construction industry ($102,000 in 1978) and the Alaska Mutual Savings Bank of Anchorage ($65,000). The oil companies gave at least $10,000 apiece. "It takes a lot of money to fight these environmentalists," Motley explained.[40] He could also count on several trade associations, the AFL-CIO, the Teamsters, and the National Rifle Association. Early in 1979 the Alaska legislature appropriated another $2 million to support its own lobbying effort. Scorning the d(2) steering council, Hammond hired former Stevens staffer and Anchorage attorney John Katz to represent the state. Together with former Representative Meeds, now a lobbyist, Katz worked closely with CMAL and Bill Horn of Young's staff.

Hammond and Natural Resources Commissioner LeResche also devised a new Alaska "consensus" plan. This time they emphasized simpler goals: cancellation of the Carter withdrawals, immediate transfer of state-selected lands, assured access to state and private lands, state management of fish and wildlife on all lands, and exclusion of "valuable resources" from parks and refuges. LaResche acknowledged that the new plan reflected the fact that "our position in Congress has worsened. ... We must be very cautious about promoting unrealistic public expectations."[41] Harry Crandell described it as "Leave us alone to do whatever we want to do, wherever we want to do it, anywhere in the State on Federal lands."[42]

The governor tried to win the backing of various interest groups. On January 21, 1979, he met Celia Hunter; Ben Shaine, now of the Fairbanks Environmental Center; Paul Lowe of the Alaska Center for the Environment in Anchorage; Will Troyer of the Alaska Conservation Society; and other environmentalists to discuss the consensus plan. In what had become a familiar pattern, Hammond was apologetic and conciliatory, admitting that he had blundered in trying to select d(2) lands. He expressed a willingness to redefine "valuable resources" to include "scenic values, wildlife values, salmon spawning stream preservation, and intangible values." He might not be perfect, he implied, but he was far more accommodating than the state's other politicians.[43] By 1979 this argument was wearing thin. Even his Alaska Conservation Society allies were becoming impatient. Soon after the January meeting they expressed a "general consensus that the Department of Natural Resources was running amok and that environmental groups were getting little response to their concerns."[44]

The most important potential obstacle of 1979, however, was Senator Jackson. The factors that had affected his behavior in 1977 and 1978 were no less influential. In addition, the political revolution in Iran and the beginning of the second domestic energy crisis increased his interest in energy development. In mid-January he called for a Prudhoe Bay gas line and the exploration of ANWR.[45] Jackson's position in turn enhanced Stevens's influence. The Alaska senator had formally joined the Energy Committee to work for legislation that would approximate the 1978 Senate bill.

During the Christmas recess Udall and his staff worked with Chuck Clusen and the coalition staff on a revised bill. Udall wanted to pass legislation similar to H.R. 39 early in the session, pressure the Senate to act quickly, and reconcile the differences in a conference committee. He recognized that the critical decisions would be made in conference. After a meeting of Udall, Jackson, and Stevens, Crandell wrote that "Stevens is counting on the House and Senate passing 'any old bill' (preferably watered down) so that a completely new bill can be written in conference."[46] The bill that Udall submitted in January provided for a total of 114 million acres of parks and refuges and 85 million acres of wilderness. It converted Carter's monuments into national parks, set aside 6 million acres of the Tongass and 1.6 million acres of the Chugach National Forest as wilderness, and added the Arctic coast to the ANWR wilderness.

The opposition was also busy. Motley explained that "A lot of guys who last year said they didn't have the time are up here working pretty hard this time."[47] They drew up a bill based on the October 1978 ad hoc negotiations and recruited Representative Jerry Huckaby (D-LA) to introduce it as a substitute for the Udall bill. Huckaby was one of the Dirty Thirty and had voted against the 1978 House bill. His bill set aside a total of 97 million acres and 50 million acres of wilderness but introduced new multiple-use areas and weakened restrictions on development, especially in wildlife refuges. Most of the Tongass wilderness lands would be placed in pulp banks, and ANWR would be open to oil exploration.

Though Udall was not surprised by the Huckaby bill, he was surprised—indeed shocked—when on February 28 his committee voted 22 to 21 to make it the markup vehicle. All 15 Republicans voted as a bloc. Seven Democrats, mostly former Meeds allies, joined them.

For the rest of that day and much of the night both sides pressured two swing voters, a Georgia Democrat and a Pennsylvania Democrat who had been a Meeds ally in the previous Congress. The president contacted the Georgian, and his lobbyists urged the Pennsylvanian, Austin Murphy, to prepare a shopping list of projects for his district.[48] Stuart Eizenstat called Murphy the following morning and offered administration support for a national historical park that it had previously vetoed.[49] However, neither representative was willing to change his vote. Murphy explained that he was reacting to rising gasoline prices. An "ebullient" Don Young had a different explanation. "That's what I call perseverance winning over intelligence," he told reporters.[50]

Insisting that the Interior Committee vote was "not a major setback," Jim Free, Carter's top lobbyist, called a meeting of representatives of the Interior and Agriculture departments, the Alaska Coalition, and Udall's staff for March 12.[51] They discussed their prospects in the wake of this "rather surprising event," but Free soon came to the point. He was "taking over the Administration's campaign because he had received a royal chewing out from the President himself" after the Interior Committee vote, and "he had no intention of getting another one." He pledged a more vigorous effort. By implication he criticized Cynthia Wilson and Jim Pepper, Interior Department lobbyists, whom coalition leaders had long viewed as ineffectual. When Pepper reacted angrily, Doug Scott "took him on and lectured him quite severely." Later Clusen and Scott proposed that Pepper and Wilson "be kept off Capitol Hill."[52]

The legislation now went to the House Merchant Marine Committee, where Fisheries Subcommittee Chairman John Breaux (D-LA) indicated that he would reconsider the 1978 bill. But in late March he and John Dingell (D-MI), the other ranking Democrat, together with the ranking Republican and Don Young, drafted a new bill that was similar to the Huckaby bill.[53] The Breaux-Dingell bill increased the total acreage to 128 million, with 54 million acres of wilderness. It reduced the national park acreage but increased the refuge acreage to 85 million, mostly by including the Pet 4 land. On ANWR and the Tongass, Breaux-Dingell was practically identical to the Huckaby bill. Breaux's subcommittee was divided, with several southern Democrats holding the balance of power.[54] Earl Hutto (D-FL), for example, had a strong environmental record in Florida but advocated a "good balance" between preserving Alaska's "natural beauty" and exploring for minerals and oil, "so much needed in the energy crunch."[55] When the subcommittee voted on March 29, Hutto and two other Democrats opted for the Breaux bill, which won over the 1978 bill 16 to 14. After making several minor amendments on April 9, the full committee also endorsed it. A motion to substitute the earlier bill lost by a vote of 14 to 25.[56]

Even before the Merchant Marine Committee had completed its work, Clusen and Scott, together with Crandell, Free, and members of Udall's staff, were working on a revised bill that Udall would offer as a substitute for the Huckaby and Breaux-Dingell bills. Their goal was to "blunt the kind of arguments we expect from our opponents."[57] The new Udall bill, announced on April 23, resembled the successful 1977 bill except for the wilderness acreage, which was 50 percent higher in the wildlife refuges and twice as great in the Tongass, 67 million acres in all. Coalition leaders worked with the National Wildlife Federation to accommodate sport hunting interests and offset Dingell's influence.[58] The proposed Misty Fiords wilderness included the U.S. Borax mine site.

Udall and his allies also made a concerted effort to win over undecided representatives. Udall recruited a Republican cosponsor, John Anderson (R-IL), and persuaded five other Republicans to join a bipartisan steering committee. In a related move, Americans for Alaska, an ad hoc group of prominent, mostly Republican individuals that Larry Rockefeller of the Natural Resources Defense Council had organized in 1977, became more active. At a well-publicized Washington press conference on May 3, Americans for Alaska presented Carter with a conservation award and Tlingit leaders made him an honorary chief.[59]

Udall's most important move, however, was to use his position to insist that the House Rules Committee schedule his bill first. Only if Udall-Anderson failed would the House consider the Huckaby or Breaux-Dingell bills. As Hession recalled, "It shows you the power of an enraged committee chairman."[60]

As the vote approached, lobbyists besieged undecided representatives. In addition to the coalition operation, which included 20 full-time lobbyists and 3 million letter-writers, the presidents and executive directors of the Sierra Club and the Audubon Society spent more than a week in Washington. Full-page ads in Washington newspapers and in hometown papers of undecided representatives reinforced the lobbyists' work. Udall described this effort as "head and shoulders above anything put together in the public interest field since the civil rights movement."[61]

Yet opponents of Udall-Anderson were also active. CMAL, the state, and the National Rifle Association mobilized a small army of lobbyists; U.S. Borax alone employed six. To siphon Udall supporters, they sponsored several amendments to the Huckaby and Breaux-Dingell bills. By the end of the House debate, Breaux-Dingell, supposedly favorable to hunters, actually permitted less sport hunting than Udall-Anderson.[62] These concessions, together with the mounting energy crisis, raised expectations. Both sides believed that the vote on Udall-Anderson could go either way.

Uncertain about the outcome, the Interior Department prepared two press releases, one proclaiming victory, the other acknowledging defeat.[63]

Nearly everyone was surprised, then, on May 16, when Udall-Anderson won by a lopsided margin, 268 to 157. When it became apparent that Udall-Anderson would win, many potential Breaux-Dingell supporters shifted to the winning side. Bill Horn moaned that "their 200 votes were hard, our 200 votes were soft."[64] The size of the margin was due to the unexpected support of many Republicans, who divided evenly for and against the bill. The Ohio delegation was illustrative. The Alaska Coalition estimated that nine Ohio Democrats and four Republicans would vote for Udall- Anderson, one Democrat and five Republicans were uncertain, and four Republicans were opposed. The final Ohio vote, therefore, could range anywhere from 13–10 to 19–4. The actual vote was 17 to 6, as all the Democrats and seven of the Republicans voted for Udall-Anderson.[65] Several congressional leaders thought they detected a backlash against the oil companies. Speaker Tip O'Neill concluded that "the members think they're voting against another rape by Big Oil." Afterward, Udall boasted that "we outhustled and outfought the oil boys."[66] "You beat the hell out of them," he told cheering followers. Breaux was equally candid. "I've got to compliment anybody who kicks the hell out of me," he later observed.[67]

The House vote was particularly embarrassing to the Alaskans. Young and Stevens responded with characteristic bluster, threatening to defy the federal government. They were careful to qualify their suggestions, but some Alaskans took them literally: merchants in Glenallen evicted Park Service employees from motels, and hunters trespassed in the Wrangell–St. Elias and Gates of the Arctic monuments.[68] Gravel threatened more filibusters. A chagrined Governor Hammond pledged to continue the fight. His growing identification with the booster campaign, symbolized by his appointment of a blue-ribbon committee of prominent boosters, including Egan, Hickel, and Atwood (as well as a reluctant Bob Weeden), and approval of the legislature's expenditure of millions of dollars on lobbyists, angered many former backers. Upset, Paul Lowe wrote that the state's environmentalists felt disenfranchised.[69]

Still, defiant gestures and exaggerated language could not obscure the discord in the boosters' ranks. Stevens called for immediate action before Senate liberals demanded more wilderness. Hammond generally followed his lead. Gravel was contemptuous of what he described as the state's "unaggressive lackluster" policies and called for a lawsuit against the Carter withdrawals.[70] Most lawyers did not take his proposals seriously, but Gravel may have been closer to the booster mainstream than either Stevens or Hammond. Summarizing an early meeting of the blue-ribbon committee, Lieutenant Governor Terry Miller wrote that there was general agreement that the state should work to weaken the 1978 Senate bill but that "delay until next year [was] a possible tactical goal ... if a satisfactory bill cannot be produced this Congress, every effort should be made to defeat a bill until a later time."[71]

THE LONG SENATE CAMPAIGN

The passage of Udall-Anderson and the support of the Carter administration meant that once again, the Senate Energy Committee and Senator Jackson were in a position to determine the fate of the Alaska legislation. Increasingly impatient with the antics of Gravel and the other Alaska politicians and unwilling to devote extended attention to the Alaska legislation, Jackson planned to approve the 1978 bill (now S. 9; the Senate version of Udall-Anderson, called Durkin-Nelson-Roth, S. 220, received no consideration) without significant change before the August recess and move on to other issues.

Alaska Coalition leaders agreed with him and Stevens on the desirability of immediate action. The House victory had raised the esprit de corps of their followers. And though they had little hope of a satisfactory Senate bill, Carter's withdrawals had created a higher standard for the conference committee. While urging friendly members of the Energy Committee to resist weakening amendments, coalition leaders were more concerned about the composition of the House delegation to the conference, hoping to minimize Merchant Marine Committee participation.

Several problems remained. Senator John Durkin faced a difficult reelection campaign and was unable to devote as much attention to Alaska as in the previous session. His role in the committee's deliberations consisted largely of proposing more generous preserves to appeal to New Hampshire's many hunters. His replacement, Paul Tsongas, was a Senate freshman who had been a Udall ally on the House Interior Committee. Among the committee members, Tsongas could count on only Durkin and Howard Metzenbaum for support; to win any contested point, he would have to attract five or six of Jackson's allies. Facing that near-impossible task, he initially sought an agreement with Stevens to rubber-stamp the 1978 bill and let the conference committee reconcile it with the House bill. Stevens, however, rebuffed him, announcing that he would propose as many as 40 amendments. Tsongas and the coalition prepared for a prolonged fight.[72]

There were other complications as well. The most obvious one was Gravel, who made no secret of his intention to obstruct the committee's deliberations. The Alaskan forced the committee to hold a hearing (with live television transmission to Alaska) on a bill to amend the Antiquities Act and nullify Carter's action. A disgusted Jackson walked out after a few minutes.[73] When the committee finally turned to the Alaska bill, Gravel introduced several frivolous amendments; Jackson characterized them as "so preposterous that I'm appalled."[74]

Though Gravel's tactics were disruptive and ultimately self-defeating, they had the desired effect of warning the Senate of the obstacles that lay ahead. In late August, Senator Alan Cranston, a Senate leader and supporter of the Alaska Coalition, met with California environmentalists and "adamantly stated that the Alaska legislation would not come before the full Senate this fall." Energy legislation, an arms treaty with the Soviet Union, and the budget would leave little time for Alaska. Furthermore, Senate Majority Leader Robert Byrd (D-WV) was "reluctant to schedule the bill for the floor when the filibuster threat is so real." Would it be considered in early 1980? "Cranston again warned that Byrd would hesitate to schedule the bill ... because of the filibuster threat!" Cranston asked what would happen if there were no vote. The environmentalists explained that only Congress could designate wilderness areas and appealed to him to pressure Jackson and Byrd. He repeated his support for the coalition but refused to commit himself to a more active role.[75]

The Energy Committee began to consider substantive amendments on October 10, 1979, and continued its deliberations off-and-on for three weeks. The first vote was on Gravel's proposal for oil leasing in both Pet 4 and ANWR. Jackson opposed the inclusion of ANWR, and the amendment lost 3 to 4, with Stevens and two western senators in favor and Jackson, Tsongas, and two Jackson supporters in opposition. The October 12 session was devoted to "grandstanding for the benefit of television," as Gravel submitted amendments that even Stevens and his proindustry supporters considered fanciful.[76] On October 15, as one observer noted, "there was a minimum of discussion or debate, and no real speech-making" because "there were no TV cameras."[77] On October 17 the committee adopted an amendment by Senator Henry Bellmon (R-OK), an oil industry ally, that authorized petroleum companies to conduct seismic studies in ANWR.

The vote was 5 to 1 (two absent senators approving via Jackson), with Tsongas casting the single negative vote. He supposedly "felt there was little he could do except vote no and acquiesce."[78]

The most dramatic clash began later that day, when Tsongas, presiding in Jackson's absence, moved to force a vote on Stevens's top priority, the removal of the U.S. Borax mine site from the Misty Fiords Monument. Tsongas attacked U.S. Borax for its "inaccurate and misleading" statements while Stevens pleaded for his amendment. Tsongas reluctantly agreed to delay the vote, noting that "your proxies are shakier than mine" and that "my office is open" for additional discussions.[79] A week later, after apparently fruitless negotiations, Stevens threatened to filibuster the final bill. Jackson "sat unmoving and silent."[80] Finally, on October 30, Tsongas and Stevens announced a deal: the mine site would remain in the monument, but the secretary of Agriculture would conduct a one-year study of Borax's proposed five-mile road and approve it unless there was "some finding of overwhelming damage."[81]

Tsongas won two other small victories in the closing session. He joined Jackson to defeat a proposal by Senator John Melcher to create a new national forest in central Alaska and a Gravel amendment, supported by all the Republicans, to ban additional executive withdrawals in Alaska. Stevens had declined to offer the amendment because it would fail; Gravel insisted on a roll call so that "senators from the West can protect themselves."[82]

The final bill set aside 94 million total acres (versus 109 million in the House bill) and 38 million acres of wilderness (versus 67 million). The Senate total included 41 million acres of wildlife refuges and 9.5 million acres of national forests and Bureau of Land Management conservation areas. It also opened many areas to hunting and trapping, authorized oil companies to study ANWR, confirmed Shee Atika logging rights on Admiralty Island, granted U.S. Borax its road subject to the one-year study, and reduced wilderness acreage in ANWR, the Tongass, and Gates of the Arctic.[83] Clusen characterized the bill as "hopelessly shortsighted," while Gravel refused to rule out a filibuster against it.[84]

The committee's action led to several months of maneuvering and intrigue as the Carter administration, the Alaska Coalition, and the Alaskans gauged their prospects. One possibility was no legislation, or a bill that Carter would veto. Andrus had promised additional withdrawals if Congress did not act, and to emphasize his resolve, he moved in early 1980 to make his earlier withdrawal of refuge land permanent. Barring an unexpected court decision, no less than 93 million acres would be set aside. Alaska Coalition leaders nevertheless continued to support congressional action. They hoped to obtain millions of acres of wilderness and worried about the legality of massive executive withdrawals. A less sympathetic Congress—not an unrealistic prospect given the Republican gains of 1978 and Carter's low poll ratings—might abolish the Alaska parks or repeal the Antiquities Act. In mid-November, Tsongas and a Republican cosponsor, William Roth (R-DE), introduced a new bill called Tsongas-Roth that combined Udall-Anderson with several provisions of the Energy Committee bill, including the Misty Fiords deal.

The Alaskans also reluctantly agreed that legislation was desirable. By fall 1979 John Katz had become the state's most influential lobbyist. Reflecting the views of Hammond and Stevens, he dismissed the "no bill" movement, sought to make S. 9 the basis of the final settlement, and tried to prevent the potentially explosive antagonism between Stevens and Gravel from affecting the outcome. As the Energy Committee completed its work, he held a unity meeting in Washington, ostensibly to brief the governor's blue-ribbon task force. The first session featured Jackson, who warned of additional withdrawals if Congress did not act. Taking his cue from Jackson, Katz attacked the no-bill option and the possibility of a successful lawsuit against Carter; he also predicted that a filibuster would fail. The greatest danger, he argued, would come on the Senate floor, where Tsongas could count on 30 to 33 votes for his substitute bill and probably attract some of the 25 to 30 uncommitted senators. If S. 9 went to a conference, the Alaskans' prospects would improve.[85] Meeds and other state lobbyists generally agreed with this analysis. As Weeden scribbled, "Lobbyists greatly fear grass roots ability of Coalition—Meeds says best in U.S.—fear losing whole thing on floor. Need to keep right to filibuster until the shape of the bill is known."[86]

Later the Alaskans had a similar session with Tsongas. Weeden reported that the senator did not want to risk his standing among his colleagues by prolonging the fight. He was "more interested in statesmanship or good politics than substance of bill. Not a crusader for parks."[87] The *Fairbanks News-Miner* published a similar analysis the following day. Tsongas told a reporter that "I'm closer now to Stevens and the chairman than I was. ... I'm better off in the committee than I was before." He implied that he would try to amend S. 9 on the Senate floor rather than push his substitute. "He said he would then have to address oil drilling on the North Slope ... and timber cutting" in the Tongass.[88]

Between November and February 1980 several efforts to bring the legislation to the Senate floor failed. A Gravel informant who attended the blue-ribbon briefing believed—perhaps reflecting the senator's paranoia—that deals between Tsongas, Stevens, and Udall had already been struck.[89] Udall and Stevens did meet on November 12. Stevens expressed his concern that a prolonged delay would "work to Gravel's advantage in an election year" and proposed several procedures for breaking the stalemate. He insisted, perhaps disingenuously, that Byrd's reluctance to schedule a vote was the biggest obstacle.[90] In the meantime Andrus and his staff tried to cultivate Jackson by pushing legislation to authorize oil exploration in Pet 4, which had not been included in the Senate bill. Andrus reported that Jackson was "less adamant now" and that other senators would be more receptive to the ANWR wilderness if the Pet 4 initiative passed.[91] In early February, when an unexpected opening in the Senate calendar created an opportunity, Stevens asked Byrd to schedule debate on S. 9. He believed that the ongoing Iranian crisis and the Soviet invasion of Afghanistan had increased public sensitivity to the need for secure energy supplies. But Gravel was unmoved. He continued to reject Stevens's plans for "his very bad bill. ... The time just isn't right. [92]

The following day Tsongas, having consulted neither the administration nor the coalition, met secretly with Stevens, Gravel, and Byrd. They agreed to bring up S. 9 in mid-July, between the Republican and Democratic national conventions. The agreement set a time limit on debate, permitted only the bill's sponsors and Durkin to offer amendments, and limited the number of amendments. After the Senate had voted on the amendments, Tsongas could propose his substitute.[93]

The key was the timing. By postponing the debate for another five months and scheduling it in the midst of the presidential campaign, the agreement had recreated the conditions of 1978. The debate would last through the summer, and the conference committee would meet during the most critical period of the election campaign. Appearing at a joint press conference, the Alaska senators were ecstatic. "Never in my wildest dreams did I think we could hold out until late summer or fall," crowed Gravel. Stevens admitted that he had thought "the longest we could delay was May."[94] These statements in the *Anchorage Daily News* embarrassed Tsongas. He attacked the Alaskans in a Senate speech for "apparently gloating over their success. ... [I] have been taken advantage of."[95] But if Tsongas was the apparent loser, Gravel was the obvious winner. He was again in a position to dictate the outcome, and he had greatly improved his reelection prospects. Indeed, no prominent Republican stepped forward to challenge him.

During the following months there were more developments unfavorable to the environmentalists. Carter's efforts to deal with the energy crisis led Brock Evans to bemoan a "drastic change of mood" in Washington.[96] Senator Edward Kennedy's challenges in the early primaries (Udall might well have taken his place had he declined) were unsuccessful, leaving Carter victorious but weakened. The disarray in the Democratic Party and the growing power of western conservatives in the Republican Party did not improve the outlook for an Alaska bill.

Other problems unique to the Alaska campaign also hurt. The coalition had raised and spent nearly $300,000 in 1979, but many supporters were beginning to tire. Declining contributions forced staff reductions. The coalition was slow to line up support for Tsongas's proposed amendments, which faced an uncertain fate as late as mid-June. The administration's effort was equally ineffectual. The White House effort was delegated to an inexperienced Tom Lambrix, who "has been a real thorn in the side of everyone because of timidity."[97] Tsongas's staff was also new and inexperienced.

Given those negatives, the critical question by early summer was whether any satisfactory legislation was possible. Harry Crandell wrote that "'to get a bill' no longer is what the struggle is all about. ... My fear is that in a push to *get a bill* passed, too much will be given away."[98] Rather than accept an eviscerated bill, many environmentalists were prepared to rely on Carter to withdraw more land.

CONCLUSION

The final chapter in the legislative campaign began in July 1980 with the long-awaited Senate debate. Despite a formidable lobbying effort by the state and CMAL, the president's declining approval ratings, and the agonizing energy crisis, environmentalists orchestrated a lobbying effort that rivaled their 1977 and 1978 campaigns and reduced the appeal of the no-bill option. Tsongas also proved to be an effective champion. Yet even after the Senate had finally acted, in late August, most activists were dissatisfied, and some SEACC leaders were openly rebellious. The presidential election in November finally brought the legislative maneuvering to an end. One of the most important congressional measures of the century satisfied almost no one.

The issues and alignments of July-August were comparatively simple and straightforward. The critical issues were the fates of the Tongass and ANWR, which had acquired a symbolic importance that transcended their roles in the legislative package. Somewhat less important were the boundaries of the Gates of the Arctic and Wrangell–St. Elias parks and the total acreage devoted to wilderness and wildlife refuges. To Hammond and especially to Stevens, whose reputation as a negotiator was at stake, specific concessions, such as access to the U.S. Borax mine site in Misty Fiords, oil exploration in ANWR, and protection for the timber industry, were all-important. The Alaska politicians also sought to create inholdings in park units as examples of state power. Still, there were no irreconcilable differences. As a result, divisions between Republicans and Democrats, liberals and conservatives, and easterners and westerners, all of which had some influence, were overshadowed by the conflict between politicians and environmentalists, who worried about the effects of legislative compromises.

Carter lobbyist Tom Lambrix summarized this distinction in a July memo to Stuart Eisenstat. He explained that the environmentalists' "major fear" is that "some type of ad hoc deal will emerge on the floor … and they will be cut out." Then, as if to confirm their fears, he urged Eisenstat not to oppose such a deal or to promise additional land withdrawals if the legislation failed. Since some of Tsongas's proposed amendments probably would fail, "we need to keep all options open. It could be that an acceptable bill might be worked out in an ad hoc manner. … It may be that we will find the enrolled bill acceptable, but the coalition will not."[99]

Kathy Fletcher, a former Carter staffer who had become a coalition lobbyist, was no less explicit about the coalition's "bottom line." First and most important, she wrote, the Tongass provisions of S. 9 "are completely unacceptable. Without improvement on the Senate floor, a House Senate conference might fail even to protect Admiralty Island and Misty Fiords … and might require overcutting the National Forest. … These three deficiencies could never be accepted by conservationists." In contrast, a "wilderness designation" for the ANWR coast "is probably impossible to achieve." Though more restrictions on oil and gas exploration were desirable, an "otherwise good bill would be acceptable to the coalition, even without an Arctic Range wilderness." Other features of the legislation "could be worked out in any reasonably balanced negotiation between the House and Senate bills." The House bill was obviously preferable as a starting point, but "given Senator Jackson's pride of authorship this may not be possible."[100] Clusen and the executive directors of the Sierra Club, Audubon Society, and National Wildlife Federation reiterated these points in a personal meeting with Eisenstat on July 11.

Their arguments were apparently persuasive. In the following week administration leaders and lobbyists made the Tongass amendments their top priority. Carter and Andrus made numerous calls, and Secretary of Agriculture Bob Bergland mobilized farm state senators. Their efforts became even more critical after Energy Secretary Robert Charles Duncan refused to endorse the ANWR wilderness amendment and publicly called for opening the entire coast to oil drilling. His unilateral action "hurt our chances significantly," Lambrix reported.[101] The likely defeat of the ANWR amendment made the Tongass amendments all the more significant.

Consideration of the Alaska legislation began on July 21 with intensive lobbying activity and a day of floor speeches. Stevens's office became a "command post" for state and industry lobbyists, while Vice-President Walter Mondale's office served a similar function for coalition and administration lobbyists and pivotal House members. "Look at Seiberling," remarked an oil company lobbyist. "He's wandering around like a piranha."[102] Andrus told senators and reporters that his staff had completed the paperwork for withdrawing an additional 20 million acres of Alaska lands if the legislation failed.[103] On the Senate floor, Gravel stalled the debate for three hours with a rambling speech that signaled his continuing hostility to any legislation. "I don't know what he's doing out there," Stevens told reporters, "and I don't think anybody else does either."[104] At the White House Carter received another award from Americans for Alaska. That evening 400 environmentalists gathered at a Senate reception. Tsongas predicted a close but favorable vote.

On July 22 the Senate considered the first and probably most popular of the Tsongas amendments, a proposal by Senator Gary Hart (D-CO) to add 14 million acres to the wildlife refuges created in S. 9. Senators Jackson, Melcher, and Hatfield each proposed modifications that would have effectively killed the Hart amendment but lost by margins of 33 to 64, 30 to 60, and 38 to 62, respectively. The Hatfield amendment, to add only 7 million acres, was the first real test of Tsongas's support. In addition to most Democrats, all but one of the northeastern and midwestern Republicans voted with Tsongas and Hart.[105] A smiling Andrus told reporters that "right will prevail." The Alaskans were disheartened. Gravel described the votes as a debacle, and Hammond was so discouraged that he seemed about to embrace Gravel's no-bill approach.[106] Stevens then announced that he would introduce a series of secondary amendments, effectively halting the vote.

An apparent violation of the February agreement, this action had two objectives. First, it was a defensive move against Gravel, who had accused Stevens of selling out to the environmentalists and had summoned Alaska business and political leaders to Washington. By prearrangement a group calling itself Commonwealth North recruited a delegation of legislators, Teamsters, professional hunters, and interest group representatives whose expenses were paid by the legislature. Walter Hickel joined them in Washington. Ken Fanning of the "REAL Alaska Coalition" explained that their goal was to pressure Stevens and Hammond.[107] By halting the debate, Stevens supposedly showed that he was still influential. To emphasize his point, he attacked Hart personally in a Wednesday morning speech, threatening to campaign against him in the next election.

The second and more meaningful goal was to force another ad hoc conference. In his account of the Senate deliberations, journalist Robert Cahn described these efforts as an assault on the democratic process of open debate that shattered the hopes of the environmentalists.[108] In fact, the environmentalists were aware of what was in store. Three weeks earlier Harry Crandell had learned from a source in the Stevens camp that "in case …. one or more of the Coalition's amendments are adopted, the goal is to arrange another informal 'ad hoc' session."[109] In the days preceding the debates administration and coalition lobbyists often made the same point. They hoped that the vote would be positive and decisive, but given the parliamentary maneuvers available to Stevens and Gravel and the support of powerful figures such as Jackson and Byrd, they expected the vote to proceed only if Tsongas's amendments were losing. Their realistic goal was to give Tsongas the greatest possible leverage in negotiations with Stevens. Tsongas and Stevens met on the evening of July 22 to discuss an informal conference off the Senate floor. The meeting was a victory for the Tsongas forces.

The negotiations continued on July 23, with each senator's aides exchanging proposals. By 2:00 p.m., with Tsongas holding firm and Gravel mobilizing his backers, Stevens decided to withdraw from the negotiations. At that point, Jackson stepped in as a peacemaker. He met privately with Stevens, Hatfield, Tsongas, Hart, and Durkin (Gravel pointedly was not invited). Stevens apologized to Hart, and Hart agreed to several face-saving concessions. Jackson assured reporters that they had all agreed to work together to resolve their differences. Byrd formally suspended the floor debate.[110]

For the next week Stevens, Jackson, Tsongas, and Cranston and their staffs (including Roy Jones from Seiberling's staff) negotiated a new Senate bill. They made Admiralty Island a national monument but confirmed Shee Atika's timber claims, removed the U.S. Borax mine site from the Misty Fiords monument and made the southern section of the monument a pulp bank, set a Tongass timber harvest target of 450 million board feet per year (rather than the 520 million Stevens favored), created a mechanism for opening the ANWR coast to private oil exploration, added 14 million acres of wilderness and a similar amount to the refuges, increased the size of Gates of the Arctic Park, and banned mining in the Gates and Wrangell parks. Tsongas briefed Carter's staff and the coalition leaders on the evening of July 29. Together with Jackson and Stevens, he urged the House to accept the compromise bill, preferably before the Senate recessed on Wednesday, August 6, for the Democratic National Convention.

July 30 saw virtually nonstop meetings between Andrus, Udall, Seiberling, and the coalition leaders as they decided how to respond. There was general agreement that the bill was still inadequate and that a "second bite" was essential. Beyond that, they were divided. Andrus urged immediate action. According to Doug Scott, the secretary insisted "that we had only one procedural option: to get fast agreement on some kind of 'nibble' or 'bite' involving the House and then to get it passed by the Senate before Wednesday." Seiberling took a similar position. His concern was that the deal would unravel during the recess and that a new agreement would be impossible during the political campaign. Clusen and Scott were skeptical. "I've been in on every key discussion of this risk assessment," Scott explained, "and I conclude that we should take the risk of slowing down ... and choose our shots for the 'second bite.'"[111] They arranged a meeting of Udall, Seiberling, and Andrus with Phillip Burton, a veteran of numerous parks battles. "It was a useful session," Scott reported, "in that John S. heard a variety of typically Burtonesque procedural alternatives laid out. ... It is now imperative that Burton assert a calming and flowing influence on John Seiberling ... and having John come to believe, with Phil's help, that getting more will not imperil the whole thing."[112] By the evening of July 30 Andrus and Seiberling had reluctantly agreed that the House should insist on a meaningful second bite, even if it meant delay beyond August 6.

Tsongas, however, disagreed. He told reporters that he was not surprised at the coalition's position, but he was "committed to using my best judgment on this issue, regardless of the Coalition's stand." Though he sought

House support "to increase momentum on the Senate floor," he was deter-mined to act before the Democratic convention. Senator Byrd scheduled the revised bill for consideration on Monday, August 4. Stevens praised Tsongas's action: "He's in control now," he told a group of Alaskans.[113]

Stevens still had to deal with Gravel and his followers. The Alaska boosters had begun a noisy campaign against the bill and indirectly against Stevens. Irritated, Stevens sent Senator Rudy Boschwitz (R-MN) to enlighten them. Boschwitz explained that Gravel had little support and would be unable to stop the legislation. Several of his listeners were "shocked."[114] The following Monday, August 4, Stevens himself confront-ed them. In response to pleas from former Governor Egan and Republican activist C. R. Lewis to join Gravel in sabotaging the bill, Stevens's temper rose. "Before [the environmentalists] are through," he snapped, "there would be such a lock up. It is a matter of vengeance." He insisted that Congress would pass a bill and that "we are still trying to get the best bill we can." When a Republican state legislator replied that "the most distin-guished citizens of the state are here begging and pleading for a delay," he could not contain himself. "What for?" he shouted. "I know what will hap-pen to us now. It's going to get worse, not better."[115]

On Monday Tsongas and Jackson signaled their intention to pass the bill by Wednesday. They were especially optimistic after Andrus pro-nounced it "nearly acceptable." When coalition leaders attempted to appeal to Carter, the secretary angrily reminded them that he was the administration's "point man."[116] That left Gravel as the principal obstacle. He announced that the bill "goes right to the jugular" and vowed to block it by any means. Complaining of a "down and dirty approach," he tied up the Senate for more than eight hours. Jackson was furious. "I can take so much nonsense," he told Gravel. "Who are we trying to fool here?" Tsongas added that "every time I try to be reasonable with Sen. Gravel, I end up with a stiletto out my back."[117] When Gravel, seemingly unmoved, continued to stall on Tuesday, Byrd suspended debate and announced a cloture vote for August 18, when the Senate reconvened. Later that day Tsongas, Stevens, and Jackson introduced a revised bill designed to satisfy proponents of a second bite. It eliminated the Misty Fiords pulp bank and made the fiords, with the notable exception of the U.S. Borax mine site and access road, a wilderness.

At that point the outcome of the Senate deliberations was still uncer-tain. Administration lobbyists expected the coalition "to work feverishly over the next 10 days to win more concessions from Stevens." They were increasingly anxious that the "most uncompromising" activists, notably Clusen, Scott, and Bill Turnage, the new head of the Wilderness Society, would try to sabotage the Tsongas bill in a desperate effort to get something better. A member of Eisenstat's staff advised Andrus before a meeting with coalition leaders, "Make it *very* clear that we expect to follow their lead the rest of the way, but that we do not want to lose the opportunity to get a bill."[118] Gravel was the other question mark. Would he be able to attract enough support to defeat the cloture vote? Many southern and western senators were wary of cloture motions. Governor Hammond publicly predicted that at least three cloture votes would be required.[119]

The actual Senate votes on August 18 were surprisingly anticlimactic. The first cloture vote won 63 to 25, with all but a handful of southern and western Democrats and 15 Republicans opposing Gravel. Several potential allies, led by Republican Barry Goldwater (R-AZ), voted for cloture because of their distrust of Gravel. The subsequent motion, to substitute the Tsongas-Jackson bill for the Energy Committee bill, was adopted 72 to 16, with a handful of southern and western senators the only holdouts. The final vote on the Tsongas bill, the first actual Senate vote on the Alaska legislation, was 78 to 14. Gravel was crestfallen. He was "very personally unhappy"; the experience had been "very depressing." His Alaska followers were equally somber. Several wept at the news of the cloture vote.[120]

The Senate vote effectively doomed Gravel's reelection campaign. By early 1980 he had alienated many Alaska Democrats, and Clark Gruening, a 37-year-old grandson of Ernest Gruening, had challenged him in the Democratic primary. Gravel outspent Gruening nearly three to one, but even that advantage backfired when reporters raised questions about Gravel's personal finances and the *Wall Street Journal* published a story suggesting that he traded favors for contributions. An early August poll showed the two candidates tied, with a large number of undecided voters.[121] A Gravel radio blitz attacking Gruening for accepting "special interest money," a reference to contributions from Jewish businessmen, alienated many voters. The Senate votes were the last straw. Polls prior to the August 26 primary showed Gruening with a large and growing lead. He ultimately won by a 56 percent to 44 percent margin.

Gravel's defeat became one more factor in a prolonged debate among administration, House, and coalition leaders about how to respond to the Senate vote. With more acreage designated for parks and refuges than the Interior Department had requested in 1973 or 1977, the issue was whether additional effort was necessary or even desirable. Clearly, the Senate vote had altered the political landscape. Jackson told reporters that Udall and Seiberling "are going to see that it's this bill or no bill. I think ... they'll decide to accept this bill."[122] Stevens threatened to join Gravel's filibuster if the House insisted on substantial changes. In the following weeks, he repeatedly rejected additional modifications. Udall's decision to insist on additional concessions was as much a reflection of his anger at the senators' cavalier behavior as a belief that additional action was necessary.

A second complication was the shifting perspective of the Carter administration, now locked in a come-from-behind reelection campaign. After the Senate vote, Tom Lambrix prepared a detailed memo showing how much more generous the Tsongas bill was than either the administration's 1977 proposal or the 1978 withdrawals. Though the bill was a substantial achievement, it was too early to declare victory because of the sensitivity of coalition leaders to "symbolic" shortcomings, such as the exclusion of the U.S. Borax site. "It will be tragic if ... the President receives unfair criticism from the Alaska Coalition, when he should be receiving their full support for protecting Alaska."[123] Andrus publicly urged House leaders not to endanger the victory by making the bill "more conservation oriented."[124] Nor was there any doubt about Carter's position. He informally asked House leaders to pass the Senate bill and urged environmentalist icon Ansel Adams to pressure Udall and Seiberling.

Given Carter's preoccupation with the election and Andrus's desire to pass a bill, Udall became the final holdout. At the time of the Senate vote he indicated that he was undecided about what to do.[125] During the following days he weighed several options. He agreed with most observers that a formal conference committee was impossible because of the likelihood of a filibuster. However, the House could still alter the Senate bill and send it back for an up-or-down vote, or it could pass a separate bill addressing the deficiencies in the Senate bill. In early September the coalition prepared a letter that 111 House members signed, asking for a stronger bill. On September 9 Udall had a "secret" meeting with Jackson and Stevens to discuss supplementary legislation. They agreed to assign aides to discuss specific proposals. Andrus and Eisenstat agreed to cooperate.[126]

For nearly a month members of the Jackson, Stevens, Tsongas, Udall, and Seiberling staffs considered various adjustments to the Senate bill. Udall and the coalition leaders hoped to win greater wilderness acreage, especially in the Tongass. In exchange they were willing to cooperate with Stevens's efforts to sustain the Tongass timber industry and to enlarge several preserves. Larger preserves would also help Udall, who faced a well-financed opponent who was appealing to hunting groups. Stevens, however, refused to cooperate.[127] He stalled in the hope that Udall and Seiberling would offer more attractive concessions. By late September coalition leaders were concerned that he was succeeding. In a sharply worded memo they demanded a tougher stand. "Thus far," they complained, "we have sweetened the kitty for nothing but Stevens' interest in further talks." [128]

In an effort to bring the negotiations to a conclusion, Udall and cosponsor Thomas Evans (R-DE) introduced H.R. 8311 on October 2. The bill increased the West Chichagof–Yakobi wilderness to its original size (the Senate bill had reduced it substantially) and forced Shee Atika to choose timberlands off Admiralty Island. It also enlarged several preserves. As Udall explained to Carter, he was "asking for much less than half the difference between the House and Senate bills."[129] Dee Frankfourth reported,

> 8311 represents the strongest position we were able to get Mo and John to forward. In fact, the previous two weeks of negotiating with Ted Stevens had seriously eroded our line—they were simply being too reasonable, and we were losing. So, when Stevens continued to be rude and walk out … Udall and Seiberling got fed up and decided to introduce a bill. … It is a better position than any of their previous proposals.[130]

Some environmentalists disagreed. Several SEACC leaders, including Kay Greenough and Ron Hawk, had long suspected that Clusen and Scott were not really committed to Southeast Alaska. As the Senate Energy Committee devoted more and more attention to the Tongass, they became increasingly critical, to the discomfort of Paul Peyton, who represented SEACC on the coalition staff. In late August, after the Senate had passed the Tsongas bill, Jack Calvin reported that SEACC had "reached the point of desperation."[131] H.R. 8311 was the last straw. Without the authorization of the SEACC board, Greenough and Hawk flew to Washington and publicly attacked both ANILCA and the supplementary legislation. On October 25 the SEACC board, which had been divided, unanimously voted to back them. It cited the exclusion of the U.S. Borax mine site from Misty Fiords, the 450 million board feet timber mandate (which had been considered a coalition victory), and the annual timber subsidy (now raised to $40 million) that Stevens had written into the Senate bill, unchallenged by Udall and Seiberling. SEACC President Marilyn Conley complained that the bill "more clearly resembles a development bill than a conservation bill."[132]

The SEACC rebellion suggested the problems that lay ahead, assuming that Congress considered the supplementary legislation. That would happen only in a lame-duck session scheduled to convene in mid-November. In a letter to Alaska boosters Lieutenant Governor Miller emphasized his uncertainty about Udall's and Seiberling's postelection plans, though he added, "there are some indications that the outcome of the presidential election may have an influence on their decision."[133]

Miller was right about the effects of the election. Ronald Reagan's victory and a new Republican majority in the Senate (including the little-known Frank Murkowski, who had defeated Clark Gruening in Alaska) brought the negotiations to an abrupt halt and dashed any hope of passing H.R. 8311. Acknowledging the new political environment, Alaska coalition leaders conceded the hopelessness of their effort. On November 12 Udall reluctantly announced that he would ask the House to pass the Senate bill. In a final, anticlimactic decision, it adopted ANILCA by voice vote the following day.[134]

The December 2 White House signing ceremony captured the bittersweet conclusion to the Alaska lands campaign. On the one hand, ANILCA protected more than 100 million acres, slightly more land than had been awarded to the state in 1959. It more than doubled the size of the national park and wildlife refuge systems and tripled the size of the wilderness preservation system. Alaska environmentalists could argue that they, not the business groups or politicians, were responsible for modernizing the economy, creating opportunities in the services and professions, and enhancing the state's appeal. Compared with what Olaus Murie had sought to preserve in the 1950s, what Interior Secretary Stewart Udall had asked President Johnson to set aside in 1969, what Interior Secretary Morton had designated in 1973, what most Alaska environmentalists would have settled for in 1977, or what the ad hoc conference of 1978 would likely have approved, it was a substantial achievement.

The new map of Alaska revealed the scope of ANILCA. The greatest changes were in the Arctic. In the northeast a greatly enlarged ANWR abutted the Canadian border. To the west a series of national park units (Gates of the Arctic, Noatak, Kobuk Valley, and Cape Krusenstern) added nearly 17 million acres of fragile tundra and magnificent mountains to the park system. Three hundred miles to the south an expanded Mount McKinley Park (renamed Denali) and an enlarged Katmai anchored another series of parks and refuges that included much of the Alaska Range and ended in an expanded Aleutian Islands Refuge. In east-central Alaska, the long-anticipated Wrangell–St. Elias Park (at 12 million acres, the nation's largest), Yukon-Charley Park and Preserve, and Tetlin and Yukon Flats wildlife refuges hugged the Canadian border. In western Alaska a series of wildlife refuges (most notably the 15-million-acre Yukon Delta Refuge) added 28 million acres to the refuge system. Finally, 5 million acres of wilderness in the Tongass National Forest marked the first important victory to date in the struggle to protect parts of the southeastern rain forest, though the cost—the $40 million annual subsidy, the cutting target, and the implied approval of Forest Service policies in the rest of the national forest—was great.

The law also addressed other issues of interest to Alaskans. It spelled out permissible subsistence activities on federal lands and included a variety of procedures for facilitating the transfer of lands to the Native corporations and the state in accord with the Alaska Native Claims Settlement Act and the Statehood Act. Thus, it directly affected more than 150 million acres and became the pivotal measure in the wholesale reallocation of Alaska public lands that had begun in 1958.

On the other hand, it was easy to point out what had not been accomplished. Udall was candid: "I make no secret of the fact that neither I nor those who support me consider this legislation to be a great victory for our cause."[135] The limited success of the second-bite campaign and the disenchantment of the SEACC activists were only the most obvious indicators of these shortcomings. A shrewd industrialist might well have applauded: ANILCA did not restrict any realistic economic prospect, and it provided an enormous boost to Alaska tourism. It preserved one-fourth of Alaska but eliminated many potential obstacles to economic activity in the other three-fourths. It was a blow for the state's boosters but only because their vision of Alaska's future had been so unrealistic.

ANILCA, however, was more than the sum of victories and defeats in the bruising congressional battles of 1977–1980. Like the larger campaign for wilderness Alaska, it reflected the strength of environmental sentiment and the ability of environmentalists to organize at the state and national levels and to translate that strength into tangible political achievements. The decade of the 1970s, the political heyday of environmentalism, witnessed far-reaching changes in federal land and resource policies and innovative efforts to regulate pollution, especially by the federal government. ANILCA was the single greatest contribution to the era's impressive increase in park, refuge, and wilderness lands. But the 1970s was also a time of energy crises, recessions, and high unemployment. By 1978 these problems had taken their toll. The 1980 elections provided decisive confirmation of their impact. Like the pipeline controversy of the early 1970s, the ANILCA campaign underlined the obstacles that were likely to arise when environmental protection seemed to clash with economic opportunity.

ALASKA IN THE 1980s
AND BEYOND

Almost exactly five years after the White House ceremony celebrating the passage of the Alaska National Interest Lands Conservation Act (ANILCA), Alaska Governor Bill Sheffield, Hammond's successor, hosted a reception to commemorate it, as well as the 25th anniversary of the Arctic National Wildlife Refuge (ANWR). The occasion provided an opportunity to reflect on those events, which bracketed the most critical years of Alaska's growth and the most sweeping changes in the history of American conservation. Sheffield, a hotel owner and Citizens for the Management of Alaskan Lands backer, described the 1980 act as a sequel to ANWR and a "positive, progressive" conclusion to the process of preserving the state's most visually and scientifically valuable areas. ANILCA, he added, had "stopped the constant fighting" and settled "many" issues.[1]

Sheffield could afford to be magnanimous. The early 1980s were the peak years of Alaska's oil boom, a time when the state and its citizens seemingly had entered a new and markedly different stage in their history. The politicians of the 1970s had assumed that Native gains would be at the expense of non-Native enterprise, that national parks and wilderness areas would "lock up" resources and doom Alaska to poverty. The social and political "fracturing" of the late 1970s had been in part an expression of these assumptions. Yet by most measures the political decisions of the 1970s had had quite different results. The boosters had gotten their pipeline; oil had become the foundation of the state's economy and had led to dramatic increases in state spending and, via a Hammond innovation, the Permanent Fund, direct payments to residents. At the same time, Alaska's Natives had received substantial grants of land and money, equipping them to preserve traditional lifestyles and combat poverty. No less impressive was the magnitude of the environmentalists' achievement. Given the political culture of Alaska, the environmentalists' modest initial objectives, and the willingness of their congressional allies to accept relatively unfavorable compromises as late as 1978, the provisions of ANILCA were remarkably generous. On paper, at least, the results of the land allocation decisions of the 1970s resembled the "grand bargain" that social scientists had proposed in the late 1960s.

Sheffield's conclusion that these developments had stopped the constant fighting and settled many issues could not have been more mistaken, however. The political divisions that had emerged in the 1960s and 1970s persisted and in cases intensified in the following decades, as the conflicts over Alaska's resources—its oil and timber but also its mountains, glaciers, rain forests, and enormously varied wildlife—continued. Ken Ross, John Strohmeyer, and others have provided lucid accounts of these contests and have made it possible to identify three critical areas of contention.[2] First, by the 1980s the coastal plain just east of Prudhoe Bay, excluded from the ANWR wilderness, had emerged as the most likely site of the next Alaska oil bonanza and a test of the environmental movement's ability to preserve sensitive lands from industrial development. Second, the southeastern rain forest remained a prize for both the Alaska-based timber industry and for environmentalists, and the Forest Service, seemingly unfazed by the political debates of the 1970s, continued to resist restrictions on its authority. Third, for more than a decade after the passage of ANILCA, politicians who were skeptical of environmental protection in general and hostile to restrictions on the exploitation of commercially valuable public resources dominated the executive branch of the federal government. Each of the ensuing conflicts had roots in the political turmoil of the 1970s, the first two in the complex provisions of ANILCA itself.

THE CONTINUING QUEST FOR ALASKAN OIL

Oil and the need to transport it to refineries and markets had inspired the dramatic political events of the 1970s. It had also ensured that the decisions of that era would not be the last word on the future of Alaska's resources. Far from insulating Alaska against the boom-and-bust pattern of its past and liberating it from its colonial status, oil made it even more dependent on outsiders. In the words of Alaska historian Stephen Haycox, "The century closed in Alaska just as it began."[3] Oil was also a continuing source of environmental conflict. The transport system created in the 1970s remained vulnerable to natural disruptions and human miscalculation, and the search for new oil threatened to compromise the parks and refuges created in 1980. It would be hard to imagine a more comprehensive challenge to the environmental movement.

The provocations began almost immediately. The Energy Committee earmarked 1.5 million acres, embracing the western two-thirds of the ANWR coast, for additional consideration. The Interior Department was to conduct wildlife and seismic studies over the next five years (specified in Section 1002 of ANILCA) and then, if Congress agreed, open the 1002 area to oil development. Yet even before the Senate voted on ANILCA, an adviser to the Reagan administration called for opening the area.[4] Three months later the new secretary of the Interior, James Watt, signaled the beginning of a systematic campaign to circumvent the legislation. Watt ordered the industry-oriented U.S. Geological Survey, rather than the U.S. Fish and Wildlife Service, to conduct the mandated ANWR studies. (A suit by Trustees for Alaska and other environmental groups blocked this initiative; the Fish and Wildlife Service remained in charge.) Watt simultaneously cancelled negotiations with the Canadian government (another ANILCA requirement) over protective measures for the Porcupine Caribou herd, whose traditional calving ground was in the 1002 area, and ordered the Bureau of Land Management to suspend wilderness reviews of its remaining lands (suggested in ANILCA) and devote its resources to oil, gas, and mineral leasing.[5] To implement these policy changes, he named Bill Horn, a former aide to Representative Don Young, as deputy under-secretary for Alaska and Vern Wiggins, the executive secretary of Citizens for the

Management of Alaskan Lands, as his representative in Anchorage. Together they would play crucial roles in the subsequent effort to open refuges and even wilderness areas to oil exploration.

Their most ingenious tactic was an effort to shrink the 1002 area and privatize the Arctic coast. Watt and Horn seized on an obscure provision of ANILCA authorizing land trades to propose swaps with several Native corporations, typically offering potentially valuable oil lands in ANWR for inholdings in wildlife refuges. Native-owned lands were not subject to federal regulations and could be leased immediately. The first of the proposed trades, in late 1981, sought to exchange wilderness land on St. Matthew Island in the Bering Sea, which the oil companies wanted for an offshore exploration base, for lands owned by the Cook Inlet Region, Inc., in the Kenai Wildlife Refuge. Though a suit eventually thwarted this plan, a 1983 swap with the Arctic Slope Native Corporation permitted Chevron to drill a test well near Kaktovik, in ANWR. In late 1986, just before the Fish and Wildlife Service released its report on the 1002 area, Horn began negotiations with 19 Native corporations. His goal was to trade the most promising areas of ANWR to the corporations, which planned to sign leases with Chevron and British Petroleum.[6] Horn believed the swaps would speed exploration and increase the likelihood that Congress would open the rest of the ANWR coast. After all, a large share of the anticipated oil revenue would now go to the lowly Native corporations rather than to the newly rich state. Alaska Senator Frank Murkowski contended that the trades would give the Alaska delegation a "tactical advantage" in dealing with Congress. Don Young was more explicit. "Without them, opening won't occur," he told a reporter. George Kriste, a representative of Cook Inlet Region, Inc., was even more forthcoming. "The only way drilling is going to be opened up is if there's something in it for everyone."[7]

In early 1987 Horn threw caution to the winds. Disregarding the advice of his staff, he "met individually behind closed doors" with representatives of the Native corporations and negotiated deals that were exceedingly favorable to them. He raised the value of Native inholdings from an average of $111 per acre to an average of $601, permitting the corporations to claim substantially more ANWR acreage.[8] This so-called megatrade would have been controversial under any circumstances, but Horn's recklessness ignited a firestorm of protest. "Interior is threatening to take the decision away from Congress," Edgar Wayburn charged in denouncing the trades.[9] Representative George Miller (D-CA), who headed a critical subcommittee of the House Interior Committee, protested loudly to Watt's successor as

Interior secretary, Donald Hodel, who reassured him that Congress would have the last word on the swaps.

By that time the proposed trades had created two other influential enemies. First were the oil companies, led by Exxon, which were not parties to the deals and would lose out to their wily rivals. Second was the state, which would forgo much of its anticipated revenue. Democratic Governor Steve Cowper favored opening ANWR and even hoped to trade state lands for part of the refuge, but the Horn plan left the state government out in the cold. Alaska politicians had already conceded that a reduction in the state's percentage of oil revenues from federal lands would be the price of congressional approval. Instead of the generous 90-10 state-federal split that had prevailed since statehood, Alaska would probably have to settle for a 50-50 division. But if the best lands had already been traded to the Native corporations (Senator Murkowski insisted that only about 15 percent of the potential wealth of ANWR would be lost, but other observers believed that as much as two-thirds of the total was involved), the 50 percent state share might be quite modest by Prudhoe Bay standards.[10] Despite calls for unity by Stevens and others, Cowper continued to oppose the trades. By mid-1987 the megatrade was in political limbo.

The most important effect of the controversy, however, was to reactivate the Alaska Coalition. In the early 1980s Tim Mahoney of the Sierra Club had succeeded Chuck Clusen as chairman and had worked with the Alaska groups to monitor the implementation of ANILCA. The megatrade and the likelihood of legislation to open the rest of the 1002 area galvanized them; by early 1987 Mahoney and the Washington representatives of the major environmental organizations were meeting weekly to exchange information and plot strategy. Although the coalition claimed 21 members (the number would double by 1988), the Sierra Club and the Wilderness Society provided most of the money and leadership.

The release of the Interior Department's report on the 1002 area in December 1986 made Congress the principal battlefield in the ANWR conflict. Young introduced a bill to open the 1002 area and waive the requirement of an environmental impact statement; Murkowski and Stevens introduced a similar bill in the Senate. Representative Morris Udall reintroduced a bill to add the 1002 area to the ANWR wilderness. By June Young had 144 sponsors, including 32 Democrats; Udall had 79, including 7 Republicans.[11] During summer 1987 delegations from the House Interior Committee, the House Merchant Marine Committee, and the Senate Energy Committee visited ANWR. Mahoney accompanied the senators. "What a hard drinking, party crew!!" he reported afterward. Yet the convivial atmosphere had little political effect. "The committed got more committed," Mahoney recalled, "and the compromisers got more confused."[12]

Because the chairs of both House committees were reluctant to take any action, the Senate became the scene of the initial confrontation. Senator J. Bennett Johnston (D-LA), one of the oil industry's most reliable allies, had succeeded Henry Jackson (who had died in 1983) as chairman of the Energy Committee. In September he polled the committee on the proposed legislation. Seven Republicans favored action; five Democrats were opposed; the other seven members did not respond. Despite this inconclusive result, Johnston argued that a "consensus" favored action. Supposedly his goal was to "coax" environmentalists to drop their opposition and propose amendments.[13] But they refused to cooperate. Buoyed by widespread hostility to the megatrade, they recruited Senator William Roth (R-DE) and a half-dozen cosponsors to introduce an ANWR wilderness bill, and Senator Timothy Wirth (D-CO), an Energy Committee member, to propose an amendment to Murkowski's bill that would require a comprehensive, multiyear energy study before Congress acted on ANWR. Johnston delayed for several months while he tried to rally support, but when the Energy Committee finally voted, in February 1988, it remained divided. Johnston and his supporters were able to defeat the Wirth amendment, but only by a single vote, and approved a version of Murkowski's bill 11 to 8. Only one other Democrat joined Johnston; eight opposed it. Murkowski admitted that "we have a tough fight ahead of us."[14]

In the House, Representative Walter Jones (D-NC), chairman of the Merchant Marine Committee, led the prodevelopment forces. In late 1987 he introduced a bill for limited drilling in the 1002 area and protections for caribou. The Alaska Coalition and Young both attacked it. When the bill failed to attract supporters, Jones dropped the restrictions, in effect siding with Young. Yet his bill languished until the new House Speaker, Jim Wright (D-TX), another oil industry ally, intervened. Wright pressured the Subcommittee on Fisheries and Wildlife and then the full Merchant Marine Committee to report Jones's bill (with a ban on early drilling on Native lands in case the administration revived the megatrade) by a two-to-one margin in early May. Wright then demanded that Udall and Miller act as well. Most observers interpreted these maneuvers as a bid to assert his authority; the ANWR bill was on his "must do" list.[15] But as Wright became absorbed in an embarrassing ethics controversy, his influence began to wane. A Fish and Wildlife Service study, leaked to the press in

May, reported significantly greater pollution and wildlife losses at Prudhoe Bay than had been forecast in the 1972 environmental impact statement, buttressing the case for caution and delay.[16] A Government Accounting Office report attacking the land swaps was probably the last straw. Wright reluctantly acknowledged that the House was unlikely to act before the presidential election. Johnston added that both the ANWR bill and the Tongass Timber Reform bill, which had had a parallel history, were too controversial for the election season.[17]

The election of George Bush in 1988 (his opponent, Democrat Michael Dukakis, opposed drilling) ensured that the ANWR debate would continue. Although the new president professed to be an environmentalist who supported only "prudent" development in the Arctic, he had close ties to the oil industry and selected Representative Manuel Lujan, one of the "Dirty Thirty" of the late 1970s, as his secretary of the Interior. Senator Wirth predicted that Bush would "run right into the meat grinder on this one."[18] In his February 1989 budget bill Bush dutifully called for opening ANWR, and Johnston and Young reintroduced their 1988 bills. A month later the Senate Energy Committee reported out Johnston's bill 12 to 7. Environmentalists hoped to delay Senate action and sabotage the House bills, but the president's "honeymoon" and apparent willingness to accept restrictions suggested that a compromise measure might emerge.

At that point disaster intervened. On March 24, 1989, the giant oil tanker *Exxon Valdez* wandered off course and struck Bligh Reef in Prince William Sound, spilling 11 million gallons of crude oil into the water. It was the most disastrous American oil spill to date. The oil devastated the sound's wildlife, fouled the beaches, provoked a national uproar, and led to one of the most laborious and expensive (and arguably ineffective) cleanups of all time. It also confirmed the suspicions of many people in and out of the environmental community that Alaska oil operations were far less safe and less well managed than the industry insisted.[19] Congress and the state launched investigations of the spill and of the Alaska oil industry. The ANWR bill quickly died. Washington observers predicted that Congress would not be willing to take up the issue again for a year, perhaps for three or four years.

The *Exxon Valdez* incident ensured that the stalemate of the late 1980s would persist for more than a decade. The Bush administration called for opening ANWR in 1991, and the oil industry's congressional allies introduced several bills in the 1990s, but the memory of the megatrade and the *Exxon Valdez*, coupled with the opposition of environmental groups, was too strong. The second Bush administration tried again, in 2002 and 2003, but ran into equally vigorous opposition. The partisan divisions of the late 1970s and the late 1980s persisted into the new century. In the intervening years a flood of books and television documentaries and the popularity of ANWR as a tourist destination exposed a growing number of people to the noneconomic values of that vast, remote, and spectacular land.

TONGASS CONFLICTS

The Tongass wilderness areas had been the other lightning rod in the ANILCA debates. And by most standards environmentalists had scored a major victory, confirming the wisdom of their decision to include national forest lands in ANILCA. The 5 million acres of wilderness created in 1980 included the most important of the 45 areas identified by the Southeast Alaska Conservation Council (SEACC)—Admiralty Island and West Chichagof-Yakobi in particular—and suggested that the Wilderness Act could curb the excesses of the multiple-use agencies. Yet many problems remained, including the fate of the other SEACC areas; several million acres of the Chugach National Forest, which had originally been considered of equal value; the ANILCA provisions for an annual cut of 450 million board feet and a unique $40 million annual subsidy, the Tongass Timber Supply Fund; and the continuing hostility between the Tongass managers and their critics. Finally, the bittersweet victory of 1980 had temporarily demoralized the organization. Although most of the local groups remained viable, SEACC itself stumbled until 1984, when Bart Koehler, a former Forest Service and Wilderness Society employee and a founder of the exuberantly radical EarthFirst!, became executive director.

In the meantime the recession of the early 1980s had a devastating effect on the Alaska timber industry. Prices collapsed, mills shut down, and unemployment rose ominously. Average employment fell from 2,700 in 1980 to 1,260 in 1984. Pulp mill workers bore the brunt of the contraction, but half or more of the loggers and sawmill workers also lost their jobs.[20] Nevertheless, the Forest Service continued to offer an additional 450 million board feet of timber every year, even when there were no purchasers. The explanation for this seeming anomaly was the $40 million subsidy, which was mostly used to build roads in the areas where the unsalable timber was located. The 1979 Tongass management plan had estimated, for example, that an annual cut of 450 million board feet would require 46 miles of "preroading." Between 1982 and 1984, when the cut averaged 232 million board feet, the Tongass managers built an average of 51 miles of road per year. At least $50 million was wasted.[21] Forest Service officials admitted that the subsidy enabled them to maintain employment at prerecession levels. At times the Forest Service labor force approached that of the timber industry.[22]

The agency's self-aggrandizing policies might have escaped criticism if it had lived up to a central assumption of the 1980 negotiations. At that time Forest Service executives had given Udall assurances that the subsidy would enable them to target remote and relatively low value hillsides, saving more of the prime old-growth forest that was the most visually striking part of the Tongass and the most valuable wildlife habitat. But the Forest Service had never honored those assurances. The loggers wanted only the highest-quality, most accessible trees, and the foresters made little effort to reorient their activities. In the 1980s and 1990s the Forest Service concentrated its road-building operations in the most desirable areas, exactly the opposite of what had been envisioned.

Everything, it seemed, had gone wrong. An ill-conceived plan to protect jobs had had a negligible effect on private employment, wasted public funds, and harmed the fragile rain forest environment. A 1985 SEACC report, prepared by Dixie Baade, Mary Ellen Cuthbertson, Ted Whitesell, Koehler, and other activists, repeated the indictment of the 1970s. The Forest Service had "continued on its destructive logging-oriented course, blaming Congress and ANILCA for this policy of senseless inflexibility." Once more, it "has shown itself to be incapable of reform on the Tongass."[23]

What was to be done? Koehler and most SEACC leaders had soured on the solution of the 1970s, the creation of new wilderness areas. ANILCA, Koehler wrote, designated "a substantial … amount of wilderness … without addressing or challenging the fundamental Tongass Timber Problem," the 50-year contracts, the Forest Service management plans, the annual cut of 450 million board feet, and the Tongass Timber Supply Fund. Rushing "to gain designated protections without curing the major ills of the forest" would simply repeat the mistakes of 1980. "We believe that Jim [Clark, attorney and lobbyist for Alaska Pulp] is counting on a repeat of this sort of political dynamic." Fortunately, "there is a real constituency in this region for getting rid of the 450, and the long term contracts and deferring timber activities in areas on the SEACC … list."[24]

By 1986 the problems of the Tongass had attracted the attention of Representative Udall and Representative John Seiberling, who conducted oversight hearings. Taking advantage of the accompanying publicity, Koehler persuaded the Henry Kendall Foundation and others to finance a SEACC-led Tongass reform campaign aimed at eliminating the obnoxious ANILCA provisions and the 50-year contracts.[25]

The campaign began in 1987 with the introduction of reform bills by Representatives Bob Mrazek (D-NY) and George Miller and Senator Tim Wirth. With the national environmental organizations immersed in the ANWR fight, SEACC did most of the initial lobbying. Still, one Wilderness Society contribution proved invaluable. With the assistance of the Underhill Foundation, the society created a research organization, the Southeast Alaska Natural Resources Center, and hired Joseph R. Mehrkens, the Forest Service's chief Alaskan economist, as director. Mehrkens had served in Alaska for many years and had been a loyal employee. In 1980 he had been given responsibility for collecting data and preparing reports on Tongass timber supplies and prices, as provided in ANILCA. The experience was a revelation. By 1985 he had become alarmed at the agency's efforts to hide its losses on timber operations. His superiors had "cooked the books … until the results became positive." They insisted these tactics were "necessary for the Alaska congressional delegation to defend and maintain the ANILCA timber subsidy."[26] Disillusioned, he resigned and joined the Wilderness Society project. Mehrkens brought an intimate knowledge of the inner workings of the Tongass management, an understanding of the agency's murky language, and helpful contacts in the bureaucracy.

Given the aggressive lobbying of SEACC, the history of the Tongass Timber Reform Act had many similarities to the earlier ANILCA campaign. In March 1988 the House Interior Committee endorsed Miller's reform bill by a narrow margin; in August the House voted down Young's substitute 102 to 311, with 80 Republicans joining the majority, and passed the Miller bill 361 to 47. It was the big victory that the reformers had sought. The outlook in the Senate was less favorable, despite indications that 67 or more senators supported the bill.[27] Senator Johnston refused to bring up the legislation during the presidential election campaign, and the Democratic leadership supported him because of a likely Murkowski filibuster. Despite this setback Koehler was encouraged by the "tremendous level of support" in the Senate. He was optimistic that a bill would pass in 1989.[28]

That support translated into stronger legislation. Miller's new bill called for abolishing the subsidy and mandated timber cut, terminating the long-term contracts, and creating 1.7 million acres of additional Tongass wilderness. An amendment for 100-foot buffer zones along streams, a response to the concerns of the local fishing community—dramatized by a new suit that fisherman-militant Alan Stein and several allies brought against the Forest Service—added another important restriction. Despite the opposition of Governor Cowper and leaders of the southeastern communities, the House voted down a weaker substitute bill by a two-to-one margin and then passed the Interior Committee version 356 to 60.[29]

In the meantime a surprisingly supportive hearing in Sitka convinced Johnston that Senate action was desirable. He predicted that environmentalists would win 80 percent of their demands.[30] He also urged Wirth and Murkowski to devise a compromise that would avoid a filibuster. Despite several meetings during summer and fall, they were unable to reach an agreement on the fate of the long-term contracts and the amount of new wilderness acreage. Finally, in January 1990, with the legislation again stalled, Johnston called the SEACC lobbyists to his office. Assured that they would accept less than the House bill, he introduced a compromise bill that contained most of the House provisions but did not cancel the contracts. Cowper and the Alaskan officials endorsed this measure, and the Energy Committee reported it out in June. The Senate vote was 99 to 0. In its final form the Tongass Timber Reform Act of 1990 repealed the obnoxious ANILCA provisions, created 300,000 acres of wilderness and 700,000 acres of roadless "wildlands," required stream buffers, and called on the Forest Service to renegotiate the long-term contracts.[31]

The survival of the long-term contracts proved to be only a temporary concession. Despite their generous terms, which were only slightly modified in the ensuing negotiations, the Ketchikan and Sitka mills remained marginal participants in a highly competitive industry. The passage of the Tongass Timber Reform Act probably made their futures seem even more problematic. In any case, Ketchikan Pulp and Alaska Pulp managers resolved to maximize short-term profits and rely on supporters in Ketchikan and Sitka to deflect criticism. Among other things, their activities led to increased discharges of industrial wastes into nearby waters. The state and the U.S. Environmental Protection Agency had long complained about this activity but had made little progress in halting it because of the companies' resistance and legal delays. By the 1990s, however, the evidence of illegal activity, including fraudulent recordkeeping and document destruction, was overwhelming. Faced with fines and expensive cleanup procedures, Alaska Pulp and later Ketchikan Pulp opted to close the plants, bringing to at least a temporary end the Forest Service plan to diversify the economy of Southeast Alaska. Because of the booming tourist industry and other opportunities, the closings had surprisingly little adverse economic impact on Ketchikan and Sitka.[32]

Despite the Tongass Timber Reform Act and the mills' perilous condition, the pace of timber cutting actually accelerated in the 1980s and early 1990s. The problem, only dimly perceived in the 1970s, was the Native land grants that had been carved out of the Tongass. These totaled a half-million acres and contained 20 percent to 25 percent of the national forest's commercial timber.[33] No one knew exactly how these selections would affect the overall situation. The Alaska Native Claims Settlement Act (ANCSA) had piously called for sustained-yield management on Native-owned lands but included no meaningful incentives or regulations.[34] In the ANILCA debates proponents and opponents estimated that somewhere between 50 million and 150 million board feet per year would be available from Native lands.

Everyone had grossly misjudged the impact of the ANCSA grants on Native expectations. Encouraged to become entrepreneurial and pressured to pay dividends, many southeastern village corporations went into the timber business in the late 1970s, either contracting with existing firms or setting up their own operations. In either case they competed with loggers who depended on national forest purchases. Their advantages were substantial: they were unregulated, exempt from even the mild restraints of the Forest Service, and could sell unprocessed logs to the Japanese. The future looked bright. Environmentalists held their criticism.

Within a year, however, the recession had reduced demand and prices, and the Native operations began to incur substantial losses. Byron Mallott, the president of Sealaska, recalled that "we thought we were at the top of a mountain. In fact, we were at the edge of a cliff and we all walked off together."[35] With few apparent options, the Native corporations sold their one salable asset, the trees, to loggers who sought to recoup their investment as quickly as possible. Harvests on Native lands rose from 19 million board feet in 1979 to 70 million in 1980, 122 million in 1981, more than 200 million every year from 1982 through 1986, and 335 million in 1987. Prices were so low that loggers often left low-value pulp logs, half or more of the total, to rot.[36]

For the Native corporations salvation came in the form of a special provision in the 1986 tax law, engineered by Senator Stevens, that allowed them to sell their losses to outside profitable corporations. Ultimately, the sales of all Native corporations totaled $1 billion.[37] In Southeast Alaska the bailout led to even more cutting because the Natives were allowed to sell "soft" losses—the paper losses on standing timber. The benefit "could only be realized by actually harvesting timber or by selling stumpage in a lump-sum sale." Purchasers of stumpage "faced pressure to harvest to realize a return on their timber investments."[38] The loss sales may have saved the Native corporations, but they contributed to the devastation of the Natives' lands and partially cancelled the effects of the Tongass Timber Reform Act and the mill closings. By the 1990s most of the Native lands had been clear-cut.

OTHER CHALLENGES

The third legacy of 1980 was a political climate less receptive to environmental activism. The most notable and obvious change was the arrival of Reagan administration and administrators such as James Watt. The Republican administrations of the 1950s, 1960s, and 1970s had not been known for vigorous leadership on conservation and environmental issues. Yet Fred Seaton and Rogers Morton and their subordinates had worked with environmental groups to preserve Alaska's wildlands and could claim responsibility for most of the policy and legislative initiatives (apart from the Udall land freeze) before 1977. In contrast Watt and his successors were aggressively hostile. They made little effort to conceal their contempt for environmentalists and worked to circumvent the laws they were charged with administering. The campaign to open ANWR was the best-known example, but there were many others.[39]

ANILCA was a complex law that would have created major administrative challenges under the best of circumstances. Watt's effort to assign the 1002 studies to the U.S. Geological Survey was a straw in the wind, the land swaps an indication of how far he was prepared to go. In addition environmentalists complained of the administration's lax management of wildlife refuges, its refusal to authorize purchases of inholdings in Denali and Wrangell–St. Elias national parks and in wildlife refuges, its failure to regulate mining activities that adversely affected nearby wild and scenic rivers, and its permissive approach to illegal hunting, fishing, and trapping.[40] Watt and his assistants and successors also sought to sabotage the wilderness studies they were required to undertake. When experts from the National Park Service and the Fish and Wildlife Service identified 68 million acres of qualified wilderness (16 million in parks and 52 million in wildlife refuges), Interior officials cut the total to a mere 8.1 million acres. Even that modest total was never reported to Congress.[41]

Those and other activities led veteran National Park Service planner John Kauffman to complain publicly that ANILCA had become a "monstrosity." The fine print "countermanded the intent of preservation," he noted, and Interior Department officials exploited and abused those provisions. "It is small wonder," Kauffman concluded, "that federal land managers have been baffled and cowed. ... Ever on the side of machines, roads, real estate development, and rife tourism, this vengeful political establishment has been determined to unravel Alaskan conservation as much as possible."[42] Political scientist Ken Ross would later agree that the "forces of exploitation got much of what they sought on federal lands."[43]

Nor was the state of much assistance. Although Hammond's successors, Sheffield and Cowper, were closer to him than to Egan or Hickel on environmental issues, they faced many of the same problems and pressures that had frustrated Hammond. One additional factor was the rapid growth of oil industry influence in state politics. By the 1980s oil accounted for most of the state's revenue, and the industry had become an important source of jobs. As the Teamsters declined (Jesse Carr died in 1985, and Local 959 declared bankruptcy in 1986), the oil companies took the union's place. "By the late 1980's," John Strohmeyer writes, "oil had everything under control."[44] The state's congressional representatives had long been accommodating; the legislature, particularly the state Senate, now became equally supportive. Legislators refused to consider oil tax increases and enthusiastically endorsed industry goals, such as the opening of ANWR.

In retrospect the most important effect of those changes was on the regulatory mechanisms that had been created in the 1970s. To win support for the pipeline, the industry, state, and Interior Department had agreed to safeguards against oil spills, including regular pipeline inspections and a permanent spill response team at Valdez. At first these systems seemed to work. There were only minor incidents (totaling, however, more than 20,000 by the mid-1980s, including fuel and other chemical spills at Prudhoe Bay). This record, coupled with industry pressures to reduce "unnecessary costs" (the Alyeska Pipeline Service Company disbanded its spill response team in the early 1980s), led to growing laxity. Alyeska's marine superintendent later testified that on assuming his responsibilities, he had been "shocked at the shabbiness of the operation. ... The only surprise is that the disaster didn't strike sooner."[45] During the 1980s state appropriations for pipeline surveillance fell from $4 million to zero. Federal regulators, including the Coast Guard, which had responsibility for navigation in Prince William Sound, became equally nonchalant, partly because of pressures from the Reagan administration. The *Exxon Valdez* disaster led the legislature to adopt a variety of new regulations.[46] Yet the kinds of problems that had made the *Exxon Valdez* spill possible persisted. State and federal employees who reported violations were criticized and demoted; oil company workers who protested were discharged. In the late 1980s and 1990s a continuing series of whistleblower controversies and more and more accidents involving the now-aging pipeline raised fears of catastrophic spills.[47]

In Alaska, as in Congress, efforts to circumvent ANILCA and the regulations imposed on the oil industry inspired vigorous resistance from a large and energetic environmental community. That resistance was also shaped by the experiences of the late 1970s. Early in 1979, as the congressional battle over Alaska lands appeared to be approaching a climax, Robert Allen of the environmentally oriented Henry B. Kendall Foundation publicly asked, "Is there life after d-2?" In August and September, he and Richard Cooley traveled extensively in Alaska, attempting to ascertain, in Cooley's words, "the status and needs of the Alaska environmental movement." A meeting with a dozen activists at the Dogpatch homes of Celia Hunter and Ginny Wood elicited widespread concern that Alaska would disappear from the public consciousness "even though post d-2 issues would be horrendous." Two important initiatives grew out of this discussion. With the assistance of Dennis Wilcher of the national Sierra Club staff, Alaska environmental leaders formed the Alaska Conservation Foundation to raise money for Alaska projects. The second, financed by the Kendall Foundation, was the Alaska Environmental Planning Project, designed to draw the groups together, set priorities, plan for the future, and answer Allen's question.[48]

Although the Conservation Foundation proved to be a welcome addition to the Alaska environmental community, the Planning Project was less successful. Recruiting participants and coordinating their work proved more difficult than Allen imagined. Meetings at Juneau and Fairbanks in spring and summer 1981 featured spirited discussions but little agreement. The organizers discovered what Alaska Conservation Society leaders had already learned: the issues were so complex and varied that a single, coherent approach was unrealistic. Rather than promoting unity and consensus, the project seemed to push them apart. In effect it reaffirmed what Celia Hunter had said on another occasion: "we can and do get together on the things that matter, and argue endlessly on those that don't."[49] In the following years groups with narrow specific interests or a distinctive focus continued to proliferate. By the turn of the century there were at least 91 Alaska environmental organizations, 20 dating from the pre-ANILCA years, 31 from the 1980s, and 37 from the 1990s.[50] The largest of them claimed an aggregate membership of 10,300 in 1980, nearly 18,000 in 1990, and 19,000 in 2000.[51]

Despite that growth, the organizational pattern of the 1970s remained largely unchanged. The environmental centers anchored activities in their respective regions, and other umbrella groups—such as the Alaska Coalition; the Alaska Lands Act Coordination Committee, formed in 1981 to monitor the implementation of ANILCA; and the Alaska Environmental Assembly, also formed in 1981—emphasized political action and government relations. Trustees for Alaska continued to provide Alaska-oriented legal action, and the Alaska Conservation Foundation financed a variety of educational programs. This structure accommodated a movement that was as varied and sprawling as the Alaska landscape it sought to preserve.

In early 1991 the Alaska groups worked with the national organizations to plan a conference and reunion called "Celebrate Wild Alaska," scheduled for February in Washington. The sessions featured officers of the various organizations, veterans of the Alaska Coalition, and congressional leaders—in short, a large percentage of the names that have appeared in this account. There were also videotaped greetings from Margaret Murie, Morris Udall, and Jimmy Carter. The printed program included a statement by John Seiberling and a poem by his wife Betty, extolling the grandeur of Alaska. Secretary of the Interior Lujan spoke, as did the head of the Yukon territorial government.[52] The mood was celebratory—similar, perhaps, to the mood at the more modest reception Governor Sheffield had hosted in 1985. But there were marked differences. The activists who gathered in February 1991 had no illusions about the finality of their earlier achievements, including ANILCA and the recently passed Tongass Timber Reform Act or about the hurdles that would confront them in the future. If the Bush administration seemed more hospitable than its predecessor, the recent election of Walter Hickel as governor of Alaska in a bizarre three-way contest dispelled any tendency toward complacency. Yet it was possible to look beyond the problems and obstacles. Despite a century of booster activity and a quarter-century oil boom, 68 million acres of

Alaska's national parks and wildlife refuges, at least 2 million acres of the Chugach National Forest, and perhaps 50 million acres of Bureau of Land Management land remained sufficiently undeveloped to qualify for inclusion in the wilderness preservation system. It would still be possible to preserve "at least" 100 million additional acres of the Alaska wilderness.[53] This reassuring total reflected the vast size of Alaska, its remoteness and relative isolation, and the ability of conservationists and environmentalists to deflect the plans of boosters and assert the public interest.

SUMMING UP: THE STRUGGLE FOR WILDERNESS ALASKA

If the continuing controversies over natural resource issues emphasized the strength and persistence of booster sentiment, the ability of environmentalists to delay, modify, or thwart most development plans was an indication of how much had changed since the 1960s. No longer was opposition an ad hoc response to booster initiatives. Even though the Reagan appointments had meant a continuation of the "constant fighting," the result was political stalemate, not a wholesale rollback of the achievements of the 1970s. The difference was associated with three inter-related developments, concentrated in the 1960s and 1970s: the rise of environmentalism, expressed in the broadening perspectives of activists, their growing numbers, and the legal and political tools available to them; an increasing national awareness of Alaska as the last unspoiled area of the United States; and the coalition of local and national organizations that worked to preserve parts of wild Alaska. Together they ensured that there would be no return to an earlier age.

In 1940 Alaska had been a vast, lightly inhabited, and little-known territory. Apart from the coast of the southeastern panhandle and widely scattered areas of the interior, it was little changed from a century or even a millennium earlier. Compared with the rest of the United States, it was inaccessible, a de facto wildlife sanctuary. Forty years later it had changed in far-reaching, mostly unanticipated ways. The population was still small and scattered, but Alaska was hardly more inaccessible than many other areas. A vast oil field on the Arctic coast, an 800-mile pipeline, and a highway connecting the Arctic with Fairbanks were the most visible and compelling symbols of change, but there were many others. Airplanes routinely penetrated the most remote areas, and hikers and hunters, as well as geologists and prospectors, had access to virtually every square mile. If accessibility had been the only measure, the struggle for wilderness Alaska had been lost, and lost decisively.

Yet there was also a growing awareness of the need for compensatory measures. A major development of the late 1950s and 1960s had been the emergence of a politically active environmental movement that translated a growing sense of loss and deterioration into tangible remedial measures. By the late 1960s powerful national organizations, riding a wave of heightened public sensitivity to real or potential environmental degradation, had become influential forces in Washington and in many states. Together with local affiliates and allies, they made public lands, public land management, and the dangers of unregulated industrial growth major issues. They became a growing presence in Alaska as the state's growing visibility attracted people who rejected the "frontier" perspective and insisted that material prosperity and environmental protection were complementary goals. As Alaska residents, familiar with specific areas and problems and making legitimate claims on the attention of state officials, they played critical roles in the long and controversial effort to preserve parts of the northern landscape.

Like other environmentalists, the Alaskans struggled to devise an effective organizational structure. By the late 1960s the Alaska Conservation Society could no longer serve the interests of an increasingly diverse environmental community. Coalitions of local groups and national organizations became an effective alternative. But the distinguishing feature of Alaska environmentalism was the regional center. Centers in the Southeast, in Anchorage, and in Fairbanks were responses to the vast distances, scattered population, and distinctive problems of Alaska. They provided a physical presence, a place to seek answers and assistance. No less important was their symbolic significance as oases of support and sympathy in a hostile setting. In the Southeast SEACC soon overshadowed its affiliates; in Anchorage the Alaska Center for the Environment and the Sierra Club coexisted harmoniously; and to the north, the Fairbanks Environmental Center (later the Northern Alaska Environmental Center) gradually overshadowed the Alaska Conservation Society. In later years, as local interest groups continued to proliferate, the centers' roles in providing organizational coherence to the environmental movement became even more important.

It was the combination of these groups and national organizations that wrote a notable new chapter in the history of American political activism. The national organizations contributed militant leadership, a broad membership base, and a potent political formula—a coupling of idealistic goals with aggressive advertising and litigation. The Alaska groups provided on-the-spot information and expertise and persuasive evidence of the diversity of Alaska opinions. The alliance of national and local groups first addressed the effects of the oil boom and the ambitious logging plans of the Forest Service and then took the offense with even greater impact in the late 1970s.

Between 1977 and 1980 they mounted one of the most impressive campaigns in the annals of American politics and brought about substantial additions to the nation's stock of legally protected land. Their achievements transformed the national park system, creating or enlarging some of the most popular parks (Denali and Glacier Bay, for example) as well as some of the least visited (the Arctic parks, Wrangell–St. Elias, and Lake Clark, which at the end of the century still had virtually no tourist facilities). The more than 5 million acres of Tongass wilderness far exceeded that of any other national forest and became an unexpected asset to the Forest Service, which began citing Tongass to "prove" its enthusiasm for wilderness.[54] SEACC activists remained bitter over the U.S. Borax mine site in Misty Fiords, the comparatively small West Chichagof–Yakobi wilderness, the Shee Atika logging operation on Admiralty Island, the clear-cutting of much of Afognak Island, and the continuing devotion of the Forest Service to timber, but nearly every wilderness battle of the 1960s and 1970s had resulted in similar trade-offs. Compared with what Jack Calvin and his friends envisioned in 1967–1968, the total was impressive. By 1990, moreover, environmentalists had managed to halt the pernicious effects of the Tongass Timber Supply Fund and reduce the loss of wildlife in the southeastern rain forest.

Although Alaska and Alaskans continued to face challenges not unlike those of earlier decades, the setting after 1980 was different. The most attractive and unusual parts of Alaska were permanently preserved in parks, wildlife refuges, public recreation areas, and wilderness tracts, and a web of voluntary organizations monitored public land management and systematically opposed industrial and commercial activities that threatened to degrade the land, water, and air. The areas that remained in contention, such as the southeastern forests and the ANWR coast, were no longer the obscure and remote lands they had been to most Americans of the 1930s or 1940s. The combination of activism, publicity, legal restraints, and tourism thus ensured that an increasingly accessible Alaska would never again be the isolated place it had been.

The struggle for wilderness Alaska was also a gauge of the larger movement for environmental protection. It illustrated the dramatic effects of
environmentalism on conservation organizations and activities and the
ability of activists to use public appeals and legal challenges to counter the
superior economic resources of their opponents. As much as any other
development of that era, the Alaska experience exposed the political fault
lines in American society. But if it symbolized a more general awakening
to the costs and implications of contemporary prosperity, it also underlined the problems that were certain to confront any initiative that could
be interpreted as compromising the promise of future prosperity.
Environmentalists insisted that environmental protection was compatible
with economic growth, particularly as the economy became less dependent on natural resource exploitation, and cited compelling evidence to
buttress their claims. But their evidence made little difference to entrenched
interests, such as the mining and petroleum industries, and their arguments tended to fall on deaf ears in periods of recession and economic
decline, such as the mid- and late 1970s. Given these hurdles, environmental activists in Alaska and elsewhere faced a persistent challenge in
reminding their friends and neighbors of the close and beneficial association between environmental protection, economic modernization, and
improved living standards.

NOTES

Prologue: Washington, December 1980

1. *Washington Post*, December 2, 1980.
2. Ibid.
3. Ronald Hawk interview, November 22, 1999; Kay Greenough interview, November 18, 1999; Kathie Durbin, *Tongass: Pulp Politics and the Fight for Alaska's Rain Forest* (Corvallis: Oregon State University Press, 1999), 102–103.
4. Cecil D. Andrus and Joel Connelly, *Cecil Andrus: Politics Western Style* (Seattle: Sasquatch Books, 1998), 67.
5. "Remarks of the President," White House Release, December 2, 1980, Carter Papers, White House Central File ST-5.
6. "Remarks of the President"; Andrus and Connelly, *Andrus*, 79; *New York Times*, December 3, 1980.
7. These totals are based on calculations by Richard Gordon. The official figures differ slightly.
8. Richard N. L. Andrews, *Managing the Environment, Managing Ourselves: A History of American Environmental Policy* (New Haven: Yale University Press, 1999), 202.
9. See John Hanrahan and Peter Gruenstein, *Lost Frontier: The Marketing of Alaska* (New York: W.W. Norton, 1977), 3; Peter A. Coates, *The Trans-Alaska Pipeline Controversy: Technology, Conservation and the Frontier* (Fairbanks: University of Alaska Press, 1993), 82.
10. Richard A. Cooley, *Alaska: A Challenge in Conservation* (Madison: University of Wisconsin Press, 1967), 65. Also see Federal Field Committee for Development Planning in *Alaska, Alaska Natives & the Land* (Anchorage, 1968), 449.

Part 1. Seedtime: Alaska in the 1960s

The quotations on the introductory page to Part I are from the following sources: George Bird Grinnell in William H. Goetzmann and Kay Sloan, *Looking Far North:The Harriman Expedition to Alaska, 1899* (New York: Viking Press, 1982), 196; Edward J. Rusing in U.S. Senate, *Hearings before the Committee on Interior and Insular Affairs, March 25-26, 1957*, 58th Congress, First Session (Washington: Government Printing Office, 1957), 18; and George W. Rogers in Gordon Scott Harrison, *Alaska Public Policy: Current Problems and Issues* (Fairbanks: Institute of Social, Economic and Government Research, 1971), 228.

Chapter 1. The Emergence of Alaska

1. William H. Goetzmann and Kay Sloan, *Looking Far North: The Harriman Expedition to Alaska, 1899* (New York: Viking Press, 1982), xi.
2. Goetzmann and Sloan, *Looking Far North*, 53.
3. Goetzmann and Sloan, *Looking Far North*, 59; Bruce Merrell, "'A Wild Discouraging Mess': John Muir Reports on the Klondike Gold Rush," *Alaska History* 7 (Fall 1992), 30–39.
4. Goetzmann and Sloan, *Looking Far North*, 41.
5. U.S. Department of Commerce, *Historical Statistics of the United States; Colonial Times to 1970, Part I* (Washington, 1975), Series A, 195–209, 24–37.
6. Ernest Gruening, *Many Battles: The Autobiography of Ernest Gruening* (New York: Liveright, 1973), 215.
7. James A. Crutchfield and Giulio Pontecorro, *The Pacific Salmon Fisheries: A Study in Irrational Conservation* (Baltimore: John Hopkins University Press, 1969), 74–98.
8. Crutchfield and Pontecorro, *Pacific Salmon Fisheries*, 58; Michael L. Weber, *From Abundance to Scarcity: A History of U.S. Marine Fisheries Policy* (Washington: Island Press, 2002), 76–77.
9. Jeannette P. Nichols, *Alaska: A History of Its Administration, Exploitation, and Industrial Development during Its First Half Century under the Rule of the United States* (Cleveland: Arthur H. Clark, 1924), 203–204.
10. Stephen Haycox, *Alaska, An American Colony* (Seattle: University of Washington Press, 2002), 205.
11. Quoted in Robert A. Stearns, "The Morgan-Guggenheim Syndicate and the Development of Alaska, 1906–1915," Ph.D. dissertation, University of California, Santa Barbara, 1967, 18. For an overview of business developments, see Elizabeth A. Tower, *Icebound Empire: Industry and Politics on the Last Frontier, 1898–1938* (Anchorage: n.p., 1992).
12. John H. Davis, *The Guggenheims: An American Epic* (New York: William Morrow, 1978), 103.
13. Phil R. Holdsworth, "Kennecott and Nabesna, Historic Mines in the Wrangall Mountains of Southcentral Alaska," in Alaska Historical Society, *Mining in Alaska's Past: Conference Proceedings, Anchorage, 1980* (Anchorage: Office of History and Archaeology, Division of Parks, 1980), 30.
14. Melody Webb Grauman, "Kennecott: Alaska Origins of a Copper Empire, 1900–38," *Western Historical Quarterly* 9 (April 1978), 204.
15. Grauman, "Kennecott," 204.
16. See Evangeline Atwood, *Frontier Politics: Alaska's James Wickersham* (Portland, OR: Binford & Mort, 1979).
17. Robert B. Weeden, *Alaska: Promises to Keep* (Boston: Houghton Mifflin, 1978), 4.
18. George W. Rogers, *Alaska in Transition: The Southeast Region* (Baltimore: Johns Hopkins University Press, 1960), 181–82.
19. Richard K. Nelson, *Hunters of the Northern Forest: Designs for Survival among the Alaskan Kutchin* (Chicago: University of Chicago Press, 1986), 276–79.
20. Ernest S. Burch, *The Inupiaq Eskimo Nations of Northwest Alaska* (Fairbanks: University of Alaska Press, 1998), 309.
21. Rogers, *Alaska in Transition*, 177.
22. Hudson Stuck, *Ten Thousand Miles with a Dog Sled* (Lincoln: University of Nebraska Press, 1988), xiii.
23. Donald Craig Mitchell, *Sold American: The Story of Alaska Natives and Their Land, 1867–1959* (Hanover: University Press of New England, 1997), 92–93; Ted Hinckley, *The Americanization of Alaska, 1867–1897* (Palo Alto: Pacific Books, 1972), 150–51.

24. Mitchell, *Sold American*, 230–31.

25. Char Miller, *Gifford Pinchot and the Making of Modern Environmentalism* (Washington: Island Press, 2000), 119–43; Samuel Hays, *Conservation and the Gospel of Efficiency: The Progressive Conservation Movement, 1890–1920* (Cambridge: Harvard University Press, 1959), chapter 8.

26. Lawrence Rakestraw, *A History of the U.S. Forest Service in Alaska* (Anchorage: Alaska Historical Commission, 1981), 17–42.

27. Nichols, *Alaska*, 363. Also see Donald Worster, *Under Western Skies: Nature and History in the American West* (New York: Oxford University Press, 1992), 182–83.

28. Miller, *Pinchot*, 206–17; M. Nelson McGeary, *Gifford Pinchot, Forester, Politician* (Princeton: Princeton University Press, 1960), 132–47; James Penick, *Progressive Politics and Conservation: The Ballinger-Pinchot Affair* (Chicago: University of Chicago Press, 1968), 30–40, 77–85, 175–89; Hays, *Conservation and the Gospel of Efficiency*, 150–70.

29. Rakestraw, *Forest Service in Alaska*, 108–10.

30. David L. Spencer, "Aleutian Islands National Wildlife Refuge," in David L. Spencer, Claus-M Naske, and John Carnahan, *National Wildlife Refuges in Alaska: A Historical Perspective* (Anchorage: Arctic Environmental Information Center, 1979), 40–41, 51.

31. Theodore Catton, *Inhabited Wilderness: Indians, Eskimos, and National Parks in Alaska* (Albuquerque: University of New Mexico Press, 1997), 22–25; G. Frank Williss, "'Do Things Right the First Time': The National Park Service and the Alaska National Interest Lands Conservation Act of 1980" (Washington: National Park Service, 1985), 9.

32. Williss, "Do Things Right," 20.

33. Williss, "Do Things Right," 15.

34. Williss, "Do Things Right," 23–26.

35. National Resource Committee, *Alaska—Its Resources and Development, Part VII, Regional Planning* (Washington: Government Printing Office, 1938), 3.

36. National Resource Committee, *Alaska*, 20.

37. National Resource Committee, *Alaska*, 20.

38. National Resource Committee, *Alaska*, 28.

39. National Resource Committee, *Alaska*, 140.

40. National Resource Committee, *Alaska*, 213. For Marshall's ideas on wilderness, see Paul S. Sutter, *Driven Wild: How the Fight against Automobiles Launched the Modern Wilderness Movement* (Seattle: University of Washington Press, 2002), chapter 6.

41. Orlando W. Miller, *The Frontier in Alaska and the Matanuska Colony* (New Haven: Yale University Press, 1975), 162–63; James M. Glover, *A Wilderness Original: The Life of Bob Marshall* (Seattle: The Mountaineers, 1986), 261.

42. Robert David Johnson, *Ernest Gruening and the American Dissenting Tradition* (Cambridge: Harvard University Press, 1998), 154; Gruening, *Many Battles*, 256–57.

43. William R. Morrison and Kenneth A. Coates, *Working the North: Labor and the Northwest Defense Projects, 1942–1946* (Fairbanks: University of Alaska Press, 1994), 72–75.

44. Lisa Mighetto and Carla Homstad, *Engineering in the Far North: A History of the U.S. Army Engineering District in Alaska, 1867–1992* (n.p.: Historical Research Associates, 1997), 256–58.

45. George W. Rogers and Richard A. Cooley, *Alaska's Population and Economy: Regional Growth, Development and Future Outlook, Vol. I, Analysis* (College: Alaska Institute of Business, Economics and Government Research, University of Alaska, 1963), 116–18.

46. Rogers and Cooley, *Alaska's Population*, 61.

47. See Evangeline Atwood, *Anchorage: All-America City* (Portland, OR: Binford & Mort, 1957), 35, and Terrence Cole and Elmer E. Rasmuson, *Banking on Alaska: The Story of the National Bank of Alaska, Vol. I* (Fairbanks: University of Alaska Press, 2000), 190.

48. Gruening, *Many Battles*, 352–54; Johnson, *Gruening*, 164–65, 171–72.

49. Johnson, *Gruening*, 163; Stephen Haycox, "Owning It All in Alaska: The Political Power of a Rhetorical Paradigm," in William G. Robbins and James C. Foster, *Land in the American West: Private Claims and the Common Good* (Seattle: University of Washington Press, 2000), 165–68.

50. Elmo Richardson, *Dams, Parks & Politics: Resource Development & Preservation in the Truman-Eisenhower Era* (Lexington: University Press of Kentucky, 1973), chapters 1–2.

51. Alaska Field Committee, "A Six Year Integrated Program for the Department of the Interior in Alaska, 1950–1955" (Washington: Government Printing Office, 1949), 66.

52. Alaska Field Committee, "Six Year Integrated Program," 66.

53. Alaska Field Committee, "Six Year Integrated Program," 66.

54. Evangeline Atwood and Robert N. DeArmond, *Who's Who in Alaskan Politics: A Biographical Dictionary of Alaskan Political Personalities, 1884–1974* (Portland, OR: Binford & Mort, 1977), 42; Rakestraw, *Forest Service in Alaska*, 119.

55. National Resource Committee, *Alaska*, 9.

56. National Resource Committee, *Alaska*, 98.

57. Paul W. Hirt, *A Conspiracy of Optimism: Management of the National Forests since World War II* (Lincoln: University of Nebraska Press, 1994), 40–41.

58. Rakestraw, *Forest Service in Alaska*, 132.

59. Rakestraw, *Forest Service in Alaska*, 139.

60. Rogers, *Alaska in Transition*, 73.

61. Mitchell, *Sold American*, 320.

62. Stephen W. Haycox, "Economic Development and Indian Land Rights in Modern Alaska: The 1947 Tongass Timber Act," in Stephen W. Haycox and Mary Childers Mangusso, *An Alaska Anthology* (Seattle: University of Washington Press, 1996), 343.

63. Haycox, "Economic Development," 350.

64. Haycox, "Economic Development," 355.

65. Rakestraw, *Forest Service in Alaska*, 127–28; Rogers, *Alaska in Transition*, 78–79.

66. Gerald E. Bowkett, *Reaching for a Star: The Final Campaign for Alaska Statehood* (Fairbanks: Epicenter Press, 1989), 15.

67. Weeden, *Alaska: Promises to Keep*, 13.

68. Johnson, *Gruening*, 187.

69. Jack Roderick, *Crude Dreams: A Personal History of Oil & Politics in Alaska* (Fairbanks: Epicenter Press, 1997), 92.

70. Bowkett, *Reaching for a Star*, 2–3; Victor Fischer, *Alaska's Constitutional Convention* (Fairbanks: University of Alaska Press, 1975), 22–23.

71. Donald Craig Mitchell, *Take My Land, Take My Life: The Story of Congress's Historic Settlement of Alaska Native Land Claims, 1960–1971* (Fairbanks: University of Alaska Press, 2001), 226–27; Claus-M. Naske, *An Interpretative History of Alaskan Statehood* (Anchorage: Alaska Northwest Publishers, 1973), 155.

72. Fischer, *Alaska's Constitutional Convention*, 130–31.

73. John Hanrahan and Peter Gruenstein, *Lost Frontier: the Marketing of Alaska* (New York: W.W. Norton, 1977), 19.

74. Gruening, *Many Battles*, 386; Fischer, *Alaska's Constitutional Convention*, 179, 184.

75. John Whitehead, "The Governor Who Opposed Statehood: The Legacy of Jay Hammond," in Haycox and Mangusso, *An Alaska Anthology*, 369.

76. Whitehead, "Governor Who Opposed Statehood," 371.

77. Richard A. Cooley, *Alaska, A Challenge to Conservation* (Madison: University of Wisconsin Press, 1967), 23.

78. Ernest Gruening, *The State of Alaska* (New York: Random House, 1954), 474–75.

79. Naske, *An Interpretative History*, 101.

80. Naske, *An Interpretative History*, 163; Cooley, *Alaska*, 25; Claus-M Naske, *Edward Lewis "Bob" Bartlett of Alaska … A Life in Politics* (Fairbanks: University of Alaska Press, 1979), 144–46.

81. Peter A. Coates, *The Trans-Alaska Pipeline Controversy: Technology, Conservation, and the Frontier* (Fairbanks: University of Alaska Press, 1993), 88–89; Ernest Gruening, *The Battle for Alaska Statehood* (College: University of Alaska Press, 1967), 97.

82. "Meet the Senators," CBS Television film, 1959. University of Alaska Library.

Chapter 2. Conservation in Transition

1.   Virginia Hill Wood to Edgar Wayburn, May 27, 1968, Sierra Club Papers (Bancroft Library, University of California, Berkeley) 228:23 [hereafter SC Papers]; Sally Corrighar, *Moonlight at Midday* (New York: A. A. Knopf, 1959), 381–83.

2.   G. Frank Williss, "'Do Things Right the First Time': The National Park Service and the Alaska National Interest Lands Conservation Act of 1980" (Washington: National Park Service, 1985), 70.

3.   Stephen Fox, *The American Conservation Movement: John Muir and His Legacy* (Boston: Little Brown, 1981), chapter 8.

4.   Margaret E. Murie, *Two in the Far North* (Anchorage: Alaska Northwest Books, 1997), parts 2, 3; Gregory D. Kendrick, "An Environmental Spokesman: Olaus J. Murie and the Democratic Defense of Wilderness," *Annals of Wyoming* 50 (Fall 1978), 213–302; David Backes, *A Wilderness Within: The Life of Sigurd F. Olson* (Minneapolis: University of Minnesota Press, 1997).

5.   Samuel P. Hays, *Beauty, Health, and Permanence: Environmental Politics in the United States, 1955–1985* (New York: Cambridge University Press, 1987), chapter 1. Hays's survey—and his later work, *A History of Environmental Politics Since 1945* (Pittsburgh: University of Pittsburgh Press, 2000), document the remarkable scope of environmentalism. Also see Curt Meine, *Aldo Leopold: His Life and Work* (Madison: University of Wisconsin Press, 1988); Linda J. Lear, *Rachel Carson: Witness for Nature* (New York: Henry Holt, 1997); and Thomas R. Dunlap, *Saving America's Wildlife* (Princeton: Princeton University Press, 1988), 98–105.

6.   Paul W. Hirt, *A Conspiracy of Optimism: Management of National Forests since World War II* (Lincoln: University of Nebraska Press, 1994), 221–22.

7.   Lawrence C. Merriman to Files, August 13, 1952, National Park Service Papers, RG 36 (Harpers Ferry, WV, Archives) [hereafter NPS Papers].

8.   Olaus Murie to Lawrence C. Merriman, October 17, 1956, SC Papers 18:24. Richard West Sellars describes the larger concerns Murie and others had with the NPS effort. *Preserving Nature in the National Parks: A History* (New Haven: Yale University Press, 1997), 185–88.

9.   Roderick Nash, *Wilderness and the American Mind* (New Haven: Yale University Press, 1967), 209–21.

10. John McPhee, *Encounters with the Archdruid* (New York: Farrar, Straus and Giroux, 1971).

11. Tom Turner, *Sierra Club: 100 Years of Protecting Nature* (New York: Harry N. Abrams, 1991), 140–219; Robert Gottlieb, *Forcing the Spring: The Transformation of the American Environmental Movement* (Washington: Island Press, 1993), 41–46, 148–51; Michael P. Cohen, *The History of the Sierra Club, 1892–1970* (San Francisco: Sierra Club Books, 1988), 325–46.

12. Mark W. T. Harvey, *A Symbol of Wilderness: Echo Park and the American Conservation Movement* (Albuquerque: University of New Mexico Press, 1994), 5.

13. Quoted in Craig W. Allin, *The Politics of Wilderness Protection* (Westport: Greenwood Press, 1982), 111. See Steven C. Schulte, *Wayne Aspinall and the Shaping of the American West* (Boulder: University Press of Colorado, 2002), chapter 4; Nash, *Wilderness*, 222.

14. Schulte, *Wayne Aspinall*, 163; Allin, *Politics of Wilderness Protection*, 115–52; Hirt, *Conspiracy of Optimism*, 229–32; Hal K. Rothman, *The Greening of a Nation? Environmentalsim in the United States since 1945* (Fort Worth: Harcourt Brace, 1998), chapter 2.

15. Morgan Sherwood argues that most Alaskans—apart from merchants and lawyers—favored utilitarian conservation. *Big Game in Alaska: A History of Wildlife and People* (New Haven: Yale University Press, 1981), 149.

16. Olaus Murie to Council of the Wilderness Society, March 22, 1956, Wilderness Society Papers (Denver Public Library, Denver), 3:200 [hereafter TWS Papers].

17. Merriman to Files, August 13, 1952, NPS Papers; transcript of interview with George Collins, May 12, 1978, 188, NPS Papers.

18. Collins interview, 189.

19. "A Preliminary Geographical Survey of the Kongakut–Firth River Area," (Washington: National Park Service, 1954), NPS Papers.

20. Collins interview, 192.

21. Claus-M Naske, "Creation of the Arctic National Wildlife Range," in David L. Spencer, Claus-M Naske, and John Carnahan, "National Wildlife Refuges of Alaska: A Historical Perspective" (Anchorage: Arctic Environmental Information and Data Center, 1979), 104.

22. Richard Leonard to O. L. Chapman, September 12, 1952, Margaret Murie Papers (University of Alaska Archives, Fairbanks), Box 2.

23. Mardie Murie to Howard Zahniser, September 15, 1953, TWS Papers 3:200.

24. Zahniser to M. Murie, September 21, 1953, TWS Papers 3:200.

25. "Tentative Estimate of Costs ...," February 19, 1954, Murie Papers, Box 2.

26. Olaus Murie to Members of Wilderness Society Council, March 22, 1956, TWS Papers 3:200.

27. O. Murie to George Collins, November 29, 1956, TWS Papers 3:200.

28. O. Murie to Fairfield Osborn, February 18, 1957, Murie Papers, Box 2.

29. U.S. Senate, *Hearings before the Merchant Marine and Fisheries Subcommittee of the Committee on Interstate and Foreign Commerce*, 86th Congress, 1st Session (Washington: Government Printing Office, 1959), 290.

30. O. Murie to Collins, November 29, 1956, TWS Papers 3:200.

31. O. Murie to Zahniser, May 26, 1956, TWS Papers 3:200.

32. M. Murie to Anne, June 13, 1956, TWS Papers 3:200.

33. O. Murie to Osborn, February 18, 1956, Murie Papers, Box 2.

34. O. Murie to Collins, August 10, 1957, Murie Papers, Box 2.

35. "Brief recount of a journey ...," June 15, 1957, Murie Papers, Box 2.

36. O. Murie to Collins, August 10, 1957, Murie Papers, Box 2.

37. Zahniser to O. Murie, September 27, 1957, Murie Papers, Box 2.

38. U.S. Senate, *Hearings*, 1959, 434.

39. O. Murie to Collins, August 19, 1957, Murie Papers, Box 2; Charles S. Jones, *From the Rio Grande to the Arctic: The Story of the Richfield Oil Corporation* (Norman: University of Oklahoma Press, 1972), 285–88.

40. Zahniser to O. Murie, September 27, 1957; Ross Leffler to O. Murie, October 21, 1957; O. Murie to L. Sumner, December 3, 1957, Murie Papers, Box 2.

41. O. Murie to Sumner, December 3, 1957, Murie Papers, Box 2.

42. U.S. Senate, *Hearings*, 1959, 434.

43. U.S. Senate, *Hearings*, 434.

44. David Brower, *For Earth's Sake: The Life and Times of David Brower* (Salt Lake City: Peregrine Smith Books), 486.

45. Theodore Catton, *Inhabited Wilderness: Indians, Eskimos, and National Parks in Alaska* (Albuquerque: University of New Mexico Press, 1997), 148; Orlando W. Miller, *The Frontier in Alaska and the Matanuska Colony* (New Haven: Yale University Press, 1975), 171–72.

46. Territorial Department of Mining, *Bulletin IV* (March 1958), 1–2.

47. O. Murie to Osborn, March 15, 1958, Murie Papers, Box 2.

48. J. C. Boswell to O. Murie, March 7, 1958, Murie Papers, Box 2.

49. Bud Boddy to O. Murie, March 31, 1958, Murie Papers, Box 2.

50. U.S. Senate, *Hearings*, 1959, 119.

51. U.S. Senate, *Hearings*, 347.

52. U.S. Senate, *Hearings*, 4.

53. U.S. Senate, *Hearings*, l0.

54. U.S. Senate, *Hearings*, 34. Alaska reporter John Greeley later recalled Bartlett's belief that state management of fishing and hunting was part of the bargain. *Anchorage Daily News*, February 7, 1988.

55. U.S. Senate, *Hearings*, 34.

56. *News Bulletin* 1 (August 1960), 1.

57. Dixie Baade to O. Murie, January 26, 1960, Murie Papers, Box 2.

58. U.S. Senate, *Hearings*, 328.

59. U.S. Senate, *Hearings*, 340.

60. U.S. Senate, *Hearings*, 328.

61. Brower, *For Earth's Sake*, 486.

62. Sigurd Olson to Fred Seaton, October 6, 1960, Murie Papers, Box 2; Backes, *Wilderness Within*, 299–301.

63. Quoted in Naske, "Creation," 110.

64. Quoted in Coates, *Trans-Alaska Pipeline*, 107.

65. Dwight D. Eisenhower, "Special Message to the Congress on the Legislative Program," May 3, 1960, *Public Papers of the Presidents of the United States, D. D. Eisenhower, 1960–61* (Washington: Government Printing Office, 1961), 393.

66. Naske, "Creation," 110.

67. Ernst W. Mueller to Frederick A. Seaton, April 17, 1972, Fairbanks Environmental Center Papers, University of Alaska Archives, Box 12 [hereafter FEC Papers].

68. U.S. Department of the Interior, Fish and Wildlife Service, "Arctic National Wildlife Range, Annual Narrative Report, 1976" (n.p., n.d.), 3.

69. Zahniser to O. Murie, July 7, 1956, TWS Papers 3:200.

70. Virginia Hill Wood to O. Murie, April 30, 1957, Murie Papers, Box 2.

71. *News Bulletin* 1 (March 1960).

72. *News Bulletin* 1 (May 1960), 11; 2 (June 1961), 2; Robert B. Weeden interview, September 9, 1999.

73. Weeden interview.

74. Dan O'Neill, *The Firecracker Boys* (New York: St. Martin's Press, 1994); Coates, *Trans-Alaska Pipeline*, chapter 4; Coates, "Project Chariot: Alaska Roots of Environmentalism," in Stephen W. Haycox and May Childers Mangusso, *An Alaska Anthology: Interpreting the Past* (Seattle: University of Washington Press, 1996), 381–95; Ken Ross, *Environmental Conflict in Alaska* (Boulder: University Press of Colorado, 2000), 96–l09.

75. See Hays, *Beauty, Health, and Permanence*, 177–82; Gottlieb, *Forcing the Spring*, 177–83.

76. Quoted in O'Neill, *Firecracker Boys*, 216.

77. Dean W. Kohlhoff, *Amchitka and the Bomb: Nuclear Testing in Alaska* (Seattle: University of Washington Press, 2002), 77.

78. Quoted in Lisa Mighetto and Carla Homstad, *Engineering in the Far North: A History of the U.S. Army Engineering District in Alaska, 1867–1992* (n.p.: Historical Research Associates, 1997), 185–88.

79. Robert David Johnson, *Ernest Gruening and the American Dissenting Tradition* (Cambridge: Harvard University Press, 1998), 272; Ross, *Environmental Conflict in Alaska*, 121–33.

80. Quoted in Coates, *Trans-Alaska Pipeline*, 141.

81. *News Bulletin* 4 (December 1963), 11.

82. Ernest Gruening Diary, September 7, 1963; Ernest Gruening Papers, University of Alaska Archives, Box 3.

83. See McPhee, *Encounters*, 170.

84. *News Bulletin* 3 (January 1962), 2; Celia Hunter interview, October 28, 1998.

85. *News Bulletin* 4 (October 1963), 9.

86. Gruening Diary, October 9, 1963, Gruening Papers, Box 3.

87. *News Bulletin* 6 (May 1965), 6–7.

88. *Alaska Conservation Review* 17(Spring 1976), 6.

89. *News Bulletin* 9 (May 1972), 2.

90. "Tanana-Yukon Chapter," December 1971, FEC Papers, Box 71.

91. "Trip Report by Stanley Cain," 1965, 14, NPS Papers.

92. Williss, "Do Things Right," 34. Also see Pamela E. Rich and Arlon R. Tussing, *The National Park System in Alaska: An Economic Impact Study* (College: University of Alaska, 1973).

93. "Trip Report by Stanley Cain," 8.

94. George B. Hartzog, *Battling for the National Parks* (Mount Kisco: Moyer Bell, 1988), 205.

95. Catton, *Inhabited Wilderness*, 150.

96. "Operation Great Land" (Washington, 1965), 7, NPS Papers, emphasis in the original.

97. "Operation Great Land," 56, 58, 59, 69.

98. Hartzog, *Battling*, 207.

99. Hartzog to W. J. Hickel, December 6, 1967, NPS Papers.

100. Hartzog to Hickel, September 10, 1968, NPS Papers.

101. James H. Husted, "History of the Johnson Proclamations," NPS Papers.

102. Husted, "History," 7.

103. John P. Grevelli, "The Final Act of the Greatest Conservation President," *Prologue* 12 (Winter 1980), 180.

104. Quoted in Grevelli, "The Final Act," 180.

105. Grevelli, "The Final Act," 187.

106. Quoted in *Christian Science Monitor*, January 23, 1969.

107. Grevelli, "The Final Act," 181, 186. Also see J. Brooks Flippen, "Mr. Hickel Goes to Washington," *Alaska History* 12 (Fall 1997), 1–22, and Flippen, *Nixon and the Environment* (Albuquerque: University of New Mexico Press, 2000), 23–24.

108. Grevelli, "The Final Act," 181.

Part II. Wilderness Politics: Alaska, 1960s–1976

The quotations on the introductory page to Part II are from the following sources: Gordon B. Wright to Jim Kowalsky, September 5, 1971, Wilderness Society Papers 12:201B; *Ketchikan Daily News*, January 22, 1975; and Potter Wickware, *Crazy Money: Nine Months on the Trans-Alaska Pipeline* (New York: Random House, 1979), 89.

Chapter 3. Alaska Upheavals

1. Bryan Cooper, *Alaska: The Last Frontier* (London: Hutchinson, 1972), 77.

2. Quoted in Cooper, *Alaska*, 82. Also see Donald Craig Mitchell, *Take My Land, Take My Life: The Story of Congress's Historic Settlement of Alaska Native Claims, 1960–1971* (Fairbanks: University of Alaska Press, 2001), 183.

3. Jack Roderick, *Crude Dreams: A Personal History of Oil & Politics in Alaska* (Fairbanks: Epicenter Press, 1997), 218, 221.

4. The standard accounts are Peter A. Coates, *The Trans-Alaska Pipeline Controversy: Technology, Conservation, and the Frontier* (Fairbanks: University of Alaska Press, 1993), and Mary Clay Berry, *The Alaska Pipeline: the Politics of Oil and Native Land Claims* (Bloomington: Indiana University Press, 1975).

5. Arlon Tussing and Gregg Erickson, "Mineral Policy, the Public Lands and Economic Development: the Case for Alaska" (Fairbanks: Institute of Social, Economic and Government Research, 1969), 31.

6. George W. Rogers, *The Future of Alaska: Economic Consequences of Statehood* (Baltimore: Johns Hopkins University Press, 1962), 102.

7. John S. Wheatley and Guy Gordon, *Economic and Transport Developments in Alaska's Future* (Seattle: University of Washington Graduate School of Business Administration, 1969), 12.

8. Cooper, *Alaska*, 114. For background, see Robert W. King, "Without Hope of Immediate Profit: Oil Exploration in Alaska, 1898 to 1953," *Alaska History* 9 (September 1994), 19–36; and Roderick, *Crude Dreams*.

9. Robert Weeden, "Kenai National Moose Range," *Alaska Conservation Review* 10 (Spring 1969), 8–9; Richard G. Smith, "The Kenai Moose Range," *The Living Wilderness* 95 (Winter 1966–67), 28–30.

10. George Laycock, *Alaska, the Embattled Frontier* (Boston: Houghton Mifflin, 1971), 69.

11. This common distinction was not literally true. Indeed, the Native death rate fell by 50 percent between 1950 and 1960, largely because of a decline in deaths due to tuberculosis. Federal Field Committee for Development Planning in Alaska, *Alaska Natives & the Land* (Anchorage, 1968), 19–20.

12. Cooper, *Alaska*, 190. Also see Joe McGinnis, *Going to Extremes* (New York: Knopf, 1980).

13. Federal Field Committee, *Alaska Natives*, 73.

14. Wendell H. Oswalt, *Bashful No Longer: An Alaskan Eskimo Ethnohistory, 1778–1988* (Norman: University of Oklahoma Press, 1990), 180.

15. Federal Field Committee, *Alaska Natives*, figure 15.

16. Norman A. Chance, *The Inupiat and Arctic Alaska: An Ethnography of Development* (Fort Worth: Holt, Rinehart and Winston, 1990), 107.

17. Margaret Lantis, "The Current Nativistic Movement in Alaska," in Gosta Berg, editor, *Circumpolar Problems: Habitat, Economic and Social Relations in the Arctic* (Oxford: Pergamon Press, 1973), 100–114; Gerald A. McBeath and Thomas A. Morehouse, *The Dynamics of Alaska Native Self-Government* (Washington: University Press of America, 1980).

18. "State Wide Native Conference, Tuesday Morning, October 18, 1966," 26, William Paul Papers (University of Washington Archives, Seattle), 1:2. For background, see Mitchell, *Take My Land*, 65–81.

19. Craig W. Allin, *The Politics of Wilderness Preservation* (Westport: Greenwood Press, 1982), 213.

20. Mitchell, *Take My Land*, 441.

21. John M. Kauffman, *Alaska's Brooks Range: The Ultimate Mountains* (Seattle: Mountaineers, 1992), 105; G. Frank Williss, "'Do Things Right the First Time': The National Park Service and the Alaska National Interest Lands Conservation Act of 1980" (Washington: National Park Service, 1985), 72–73.

22. Quoted in Mitchell, *Take My Land*, 443.

23. Art Davidson to George Alderson, n.d., FEC Papers, Box 76. Also Berry, *Alaska Pipeline*, 117–121.

24. See George Marshall to Stewart M. Brandborg, March 25, 1970, TWS Papers 12:200; David Hickok to Denny Rapp, March 17, 1970, TWS Papers 12:200.

25. Edgar Wayburn, Stewart M. Brandborg, and Charles H. Callison to Walter J. Hickel, February 24, 1970, SC Papers 129:30.

26. Davidson to Alderson, n.d.

27. Stewart Brandborg interview, March 25, 2003.

28. Berry, *Alaska Pipeline*, 132.

29. Robert Weeden to George Marshall, July 25, 1969, SC Papers 224:5.

30. Weeden to Walter Hickel, December 9, 1968, SC Papers 224:5.

31. Michael McCloskey interview, November 2, 1998.

32. See M. Rupert Cutler to Celia M. Hunter, March 7, 1967, TWS Papers 12:300.

33. Thomas L. Johnson to S. M. Brandborg, January 27, 1968, TWS Papers 12:300.

34. "Wilderness Workshop, Juneau, Alaska, Feb. 15–16, 1969," TWS Papers 12:201B.

35. Celia Hunter to Mrs. Joseph W. Greenough, January 11, 1967, TWS Papers 12:200.

36. Rich Gordon, "Early Alaskan Conservation Efforts," Richard Gordon Papers (privately held).

37. See Michael P. Cohen, *The History of the Sierra Club, 1892–1970* (San Francisco: Sierra Club Books, 1988), chapter 8, Afterword; Tom Turner, *Sierra Club: 100 Years of Protecting the Environment* (New York: Harry Abrams, 1991), 179–91.

38. Edgar Wayburn interview, August 27, 1998; Wayburn interview with Frank Norris, July 29, 2003 (National Park Service, Anchorage). Wayburn's autobiography, *Your Land and Mine: Evolution of A Conservationist* (San Francisco: Sierra Club Books, 2004) appeared just as this manuscript was going to press.

39. McCloskey interview.

40. Mark Hickok interview, May 12, 1999; Alaska Chapter *Newsletter*, n.d.

41. Wayburn interview, 1998; Rich Gordon interview, November 4, 1999; Gordon, "Early Alaskan...."

42. Gordon Wright to Edgar Wayburn, May 28, 1970, FEC Papers, Box 70.

43. Edgar Wayburn to Scott D. Hamilton, January 17, 1968, SC Papers 224:1.

44. See Kathie Durbin, *Tongass: Pulp Politics and the Fight for the Alaska Rain Forest* (Corvallis: Oregon State University Press, 1999), 26–28; Julie Cannon, "Heritage in Probate: Our Tongass Forest," *Sierra Club Bulletin* 59 (April 1974), 5–8, 24.

45. Thomas L. Johnson to S. M. Brandborg, January 27, 1968, TWS Papers 12:300.

46. Durbin, *Tongass*, 30–31.

47. Peggy Wayburn Diary, August 12, 1969, SC Papers 224:1; Rakestraw, *Forest Service in Alaska*, 153.

48. Cannon, "Heritage in Probate," 6.

49. Wayburn to Howard Johnson, August 16, 1968, SC Papers 228:33.

50. Johnson to Wayburn, August 22, 1968, SC Papers 239:20.

51. Johnson to Celia M. Hunter, September 10, 1968, TWS Papers 12:200; Johnson to Roger DuBrock, September 19, 1968, TWS Papers 12:300.

52. Hunter to Mardie Murie, October 9, 1968, TWS Papers 12:200.

53. Roger DuBrock, "Re Proposed Wilderness Area," TWS Papers 12:300.

54. Allin, *Wilderness Preservation*, 148.

55. Gordon to Invitees, January 4, 1969, Gordon Papers.

56. *ACR* 9 (December 1968), 12; *Alaska Newsletter*, February 11, 1969.

NOTES (pages 76–95)   279

57. *Southeast Alaska Empire*, February 1969; John M. Hall, "Wilderness Conference Wrap-Up," *Sierra Club Bulletin* 54 (April 1969), 6–7; Gordon, "Early Alaskan…"

58. *Alaska Newsletter*, April 15, 1969, n.p.; *ACR* 10 (Spring 1969), 12.

59. Dixie Baade to Rich Gordon, April 22, 1970, Gordon Papers.

60. Gordon, "Early Alaskan…."

61. Gordon to McCloskey, July 31, 1969, SC Papers 235:22.

62. *New York Times*, September 21, 1969.

63. Margaret H. Piggott to John L. Hall, August 5, 1969, TWS Papers 12:300.

64. *Anchorage Daily Times*, December 15, 1969; *Sitka Sentinel*, December 15, 1969.

65. McCloskey interview.

66. Gordon to McCloskey, July 31, 1969, SC Papers 235:22.

67. Jack Calvin to Wayburn, December 30, 1969, SC Papers 129:26.

68. Richard Myren interview, October 26, 1999.

69. *Southeast Alaska Empire*, February 14, 16, 26, March 6, 20, 1970.

70. Brock Evans to Bob Weeden, March 19, 1970, SC Papers 129:27.

71. *Southeast Alaska Empire*, February 26, 1970.

72. Gordon to Gordon Robinson, April 29, 1970, SC Papers 145:12.

73. Warren Matthews to Don Harris, November 23, 1970, SC Papers 238; Tom Turner, *Wild By Law: The Sierra Club Legal Defense Fund and the Places It Has Saved* (San Francisco: Sierra Club Legal Defense Fund, 1990), 37.

74. *Southeast Alaska Empire*, July 21, 1971.

75. George Marshall to Robert B. Weeden, April 27, 1969, SC Papers 224:5.

76. E. H. Hilliard to Weeden, July 18, 1969, SC Papers 235:22.

77. Gordon to Clifton R. Merritt, April 26, 1970, TWS Papers 12:200.

78. Celia Hunter to Wayburn, May 12, 1969, SC Papers 224:5.

79. "Weeden's New Job," *ACR* 10 (Fall 1969), 5.

80. Weeden interview.

81. "Weeden's New Job," 5.

82. Quoted in *ACR* 11 (November 1970), 6; "Conservation and Development in the Possible Alaska," March 5, 1970, Alaska Center for the Environment Papers (University of Alaska Anchorage Archives), Series 2, Box 1 [hereafter ACE Papers].

83. McCloskey interview.

84. *Alaska Newsletter* 2 (October 19, 1970), 9.

85. Weeden interview.

86. George Marshall to Sigrid Olson, August 13, 1970, TWS Papers 12:300.

87. *Alaska Newsletter* 2 (July–August, 1970), 2.

88. Wayburn interview.

89. John McPhee, *Coming into the Country* (New York: Farrar, Straus, and Giroux, 1977), 80.

90. Arthur Marwick, *The Sixties: Cultural Revolution in Britain, France, Italy and the United States, c. 1958–c. 1974* (New York: Oxford, 1998), 16–20.

91. *Alaska Newsletter* 1 (November 1969), 6.

92. *Alaska Newsletter* 2 (October 1970), 4.

93. Minutes, Alaska Wilderness Council, March 10, 1969, Gordon Papers. The reports are in the Brock Evans Papers (University of Washington Archives, Seattle), Box 3.

94. "Alaska Priority Areas," June 12, 1969, TWS Papers 12:300; *Alaska Newsletter* 1 (September 1969), 4.

95. Gordon to Wayburn, April 1, 1970, Evans Papers, Box 3.

96. News Release, March 25, 1970, Evans Papers, Box 3.

97. Baade to Alaska Wilderness Council, April 22, 1970, Gordon Papers.

98. *Alaska Newsletter* 3 (January 1971), 3.

99. Celia Hunter to Mark Ganapole, March 3, 1971, Evans Papers, Box 3.

100. Baade to Alaska Wilderness Council, April 22, 1970, Evans Papers, Box 3.

101. Gordon to Cooperators, c. June 1970, Gordon Papers.

102. *Alaska Newsletter* 3 (April 1971), 2.

103. *Alaska Newsletter* 2 (December 1970), 2, 6.

104. *Alaska Newsletter* 2 (December 1970), 3.

105. Gordon Wright to Executive Committee, Friends of the Earth, June 14, 1971, FEC Papers, Box 72; Celia Hunter interview, October 28, 1998.

106. Ibid., James Kowalsky to Gary Soucie, June 10, 1971; David Brower to Friends of the Earth Executive Committee, June 10, 1971, FEC Papers, Box 72.

107. Gordon Wright interview, February 4, 2000.

108. James Kowalsky interview, January 26, 2000; Wright interview.

109. Wright interview.

110. Charles Konigsberg interview, July 22, 1999.

111. *Alaska Newsletter* 2 (June 1970), 6–7.

112. David Brower to Friends of the Earth Executive Committee, July 10, 1972, FEC Papers, Box 73.

113. Charles Konigsberg, "Proposal," August 2, 1971, ACE Papers, Series 2, Box 1.

114. *Alaska Newsletter* 4 (October 1971), 4–5.

115. "ACE early history...," 1986, Helen Nienhauser Papers (privately held).

116. Charles Konigsberg, "Progress Report," December 21, 1971, ACE Papers, Series 2, Box 1.

Chapter 4. Congressional Responses

1. W. J. Hickel, "A Special Report to the People; the Potential and Promise of the Arctic" (Washington, 1970) in NPS Papers, RG 36.

2. See J. Brooks Flippen, *Nixon and the Environment* (Albuquerque: University of New Mexico Press, 2000).

3. Robert Weeden to Mike Gravel, October 29, 1970, TWS Papers 12:200

4. *Washington Post*, August 9, 1970.

5. Richard Corrigan, *CPR National Journal*, April 17, 1971, Lloyd Meeds Papers (University of Washington Archives, Seattle), 219; statement of Donald R. Wright, April 6, 1971, Meeds Papers, 219.

6. Donald R. Wright to Lloyd Meeds, November 16, 1971, Meeds Papers, 218.

7. See Gerald A. McBeath and Thomas A. Morehouse, *The Dynamics of Alaska Native Self-Government* (Washington: University Press of America, 1980), 60–64. The Federal Field Committee had reported 178 villages with 25 or more inhabitants in 1967. See Federal Field Committee for Development Planning in Alaska, *Alaska Natives and the Land* (Anchorage: Government Printing Office, 1968), 6. Ultimately, a total of 45.5 million acres was awarded to Native communities.

8. *Sierra Club Bulletin* 58 (June 1973), 16.

9. Donald Craig Mitchell, *Take My Land, Take My Life: The Story of Congress's Historic Settlement of Alaska Native Land Claims, 1960–1971* (Fairbanks: University of Alaska Press, 2001), 441.

10. David Hickok to Robert Weeden, August 4, 1971, Harry Crandell Papers (Denver Public Library), 3:2.

11. Alaska Coalition to Morris Udall and John Saylor, October 14, 1971, Crandell Papers 3:2.

12. Douglas Scott interview, August 26, 1999; Alaska Coalition to President, September 30, 1971, FEC Papers, Box 76.

13. George Hartzog, *Battling for the National Parks* (Mount Kisco: Moyer Bell, 1988), 213.

14. G. Frank Williss, "'Do Things Right the First Time': The National Park Service and the Alaska National Interest Lands Conservation Act of 1980" (Washington: National Park Service, 1985), 75–77.

15. Mary Clay Berry, *The Alaska Pipeline: The Politics of Oil and Native Land Claims* (Bloomington. Indiana University Press, 1975), 195.

16. Morris Udall to Colleague, October 15, 1971, Meeds Papers, 215.

17. Berry, *Alaska Pipeline*, 187. Mitchell's account has some variations. *Take My Land*, 448.

18. Mitchell, *Take My Land*, 448.

19. James Kowalsky to George Alderson, October 26, 1971, FEC Papers, Box 76.

20. Scott interview.

21. *New York Times*, October 25, 1971.

22. Mitchell, *Take My Land*, 470; Berry, *Alaska Pipeline*, 198–200.

23. *Anchorage Daily News*, November 12, 1971.

24. Berry, *Alaska Pipeline*, 210.

25. Memo, December 12, 1971, Crandell Papers 3:2; *Anchorage Daily Times*, December 9, 10, 1971.

26. See Mitchell, *Take My Land*, 477–79.

27. *U.S. Code*, 92nd Congress, 1st Session, 1971, Volume 1, 786, 801–802.

28. Berry, *Alaska Pipeline*, 211–12.

29. Robert Weeden to Edgar Wayburn, Stewart Brandborg, February 20, 1970, SC Papers 129:30, emphasis in the original.

30. *Fairbanks News-Miner*, April 7, 1970; Celia Hunter to James Dean, April 6, 1970, TWS Papers 12:200.

31. "Statement of Celia M. Hunter," April 28, 1970, TWS Papers 12:203.

32. Wayburn to Walter Hickel, April 21, 1970, SC Papers 129:30.

33. Mike McCloskey to file, July 12, 1970, SC Papers 129:31.

34. Celia Hunter to James Dean, April 8, 1970, TWS Papers 12:200.

35. "Lawyers Seek Pipeline Pacts," *The Living Wilderness* 34–112 (Winter 1970–71), 64.

36. Berry, *Alaska Pipeline*, 141.

37. Celia Hunter to Brandborg, January 27, 1972, TWS Papers 12:200; Wilbur Mills to Brandborg, February 21, 1972, TWS Papers 12:203.

38. Tony Smith to Brandborg, February 9, 1972, TWS Papers 12:200; "The Pipeline Story: Another Chapter," *ACR* 12 (Spring 1971), 80; "News Items of Interest," *TLW* 35–113 (Spring 1971), 45.

39. "News Item of Interest," *TLW* 35–113 (Spring 1971), 45; Peter A. Coates, *The Trans-Alaska Pipeline Controversy: Technology, Conservation, and the Frontier* (Fairbanks: University of Alaska Press, 1993), 199.

40. Berry, *Alaska Pipeline*, 218–20.

41. *Homer News*, February 12, 25, March 4, 1971.

42. Berry, *Alaska Pipeline*, 220–21.

43. James Marshall, "Memorandum," March 23, 1972, TWS Papers 12:200.

44. H. Lee Watson to File, August 3, 1971, TWS Papers 16:201A.

45. Charles J. Cicchetti, *Alaskan Oil: Alternative Routes and Markets* (Baltimore: Johns Hopkins University Press, 1972), 117–19.

46. Quoted in Berry, *Alaska Pipeline*, 221.

47. *The Thunder Mug*, July 15, 1971.

48. Les Aspin, "Why the Trans-Alaskan Pipeline Should Be Stopped," *Sierra Club Bulletin* 56 (June 1971), 16–17.

49. Allen J. Matusow, *Nixon's Economy: Booms, Busts, Dollars, Votes* (Lawrence: University Press of Kansas, 1998), 242–46.

50. Berry, *Alaska Pipeline*, 228–29; Coates, *Trans-Alaska Pipeline*, 227; Robert Douglas Mead, *Journeys Down the Line; Building the Trans-Alaska Pipeline* (Garden City: Doubleday, 1978), 159.

51. Berry, *Alaska Pipeline*, 234–35; Senators to Rogers Morton, May 5, 1972, TWS Papers 12:200; House of Representatives to Morton, March 14, 1972, TWS Papers 12:200. Also see Donald Worster, *Under Western Skies: Nature and History in the American West* (New York: Oxford University Press, 1992), 202–203.

52. Quoted in Stewart Brandborg to John Melcher, June 14, 1973, TWS Papers 12:200.

53. "Confidential Memo for the Clients," February 21, 1973, Crandell Papers 3:3.

54. "Letter from Washington," *TLW* 36–118 (Summer 1972), 3; C. Robert Zelnick, "The Darkness at the End of the Pipeline," *TLW* 36–118 (Summer 1972), 7.

55. *Wall Street Journal*, February 12, 1973; *Alaska Newsletter* 7 (April 1973), 5.

56. Brock Evans, "Excerpts of Observations," SC Papers 210:35.

57. Len Arrow, "The Pipeline: How Not to Make a Decision," *Environmental Action* (August 14, 1973), 16.

58. "Opening Statement by Chairman John Melcher...at the July 17 Public Lands Subcommittee Markup Session," John Melcher Papers (Denver Public Library), Box 1.

59. Rogers Morton to Senators, April 14, 1973, TWS Papers 12:200.

60. Dennis Flannery to Environmental Defense Fund, Friends of the Earth, Wilderness Society, August 13, 1971, TWS Papers 12:201B.

61. Quoted in Jack Roderick, *Crude Dreams: A Personal History of Oil and Politics in Alaska* (Fairbanks: Epicenter Press, 1997), 380.

62. Mitchell, *Take My Land*, 274.

63. Roderick, *Crude Dreams*, 380.

64. Roderick A. Cameron, Stewart M. Brandborg, George Alderson to John Melcher, July 17, 1973; Melcher Statement, July 19, 1973, Melcher Papers, Box 1; Brock Evans, "Oily Politics: The Canadian Caper," *Sierra Club Bulletin* 58 (September 1973), 17.

65. Roderick, *Crude Dreams*, 382.

66. Ibid.

67. Berry, *Alaska Pipeline*, 274.

68. Coates, *Trans-Alaska Pipeline*, 249.

69. Brandborg to Governing Council, February 1, 1974, TWS Papers 12:201A.

70. Evans, "Oil, Gas, and Alaska," *Sierra Club Bulletin* 58 (July–August, 1973), 19.

71. Wayburn to Raymond Sherwin, September 17, 1973, SC Papers 210:35.

72. Evans, "Excerpts of Observations," SC Papers 210:35.

73. Mead, *Journeys Down the Line*, 169.

74. Wayburn to Sherwin, September 17, 1973, SC Papers 210:35.

75. Evans, "Excerpts of Observations," SC Papers 210:35.

76. Evans, "Excerpts of Observations," SC Papers 210:35.

77. Jack Hession to Mike McCloskey, December 23, 1971, SC Papers 227.

78. "ANCSA," February 3, 1972, Crandell Papers 3:3.

79. Hartzog, *Battling*, 214–15.

80. See Robert Weeden, "Letter from Alaska," *TLW* 35–114 (Summer 1971), 35–40.

81. Nathaniel Reed to George Hartzog and Spencer Smith, December 21, 1971, Crandell Papers 3:2.

82. Ernest J. Borgman to Director, Pacific Northwest Region, September 27, 1971, NPS Papers, RG 36.

83. Richard Stenmark to Fred Dean, April 8, 1971, NPS Papers, RG 36.

84. Borgman to Director, Pacific Northwest Region, May 12, 1971, NPS Papers, RG 36.

85. Hession to McCloskey, December 23, 1971, SC Papers 227.

86. Hession to McCloskey, December 23, 1971, SC Papers 277.

87. McCloskey, "Outline of Possible Strategy   ," December 29, 1971; McCloskey and Denny Wilcher, "Proposed Advertising Campaign," December 20, 1971, SC Papers 227.

88. Harry Crandell to John Saylor, January 10, 1972, Crandell Papers 3:3; Morris Udall and John Saylor to Rogers Morton, January 11, 1972, SC 225:7; Berry, *Alaska Pipeline*, 224–25.

89. William Egan to Wayne Aspinall, January 28, 1972, TWS Papers 12:300.

90. Richard C. Olson to McCloskey, January 29, 1972, Crandell Papers 3:3.

91. Berry, *Alaska Pipeline*, 226.

92. Olson to McCloskey, January 29, 1972; "Alaska's Wildlands: Secretary Morton's Biggest Test," Crandell Papers 3:3.

93. Berry, *Alaska Pipeline*, 226.

94. Williss, "Do Things Right," 98–99.

95. *Alaska Newsletter* 6 (January 1972), 2.

96. Mark Hickok interview, May 12, 1999.

97. Hickok interview.

98. Nathaniel Reed to Morton, March 2, 1972, Crandell Papers 3:3

99. *Anchorage Daily Times*, March 16, 1972.

100. *Alaska Newsletter* 6 (April 1972), 12.

101. McCloskey, "Conversation with Nat. Reed," April 19, 1972, SC Papers 227.

102. *Anchorage Daily News*, March 16, 1972.

103. McCloskey, "Conversation," April 14, 1972, SC Papers 227.

104. Hession to San Francisco, August 8, 1972, SC Papers 227.

105. "Secretarial Meeting on Alaska Land Withdrawals," August 11, 1972, NPS Papers, RG 36.

106. Crandell to George Marshall, August 29, 1972, Crandell Papers 3:3. An obscure provision of the agreement opened part of the proposed Aniakchak Crater National Monument to sport hunting. This was a significant step toward the creation of national preserves, which Congress embraced in 1974. Frank Norris, *Alaska Subsistence: A National Park Service Management History* (Anchorage: U.S. Department of the Interior, 2002), 54.

107. James W. Moorman to Wayburn, McCloskey, August 29, 1972, SC Papers 227.

108. *Alaska Newsletter* 6 (September 1972), 4–5; Press Release, September 7, 1972, SC Papers 226:10; Groups to Morton, September 8, 1972, Crandell Papers 3:3.

109. *Fairbanks News-Miner*, September 5, 1972.

110. Williss, "Do Things Right," 123.

111. *The Northern Light* 2 (September 18, 1973), 2.

112. *Alaska Newsletter* 7 (May 1973), 1–2.

113. George Marshall to Brandborg, May 23, 1973, Crandall Papers 3:3; also Clifton R. Merritt to Celia M. Hunter, March 29, 1973, Crandell Papers 3:3.

114. Hession to San Francisco, January 10, 1973, Brock Evans Papers, Box 3.

115. Rich Gordon to Wayburn, March 2, 1973, Gordon Papers.

116. Rich Gordon to Wayburn, March 2, 1973, Gordon Papers.

117. Edgar and Peggy Wayburn, "Alaska—the Great Land—America's Last Legacy," *Sierra Club Bulletin* 58 (June 1973), 16–25.

118. Williss, "Do Things Right," 131–37.

119. Williss, "Do Things Right," 129, 139.

120. Jack Shepherd, *The Forest Killers: The Destruction of American Wilderness* (New York: Weybright & Talley, 1975), 327; Williss, "Do Things Right," 140.

121. "Notes on Meeting at USDI," November 16, 1973, Gordon Papers; Williss, "Do Things Right," 141–42.

122. Ted Swem to Ron Walker, November 9, 1973, NPS Papers, RG 36.

123. "Senator Stevens' Comments," June 1, 1974, NPS Papers, RG 36.

124. Swem to Ron Walker, December 6, 1973, NPS Papers, RG 36; also Hession to Mike, Ed, Brock, December 7, 1973, SC Papers 225:27.

125. *Anchorage Daily News*, January 27, 1974.

126. *New York Times*, January 13, 1974.

127. *Christian Science Monitor*, December 19, 1973.

128. *Christian Science Monitor*, December 19, 1973.

Chapter 5. Southeast Alaska and the Wilderness Movement

1.   Dixie Baade, "Opinion: 'Progress' in Ketchikan," *Alaska Newsletter* 7 (February 1973), 3.

2.   Baade to Darlene Larson, November 27, 1972, Alan Stein Papers (Alaska State Library, Juneau), Box 1; Kathie Durbin, *Tongass: Pulp Politics and the Fight for the Alaska Rain Forest* (Corvallis: Oregon State University Press, 1999), 26–27, 37.

3.   "The DeFacto Wilderness Case," January 27, 1973, FEC Papers, Box 14.

4.   John J. Schnabel to Jack Hession, November 18, 1972, SC Papers 238:6

5.   *Ketchikan Daily News*, November 10, 1972.

6.   *Anchorage Daily News*, November 16, 1972; Baade to Brock Evans, December 8, 1972, SC Papers 238:29.

7.   Evans to Mike McCloskey, Edgar Wayburn, December 19, 1972, SC Papers 238:29.

8.   Gordon Robinson to Ray Sherwin et al., November 1, 1971, SC Papers 238:29; *The Northern Light*, April 10, 1973, 3.

9.   *Anchorage Daily News*, September 24, October 2, 1974.

10. James Moorman to Clients, November 21, 1974, SC Papers 223:24.

11. Moorman to George W. Rogers, January 7, 1975, SC Papers 238:29.

12. Jack Hession, "Memorandum," February 28, 1975, SC Papers 234:26.

13. Hession to Mike, July 5, 1975, SC Papers 234:26.

14. Durbin, *Tongass*, 54.

15. Durbin, *Tongass*, 53.

16. Hession to Daniel Johnson, July 6, 1975, SC 223:24.

17. Ernst W. Mueller to Guy R. Martin, April 8, 1975, Stein Papers, Box 3.

18. *Anchorage Daily News*, March 13, 1976; Anchorage Daily Times, March 14, 1976.

19. Durbin, *Tongass*, 55.

20. Hession to Mike, May 17, 1974, SC Papers 238:29; *The Northern Light*, January 1973, 1–3; *Anchorage Daily Times*, May 2, 1975; *Anchorage Daily News*, May 13, 1975.

21. David McCargo to Clifton R. Merritt, October 28, 1975, TWS Papers 12:300.

22. *Ketchikan Daily News*, November 25, 1972.

23. Baade to Darlene Larson, Alan and Sandra Stein, November 27, 1972, Stein Papers, Box 1.

24. *Southeastern Log*, February 1973; Alan Stein interview, September 30, 1998.

25. Hession to Baade, December 10, 1972, Stein Papers, Box 1.

26. Richard M. Wilson to Don Finney, June 10, 1974, Stein Papers, Box 1.

27. *Ketchikan Daily News,* November 9, 1973, December 12, 1973.

28. Hession to Baade, June 17, 1973, Stein Papers, Box 1.

29. Baade to Hession, July 18, 1973, Stein Papers, Box 1.

30. Hession to Brock, Mike, Doug, February 13, 1974, SC Papers 99:14.

31. Hession to Joe Upton, April 9, 1974, Stein Papers, Box 1.

32. Baade to Barry Fisher, July 19, 1973, Stein Papers, Box 1.

33. Richard Myren Interview, October 26, 1999.

34. Alan Stein, "Point Baker Law Suit," *ACR* 16 (Winter 1975), 9.

35. See Alan Stein, "Point Baker Law Suit," 9; Brock Evans and Gordon Robinson, "The Beautiful, Incredible Monongahela Decision," *Sierra Club Bulletin* 60 (October 1975), 22.

36. Richard Folta to Marvin Dunning, April 14, 1975, Stein Papers, Box 1.

37. *Southeast Alaska Empire,* January 1, 1976; Ketchikan Daily News, December 31, 1975, January 1, 1976.

38. R. C. Folta to Herbert Zieske, Alan Stein, October 18, 1976, Stein Papers, Box 1.

39. Durbin, *Tongass,* chapters 5–6.

40. Craig W. Allin, *The Politics of Wilderness Preservation* (Westport: Greenwood Press, 1982), chapters 5–6.

41. Hession, "Alaska," *Sierra Club Bulletin* 57 (January 1972), 21.

42. Robert B. Weeden, *Alaska: Promises to Keep* (Boston: Houghton Mifflin, 1978), 113.

43. Jack Calvin, "Moratorium on Logging," *ACR* 12 (Summer 1971), 7.

44. Ernst W. Mueller to McCloskey, April 19, 1973, SC Papers 239:40.

45. Rich Gordon to Wayburn, March 2, 1973, Gordon Papers.

46. Gordon Robinson to Brock Evans, March 4, 1974, SC Papers 240:1.

47. See Allin, *Politics of Wilderness Preservation,* 158–62; Richard N. L. Andrews, *Managing the Environment, Managing Ourselves: A History of American Environmental Protection* (New Haven: Yale University Press, 1999), 309.

48. "Forest Service Wilderness Areas," *Alaska Newsletter* 7 (February 1975), 5.

49. Hession to Barry Fisher et al., November 20, 1972. SC Papers 234:26.

50. William R. Overdorff, "Tongass National Forest Land Use Plan," *ACR* 16 (Winter 1975), 21; Michael Frome, *The Forest Service* (Boulder: Westview Press, 1984), 88.

51. Moorman to Hession et al., March 20, 1975, SC Papers 238.

52. *The Northern Light,* August 24, 1975.

53. Edward A. Whitesell, "Southeast Wildlands Study," *ACR* 16 (Winter 1975), 7.

54. Rich Gordon to Yates, April 25, 1975, Stein Papers, Box 1; Gordon interview, November 4, 1999.

55. Gordon to SEACC leaders, July 14, 1975; Edward Whitesell to Conservation Leaders, August 28, 1975; Whitesell to various, December 17, 1975, SC Papers 238; Whitesell, "Southeast Wildlands Study," 8.

56. Whitesell to Stein, December 9, 1983, Stein Papers, Box 1.

57. Kay Greenough interview, November 18, 1999.

58. Ron Hawk interview, November 22, 1999.

59. Whitesell and Greenough, "Progress Report," March 29, 1976, FEC Papers, Box 74.

60. Whitesell to Wayburn, Moorman, June 2, 1976, SC Papers 238:16.

61. *Southeast Alaska Empire,* July 20, 1976.

62. *Raven Call* 1 (September 17, 1976), 2.

63. *Raven Call* 1 (September 17, 1976), 9–10; Paul W. Hirt, *A Conspiracy of Optimism: Management of the National Forests Since World War II* (Lincoln: University of Nebraska Press, 1994), 262–63.

64. Hawk to John Sandor, April 4, 1976, SC Papers 238.

65. Lee Schmidt to R. L. Engelbach, April 17, 1976, SC Papers 238:14.

66. Wayburn to Hawk, April 27, 1976, SC Papers 238.

67. Moorman to File, August 3, 1976, SC Papers 240:2.

68. Jack Calvin to Sandor, September 9, 1976, SC Papers 238:30.

Chapter 6. Oil Age Discontents

1. Quoted in Robert Douglas Mead, *Journeys Down the Line; Building the Trans-Alaska Pipeline* (Garden City: Doubleday, 1978), 240.

2. John Hanrahan and Peter Gruenstein, *Lost Frontier: The Marketing of Alaska* (New York: W. W. Norton, 1977), 212–13.

3. Mim Dixon, *What Happened in Fairbanks? The Effects of the Trans-Alaska Oil Pipeline on the Community of Fairbanks, Alaska* (Boulder: Westview Press, 1978), 29.

4. Dermot Cole, *Amazing Pipeline Stories* (Fairbanks: Epicenter Press, 1997), 158.

5. Matthew D. Berman, "Interstate Migration in Alaska" (Fairbanks: Institute of Social and Economic Research, 1982), 4.

6. Dixon, *What Happened in Fairbanks*, 118.

7. Dixon, *What Happened in Fairbanks*, 174; Cole, *Amazing*, 176–81; Hanrahan and Gruenstein, *Lost Frontier*, 169–71.

8. Dixon, *What Happened in Fairbanks*, 135.

9. Dixon, *What Happened in Fairbanks*, 41.

10. *Center News* 3 (July 15, 1975), 5.

11. See Gordon Scott Harrison, editor, *Alaska Public Policy: Current Problems and Issues* (Fairbanks: University of Alaska, 1971).

12. Robert B. Weeden, *Alaska: Promises to Keep* (Boston: Houghton Mifflin, 1978), 147.

13. Weeden, *Alaska*, 146–47.

14. Weeden, *Alaska*, 146–47; Mead, *Journeys Down the Line*, 350–51.

15. Quoted in Dixon, *What Happened in Fairbanks*, 141.

16. Jack Hession, "Pipeline and Politics in America's Last Frontier," *Sierra Club Bulletin* 58 (April 1973), 16; Ernst W. Mueller, "On Environmental Backlash," *ACR* 14 (September 1973), 6; "Editorial Comments," *ACR* 14 (Spring 1973), 3.

17. Dixon, *What Happened in Fairbanks*, 8.

18. Gordon Wright interview, February 4, 2000.

19. James Kowalsky interview, January 26, 2000.

20. Fairbanks Environmental Center, "Administration and Finances," n.d., TWS Papers 12:201B.

21. Kowalsky to Cornelia, November 20, 1973, TWS Papers 12:201B.

22. *The Northern Light*, March 12, 1973.

23. Kowalsky Memo, October 17, 1974, TWS Papers 12:201B; Stan Stenner to Cooperator, June 1976, FEC Papers, Box 72..

24. Kowalsky, "Alaska Status," July 9, 1975, FEC Papers, Box 72.

25. Alaska Center for the Environment, "Progress Report," December 21, 1971, ACE Papers.

26. Minutes, ACE Board, February 25, 1972.

27. Minutes, ACE Board, February 25, 1972.

28. *Alaska Newsletter* 6 (May 1972), 9.

29. Charles Konigsberg to Board, August 30, 1972, ACE Papers.

30. Helen Nienhauser, December 1986 speech, Helen Nienhauser Papers (privately held).

31. Minutes, ACE Board, May 2, 1973.
32. Nienhauser, December 1986 speech.
33. Minutes, ACE Board, February 2, 1975, ACE Papers.
34. Helen Nienhauser interview, July 22, 1999; Sharon Cissna interview, July 19, 1999; Peg Tileston interview, July 22, 1999; *The Northern Light*, October 9, 1973.
35. *The Northern Light*, October 9, 1973.
36. Minutes, ACE Board, February 2, 1975, ACE Papers.
37. *The Northern Light*, May 21, 1974.
38. "Past and Present Involvement of SCLDF, TFA, NRDC in Alaska Legal Issues," Alaska Coalition Papers (Denver Public Library), Box 2 [hereafter AC Papers].
39. Kowalsky to Recipients, April 3, 1974, SC Papers 99:19; *The Northern Light*, July 17, 1973, 1.
40. Mike McCloskey to Charles Naughton, March 27, 1975, SC Papers 227.
41. Hanrahan and Gruenstein, *Lost Frontier*, 5.
42. Hession to Roger Olmstead, April 8, 1974, SC Papers 227.
43. Theodore Catton, *Inhabited Wilderness: Indians, Eskimos, and National Parks in Alaska* (Albuquerque: University of New Mexico Press, 1997), 198–201; David Hickok to George Marshall, December 2, 1973, SC Papers 231:28.
44. Ginny Harris to ACS Committee Members, December 15, 1974, FEC Papers, Box 71.
45. Jack Roderick, *Crude Dreams; A Personal History of Oil & Politics in Alaska* (Fairbanks: Epicenter Press, 1997), 375.
46. Nancy Munro, "Oil in Kachemak Bay," *Seas and Coasts* 2 (February 15, 1974), 1, 6.
47. *Homer Weekly News*, December 20, 1973; January 24, 1974.
48. *Homer Weekly News*, February 21, 1974.
49. Clem Tillion interview, August 25, 2000.
50. Jay Hammond, *Tales of Alaska's Bush Rat Governor* (Fairbanks: Epicenter Press, 1994), chapters 15–21; Richard Saltonstall, "The New Man in Juneau," *The Living Wilderness* 38 (Winter 1974–75), 10–15.
51. *Homer Weekly News*, March 7, 1974.
52. *Homer Weekly News*, June 6, 1974.
53. *Homer Weekly News*, May 23, 1974.
54. *Homer Weekly News*, October 10, 1974.
55. *Homer Weekly News*, October 3, 1974.
56. "Report of the Directors' Meeting," *ACR* 16 (Spring 1975), 8.
57. James Kowalsky to David Brower, July 9, 1975, FEC Papers, Box 73.
58. *Homer Weekly News*, November 21, 1974.
59. *The Northern Light*, November 16, 1975; also see *Center News* 3(May 20, 1975), 4.
60. *Homer Weekly News*, February 19, 1976.
61. *Homer Weekly News*, March 14, 1976.
62. *Homer Weekly News*, May 20, 1976.
63. *Homer Weekly News*, May 20, 1976.
64. *Homer Weekly News*, May 13, 1976.
65. "Background of Southeast Alaska Forest Service Issues," October 10, 1975, Stein Papers, Box 3.
66. Raymond Estes to Charles Yates, April 25, 1975, SC Papers 238:7.
67. Charles Yates to James M. Brooks, April 25, 1975, Stein Papers, Box 1.
68. Hanrahan and Gruenstein, *Lost Frontier*, 165.
69. Mead, *Journeys Down the Line*, 419.

70. Robert B. Weeden to Ernst Mueller, August 22, 1973, TWS Papers 12:201B; "Pipeline Surveillance," *ACR* 14 (Summer–Fall 1973), 3.

71. George Alderson to National Cooperative Groups, January 4, 1974, TWS Papers 12:200.

72. Kowalsky, "Pipeline Surveillance Scored," *The Northern Light*, June 1975, 3.

73. Hanrahan and Gruenstein, *Lost Frontier*, 163–64.

74. Joe La Rocca, "Pipeline Coordinator's Annual Report—A Review," *ACR* 16 (September 1975), 16.

75. Mead, *Journeys Down the Line*, 316–17; Gil Zemansky, "Pipeline Monitoring," *The Northern Light*, June 1975, 1–3; Pat Senner and Gil Zemansky, "Line Surveillance Falls Short," *The Northern Light*, October 14, 1975, 2, 4.

76. Hanrahan and Gruenstein, *Lost Frontier*, 180–309; Ken Ross, *Environmental Conflict in Alaska* (Boulder: University Press of Alaska, 2000), 164–66.

77. *The Northern Light*, July 11, 1972.

78. *Alaska Newsletter* 7 (November 1973), 7.

79. Alaskan Arctic Gas Press Conference, March 21, 1974, TWS Papers 12:201A.

80. "Meeting with El Paso Gas Representatives," November 20, 1974, TWS Papers 12:201A.

81. See Walter J. Mead, *Transporting Natural Gas from the Arctic: The Alternative Systems* (Washington: American Enterprise Institute, 1977), especially the essay by George W. Rogers, 21–52.

82. See McCloskey to Stewart Brandborg, June 26, 1975; Tina Stonorov to McCloskey, June 4, 1975; Celia M. Hunter to Robert B. Weeden, December 17, 1977, TWS Papers 12:201A.

83. See Celia M. Hunter, "Slipshod Mining Sears McKinley Addition," *The Northern Light*, November 18, 1975, 1, 4.

84. See *Southeast Alaska Empire*, March 11, 1976; Hession to Sharon Lobaugh, Ron Hawk, Rich Gordon, March 17, 1976, SC Papers 229:29.

85. Hession interview, May 6, 1999; *Raven Call*, September 17, 1976, 11; Hession to Chuck Clusen, July 20, 1976, SC Papers 234:26. For a thorough account of the fight over Glacier Bay, see Theodore Catton, "Land Reborn: A History of Administration and Visitor Use in Glacier Bay National Park and Preserve" (Anchorage: National Park Service, 1995), 178–89.

86. Jan to Senator, February 18, 1974, Mike Gravel Papers, Box 573.

87. Edgar Wayburn to D-2 Cooperators, August 26, 1975, AC Papers, Box 6.

88. Hession to Mike, February 16, 1976, SC Papers 225:11; also George Alderson, "Capitol Watch," *The Living Wilderness* 38 (Autumn 1974–75), 60.

89. Hession to Mike, February 16, 1976, SC Papers 225:11. Also George Hartzog, *Battling for the National Parks* (Mount Kisco: Moyer Bell, 1988), 216–18.

90. G. Frank Williss, "'Do Things Right the First Time': The National Park Service and the Alaska National Interest Lands Conservation Act of 1980" (Washington: National Park Service, 1985), 171.

91. *Homer Weekly News*, October 10, 1974.

92. Wayburn to Brock Evans, January 15, 1975, SC Papers 225:9.

93. Weeden to Members of 17d(2) Task Force, April 2, 1975, Gordon Papers; McPhee, *Coming into the Country*, 185.

94. Weeden to James G. Dean, May 19, 1975, TWS Papers 12:200.

95. See Jack Hession to Stan Abbott, January 3, 1978, Morris Udall Papers (University of Arizona Archives), 327.

96. Sanford Sagalkin to Wayburn, November 14, 1975, SC Papers 210:32.

97. Press Release, October 25, 1975, SC Papers 210:32.

98. Various to Leader, ATFO, December 1975, NPS Papers, RG 36.

99. Handwritten notes on Harry B. Crandell to John F. Seiberling, n.d., Seiberling Papers (University of Akron Archives), Box 10.

100. *Center News* 3 (November 30, 1975), 1.

101. J. E. K. to Gordon, Pat and Stan, November 10, 1975, AC Papers, Box 6.

102. Kowalsky to Alaska Coalition, February 24, 1976, ACE Papers, Series 2, Box 1.

103. Tina Stonorov to ACS Board of Directors, December 16, 1974, SC Papers 25:8; Celia to Richard Leonard, January 8, 1975, SC Papers 25:9; Richard H. Bishop to McCloskey, January 17, 1975, SC Papers 25:9.

104. "Present at D-2 Summit Meeting," Crandell Papers 3:3.

105. "D-2 Summit Meeting Discussion Guidelines," Crandell Papers 3:3.

106. Brock Evans to Wayburn, February 27, 1975, SC Papers 225:9.

107. Hession to Mike, January 21, 1975. SC Papers 225:9.

108. Evans to Wayburn, February 27, 1975, SC Papers 225:9.

109. Gordon to Wayburn, March 21, 1975, Crandell Papers 3:3; Nienhauser interview.

110. Evans to Wayburn, February 27, 1975, SC Papers 225:9.

111. Minutes, Alaska Task Force, April 30, 1976, SC Papers 210:35.

112. Kowalsky to various, February 24, 1976, ACE Papers, Series 2, Box 1. Hession to Mike, February 16, 1976, SC Papers 225:11, differs slightly.

113. ACS Annual Board of Directors Meeting, Report, 1976, 2.

114. Kowalsky to Kay Greenough, March 15, 1976; Kowalsky and Tina Stonorov to Cooperators, April 22, 1976, AC Papers, Box 6.

115. Draft Agenda, D-2 Planning Meeting, April 22, 1976, AC Papers, Box 6.

116. Hession to McCloskey, May 24, 1976, SC Papers 225:11.

117. "A Report of the Second Alaska Coalition Meeting on the National Interest Lands," Murie Papers, Box 2.

118. Bob Roark to SEACC member groups, April 28, 1976, SC Papers 238:14.

119. Celia Hunter interview, August 10, 1985, University of Alaska Archives; Gordon to Kowalsky, April 30, 1976, Gordon Papers.

120. "A Report of the Second Alaska Coalition Meeting on the National Interest Lands," Murie Papers, Box 2; also SC Papers 225:11.

Part III: The ANILCA Campaign: Alaska and Washington, 1977–1980

The quotations on the introductory page to Part III are from the following sources: *Alaska Advocate*, August 25, 1977; Nathaniel P. Reed to Harry Crandell, August 3, 1979, Harry Crandell Papers 1:1.

Chapter 7. Congress Deliberates

1. John McPhee, *Coming into the Country* (New York: Farrar, Straus, Giroux, 1977), 21. After reviewing the situation with Interior Department lawyers, one of the president's assistants wrote that "more than one hundred public land orders and proclamations must be reviewed before we will actually know what would happen if Congress does not act this year." Bill Deller to Stu Eizenstat, June 28, 1978, Carter Papers, White House Central STR-3.

2. Craig W. Allin, *The Politics of Wilderness Preservation* (Westport: Greenwood Press, 1982), 224.

3. Jay Hammond to Dee Frankfourth, December 9, 1976, ACE Papers, Series 2, Box 1.

4. Alaska Chapter Special Executive Committee Meeting, February 3, 1977, SC Papers 235:22.

5. Pam Rich to Frankfourth, February 4, 1977, TWS Papers 12:301.

6. Frankfourth to Rich, November 7, 1977, TWS Papers 12:301.

7. Frankfourth to Rich, November 7, 1977, TWS Papers 12:301.

8. Sierra Club Executive Committee, February 9, 1977, SC Papers 235:22. Also Bob Weeden to Rich Gordon, January 28, 1977, Gordon Papers.

9. Sierra Club Executive Committee, March 2, 1977. SC Papers 235:22.

10. Stan Sloss, Memo to Mr. Seiberling, February 22, 1977, Seiberling Papers, Box 7. Also *Anchorage Daily News*, February 16, 1977; *Anchorage Daily Times*, February 6, 1977.

11. Sierra Club Executive Committee, March 2, 1977, SC Papers 235:22.

12. James Kowalsky, "My Impressions of the Meeting," February 21, 1977, SC Papers 225:13.

13. G. Frank Williss, "'Do Things Right the First Time': The National Parks and the Alaska National Interest Lands Conservation Act of 1980" (Washington: National Park Service, 1985), 174–80.

14. *Southeast Alaska Empire*, April 14, 1977.

15. Tony Motley to Gregg O'Clarey, April 24, 1977, FEC Papers, Box 72.

16. Michael McCloskey to Wayburn, Hession, and Clusen, July 16, 1976, AC Papers, Box 6.

17. Chuck Clusen to Files, August 10, 1976, SC Papers 210:31.

18. Pam Rich to Alaska Coalition, November 8, 1976, AC Papers, Box 6.

19. Jack Hession interview, May 6, 1999; Hession to Alaska Coalition, October 12, 1976, SC Papers 225:12; Ron Hawk to Mike McCloskey, November 18, 1976, SC Papers 238:15.

20. *Raven Call*, February 1977, 4, 6, 7.

21. Mary Ellen Cuthbertson to SEACC Board, March 5, 1977, SC Papers 238:15.

22. Jeffrey K. Stine, "Environmental Policy During the Carter Presidency," in Gary M. Fink and Hugh Davis Graham, *The Carter Presidency: Policy Choices in the Post–New Deal Era* (Lawrence: University Press of Kansas, 1998), 180–81.

23. Mary Ellen Cuthbertson to SEACC Board, March 5, 1977, SC Papers 238:15.

24. Cuthbertson to SEACC Board, March 5, 1977, SC Papers 238:15.

25. Jack Calvin to Sandy Sagalkin, April 2, 1977, SC Papers 240:3.

26. *Southeast Alaska Empire*, April 14, 1977. For Seiberling's background, see his introduction to Steve Love, *Stan Hywet Hall & Gardens* (Akron: University of Akron Press, 2000), xi–xx.

27. Edgar Wayburn to James Kowalsky, May 10, 1976, SC Papers 225:11; Alaska Task Force Steering Committee Meeting, April 30, 1976, SC Papers 210:35.

28. Mike McCloskey to Clusen, December 22, 1976; Nick Clinch to McCloskey, October 24, 1977, SC Papers 210.

29. Dee Frankfourth to Pam Rich, February 11, 1977, TWS Papers 12:301.

30. Celia Hunter to Frankfourth, May 13, 1977, TWS Papers 12:301.

31. See Kowalsky to Alaska Coalition, December 18, 1976, TWS Papers 12:301.

32. Peter Scholes and Pam Rich, "Alaska Coalition Meeting," April 23, 1977, TWS Papers 12:301.

33. Edward Ricinski, "A Report on the Alaska Coalition Lobbying for Protective Legislation," June 10, 1979, AC Papers, Box 4.

34. Michele Perrault to Wayburn, April 5, 1977, SC Papers 210:31.

35. Tony Motley to Gregg O'Clarey, April 24, 1977, FEC Papers, Box 72.

36. *Fairbanks News-Miner*, January 1986, special issue.

37. Cathy Smith to Alaska Coalition, May 10, 1977, TWS Papers 12:301.

38. Smith to Alaska Coalition, May 10, 1977, TWS Papers 12:301.

39. *University of Washington Daily*, June 23, 1977.

40. *Seattle Times*, June 19, 1977.

41. Cuthbertson to SEACC Board, March 5, 1977, SC Papers 238:15.

42. *Raven Call*, April 1977, 5–6.

43. Alaska Chapter Minutes, May 9, 1977, SC Papers 235:22.

44. See Itinerary, July 2–9, Crandell Papers 3:4; Trip Notes, July 3, 1977, Crandell Papers 3:12.

45. Petersburg Notes, July 4, 1977, Crandell Papers 3:12; *Ketchikan Daily News*, July 5, 1977; *Southeast Alaska Empire*, July 8, 1977.

46. *Southeast Alaska Empire*, July 5, 1977.

47. *Anchorage Daily News*, August 8, 1977.

48. *Southeast Alaska Empire*, July 5, 1977; *Sitka Daily Sentinel*, July 5, 1977.

49. R. Stoertz, "President's Workshop," July 24, 1977, Seiberling Papers, Box l.

50. *Southeast Alaska Empire*, July 8, 1977.

51. *Southeast Alaska Empire*, July 12, 1977.

52. *Southeast Alaska Empire*, July 12, 1977.

53. This anecdote is from a private conservation with John Seiberling. The potential streaker seems to have been Steve Kron. See House of Representatives, *Hearings before the Subcommittee on General Oversight and Alaska Lands of the Committee on Interior and Insular Affairs*, 95th Congress, lst Session, Part X (Washington: Government Printing Office, 1977), 60.

54. John Rowley to Seiberling, n.d., Seiberling Papers, Box 7.

55. See Karen to Morris K. Udall, July 28, 1977, Udall Papers, Box 328; Cuthbertson to Harry and Stan, July 13, 1977, Crandell Papers 3:12.

56. Kay Greenough to Seiberling, July 20, 1977, Crandell Papers 3:12.

57. Articles by Jim Barnett and Jack Hession, *Alaska Newsletter* 11 (June 1977), n.p.

58. Sierra Club Executive Board, August 10, 1977, SC Papers 235:22.

59. *Alaska Advocate*, August 18, 1977.

60. *Alaska Advocate*, August 18, 1977.

61. *Southeast Alaska Empire*, August 19, 1977.

62. George Matz to Alaska Coalition, n.d., SC Papers 225:16.

63. George Matz to Alaska Coalition, n.d., SC Papers 225:16.

64. *Fairbanks News-Miner*, August 22, 1977; *Anchorage Daily News*, August 22, 1977; *Alaska Advocate*, August 25, 1977.

65. Udall to Fran and Scoville, June 7, 1977, Udall Papers, Box 328.

66. *Anchorage Daily News*, August 20, 1977.

67. Francis Sheehan to Udall, June 13, 1977, Udall Papers, Box 328.

68. Alaska Task Force Meeting, reported in *Alaska Newsletter* 11 (June 1977).

69. "Summary of Actions," Crandell Papers 3:4.

70. *Fairbanks News-Miner*, November 29, 1977; *Anchorage Daily News*, November 26, 1977.

71. Robert Weeden to Robert LeResche, December 10, 1977, Robert B. Weeden Papers (University of Alaska Archives, Fairbanks), Series 2, Box 5.

72. Weeden to LeResche, April 14, 1978, Weeden Papers, Series 2, Box 5.

73. *Los Angeles Times*, September 6, 1977.

74. See Harry Crandell to Seiberling, n.d. (ca. August 1977), Seiberling Papers, Box 10.

75. McCloskey, "Carter's First Year," *Sierra* 63 (February 1978), 27.

76. Williss, "Do Things Right," 183–91.

77. Hession to Mike McCloskey et al., July 29, 1977, SC Papers 225:15; Chuck Clusen to Mike McCloskey, July 25, 1977, SC Papers 227; *Anchorage Daily Times*, July 19, 1977.

78. *Washington Post*, September 23, 1977.

79. Williss, "Do Things Right," 194–95.

80. Crandell to Seiberling, September l, 1977, Crandell Papers 3:13.

81. Williss, "Do Things Right." 199; "Major Changes in Committee Print," n.d., Seiberling Papers, Box 10.

82. Doug Scott to Wayburn et al., November 17, 1977, SC Papers 225:16. Also see Nancy Gates, *Lloyd Meeds: Democratic Representative from Washington* (New York: Grossman, 1972), 8, 12.

83. Scott to Wayburn, November 17, 1977. Also Margie Gibson to Pam Rich, November 27, 1977, AC Papers, Box 5.

84. See Lloyd Meeds Papers (University of Washington Archives, Seattle), Box 215.

85. Mike McCloskey to Board of Directors, October 27, 1977, SC Papers 121.

86. Mike Holloway to Brock Evans, December 18, 1977, SC Papers 121.

87. David Bordon to Chuck Clusen, November 14, 1978, AC Papers, Box 2.

88. Ceil Giudici to Sierra Club officers, February 22, 1978, SC Papers 229.

89. *Fairbanks News-Miner*, October 18, 1977.

90. *Bellingham (WA) Herald*, November 4, 1977.

91. Jack Hession to Ogden Williams, "Alaska Coalition Special Report," January 27, 1978, SC Papers 225:16.

92. Ogden Williams, "Mark-Up Report No. 2," SC Papers 225:7; "What's New with D-2," *Center News*, March 17, 1978.

93. Ogden Williams, "Highlights Report No. 1," SC Papers 225:17.

94. Ogden Williams, "Highlights Report No. 1," SC Papers 225:17.

95. Ogden Williams, "Highlights Report No. 1," SC Papers 225:17.

96. Ogden Williams, "Highlights Report No. 1," SC Papers 225:17.

97. Ogden Williams, "Highlights Report No. 3," SC Papers 225:17.

98. Williss, "Do Things Right," 201.

99. Crandell to Seiberling, April 13, 1978, Seiberling Papers, Box 10.

100. F. Sheehan to Udall, April 14, 1978, Udall Papers, 332; Crandell to Seiberling, April 14, 1978, Crandell Papers 3:4.

101. Ogden Williams, "Highlights Report," April 27, 1978, SC Papers 225:18.

102. Crandell to Udall and Seiberling, May 3, 1978, Seiberling Papers, Box 10.

103. Paul Swatek to Mary Ann Erickson et al., March 23, 1978.

104. Sandy Turner and Doug Scott to Alaska Coalition, March 14, 1978, SC Papers 225:17.

105. Robert Cahn, "The Fight to Save Wild Alaska" (Washington: National Audubon Society, 1982), 20–21.

106. Scott, "The Fight to Save Alaska," *Sierra* 76 (January–February 1991), 44. Also see Steve H. and Sandy to Chuck, Doug, May 17, 1978, AC Papers, Box 5.

107. To Sandy and Steve, May 17, 1978, AC Papers, Box 5.

108. Williss, "Do Things Right," 203–204.

109. Douglas Scott interview, August 26, 1999.

110. Cecil Andrus and Joel Connelly, *Cecil Andrus: Politics Western Style* (Seattle: Sasquatch Books, 1998), 79.

111. *Raven Call* 2 (June 1977), 7.

112. *Alaska Advocate*, April 6, 1978.

113. Crandell to Seiberling, April 24, 1978, Seiberling Papers, Box 10.

114. *Washington Post*, September 30, 1978.

115. "A Frustrated Constituent," March 9, 1978, SC Papers 225:17.

116. *Seattle Post-Intelligencer*, November 16, 1977.

117. *Ketchikan Daily News*, July 8, 1977.
118. "Reporter at Large," June 2, 1978, TWS Papers 12:301.
119. *Anchorage Daily Times*, November 25, 1977.
120. *Alaska Advocate*, April 6, 1978.
121. *Southeast Alaska Empire*, August 19, 1977.
122. *Washington Post*, September 30, 1978.
123. Stonorov to Rich Gordon, March 29, 1978, Gordon Papers.
124. Stan Sloss to Seiberling, April 13, 1978, Seiberling Papers, Box 10.
125. Clusen to McCloskey and Wayburn, June 24, 1978, SC Papers 225:18.
126. Clusen to McCloskey and Waynburn, June 24, 1978, SC Papers 225:18.
127. Clusen to McCloskey and Wayburn, June 24, 1978, SC Papers 225:18.
128. Clusen to McCloskey and Wayburn, June 27, 1978, SC Papers 225;18
129. See Alaska Coalition Memo, July 6, 1978, SC Papers 226.
130. Alaska Coalition, "Status of d-2 in Energy and Natural Resources Committee," July 6, 1978, SC Papers 226.
131. S. Sloss to Seiberling, July 24, 1978; Sloss to Seiberling, July 25, 1978, Seiberling Papers, Box 10.
132. *Anchorage Daily News*, August 26, 1978.
133. Crandell to Udall, Seiberling, August 30, 1978, Udall Papers, Box 329.
134. Crandell to Udall, Seiberling, August 16, 1978, Seiberling Papers, Box 10.
135. Williss, "Do Things Right," 208.
136. "Summary of Energy Committee's Decisions on Alaska Lands Bill," Seiberling Papers, Box 11; Crandell to Udall, Seiberling, September 15, 1978, Seiberling Papers, Box 10.
137. S. Sloss to Seiberling, October 5, 1978, Seiberling Papers, Box 10.
138. Crandell to Udall, Seiberling, July 31, 1978, Seiberling Papers, Box 10.
139. Udall and Seiberling to Henry Jackson, August 1, 1978, SC Papers 226.
140. S. Sloss to Seiberling, August 1, 1978, Udall Papers, Box 329.
141. *Fairbanks News-Miner*, September 30, 1978.
142. See *Fairbanks News-Miner*, August 21, 1978; *Anchorage Daily Times*, July 8, 1978.
143. *Anchorage Daily Times*, August 20, 1978.
144. Crandell to Seiberling, Udall, September 29, 1978, Udall Papers, Box 329.
145. *Ketchikan Daily News*, October 12, 1978.
146. Mike Gravel to Ted Stevens, October 12, 1978, Gravel Papers, Box 573.
147. Crandell to Seiberling, October 27, 1978, Crandell Papers 3:4.
148. Cahn, "Fight to Save Wild Alaska," 22.
149. Williss, "Do Things Right," 211; Cahn, "Fight to Save Wild Alaska," 22.
150. "Dear ___," October 19, 1978, Gravel Papers, Box 573.
151. Williss, "Do Things Right," 213.
152. Martha Gerhard-Stein to Crandell, October 18, 1979, Crandell Papers 3:2.
153. *Fairbanks News-Miner*, August 30, 1978.

Chapter 8. Birth of ANILCA

1. Ginny Hill Wood, "Woodsmoke," *ACR* 19 (Fall–Winter 1978), 15.
2. Wood, "Woodsmoke," 15.
3. W. Carl Biven, *Jimmy Carter's Economy: Policy in an Age of Limits* (Chapel Hill: University of North Carolina Press, 2002), 83.

4. *Washington Post*, September 30, 1978.

5. *Fairbanks News-Miner*, October 24, 1978.

6. *Washington Post*, September 20, 1978.

7. *Washington Post*, September 20, 1978.

8. Matthew Berman, "Economic Impact of Proposed Alaska National Interest Lands Conservation Act," July 24, 1978, in Weeden Papers, Series 2, Box 3.

9. Congressional Scheduling Proposal, October 16, 1978, Carter Papers, White House Central ST-5.

10. *Anchorage Daily News*, December 15, 1978.

11. Cecil Andrus and Joel Connelly, *Cecil Andrus: Politics Western Style* (Seattle: Sasquatch Books, 1998), 79.

12. Jack Hession to Fran Sheehan, November 29, 1978, Udall Papers, Box 330.

13. Harry Crandell to Seiberling, Udall, November 15, 1978, Seiberling Papers, Box 11.

14. Crandell to Udall, Seiberling, January 19, 1979, Seiberling Papers, Box 7.

15. *Alaska Newsletter* 11 (January 1979), 4.

16. "D-2 Steering Council Meeting," December 8, 1978, SC 226.

17. "D-2 Steering Council Meeting, December 18, 1978, SC 226.

18. Chuck Clusen to Stuart Eizenstat, November 9, 1978, Carter Papers, Box 141.

19. *Center News*, November 17, 1978; Laurence Rockefeller et al. to Anne Wexler, November 30, 1978, AC Papers, Box 5.

20. Stuart Eizenstat, Kathy Fletcher to Carter, November 17, 1978, Carter Papers, Box 141.

21. Andrus and Connelly, *Cecil Andrus*, 68.

22. Crandell to Seiberling, December 3, 1978, Crandell Papers 3:4.

23. Kathy Fletcher to Stu Eizenstat, November 18, 1978, Carter Papers, Box 141.

24. Fletcher to Eizenstat, November 18, 1978, Carter Papers, Box 141.

25. *Fairbanks News-Miner*, December 1, 1978.

26. *Anchorage Daily Times*, January 6, 1979; *Fairbanks News-Miner*, January 1986 special issue.

27. Jay Hammond, *Tales of Alaska's Bush Rat Governor* (Fairbanks: Epicenter Press, 1994), 242.

28. *Raven Call* 2 (June 1978), 10.

29. Leonard Steinberg, "Confidential Report," November 1978, SC Papers 226.

30. Kay Greenough interview, November 18, 1999.

31. *Raven Call* 2 (November 1978), 19–20.

32. *Fairbanks News-Miner*, December 4, 1978.

33. *Fairbanks News-Miner*, December 4, 1978.

34. Brock Evans to Paul Swatek, April 4, 1979, SC Papers 121:29.

35. "Alaska Coalition Budget, 1979," TWS Papers 12:301.

36. Starr Report, February 1979, AC Papers, Box 8.

37. Mike Wack Report, July 15, 1980, AC Papers, Box 8.

38. Report, January 16, 1979, AC Papers, Box 5.

39. Alaska Targeting, March 17, 1979; Interior Committee Members, February 14, 1979, AC Papers, Box 8.

40. *Anchorage Daily News*, May 8, 1979.

41. Robert LeResche to Hammond, January 18, 1979, Weeden Papers, Box 6.

42. Harry Crandell to Morris K. Udall and John F. Seiberling, July 17, 1979, Seiberling Papers, Box 13.

43. Memo by Celia Hunter, n.d. (c. 1979), Weeden Papers, Box 6; *Center News*, February 2, 1979, 1.

44. Mike Gravel to Hammond, January 23, 1979, Mike Gravel Papers, Box 573.

45. *Fairbanks News-Miner*, January 17, 1979.

46. Crandell to Seiberling, January 26, 1979, Seiberling Papers, Box 11; also *Fairbanks News-Miner*, January 26, 1979.

47. *Washington Post*, March 2, 1979.

48. *Anchorage Daily News*, March 3, 1979.

49. Kathy Fletcher to Stu Eizenstat, March 1, 1979, Carter Papers, White House ST-4.

50. *Washington Post*, March 2, 1979, *Anchorage Daily News*, March 3, 1979.

51. Alaska Coalition, "Alaska Status Report," March 6, 1979.

52. Crandell to Udall and Seiberling, March 13, 1979, Seiberling Papers, Box 8.

53. *Fairbanks News-Miner*, March 29, 1979.

54. "Merchant Marine Committee Members," March 15, 1979, Udall Papers, Box 331.

55. *Fairbanks News-Miner*, March 12, 1979.

56. *Fairbanks News-Miner*, March 12, 1979.

57. Doug Scott to Udall, March 26, 1979, Udall Papers, Box 331.

58. See Karen to MKU, July 28, 1977, Udall Papers, Box 328; Cuthbertson to Harry and Stan, July 13, 1977, Crandell Papers 3:12.

59. Transcript, May 3, 1979, Udall Papers, Box 333. Also Margaret Booth to Larry Rockefeller, December 2, 1977, AC Papers, Box 11.

60. *Fairbanks News-Miner*, January 1986 special issue.

61. *Washington Post*, June 2, 1979; Research/background material, 1979, AC Papers, Box 2.

62. *Washington Post*, May 15, 16, 1979.

63. *Washington Post*, May 17, 1979.

64. *Fairbanks News-Miner*, May 25, 1979.

65. Marshall Silverberg to Seiberling, n.d., Seiberling Papers, Box 11.

66. *Fairbanks News-Miner*, May 16, 1979.

67. "Backlash Against Big Oil," *Time*, May 28, 1979; *Fairbanks News-Miner*, May 17, 1979; *Washington Post*, June 2, 1979.

68. Wayburn, "What They're Saying in Alaska," *Sierra* 64 (September–October 1979), 16.

69. Paul Lowe to Jay Hammond, May 31, 1979, TWS Papers 12:301; *Ravencall* 4 (June 1980), 10.

70. *Anchorage Daily News*, June 29, 1979.

71. Terry Miller to Robert Weeden, June 27, 1979, Weeden Papers, Box 6.

72. Crandell to Udall and Seiberling, July 25, 1979, Udall Papers, Box 332.

73. Stan Sloss to Seiberling, September 13, 1979, Seiberling Papers, Box 13.

74. Sloss to Udall and Seiberling, October 12, 1979, Udall Papers, Box 330.

75. Winky Miller to Barbara Blake et al., August 31, 1979, TWS Papers 12:301.

76. Sloss to Udall, Seiberling, October 12, 1979, Udall Papers, Box 330.

77. Sloss to Udall, Seiberling, October 15, 1979, Seiberling Papers, Box 12.

78. Sloss to Udall, Seiberling, October 16, 1979, Seiberling Papers, Box 13.

79. Sloss to Seiberling, October 17, 1979, Seiberling Papers, Box 13.

80. Sloss to Seiberling, October 24, 1979, Seiberling Papers, Box 13.

81. Sloss to Udall, Seiberling, October 31, 1979, Seiberling Papers, Box 13.

82. Sloss to Seiberling, October 30, 1979, Seiberling Papers, Box 13.

83. Wayburn, "Alaska in the Senate," *Sierra* 64 (November–December, 1979), 46.

84. *Fairbanks News-Miner*, October 31, 1979.

85. Chuck Fishman to Gravel, October 31, 1979, Gravel Papers, Box 575.

86. Weeden Notes, Weeden Papers, Series 2, Box 5.

87. Weeden Notes, Weeden Papers, Series 2, Box 5.

88. *Fairbanks News-Miner*, November 1, 1979.

89. Fishman to Gravel, October 31, 1979, Gravel Papers, Box 575.

90. Crandell to Seiberling, November 13, 1979, Seiberling Papers, Box 13; *Fairbanks News-Miner*, November 9, 1979.

91. Tom Lambrix to Stu Eizenstat, January 12, 1980, Carter Papers, Box 141.

92. *Anchorage Daily Times*, January 5, 1980.

93. Sloss to Udall and Seiberling, February 8, 1980, Crandell Papers 3:16.

94. *Anchorage Daily News*, February 8, 1980. Also see Robert Cahn, "The Fight to Save Wild Alaska" (Washington: National Audubon Society, 1982), 26.

95. *Congressional Record*, February 8, 1980, S1379; Alaska Coalition, "Alaska Status Report," February 20, 1980, SC Papers 224:11.

96. Brock Evans, "The New Decade—Dawn or Dusk?" *Sierra* 65 (January–February, 1980), 8.

97. Crandell to Seiberling, July 9, 1980, Crandell Papers 3:8.

98. Crandell to Seiberling, July 9, 1980, Crandell Papers 3:8.

99. Lambrix to Eizenstat, July 10, 1980, Carter Papers, Box 141.

100. Kathy Fletcher to Eizenstat, July 10, 1980, Carter Papers, Box 131.

101. Lambrix to Eizenstat, July 19, 1980, Carter Papers, White House Central File ST-5.

102. *Anchorage Daily News*, July 22, 1980.

103. *Washington Star*, July 24, 1980.

104. *Anchorage Daily News*, July 22, 1980.

105. "Senate Votes," July 22, 1980, Seiberling Papers, Box 13; Cahn, "Fight to Save Wild Alaska," 27.

106. *Anchorage Daily News*, July 22, 1980.

107. *Anchorage Daily Newss*, July 24, 1980.

108. Cahn, "Fight to Save Wild Alaska," 28.

109. Crandell to Seiberling, July 9, 1980, Crandell Papers 3:8.

110. *Anchorage Daily News*, July 24, 1980.

111. Doug Scott to Wayburn, McCloskey, July 31, 1980, SC Papers 224:11.

112. Scott to Wayburn, McCloskey, July 31, 1980, SC Papers 224:11.

113. *Anchorage Daily News*, August 1, 1980.

114. *Anchorage Daily News*, August 2, 1980.

115. *Anchorage Daily Times*, August 5, 1980.

116. *Anchorage Daily News*, August 7, 1980.

117. *Anchorage Daily News*, August 5, 6, 1980; *Anchorage Daily Times*, August 6, 1980.

118. Erica Ward to Stu Eizenstat, August 7, 1980, Carter Papers, Box 141.

119. *Anchorage Daily News*, August 18, 1980.

120. *Anchorage Daily News*, August 19, 1980; Alaska Coalition, "Special Status Report," August 22, 1980, SC Papers 224:11.

121. *Anchorage Daily News*, August 4, 9, 1980.

122. *Anchorage Daily News*, August 20, 1980.

123. Lambrix to Eizenstat, August 23, 1980, Carter Papers, Box 141.

124. *Anchorage Daily News*, August 19, 1980.

125. *Anchorage Daily News*, August 20, 1980.

126. *Anchorage Daily News*, September 10, 1980; Scott to Udall, September 10, 1980, Udall Papers, Box 329.

127. William Turnage to Alan Cranston, October 6, 1980, TWS Papers 12:301.

128. John McComb, Scott, Clusen to Udall and Seiberling, September 26, 1980, Udall Papers, Box 330.

129. Udall to Carter, October 14, 1980, Seiberling Papers, Box 13.

130. Dee Frankfourth to Celia Hunter, October 9, 1980, TWS Papers 12:301.

131. Jack Calvin to Seiberling, August 25, 1980, Crandell Papers 3:7.

132. SEACC Board to Alaska Coalition, October 26, 1980, TWS Papers 12:301.

133. Terry Miller to Weeden, October 31, 1980, Weeden Papers, Box 2.

134. *New York Times*, November 13, 1980.

135. Quoted in *Ravencall* 4 (December 1980), 1.

Postscript: Alaska in the 1980s and Beyond

1. Sheffield Reception, Recording, University of Alaska Archives.

2. See Ken Ross, *Environmental Conflict in Alaska* (Boulder: University Press of Colorado, 2001); John Strohmeyer, *Extreme Conditions: Big Oil and the Transformation of Alaska* (New York: Simon & Schuster, 1993).

3. Stephen Haycox, *Alaska: An American Colony* (Seattle: University of Washington Press, 2003), 307, 312.

4. *Wall Street Journal*, November 10, 1980.

5. Ross, *Environmental Conflict*, 207.

6. *Anchorage Times*, February 22, 1987.

7. *Juneau Empire*, January 13, 1987; *Anchorage Daily News*, February 26, 1987; *New York Times*, February 28, 1987.

8. *Anchorage Daily News*, December 10, 1987.

9. *Sierra Club National News Report* 19 (March 13, 1987), 1.

10. *New York Times*, February 28, 1987; *Anchorage Daily News*, February 22, 1987.

11. "Legi-slate Report on the 100th Congress," Harry Crandell Papers, Box 17.

12. Tim Mahoney to Alaska Coalition, August 31, 1987, Crandell Papers, Box 17.

13. *Sierra Club National News Report* 19 (October 1, 1987), 1; *Anchorage Daily News*, September 24, 1987.

14. *Wall Street Journal*, February 26, 1988; Mike Matz to Alaska Coalition, February 22, 1988, Crandell Papers, Box 17.

15. Cindy Shogan to Alaska Coalition, June 28, 1988, Crandell Papers, Box 17.

16. *New York Times*, May 11, 1988.

17. Billy Kenny to Alaska Coalition, July 25, 1988, Crandell Papers, Box 17.

18. Quoted in Tim Mahoney to Alaska Coalition, January 30, 1989, Crandell Papers, Box 17.

19. SEACC, "Last Stand," 12.

20. U.S. Government Accounting Office, "Report to Congressional Requesters, Tongass National Forest, Timber Provisions of the Alaska Lands Act Needs Clarification," April 1988, 31.

21. Morris Udall to Richard E. Lyng, July 31, 1986, TWS Papers 12:400.

22. See SEACC, "The Troubled Tongass," November 1, 1985, TWS Papers 12:401.

23. SEACC, "Troubled Tongass," 3.

24. Bart Koehler to Randy Snodgrass and Steve Richardson, November 20, 1985, TWS Papers 12:401.

25. Kathy Durbin, *Tongass: Pulp Politics and the Fight for the Alaska Rain Forest* (Corvallis: Oregon State University Press, 1999), 169–71.

26. Joseph R. Mehrkens to Emily Smith, February 16, 1989, TWS Papers 12:400..

27. SEACC, "Tongass Timber Reform Act," September 26, 1988, TWS Papers 12:400.

28. Bart Koehler to Alaska Coalition, October 24, 1988, TWS Papers 12:400.

29. Leslie England to Alaska Coalition, April 11, May 1, July 17, 1989, Crandell Papers, Box 17.

30. Leslie England to Alaska Coalition, September 8, 1989, Crandell Papers, Box 17.

31. Durbin, *Tongass*, 198–201.

32. Durbin, *Tongass*, chapters 15–16, 19; Stephen Haycox, *Frigid Embrace: Politics, Economics and Environment in Alaska* (Corvallis: Oregon State University Press, 2002), 138; Erickson & Associates, "Beyond Tongass Timber" (Juneau, 1999), 10–16.

33. SEACC, *The Citizens' Guide to the Tongass National Forest: A Handbook for Conservation Activists of Southeast Alaska* (Juneau: SEACC, 1985), 16.

34. U.S. Department of the Interior, *ANSCA, 1985 Study* (Washington: Government Printing Office, 1984), III, 78, argued cryptically that "the plan of action has reportedly worked well."

35. Quoted in Gunnar Knapp, *Native Timber Harvests in Southeast Alaska* (Anchorage: Institute of Social and Economic Research, 1989), 36.

36. Knapp, *Native Timber Harvests*, 35–36; ANCSA, 1985 Study, IV, 1.

37. Haycox, *Frigid Embrace*, 132.

38. Knapp, *Native Timber Harvests*, 37–38. Also see Donald Craig Mitchell, *Take My Land, Take My Life: The Story of Congress's Historic Settlement of Alaska Native Land Claims, 1960–1971* (Fairbanks: University of Alaska Press, 2001), 517–18.

39. See Jeffrey K. Stine, "Natural Resources and Environmental Policy," in W. Elliot Brownless and Hugh Davis Graham, *The Reagan Presidency: Pragmatic Conservatism and Its Legacies* (Lawrence: University Press of Kansas, 2003), 233–56.

40. See Wilderness Society, "The Alaska Lands Act: A Broken Promise" (n.p., 1990).

41. Wilderness Society, "The Alaska Lands Act," 6–7; "Alaska in the Twenty-First Century" (n.p., 1991), 13.

42. John Kauffmann, *Alaska's Brooks Range: The Ultimate Mountains* (Seattle: Mountaineers, 1992), 161.

43. Ross, *Environmental Conflict*, 226.

44. Strohmeyer, *Extreme Conditions*, 213.

45. Quoted in John Keeble, *Out of the Channel: The Exxon Valdez Oil Spill in Prince William Sound* (New York: HarperCollins, 1991), 18.

46. Alaska Department of Environmental Conservation, *The Exxon Valdez Oil Spill: Final Report. State of Alaska Response* (Anchorage: Alaska Department of Environmental Conservation, 1993), 156.

47. For various incidents, see *Wall Street Journal*, November 1, November 6, 1991; February 22, October 10, October 18, 1993; November 9, November 12, 1999; November 3, 2000; November 9, 2001.

48. Richard A. Cooley, "Evaluation," SC Papers 224:13.

49. Celia Hunter to Dee Frankfourth, May 13, 1977, TWS Papers 12:301.

50. Ross, *Environmental Conflict*, 308–309.

51. Ross, *Environmental Conflict*, 299.

52. Celebrate Wild Alaska," Crandell Papers, Box 20.

53. Wilderness Society, "Alaska in the Twenty-First Century," 13.

54. Dennis M. Roth, "The Wilderness Movement and the National Forests, 1964–1980" (Washington: U.S. Forest Service, 1984), 57.

INDEX